HUNTING IN ALASKA

A Comprehensive Guide

Christopher Batin

Photos by Christopher and Adela Batin
Foreword by Craig Boddington
Illustrations by Jeff Schuler

D1644012

Published by

ALASKA HUNTER™

An Imprint of Alaska Angler Publications™

Fairbanks, Alaska

Hunting in Alaska: A Comprehensive Guide and How to Catch Alaska's Trophy Sportfish are part of the Alaska Angling and Hunting LibraryTM, which is dedicated to providing only the very finest in Alaska hunting and fishing literature.

Cover on trade edition: Bill Batin overlooking prime, mountain goat terrain in southcentral Alaska's Kenai Mountains.

Published by Alaska HunterTM, an imprint of Alaska Angler® Publications, P. O. Box 83550, Fairbanks, Alaska, 99708. (907) 456-8212.

First Printing, April 1987
Second Printing, October 1987
Third Printing, Revised Edition, October 1989

Book and cover design: Adela Ward Batin
Typography and production: Award Design, Fairbanks, Alaska

Library of Congress Cataloging in Publication Data
Batin, Christopher,
　　　Hunting in Alaska: a comprehensive guide.

　　　Includes index.

　　　1. Hunting--Alaska. 2. Big game hunting--Alaska. 3. Big game animals--Alaska. I. Title.
SK49.B37 1987　　　　　　　86-081185

ISBN 0-916771-07-5 (Trade Edition)
ISBN 0-916771-08-3 (Hardbound Edition)

Produced in the State of Alaska
Printed in the United States of America

Dedication

To my uncle, Robert Batin, who showed me how.

To my father and mother, Bill and Sara Batin,
who in the beginning, showed me why.

And to the Creator,
for the opportunity to celebrate His glory,
through hunting, in the greatest land of all; Alaska.

Table of Contents

A hunter glassing for spring black bear.

Craig Boddington, Editor of Petersen's Hunting magazine, with a 10 foot, 8 inch brownie taken near Moller Bay on the Alaska Peninsula. (Photo courtesy of Petersen Publishing).

Foreword

Alaska—the Great Land, the Last Frontier...what hunter hasn't thrilled to the works of Rusty Annabel, Jack London, Robert Service, and so many others who helped create the legend of the Far North? And who among us hasn't dreamed of glassing a heavy-palmed bull moose in a high alpine meadow, facing a charging brown bear in dense alder, traversing loose scree to stalk a bedded ram, or witnessing the spectacle of a caribou migration? Alaska holds all these and so many more matchless moments for the hunter, but she can be a deceptive hostess. Her unquestionably vast game populations are widely and unevenly distributed across her huge land mass, and her rugged terrain and unpredictable arctic weather are steel-jawed traps poised for the unready.

She can offer some of the finest hunting on Earth, but nowhere is planning and preparation so essential for success—and sometimes for survival. The legend of Alaska is such that hunters from the Lower 48 envision it a simple task to fly into Anchorage or Fairbanks, head into the back country, and soon head south again with their trophies. In fact, such things can happen—but not as a matter of course nor by accident—only through research and planning. Consider that the density of the moose in Alaska is many times less than the density of whitetail deer in Pennsylvania, and consider further that there are thousands of square miles of Alaska holding little or no game. Consider, too, that in most of Alaska's game country there are no roads, no people, and no source of immediate help.

Consider finally that Alaska's weather can be deadly, not just an inconvenience, and you begin to have some idea of the magnitude of planning an Alaska hunt.

The problem is that, until now, there has been no comprehensive guide available to assist in such planning. The earlier writers were adventurers in the truest sense; they shared those adventures with sportsmen of their day and ours, and they gave us the dream of hunting in Alaska. But while such writings may stir the blood, they give little practical information for today's generation of would-be Alaska hunters.

Modern writers, myself included, have reported—hopefully with some accuracy—on hunting experiences in the Land of the Midnight Sun, and perhaps we've done our bit to further the dream. We have also attempted to impart useful information, but that information has been based on a necessarily limited outsider's point of view.

I have been fortunate to hunt Alaska's great game on several occasions. She has given me some of my finest hunting memories, and has provided the backdrop for what I consider some of my finest writing. But in truth I have been merely a visitor to Alaska's magnificent wilderness, a reporter able to describe only my limited personal experience. The author of this volume, on the other hand, is neither visitor to nor outsider in Alaska.

Chris Batin is a fine writer and dedicated hunter, that last qualification being somewhat rare amongst today's outdoor writers. I won't compare him to his peers, because such comparison would be both subjective and suspect. Suffice it to say that he's *good*. But more importantly, he's an *Alaskan*—he's part and parcel to the Great Land, and his deep feeling for Alaska and her game shines on every page.

It's been a number of years now since I first met Chris Batin at an outdoor writers' convention. He hasn't changed much—quiet, unassuming, but with a sly sense of humor once you get to know him. He seems a studious sort; then and now I have trouble picturing him digging a grizzly out of an alder patch or crossing a treacherous glacier to get to a trophy billy. But such things are stock-in-trade for Chris Batin; he's an Alaskan, perhaps at heart an Alaskan of an earlier day. He hunts the Great Land as you or I would hunt our grouse covers, whitetail woods, or hedgerows.

It's a simple fact that *only* an Alaskan such as Chris Batin could write this book. It's his land, and he knows it better than any visitor ever could. For those who dream of experiencing Alaska, whether for the first time or the twentieth, this book will provide an invaluable reference that has never before been available. I have hunted Alaska both guided and unguided, and I wish this volume had been available when I planned each trip. I will return to see the northern lights again and hunt more of Alaska's great game—but I will be better prepared for having read—and undoubtedly reread—*Hunting in Alaska*. I won't find it hard to reread, either; the writing is crisp and lively, the author's detailed knowledge of his subject glaringly apparent.

Hunting in Alaska is a true milestone—good reading and good information from a man who lives his subject—and took the time to share his land and her game with all of us.

Craig Boddington
Editor, Petersen's Hunting
Los Angeles, California
January 1987

Acknowledgements

A book of this magnitude is not the work of one, but of many. My heartfelt appreciation goes to my wife Adela, for treating my long evenings at the word processor with patience and understanding, and for her graphic design skills in producing a first-class book that best exemplifies hunting in Alaska.

A special thanks to Sharon Durgan Wilson for her skills in editing this revised edition, and to Jeff Schuler for his illustrations. A very special thanks goes to my mentor and friend, Silver Stanfill, who critically reviewed this manuscript.

For a variety of help, thanks to John Gaudet, Ned Pleus, Jim Bailey, and Joe Want. A special thank you goes to ADF&G biologists, especially Dave Kellyhouse, Roy Nowlin, Herman Griese, Sam Patten, Jack Whitman, Bob Tobey, Doug Larsen, Howard Golden, Ed Crain, Ken Taylor, Ray Cameron, John Cody, Mark McNay, Tim Osborne, Bill Gasaway, Wayne Heimer, Sarah Watson, Jerry McGowan, Randy Zarnke, Patrick Valkenburg, Roger Smith, Chris Smith and the game researchers whose work has made much of this book possible.

Thanks are in order to many of my peers, including Burt Twilegar, Jay Cassell, Tony Acerrano and Jack Brown for their support. And a tip of the hunting hat to Charlie Warbelow, Ron Dixon, Doug and Danny Brewer, Max Grill and Diane and Mike McBride.

If I've forgotten anyone in this listing, my apologies and heartfelt thanks and appreciation for your help.

Christopher Batin

Chris Batin with a late-season caribou taken on a solitary hunt in western Alaska with Alaska West Air.

Introduction

Hunting in Alaska! The very thought of it evokes images of wilderness mountains and forests, unmarred by fences and "No Hunting" signs; of thousands of caribou migrating across endless arctic plain, and of waterfowl so plentiful they still darken the sky.

Hunting in Alaska is also excitement! You can pursue 10-foot Kodiak brown bear, and at the flip of a coin, be the hunter...or the hunted. Or how about calling in a 1,100 pound, 55-inch bull moose to within 20 feet of your stand, only to pass him up because he isn't large enough? You can lace up your hiking boots and travel for miles down a glacial-ravaged coastline where you can find brown bear, black bear, mountain goat and black-tail deer. Looking for a challenge? Then try jumping over a seemingly bottomless glacial crevasse, all for the chance of getting a shot at a 40-inch Dall sheep. If you're looking for hunting excitement and adventure, Alaska has it!

The thrill of the chase is only one part of hunting in Alaska. You can be a true hunter in the 49th State. On a fly-out hunt, you can concentrate on pursuing the game animal. You can study it, learn about it, and stalk it for a week if you want, and not worry about another hunter jumping out of the bushes and shooting it. An Alaska hunt is also the ultimate getaway where you can leave all business pressures behind for a week or a month, and concentrate on the simple pleasures in life, such as the sedating effects of pure and simple quiet, the tinkling of a brook, the tangy aroma of Labrador tea foliage, or a quick bath in a remote hot spring bubbling out of a mountainside.

Hunting in Alaska can be very easy or terribly difficult to where it's life threatening. Game is plentiful, but it's not overflowing into Canada. It may be hard to believe, but in many areas, big game is severely lacking or non-existent. "Outside" hunters, and a few writers and in-state outfitters are part of Alaska's "hunting image" problem. Their exaggerated tales of large bag limits and abundant game populations are responsible for the state's stereotype of having a "trophy behind every bush." When hunters discover they need to hunt as hard, if not harder in Alaska than anywhere else, they return home, bewildered and disappointed.

The reasons for this misunderstanding are many: some hunters don't do their homework. Techniques effective for game animals found elsewhere often fail miserably on Alaska's big game. There are those who don't bother to get in shape, or use cheap equipment meant for a backyard camping trip. Others sensationalize Alaska in order to book clients for their hunting trips. Remember, an Alaska hunt can KILL you if you're not physically and mentally prepared.

I've lived in Alaska for over 15 years, and have been privileged to hunt areas most men have never seen. Yet at times, this experience (a mere drop in the bucket compared to some sourdough guides I know) seems like 15 seconds. There are situations when a game animal will leave me baffled for hours, days, even years as to its behavior in a particular incident. It happens to the best of us. That's why this book is a compilation of techniques based not only on my personal observations, but also from a variety of experts in the Alaska hunting field.

But it takes more than just knowing technique to be a successful Alaska big game hunter. You must also be a naturalist, which is why this book is loaded with scientific and biological fact. Science offers you the opportunity to be a "thinking" hunter rather than a "passive" hunter. And due to Alaska's varied geographical and biological environments, and the different habits of the game animals in each, the "thinking" hunter receives the most benefits, both in enjoyment and game harvested.

The trophy hunter as well as the meat or sport hunter can use the facts and techniques in this book with equal success.

I've generally avoided record-book jargon in **Hunting in Alaska** because it sometimes detracts from the true purpose of the hunt: an interaction between man and Nature. Some hunters pursue animals for the sole purpose of record-placement, and get upset if their trophy is 1/8-inch less than their desired goal. Don't get me wrong. I'm not against trophy hunting or record book hunts. Each has its place. In this book, they both rank second, with the total experience of the hunt taking first priority. Enough said.

Therefore, treat the information in this book like a family heirloom: with respect and pride. Do not use it to rape the resource, to bag limits day in and day out. Use it as a guide to better understand Alaska's game resources and their importance in this complex web of life on Earth. Do it while you still can. Because Alaska hunting, as we know it today, will eventually become tomorrow's memory.

The handwriting is on the wall. Population increases in many villages are placing a heavy demand on wild game. Subsistence overharvest of waterfowl is responsible for severe declines in Alaska's goose population. Access to prime hunting areas is gradually being eroded by additions to the Federal Park System and land swaps with Native corporations. This is causing more hunters to concentrate in prime areas. As a result, more permit hunts will be initiated, seasons shortened and bag limits reduced. The last hope and dream of hunters—of a land with plentiful game and wilderness—will be no more. When we lose Alaska, a part of mankind will be lost forever.

Alaska hunting has its problems. But we, as sportsmen, are its answer. So let's become good friends as we hike across tundra and climb mountains, discussing as friends do the complexities of a shared pleasure and knowing all the while that it is the experience, and not whether we harvest a game animal, that makes an Alaska hunting trip worthwhile.

How To Use This Book

The harvest statistics in **Hunting in Alaska** are based on the most up-to-date figures available at press time. At the end of each chapter, you'll find a complete Where-to-Hunt section that provides specific information on a particular species as it is found in each of Alaska's Game Management Units. You'll find success ratios, bull:cow and population estimates, hunting hotspots and other building blocks you need for a successful Alaska hunt. This information is the result of several hundred hours of research and interviews.

Before you actually hunt an area, write the Alaska Department of Fish and Game (address listed in appendix) for a copy of their current regulation booklet. Also ask for copies of the drawing and registration hunt permit supplements and application forms, which are usually available in April or early May.

One last point. Alaska is a state of 585,000 square miles, and regulation checking is a small price to pay for hunting in such a great state. Know the regulations before heading afield.

Christopher Batin
Fairbanks, Alaska

CHAPTER 1

Alaska-Yukon Moose

The Alaska-Yukon moose, otherwise known as *Alces a. gigas*, is one big hombre. He's the largest species of deer found in the world. Standing on all fours, he wouldn't fit into the living room of most houses, his length of ten feet would leave little room for socializing, and I doubt if many floors could withstand his 1,200 pounds, especially the top floor of an Anchorage skyrise.

Ol' *Alces'* headgear is wider than most men are tall, with palm length attaining over half that width. This antler growth is one of the marvels of the deer kingdom. In less than 20 weeks, bulls grow antlers that can weigh up to 75 pounds and carry them well into November before shedding them. It takes extraordinary stamina and muscle to carry this kind of load continually for several months.

A prime bull can perform other superior feats, such as swimming non-stop for 12 miles, or ripping small birch trees out of the ground with his heavily tined rack. He can easily hold off a pack of arctic wolves—the most efficient predators in the northcountry—with nothing more than his hooves and headgear.

To top it off, he thrives in some of the wildest country in North America, where glaciers are overseers of the land and silver-tipped grizzlies roam the open tundra. It's a land where bald eagles are numerous in a sky that sports over 14 hours of daylight during the autumn months. Alaska not only claims the world's trophy moose, but material for trophy memories.

Biologists assume the moose is a direct descendant of the giant elk-moose, *Cervalces*, that roamed the European continent thousands of years ago. Fossil remains show that the North

Alaska has the world's largest bull moose. This monster was shot by Anchorage hunter Joe Susi while on an outfitted float trip in western Alaska. The rack measured 61 inches.

American variety began inhabiting the continent during the mid-Pleistocene Era. Some biologists theorize that the species slowly migrated from east to west, while others claim the Bering Land Bridge allowed the moose to migrate over from Siberia. The latter is the more widely accepted theory. Small groups of moose likely spread throughout much of Alaska as a result of the proliferation of shrubs and forage plants at the end of the glacial period (LeResche et al. 1974). This may indicate why the moose is a relative newcomer to Alaska, or at least parts thereof. Sporadic distribution is typical of moose populations. Archeological evidence indicates that moose may have existed in arctic Alaska before 1000 A.D. (Hall, 1973). But, Alaska Natives living on the Kenai Peninsula at the turn of the century remember when no moose could be found there. Today, the area is home to the Kenai National Wildlife Refuge and is currently a popular hunting area for the big deer, as are most areas of Alaska.

Technically speaking, the moose should be called the American elk. When early French and English pioneers settled this country, they had heard of the great *"elk"* of the north that lived in Sweden and Norway. When the settlers pushed west, they mistakenly gave the name of *"elk"* to the wapiti, and the moose was forced to keep its Algonquin Indian name, which means *"wood eater."* French Canadian explorers gave the species the Basque word *"orenac"* meaning *"deer."*

Life History

The life cycle of the moose begins with the September/October rut. Cows stay in estrous for about two days a month, while the bulls are trying to find and service as many receptive cows as possible. However, bulls do not form harems, as commonly believed by many sportsmen. Because they are so active during the rut, bulls typically lose about 20 percent of their body weight, or up to 200 pounds.

The gestation period is approximately eight months, with cows giving birth to calves in late May and June. For birthing, cows usually prefer islands that keep newborn fawns isolated from predators, particularly grizzly and brown bears.

Antler Growth

Calves grow rapidly during the first five months of life, and can weigh up to 400 pounds by October (Franzmann, 1978). A bull calf has small brownish knobs, and a yearling calf has spikes of eight to ten inches long. A two-year-old moose ex-

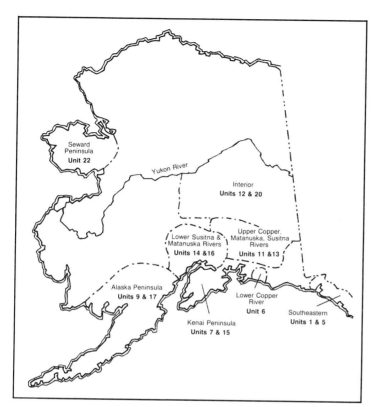

Moose antler growth was studied in the eight areas indicated at the left.

(Below) In a study of Alaska moose, antler spread and Boone and Crockett scores were compared with age in five regions of the state. To simplify the graph, average values are shown for each area. Note that there is a wide variation in spread on Boone and Crockett scores for each age class. The age and Boone and Crockett scores for 50 and 60 inches of spread are marked on the graphs by dotted lines. Comparisons of these points can easily be made. See the text for more information on the differences between areas. (Courtesy Bill Gasaway, ADF&G)

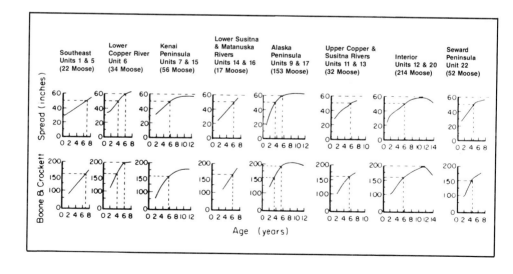

hibits a "crotch horn" with two prongs, and a three-year-old generally has three prongs. Four-year-old moose have a typical adult pattern of palmation. However, the truly impressive racks come in the seventh and eighth year of life. After about the tenth year, a bull is past his prime, and antlers begin to show atrophy. They lose both size and symmetry.

The antlers are used to establish social hierarchy during the rut. Because of their extensive palmation between antler tines, moose are especially advanced in antler evolution compared to other deer species (Bubenik, 1974). It's no small wonder why a hunter wants a moose rack on the wall.

ADF&G biologist Bill Gasaway conducted a study on moose antler growth to determine how many years it takes a moose to grow a large set of antlers. He also compared the trophy potential of moose antlers coming from various parts of the state. One of his goals was to determine if antlers got smaller with old age.

First Gasaway found that moose antlers reach different sizes in different parts of Alaska. The antlers a particular moose wears are a product of many factors: food, habitat, climate, weather, and heredity.

After three years of research in eight different regions throughout Alaska, Gasaway found that the biggest antlers on the youngest moose occur on the lower Copper River drainage and the Alaska Peninsula. Four-year-old moose had antlers averaging 50 inches or greater in these areas. By age five, moose there had antlers about 60 inches in spread. The rate of increase in spread slowed rapidly after the fifth or sixth year. By age six, bulls had nearly reached their maximum antler spread. Moose from the Kenai Peninsula, interior Alaska, southcentral Alaska and the Seward Peninsula generally had smaller antlers at the same ages. On the average, they required five to six years to reach a 50-inch spread. The average size of antlers never quite reached 60 inches in these areas at any age. Antlers from Kenai moose were the smallest and possibly the slowest-growing compared to other areas. The moose of southeast Alaska were the only exception to this six-year/50-inch standard. Southeastern moose generally required seven years to produce 50-inch antlers.

In spite of the smaller average spread for moose antlers from the interior, southcentral and southeast Alaska, and the Kenai and Seward peninsulas, some moose with antlers exceeding 60 inches were taken in these areas. The average spread of antlers in the sample from Units 12 and 20, interior Alaska, is worth

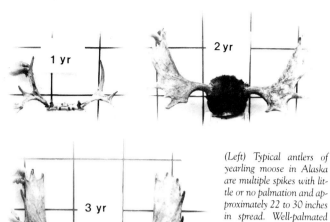

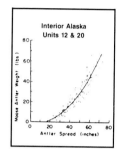

(Below) Average moose antler weight from interior Alaska, Unit 20, increases with spread up to 65 pounds and 70 inches. The line indicates average values and individual moose are marked by points.

(Left) Typical antlers of yearling moose in Alaska are multiple spikes with little or no palmation and approximately 22 to 30 inches in spread. Well-palmated antlers develop during the second year and continue to increase along with their antler spread until ages 10 or 11. Antlers appear to atrophy after the 11th year. (Charts courtesy ADF&G.)

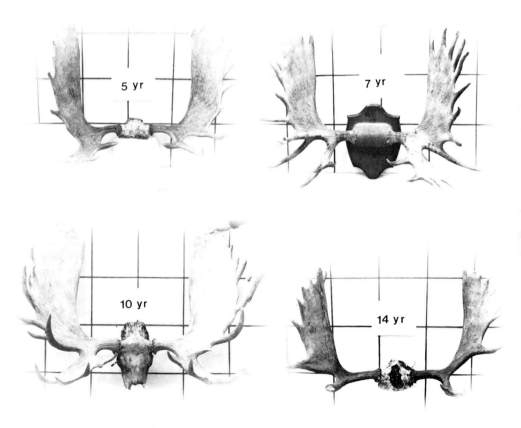

Moose antlers in a variety of forms and sizes as shown by this series of racks from 11-year-old moose of interior Alaska. The bottom two sets of antlers are exceptionally fine racks that would rank high in the Boone and Crockett records. The top rack is an example of a very small set of antlers from an 11-year-old moose. (Chart courtesy ADF&G.)

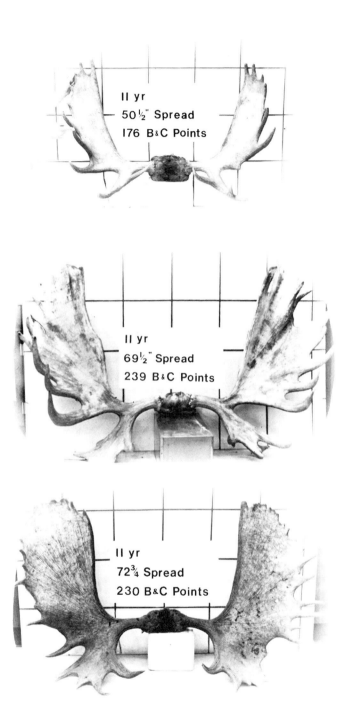

11 yr
50½" Spread
176 B&C Points

11 yr
69½" Spread
239 B&C Points

11 yr
72¾ Spread
230 B&C Points

noting. Some nine- and ten-year-old moose had antlers as small as 45 inches, while others measured up to 70 inches. Some old moose with a well-below-average spread had probably gone throughout life without ever growing a trophy rack. In Units 12 and 20, more than one-third of all eight- to 12-year-old moose measured had less than 55-inch antler spreads. Gasaway said that these moose would probably never grow large antlers.

As spread increases in antlers, their weight rapidly increases up to 60 or more pounds. In Gasaway's study, the average antler weights from large, mature bulls (8- to 12-years old) were 45 to 50 pounds. It's very likely that some very large moose antlers weigh 75 pounds.

Gasaway also made an interesting connection between moose populations and antler spread as they pertain to Boone and Crockett classification. Moose in the lower Copper River drainage and Alaska Peninsula produced antlers that not only have a greater spread at an early age, but also score higher when compared with antlers from other areas. On the average, 50-inch moose antlers from all the areas scored about 150 to 160 B and C points. However, in the lower Copper River drainage, Alaska Peninsula and the interior, 60-inch antlers scored about 195 points. Therefore, spread and B and C scores are closely related in these moose populations. As if in response to a trophy hunter's concerns, Gasaway stated that a given antler spread in any area will usually result in a similar B & C score. However, since there is a wide variability in antlers, you might find a 60-inch rack scores higher than some 65-to 70-inch racks.

Several years ago, a biologist studied the relationship between body weight of rutting moose and the size of their antlers. He spent the entire moose season in a popular hunting area in the river country of interior Alaska. When he heard a gunshot, the biologist would motorboat to the location, and with the hunter's permission, set up his mammoth tripod and weigh the moose. His findings were:

Moose weight	Antler spread
1480 pounds	48 inches
1380 pounds	61 inches
1360 pounds	47 inches
1260 pounds	57 inches

He found that the more active a bull is during rut, the more body weight the animal loses. As the chart indicates, the biggest-bodied moose may not always have the largest antlers. This is food for thought, especially if you're after meat for the freezer rather than a rack for the wall.

Big moose are easy to find during daylight hours. Just look for the sunlight flashing off their sun-bleached antlers.

Moose Behavior

Moose are most active during clear days, apparently regardless of ambient temperature (Mould, 1977). It is rain, snow, heavy overcast, and high winds that appear to reduce the amount of moose activity. Material obstacles do little to deter moose. Extremely dense stands of willow and alder along river bottomlands are generally not a barrier to moose. Harry (1957) and Milke (1969) also noted that moose were unaffected by dense vegetation.

Many hunters won't hunt the thickets in Alaska because they figure a moose and its large rack just couldn't get through the tangle. But I've seen moose mow a path through alders that would have put a bulldozer to shame. If you jump a moose at close range, don't follow him into the thick stuff. Rather, hunt the perimeters. More than likely, you'll have a better shot when the animal comes out.

When hunting alpine areas, it's important to understand how Alaska-Yukon moose respond to various types of habitat. Movement through alpine shrubs is often random and complex: stops, browsing, and changes in direction are frequent. In contrast, movement across alpine tundra is usually straight and directional. Moose usually approach an open area with caution, often surveying the area for a short time before crossing. But on exposed areas of tundra, moose maintain a relatively swift pace and rarely stop.

Mould's extensive studies on the disturbance of moose can benefit hunters. On one of his studies, Mould encountered several moose that normally fled 130 feet before stopping to look back toward him. The moose remained motionless for up to a minute before trotting into thick cover. Other biologists have noted similar reactions.

Flight distances for moose on the tundra, however, were sometimes nearly a half mile compared to less than 300 feet in brushy areas. In open areas, Mould was never able to approach moose closer than 600 feet, though observation distances of less than 160 feet were common while moose were in shrub stands. Mould also noted that moose reacted to passing aircraft more frequently when the animals were caught in open terrain.

Studies show moose behavior is often learned. Calves' remember their mothers' annual movements from high alpine areas to wintering areas. Once chased off by its mother, a young moose follows maternal seasonal migratory routes. The timing of these migrations varies, depending on food availability and sex of animal. That moose behavior is learned explains why hunters often find the animals using the same alpine areas, year after year. This learned pattern also applies to moose living year-round in alpine areas, such as the moose population in the Yanert River area. Of course, major influences such as fires, human habitation, and heavy hunting pressure can alter these movements.

When choosing an alpine area for a moose hunt, avoid mountain passes that receive heavy aircraft traffic. More hunters are in the air during moose season than at any other time of year. Mould's research indicates that an increase in aircraft traffic disturbs moose. Many hunters agree with this assessment. All too often, a hunter stalking a moose has his stalk interrupted by an aircraft of curious hunters. The plane suddenly appears, circles the moose and chases the animal off.

While I'm not for scouting for moose by flying 300 feet off the ground and harassing hunters, I believe there is a place for aircraft in locating moose populations. That place is high, for getting a better view of any moose in the area. And should you schedule a flight to scout for moose, timing is critical. Linkswiler (1982) conducted aerial surveys of high alpine moose during and after the rut. She found that afternoons were the best time to locate moose. In the fall, activity levels of moose were very low in late morning.

Data from my numerous moose hunts support Linkswiler's findings. At daybreak in high alpine country, moose move around. They tend to disappear during mid-day, and then reappear in late afternoon. Of course, you can spot bulls throughout the day in heavy cover. But it's foolish to pursue a bull in such cover, as the hunters will usually end up spooking the animal. Better to wait until the bull heads out of cover in late afternoon.

Hunting Techniques

It's ludicrous to think that one hunting technique works for all large moose. Trophy bulls are like cantankerous old hermits. Years of surviving Alaska's wilds have made them eccentric in their ways. What may work in one instance may be a complete flop in another.

My most action-packed moose hunt took place in western Alaska, hunting trophy bulls with Jake Gaudet of Alaska Wilderness Outfitters. It was a balmy, mid-September day, and my eyes occasionally tired from glassing the yellow-tinged birch and alder patches surrounding us. Earlier, we had heard two bulls grunting and bellowing in the area. But by the time we scurried to the spot, the two bulls had disappeared into the nine-foot-high alders.

Realizing that too much walking could easily spook every bull in the area, we waited for the moose to come to us. We took a stand at the end of a swamp, and called several times. Nothing. Minutes dragged on. Just as the afternoon sun was beginning to make me feel a bit sleepy, I heard a snap. Jake's head popped up: he looked to my right, and then back to me. He pointed and smiled. A large moose was ambling our way, grunting and snorting with each step he took. The bull stopped in the middle of the swamp and looked around before heading straight for our stand. I eased up my rifle, but thick brush obscured my view of the bull's chest. When the bull was about 40 yards out, I stood up and took a rest on a nearby birch tree. Through the scope I could see the bull stop, his eyes bulging with rage. His neck was puffy and the hairs on his back stood on end. He grunted a few times. Not knowing exactly what I was yet, the bull started to amble to the right in an attempt to scent me. Just before he entered the brush, he stepped into the open. I placed the crosshairs on his shoulderblade and touched off. The big bull crumpled like a

piece of foil. I ran up and put a final shot into the base of his skull.

The bull was a mean one. When we skinned the animal, he had bruise marks on his flanks and hindquarters. One side of his rack had a plum-sized hole punched through it. One tine was impacted several inches into the palm of the antler.

The rack, only 50¼ inches, won't ever make the record book. But it says so much about the bull's personality—a battle scarred veteran that died ready to do battle one more time—that this rack is one of my most treasured trophies. The excitement I felt from calling this rut-crazed bull into range was electrifying. Indeed, trophy moose hunting is ironic. It can be easy, or it can require plenty of hard work, patience, and enough glassing to induce trophy moose hallucinations. Either way, a thorough knowledge of hunting techniques and areas trophy moose frequent are prerequisites for hunters desiring the "joy" of lugging home a 55-inch-plus moose rack.

Veteran moose guide Jim Bailey considers the month of September, when moose are still in the mountains, an excellent time to try for a trophy bull. But if you're looking for dumb, rut-crazed animals, you're looking in the wrong place. Alpine moose are smart, wary creatures that behave more like Dall sheep than deer. They habitually spend all summer and fall grazing in mountain pastures, not venturing far from the safety of timberline. Large bulls remain in this area until foul weather drives them into the flatlands.

Hunting these old-time hermits calls for considerably more work than river floating, but in the mountains you'll have a slightly better chance of spotting trophy bulls. Access to alpine

This party of hunters understood moose habits and hunting techniques. They hunted from September 9 through 20 in the alpine tundra of interior Alaska.

A 50-inch-plus moose will generally have three tines on one brow and four tines on the other.

areas is by chartered Super Cub or float plane. Most air taxi operators and guides can drop you off at or above timberline: avoid dropoffs where extensive climbing through timber is required.

Once you've landed in an area, establish your camp far above timberline. You can glass more ground effectively by situating yourself above alpine meadows and grassy plateaus. I've seen grasses in some alpine meadows reach a height of over seven feet. A ridgeline connecting several low-lying areas is also an asset, enabling me to glass several potential areas quickly and inconspicuously.

Guide Kelly Vrem is a sincere believer in rising long before dawn and staying out past dusk. Trophy bulls don't move far from timberline during late evening and early morning hours, so glass slowly and carefully. What you may deem a shadow in the timber may be a trophy bull waiting for darkness to fall. Remember, timberline is open country. Moose may not see as well as Dall sheep, but they are not blind! A hunter silhouetted against the sky will spook the most immature of bulls, let alone a trophy specimen. Also, moose do have the ability to "bug-out" their eyes, and increase their field of vision to nearly 360 degrees. Whether the moose is grazing, or is facing away from you, if you're obvious about your actions, the moose will see you and vanish.

Moose often stand in the middle of a stretch of alpine tundra without a branch to be found for 100 or more yards. The openness of alpine tundra lets air move more rapidly than in a shrub-saturated river valley (Mould, 1977). In early September, moose often seek relief from insects in these high-alpine breezes.

Many times snowstorms will hit an alpine area when a hunt is in progress. While snow causes some game to move into the lower elevations, I've not noticed any lack of moose in the high alpine areas after an accumulation of six or eight inches of snow. While deeper snow restricts moose movements, snow depths of less than 29 inches have no marked effect on moose movements (Coady, 1974). However, snow and geography influence distribution of moose populations. In some mountain ranges in Alaska, moose spend most of the winter in the high alpine country of north-facing mountains. There, wind blows snow off the ridges, making browsing easier for the moose. However, on the opposite side of the same range, snow may accumulate up to 10 or more feet, forcing moose into the flatlands for the duration of the winter. Knowledge of these patterns is vital for a late-winter hunt.

Lakes

For years, veteran moose hunters have praised the advantages of hunting lakes for moose. Unlike a river float hunt, where towering stands of trees usually grow right down to the bank, hunting from a lake offers a panoramic view of mountainsides and moose pastures, all at a glance. A lake hunt is safer, lacking such river hazards as sweepers, rapids and underwater obstructions. Also, lake hunting allows the hunter the opportunity to become knowledgeable about an area without letting the moose know this education is happening.

Many moose hunters like to hunt the perimeter of a lake on foot. But more and more are using an inflatable, which has become the key transport and hunting vessel in the alpine lake country of Alaska. Hunting from an inflatable allows silent and unobtrusive travel from hotspot to hotspot through what is usually noisy and difficult terrain. Keeping hunters on the water, this craft also aids them by reducing the amount of their scent left in an area. Moreover, an inflatable makes more country available for glassing, and more time for doing it. Most Alaska professional hunting guides agree that people would bag more moose if they would stop hunting the animals like whitetail deer and discipline themselves to glass more and walk less. Lake hunting for moose from an inflatable enables a hunter to do just that.

Chris Batin examines the tracks left by a large bull on the shore of an alpine lake. Early morning and late evening are good times to find bulls out on open sand bars.

However, to hunt a large lake for moose effectively also requires knowledge of moose habits and lake topography.

While most lakes, large and small, eventually attract moose at one time or another, the best ones to hunt are those in the high alpine country. During the months of September and October, big moose are commonly found up high where ample forage exists, along with steady breezes that keep bothersome mosquitoes and deerflies at bay. Even if you find an alpine lake with no apparent aquatic vegetation attracting moose, keep an eye on it. Moose often use these alpine lakes to avoid insects. On particularly warm days, moose may stand in lakes for long periods of time to cool themselves off (Kelsall and Telfer, 1974).

While most all alpine lake country looks like top-notch moose habitat, don't be deceived by appearances. You need to select areas with features conducive to hunting success.

Alpine lakes come in all sizes. In heavily hunted areas, choose the largest lakes where hunting pressure is probably more evenly dispersed. In wilderness areas, or when hunting by yourself, a lake with several miles of shoreline is satisfactory.

Keep topography in mind when choosing a lake. Avoid lakes surrounded by miles of dense spruce/birch forests. Of course, some stands of heavy timber are necessary for shelter. But overall, moose prefer lakes near two kinds of vegetation: patches of alder, willow and similar scrub, and grassy meadows and barren tundra knolls. These are prime areas, especially when found on flat or gradually sloping mountainsides. Large alpine bowls and amphitheatres are also fine concentration points. Don't pass up areas drained by feeder streams and gullies, because bulls like to hide in these topographical structures during storms and at mid-day. In general, a lake with any or all of these features is a good area for moose.

Once you've decided what lake and surrounding area to hunt, concentrate on the south side, or areas that receive the most sun. These are likely to be moose hotspots because fertile lakes usually support an abundance of aquatic vegetation and marshy surroundings. Early-season bulls and also cows will feed on these sunny-side plants. After rutting starts, bulls stop feeding. However, they stay around these marshy grazing areas looking for a receptive cow. At this time you'll need to glass long and hard to find bulls, as they're often hesitant about coming out into the open during the daylight hours. They do, however, watch the feeding areas for cows and other bulls trespassing in their territory.

Here's a trick that many sourdough moose hunters use to prod stubborn bulls out of the brush near a lake. Fill a large cup or canteen with water, hold it about four feet from the lake's surface, and slowly pour it out until empty. This imitates a cow urinating and attracts rutting bulls from up to a quarter mile away. Extremely effective on a quiet day, this trick has a biochemical basis. The urine of both sexes of moose have pheromones. The large, molecular structures of these substances hinders evaporation. Splashing in the water promotes evaporation. In the bull's nose is what's known as the Jacobson's organ, highly sensitive to these pheromones. Upon hearing this "urinating" sound, the bull searches the area visually, deeply inhaling samples of air in an effort to locate the cow and determine whether she is in heat. The bull's visual search is also an attempt to learn whether the urination was caused by another bull, which would prompt a defense of territory. If you try this trick, it's important that you stay hidden near shoreline cover, as the bull's senses are on full alert.

Prior to employing this trick or before taking a stand, I prefer to row my inflatable into the downwind section of the lake, anchor where I can see the entire weedbed and surrounding marsh, and wait. I usually do this two hours before daybreak, and several hours prior to dusk. It's important to stay well hidden in the boat to keep from being silhouetted against the lake. Shapes don't alarm moose, but moving shapes do. Staying low in the boat gives a hunter the option of limited movement without giving away his presence.

Prepare your inflatable beforehand. Have a foam pad to lie

on, insulating your underside from the cold lake. Also, have binoculars, a thermos of coffee or tea, and rifle all within reach. If you move, do it ever so slowly. Moose often watch an opening for 15 minutes or longer for any sign of movement before venturing out into the open.

Also pay attention to structure surrounding the lake, such as draws and gullies. Large as moose are, they can quickly appear and disappear from an area via these shady avenues. Friends Deb and Will Tinnesand and I discovered the importance of glassing this type of terrain several years ago while hunting for moose in Alaska's upper Chugach Mountains.

While flying into the area, we spotted a 60-inch-plus, bone-white antlered moose. He was standing about half-way up a long, winding gully about 800 yards from the small lake that would be our base camp. Before daybreak on the next day, (hunting same day airborne is illegal in Alaska) Will was glassing one section of hillside along with Deb, who was not hunting. I opted to watch from a large boulder overlooking the other major gully emptying into a large basin some 200 yards farther down the lake.

Five hours later, we had yet to see our first sign of life, let alone a moose. With the early afternoon September sun blazing away, I felt like a lizard on a rock: I would open my eyes to check out the surroundings every ten minutes or so before dozing back off again. Suddenly, I awoke to the sound of something running my way. I grabbed my rifle, relieved to discover it was Deb.

"Come quick," she said between breaths. "I was glassing the hillside when from out of nowhere this moose walks out and starts feeding. He'll go an easy 60 inches. Will's off scouting another gully."

Of course, by the time we reached her stand, the bull had high-tailed it up the mountain. After Will learned what happened, he learned to stay on stand, not only for the remainder of that day, but throughout the rest of the hunt. His effort and patience paid off, however, as he bagged a smaller bull two days later. And what about the larger bull? I caught a brief glimpse of the ol' timer late one evening as he was heading for other pastures, possibly to round up a few cow moose, or we may have spooked him with our approach. Either way, we learned that careful glassing reinforced with plenty of patience pays big dividends.

Glassing while drifting the length of a lake is undoubtedly the most silent method of hunting for big moose. It's also one of the most versatile, as you can keep tabs on several areas at once. Depending on the steepness of the hillside and amount of country you wish to glass, set your drift anywhere from 75 to 300 yards or more offshore. Between glassing for moose, look through the alders for the best routes up to get you within shooting range if you do spot a bull. This strategy not only allows you to spring quickly into action, but also tends to relieve some of the monotony incurred by hours of glassing.

If you are seriously glassing, you have little time for boat handling, so keep the oars in the water. An occasional dip of the oars should keep the inflatable drifting parallel to shore. However, in areas with ample sign, toss out an anchor and glass every square inch of alder thicket, open meadow and timber's edge. Chances are that moose will usually materialize right in front of you.

If you're prone to sea sickness, glassing from an inflatable may not be for you, especially if the water has a slight chop. Glassing while waves hit a boat greatly intensifies the rocking motion, and may cause dizziness. Under most conditions, I've found that seven-to eight-power binoculars work fine, but 10-power is too strong in choppy water and makes me queasy.

Excessive chop means you should keep close tabs on the weather. Alaska's alpine lakes are often situated in mountain passes, which create gusts of wind up to a recorded 200 mph, along with white-capped nightmares. At the first change in wind velocity or wave build-up, head for shore. Wait out the storm. However, be ready to head back out after it clears, as that's when moose leave shelter to resume their feeding or rutting activities.

If the storm drags on for several days, or you just can't get the knack of glassing from a moving object, don't despair. During September and October, the water level in many lakes is way down, creating a smooth gravel or boulder walkway along the perimeter of the lake. Here's easy and virtually quiet walking, even with a large hunting party. Two years ago, Otto, Elmer and Randy Schuster, Curtis Creen Jr. and I opted to use the shoreline to reach five bulls we spotted about two miles from camp.

We carefully picked out a landmark on the shore nearest the best route up to the bulls. At daybreak, we jumped and hobbled our way along the part-sand, part-rock shoreline. About halfway to our landmark, both Otto and Elmer heard a bush rattle on the hillside above the beach. Uncommonly dense brush prevented an effective visual scouring with our binoculars.

Otto and Elmer opted to walk up a small tundra ridge exten-ding above the thicket, while Randy, Curtis and I continued on down to our original destination. Minutes later, two rifle shots cracked the mountain silence. We raced back and found the pair smiling from ear-to-ear over a huge bull with a 52-inch rack. We soon had the moose quartered and ready to pack to the inflatable that Curtis had retrieved from camp. We never did pursue the five bulls down the lake. After the pack-out (eight, 75-to 100-pound sections of meat and the rack) some 300 yards to the boat, complicated by three busted pack frames, we arrived at an understanding: one moose was enough for the group, and that a pack from farther up on the mountainside would have been suicide. Successful lake hunting for moose can spoil a man!

When bulls are holding high on a mountainside, you can use a lake and its topography to stalk within shooting range without being detected. First, study the moose you want. Memorize the features of its rack and body color before drift-ing or rowing about a half-mile downwind. Find a route up the mountain, to a ridgeline that will get you to within several hundred yards of the moose. Stalk the moose along the backside of the ridge to avoid being silhouetted against the skyline. Remember: always keep the moose below you and walk into the wind. In alpine country, researchers say that moose can pick up a human scent from as far away as one mile. By keep-ing your nose in the wind and maintaining a "low and slow" stalk to within shooting range, you stand an excellent chance

Always leave a fluorescent jacket or scarf high in a tree near a kill. Relocating a moose on an alder-infested hillside can be extremely difficult.

Field dressing and packing out a moose is a big job for several hunters, not to mention the do-it-yourself hunter. Expect to pack out from 500 to 600 pounds of boned-out meat.

of bagging that moose. But mountain winds can be tricky. Be ready to shoot should a moose catch your scent on a sudden and unexpected crosswind.

If you spot a moose from your inflatable late in the day, you probably won't have enough time to make a successful stalk and to shoot. To deal with that situation, the next morning, pack your sleeping bag and provisions for one day. Just prior to dusk, hike up to the outskirts of the area you last saw the moose. Overnight there. At daybreak, you'll be ready to hunt (providing you don't oversleep). Chances are, you'll either nab the bull at first light as he heads down to feed in the lowlands, or before mid-day when he returns to the alpine pasture to sun himself and look for cows.

If you bag a moose, don't rush to the inflatable without marking your way back. While it's easy to see a kill from the broad expanse of a lake, once you get into those hillside alders, it's even possible to lose sight of the sun, not to mention your downed trophy. With a generous amount of fluorescent ribbon or tape, mark your kill and also the path down to the lake. If you don't have tape or ribbon, use a brightly colored shirt or scarf.

One more tip: when hunting moose from a lake, glass areas that you wouldn't expect to find moose in a thousand years. Invariably, that's where you'll find one. On several occasions, I've glassed hillsides from my inflatable for hours, only to take a break and find a moose swimming across the opposite end of the lake. If you find yourself in this situation, without time to get close enough for a shot, slowly row up to the area and examine the shoreline on each side of the crossing. You'll probably find a well-used trail. Expect other moose to use this "swimming trail."

To hunt such an area, anchor the boat near shore or make a tree blind (where legal) near the trail and wait. Outlets and inlets of lakes are excellent areas to hunt because they are usually the narrowest part of the lake. Moose prefer simply wading across such an area rather than swimming across the width of a lake. Remember: never shoot a moose in the water. Not only would you find it a nighmare to dress out, but also wet meat will not crust. Crusting is important for the meat to preserve properly. Moose meat is fine eating, deserving the very best of care. Before making that shot, wait until the bull is actually onshore and preferably five to 10 yards up the bank.

Float Hunting Rivers

For several reasons, float hunting is a more productive method than the pack-in type of hunt. Alaska's prime moose areas are in the northern, central, southwestern and western parts of the state where the geography dictates that the moose will be found near rivers. That's where alders and willows (prime moose forage) plus cottonwood and spruce (prime cover) thrive. These trees grow in a band generally extending one-quarter to one-mile wide along the rivers. Beyond that, the terrain abruptly changes, becoming open tundra in all directions. Locating moose, which is the most difficult problem a hunter encounters, is simplified by floating rivers because moose are concentrated within the band of vegetation rather than spread out over the tundra.

Mould's work best describes moose in riparian habitat. His observations show that while many areas of the state have habitat forcing moose to be migratory, (migrations of up to 110 miles have been noted in some Alaska moose populations), moose found along waterways as described above are non-migratory. In these regions, moose appear to stay year-round in or near the river flood plain. However, seasonal movement both upriver and downriver is possible, especially during the rutting period. Therefore, floating is the best way to hunt this type of area, and perhaps one of the best ways to locate moose anywhere in Alaska.

Floating offers another significant advantage. Packing out a quartered moose to the pick-up site on a non-float type of hunt is humorously defined as two steps backward for each step

Shallow water bays and lakes are good places to find early-season bulls feeding on aquatic plants. Once rut commences, the bulls stop feeding and change behavioral patterns.

forward. Floating greatly alleviates a backbreaking task. Not one out of 28 moose taken by members of my float hunting group over the past several years was bagged more than a half-mile from the river. Most were within 300 yards.

Thirteen years ago, I had to do it the hard way. I had shot a moose two miles from camp. It took three days and ten trips, covering a total of 40 miles, to pack it out on my back. But on last year's float, I walked a total of 40 yards from the kill site to the boat, and had everything packed and hung in camp by late afternoon. The remainder of the trip was spent hunting waterfowl, grouse, and black bear. That's the way a moose hunt should be.

Other advantages of floating include the possibility of making a virtually quiet approach, relative ease in transporting gear from one camp to another, plus the option of hunting different terrain each day. There is also the esthetic effect of quietly drifting down a wilderness river, taking in the autumn sights and observing wildlife.

The planning stage is the most important part of a moose float. First, you have to determine the length and means of access. In Alaska, the choice is between aircraft and boat. Each offers advantages in price and experience.

Aircraft transportation is the most popular—and the most expensive. Floatplanes ferry gear and hunter to a stream or river. Of course, the farther you fly from a population center, such as Fairbanks or Anchorage, the better the hunting due to less hunting pressure. Fly-outs also allow a preview of the area to

be floated, invaluable on a first float. A fly-out also provides access to areas unreachable by any other means. The main disadvantage of a fly-out is that transporting the gear becomes expensive. This means you pack light.

On the other hand, boat access to many prime hunting areas can be accomplished by launching from any of the river-highway intersections throughout Alaska. A road pick-up is arranged. For floats into remote areas, pick-up is via aircraft. Larger boats than those used on a fly-out type of hunt are necessary on the larger rivers due to the strong currents. Otherwise, most hunters prefer a standard 12-or 14-foot inflatable boat powered by a 3-to 15-horse outboard. The outboard is optional.

It's always better to have too much boat than not enough. Canoes and life-raft-type inflatables are unsuitable and often-times dangerous for the type of load and hunting conditions encountered in the wilderness of Alaska.

Before going afield, always obtain a geological survey map of the hunting area. Mark potential fields, marshes, and clear-ings along the route. Also, use the map to note potential hazards such as logjams and rapids not shown. Don't forget to look for animal concentrations and possible locations for spike camps. If flying in, ensure your pilot is familiar with the pickup point.

When loading an inflatable, it's important to keep all the gear off the boat's floor. You will need a frame (either com-mercial or constructed on the spot from timber) supported by the side chambers. With this the boat can carry more weight

Riparian moose habitat in western Alaska. Moose are concentrated in timber and brush along the river's edge. Rarely do bulls venture out into the surrounding open tundra.

A pair of successful moose hunters floating a river in southcentral Alaska. Floating not only allows easy access to prime moose areas, but also is a non-strenuous way of transporting meat and rack to a pick-up point.

with less risk of bottoming out and being damaged by snags. Such a frame also provides a means for lashing gear securely as preparation for encountering turbulent water.

Although floating may appear easy, it demands adherence to timetables and techniques. Here is what has worked out well for our group: We spend the first day preparing the inflatable, reviewing the route and marking any changes viewed on the flight or float in. Gear is placed in waterproof riverbags, and if needed, platforms built for gear from nearby birch.

Later that afternoon, after base camp is set up, we take an exploratory trip upriver and scout the immediate area. We look for tracks along the bank and trails through the willows and alders. This suggests whether moose are utilizing the riverbank forage for food, cover or both. If there is plenty of sign, we find a stretch of river that allows good viewing of both sides and set up a stand. Moose aren't hesitant about swimming, and can ford rivers with relative ease. If fields and marshes are predominant along the riverbank, we glass these edges thoroughly...and listen. Moose can be unbelievably quiet for their size, but during rut bulls are generally noisy!

If moose sign is abundant along the entire river, you should motor upstream several miles, cut the motor, and drift downriver. Allow sufficient time to drift completely back to base camp without the aid of an outboard. Along the way, stop, observe, and listen for periods of five to ten minutes. Most activity will occur just before dusk. If an animal is seen and it's too dark to shoot, head back to camp and return before light the next morning. The bull will invariably be in the immediate area. If not, pick up camp and float the river downstream to the first "moosey" location previously marked on the map.

Moose can be hunted with some success during mid-day. If the river courses through hills or bluffs that will afford a good view of the terrain, spend a few hours glassing from the edges of heavy timber, marshes and brushy areas. Even when a moose is bedded down, the wide, palmated antlers will act like a mirror, readily revealing them to the observant hunter.

In heavily timbered areas, slowly walk the edges and listen for any noise such as the snap of a twig or rustling of leaves. It could mean a bull or cow is looking you over. An older bull's tendency to defend territory and cows will generally subordinate his instinct to flee, at least long enough for you to get off a shot.

As soon as you've located a moose, half the battle is won. For instance, several years ago I was floating a section of the Kuskokwim River with Kurt Rinehardt, who was operating the boat, and Bengt Karlsson, the only person in our party who had not yet bagged a moose. Working from base camp, the group was spread out along 44 miles of river. There were plenty of moose. Within the first seven miles of our last-day float, we saw four bulls, all sporting racks less than the 36-inch minimum Bengt had set for himself.

We were growing concerned. Twilight was setting in, and we had not seen any other bulls. Just as we were about to give up, Kurt forcefully put oars to water. Up ahead, a darkened form was fording the river. We nodded to each other in silence. A crown of white antler adorned the swimming bull. It would go an easy 40 inches, but much to Bengt's despair, it was too dark to chance a shot.

We beached the inflatable and listened as the bull climbed the bank, ripped up brush, and grunted excessively. There was no worrying about this one. Cupid's arrow was lodged deep. Marking the area, we returned the next morning before first light. Fifty minutes after sunrise and less than 40 yards from the river, Bengt nailed the bull with one shot. We quartered and floated the moose to base camp in time to catch the floatplane and return to civilization that afternoon.

After the moose is quartered and carried to the boat, it is important to pack the meat so air can circulate around it. This can be accomplished by lashing the quarters to the frame: the hindquarters on the bottom, followed by the front quarters, neck and ribs. Six to eight large gamebags are necessary to protect the meat from dirt and contamination. Do not use plastic bags

for storage, but keep the meat as dry as possible. If rough water is expected, then place the meat in plastic garbage bags just prior to the run, but remove them immediately after.

Riverboats are often used in areas where roads or villages intersect major rivers. Inflatables are generally used on fly-in hunts.

Bears are a potential problem. Meat stored in the boat overnight is an invitation to serious trouble. Quarters should be removed from the boat and hung on a makeshift meat pole each night. It should be constructed at least 100 yards from the main camp. In areas lacking sufficient timber, place cut alders or willows in a large pile away from the shoreline, lay the quarters out in a single layer, and top with more brush.

Calling

During rut, moose follow a consistent pattern of behavior. During the hours of mid-day (from 10 a.m. to 4 p.m.) moose are inclined to take shelter in the heavily timbered areas along a river. It has been during the early morning and evening hours when I've found bulls to be active and vocal, offering the best chance for sighting a trophy.

Large bulls won't leave you guessing it's their territory. During pre-rut and rut, mid-September through October, you'll hear bulls crashing through brush, breaking the night silence with their lovesick grunts and other vocalizations. They will generally respond to any sound indicating an invasion of territory. However, a call that will attract trophy bulls at the beginning of the rut will usually bring in only smaller bulls two weeks later. The reason for this is that most dominant bulls have already paired up with a cow and show disinterest in any stimuli suggesting they have to do the work. However, bulls can mate with receptive cows within 36 hours and be on their way.

It's also important to know that moose may react even more readily to stimuli other than grunting and calling. Most hunters who've called in Canadian moose don't do quite as well when they go after Alaska moose with the same method. The "roar" call often used in Canada's dense timber to imitate a rutting bull moose is often inappropriate for Alaska's big bulls. Studies have indicated bulls living in a more forested habitat vocalize more than bush thrash, a common practice of Alaska-Yukon moose. The following methods work well either at timberline or in the lowlands.

I've found that Alaska moose respond best to a series of low grunts or bellows. In fact, the grunts are more like the croakings of a raven. Scientific studies indicate that when moose "croak," they're often infuriated and ready to do battle. And among moose, one hot temper will attract another. But grunting at moose can spook them as easily as attract them. The trick is to avoid the long, drawn-out calls that hunters typically use. You can imitate the "croak" by forming a guttural "bark" in the base of your throat. Make sure it lasts no more than a few seconds. Do two or three, then no others for at least 10 to 15 minutes. Most important, call only in stands of brush or timber, preferably in conjunction with the scraping method. As a general rule, smaller bulls rarely threaten larger bulls. It's the larger bulls that address more threats, and the ones that hunters can expect to approach.

Don't exclude the use of a cow call. It is best described as a drawn-out yelp made by a contralto with a head cold. In many instances a cow call works extremely well, and often produces a response when a bull call would not. Avid bowhunter Jay Massey, author of the book, *Bowhunting Alaska's Wild Rivers*, offers plenty of expert advice for hunters wishing to learn about using birch bark calls and calling. It's worthwhile reading.

If a bull responds to a cow call, wait and see what happens. If he comes to you, don't move. The bull will search you out. Oftentimes the bull will play hard to get, especially a big one. Then, you'll need to move quietly to the area where the bull is holding, and make another cow call. If the bull still doesn't come out of the brush, instill some jealousy in the ol' boy's heart. Give a deep, guttural bull call. I haven't met a bull yet that would let a rival bull steal away a flirting cow right in his back yard.

Rattling or scraping up a moose is a prime way to get a trophy bull enraged, either in conjunction with croaking or when used by itself. But first, rest at ease. This technique doesn't call for lugging a set of 50-inch antlers around or clashing them together.

First, obtain two scapula bones from either a moose, steer, or other large game animal, or locate some shed moose antlers, usually commonplace in interior woodlands. Biologist Bill Gasaway uses a large, four-foot spruce or birch pole if he can't find a suitable caribou or moose antler. You want to imitate the smacking sound made by sparring moose or the scraping and polishing sounds of moose ridding their antlers of velvet. Be noisy about either rubbing an antler on a nearby shrub, making the loudest scraping noise possible, or by rattling the pieces together with moderate force.

Bush thrashing aggressively advertises presence and readiness to interact (Knowles, 1983). Knowles studied the various types of thrashing, their purposes and their effects on bulls in rut.

Hunters wishing to experience the excitement of calling a bull in should study these pointers.

High-intensity bush thrashing results in the moose thrashing his rack in horizontal and vertical head movements. The resulting sound is very loud, a result of twigs and branches snapping and breaking. It is an auditory challenge to spar. In Knowles' study, all high-intensity bush thrashing answered by high-intensity bush thrashing led to preliminary sparring actions. Moose that did not respond with high-intensity bush thrashing or a threat soon left the area. Therefore, if you want a big bull, or to pull one out of cover, high-intensity thrashing is the way to go.

I've heard high-intensity thrashing on many occasions in western and southcentral Alaska. I've heard it clearly almost half mile or so downriver. Knowles reports hearing this about one mile away. Moose, of course, can hear high-intensity thrashing over a longer distance. Therefore, it pays to stay on stand for several hours if you know trophy moose are in the area. It may take them a while to walk the mile to your location.

Low intensity bush thrashing is distinctively different. Features of low-intensity thrashing include: the bull's thrashing whatever vegetation is available; its head movements are almost always horizontal; there is little damage to the plant; and it's not very loud. Low-intensity thrashing is most frequently addressed to cows.

Another good tactic I employ requires no work, at least on

John Gaudet called this large bull into easy shooting range for the author. Calling is an effective method of hunting, especially in heavy brush.

my part. I'll glass an area until I find a small bull and permit him to do the work for me as visual stimuli. Visual stimuli can be real—or fake, which involves work. World-renowned moose biologist Tony Bubenik once experimented with a paper mache' model of antlers from a mature bull moose. He wore the head-piece to observe what visual effect antlers play during rut. Just the sight of those antlers drew larger bulls out of cover where none where observed before. And the headpiece also established a social order among cows and smaller bulls.

While I don't recommend you construct such a headpiece, I do suggest that you wait before pulling the trigger on that 36-incher. Glass the area well if time permits. A larger bull may be in the area, itching for a fight with any and all intruders. And he'll undoubtedly sport a larger rack! However, patience is the key word here: I can never tell whether the first moose is the challenger or defender! A general rule of thumb is that a bull with a group of cow moose is usually the dominant bull. However, it's not uncommon to see several "satellite" bulls in the vicinity, waiting for the opportunity to challenge the dominant bull.

If there are no bulls in the area, and I have a discarded antler with me, I usually have some fun while moose hunting. When a moose responds to the call, or you spot one along the river-bank, hold the antler high over your head. Swing it back and forth as you walk toward the moose, and watch how the animal responds. Bill Gasaway is an expert in "talking" to moose in this manner. To him, this is one of the highlights of moose hunting season. Some moose will try to challenge you, while others will run off. Still others aren't sure exactly what you are. Yet, the mere presence of a rack, and a rack in motion, communicates social competition to a bull. While you can have fun with moose, always have your rifle ready, just in case. And don't try talking with antlers in heavily hunted areas.

A wallow is the "silent indicator" of a big bull in the area, and usually announces the presence of a territorial bull. It serves many functions, among them attracting cows, and communicating and generating excitement, especially among cows. A bull makes a wallow by digging into the mud or soil, urinating in it several times, and rolling in it repeatedly. All size bulls dig wallow pits, and often a young bull wallows in the recently abandoned pit of a prime bull. So check the tracks in and around the wallow. If there's more than one pit, or a series of freshly made, large tracks, chances are it's a good place to set-up a stand.

Making the Shot

When you're sneaking into range for a shot, remain downwind. Avoid any unnecessary noise when stalking. Ideally, let the moose come to you, especially if you're calling or thrashing. But if the bull is stubborn, take it slow and easy. Look over every bit of cover. In heavily timbered areas, slowly walk the edges and listen for any noise such as the snap of a twig or rustling of leaves. It could mean a bull or cow is looking you over. An older bull's tendency to defend territory and cows will generally subordinate his instinct to flee, at least long enough for you to get off a shot.

Because moose are often difficult to kill, I prefer the heavy 30 caliber rifles. I've seen too many moose run off after taking several 7mm and .270 slugs, right in the vitals. Many hunters aim for the heart-lung area. When the situation allows, I prefer the upper shoulder area. A shot there ruins less meat, severs major arteries and breaks down the shoulderblade and spine. The hydrostatic shock of the bullet hitting such a large mass of bone is usually enough to dispatch the animal. When hit in this area, the biggest bulls are put out of commission, fast. Only if you're an expert marksman should you try for the neck, especially at a distance.

Be prepared to shoot more than once. Some moose go down with one shot, but rarely are they killed with one shot. Fire as many times as necessary to dispatch the animal. As for meat preparation, turn to the Field Care of Meat Chapter.

Hunting moose is a chance for the average hunter to enjoy a true wilderness hunting experience, going for North America's largest deer in its largest state. Not only can you enjoy the excitement of the hunt, but also the serenity of wilderness Alaska, watching otters slide down mud banks, flushing hundreds of ptarmigan from a streamside thicket, and frying fresh moose steaks over an open birch fire as snow geese wing their way south. This is what an Alaska moose hunt is all about. Experience it soon.

(left) A moose hindquarter can weigh as much as 125 pounds. Take your time, especially when going uphill or crossing marshy tundra.

(right) A hunter examining a tree scrape or rub made by the moose he shot earlier that day. Brush thrashing is a popular way of calling in big bulls.

Where to Hunt Moose

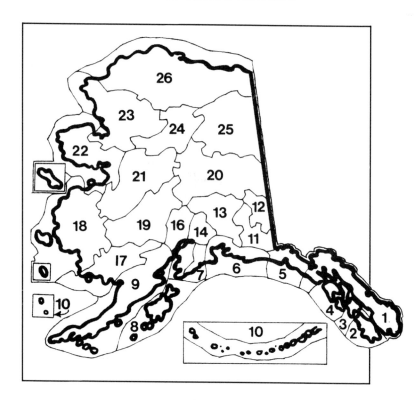

Subunits 1A, 1B, and Unit 3

As a result of a 1963-64 transplant of 14 moose from Cook Inlet and Chickaloon Flats, a remnant herd is present in the drainages of the Chickamin River in subunit 1A. Limited moose hunting occurs in the Unuk River drainage.

The northern portion of subunit 1B is seeing an increase in its moose population. Popular hunting areas in this unit are Thomas Bay and the Farragut River. Success ratios vary from 10 to 15 percent. Most hunters reach their hunting areas by boat. Over the last 10 years, harvests generally have been good.

The southern portion of subunit 1B receives much of the hunting pressure in this area. Most of the successful hunters in this unit use boats, while very few hunters use aircraft as a means of access. Harvest reports indicate that on the Stikine River, 35 percent of the bulls were taken during the first week, 10 percent during the second week, 35 percent during the third week, and 20 percent during the fourth week. An early frost in September can cause an early leaf drop, which creates good visibility for the hunters in this area.

Unit 1C

The most popular areas to hunt are Hunt Area 956, the Taku River and the Chilkat River, as well as Berners Bay drainages. Moose population is currently in good condition in the Chilkat Range. Try hunting on the Excursion Inlet side. Current season runs from September 15 through October 15.

Unit 1D

The area that stands out as producing the most moose is the Chilkat drainage. Successful hunters use riverboats. It's a toss-up as to the success of hunters above Wells Bridge and below Wells Bridge; however, many hunters interviewed prefer the lower sections of the drainage. At present, hunting is by registration permit only.

Unit 5

In subunit 5A, the Yakutat Forelands, the Dangerous River and vicinity immediately to the east are popular with most hunters, while success is somewhat lower to the west of the river. In this area, most of the moose are taken within the first week of the season.

Subunit 5B; the Malaspina Forelands: The popular spot here is east of Sitkag Bluffs.

Unit 6

The 1988 estimated moose population for Unit 6 after hunting was near 1,500. Calf production and survival was excellent.

Subunit 6A; Katalla to Icy Bay: Most of the unit's moose are here, with others east of Suckling Hills. Ratio of 30 bulls:100 cows; high percentage of antlers reaching 60-plus inches. Hunter success near 70 percent. Game department encouraging cow or calf harvest to slow rapid population growth.

Subunit 6B; Martin River: Currently restricted to resident-only participation. Population has reached nearly 340. Antlered moose hunting by registration permit; antlerless moose by drawing permit. Up to 30 antlered moose will be taken in 1989.

Subunit 6C; West Copper River Delta: Currently restricted to residents; up to 40 permits by drawing. Population nearing 260.

Units 7, 15

Kenai Peninsula

Hunter success rate for Unit 7 hovers between 15 and 20 percent. Nearly 70 percent of the successful hunters access the area via highway vehicle or horseback. Hunters using horses typically had the highest success rate (31 percent).

Subunit 15A; Kenai Peninsula: Most of the harvest in this area comes from the 85,000-acre 1969 burn, which is continuing to provide excellent browse for moose and opportunities for hunter success. However, areas that make up "good" moose habitat comprise 12 percent of the subunit, with the remainder classified as unproductive. Only bulls with spike-fork or

50-inch-plus antlers may be taken. There is an August bow season for moose in this subunit.

Subunit 15B; Kenai Peninsula: This unit shows a continuing trend toward a high bull/cow ratio. The current, minimum ratio is 40:100. This area offers a prime, trophy moose hunt that is popular among resident and non-resident sportsmen.

Subunit 15C; Kenai Peninsula: Moose are moderately abundant and are nearing the carrying capacity of this subunit. The primary means of access in this region are highway vehicles, horses and foot travel. Successful hunters concentrate on the Tustemena Lake, Deep Creek, Anchor River, Kachemak Bay and Ninilchik drainages for their moose.

Unit 9

Alaska Peninsula

Some portions of Unit 9 still have good moose hunting, with a bull/cow ratio of 35 to 40:100 in the area northwest of Lake Clark in 9B, all of 9C and the northern half of 9E. While 9C used to offer top trophy moose hunting, the harvest in that area tripled from 1984 to 1986. Subunit 9E has been experiencing a decrease in moose populations since the early 1970s. This subunit requires a 50-inch minimum on any bull moose.

Unit 11

Chitina Valley

Low moose population. Success ratio is around 25 percent.

Unit 12

Upper Tanana River and White River

Hunters pursue moose in the Tok and Little Tok drainages, with the remaining moose population spread throughout the Tanana, Nabesna, Chisana and White River drainages. Hunter success is over 20 percent.

Unit 13

Nelchina and Upper Susitna Rivers

A harvest of 1,200 moose was recorded for 1988. Larger numbers of moose are found at the higher elevations in this unit. Moose are distributed throughout the region.

Unit 14

Subunit 14A; Matanuska Valley: Both antlerless and antlered moose hunts are available. Harvest is approximately 400 to 500 moose per year.

Subunit 14B; Willow to Talkeetna: Hunters experience a 20 percent success rate, taking over 200 moose from this area. Population is stable.

Subunit 14C and Unit 7; Portage and Placer River Drainages: A young and growing moose population with a bull/cow ratio of 48:100. A special, Fort Richardson permit hunt is offered later in the season. Also, several archery-only hunts are offered in this unit.

Unit 16

West Side of Cook Inlet

There are over 9,000 moose in this area, and about 8 to 10 percent are harvested annually. Some of the most productive areas include Mount Susitna, Alexander Creek, Yenlo Hills and Willow Mountain.

Subunit 16B; Kalgin Island: This area offers a good opportunity for hunters to bag a meat moose. Most moose are killed within the first four days of the season. After the first few days of hunting, moose move into heavy cover, which reduces hunting success.

Unit 17

Northern Bristol Bay

This area has seen an increase in numbers of moose; however, antler size is quite significant among successful hunters. In a recent survey, over 56 percent of those hunting indicated their moose racks exceeded 50 inches. Aircraft is used extensively in 17B, while boats were most used in 17C. Approximately 150 to 200 moose are harvested from this unit.

Unit 18

Yukon-Kuskokwim Delta

The moose population along the Yukon River from Ohagamuit to Paimuit increased in 1988 from low to moderate density. Low numbers of moose in the Kuskokwim drainage led to a closure of the lower Yukon Delta. There's about 1,000 moose in the Yukon drainage, although they are partially migratory, retreating up river towards Unit 21E in winter.(Patten, 1989).

Unit 19

Middle and Upper Kuskokwim Drainages

The moose population appears to be stable or slightly increasing in this unit, although deep, crusted snow during the 1988-89 winter might have led to a higher than normal winterkill. About 600 moose are reported in the annual harvest, but suspected kill is thought to be near 900. Hunters usually access subunits 19A and 19D by boat. Most of the hunting effort in subunit 19A is centered along the lower Holitna-Hoholitna drainages. In subunit 19B the upper Hoholitna, especially around Whitefish Lake, and upper Stony River drainages generally produce the greatest kill.

In subunit 19C, the upper South Fork of the Kuskokwim and Hartman Rivers produce quite a few moose, as well as the Farewell Burn area and Big River drainages. A large airstrip and roads throughout the subunit make the area easily accessible to hunters who fly in.

In subunit 19D, the main Kuskokwim River, Takotna River and the North Fork of the Kuskokwim are popular and productive. During the 1987-88 season, the reported success rate in Unit 19 was 54 percent, with a mean reported antler spread of 48 inches.

Unit 20

Subunit 20A; Tanana Flats, Central Alaska Range: The subunit harvest in this area has increased annually since 1978. Most hunters prefer to hunt on the Tanana Flats between the Wood and Little Delta rivers, the Totatlanika River and the Healy and Ferry areas. Also, the foothills of the Alaska Range are an excellent area for large bulls. Aircraft and boats are the two most popular means of accessing this subunit.

Subunit 20B; Fairbanks and Central Tanana Valley: Young bulls (with antler spreads of less than 50 inches) comprise most of the harvest in this area. The Chena drainage, Minto Flats Management Area and Chatanika and Tolovana River drainages are the top producers.

Subunit 20C; Kantishna, Cosna and Nenana River Drainages: This area has a fair number of moose. Try the Nenana, Kantishna and Teklanika river areas.

Subunit 20D; Central Tanana Valley: Most successful hunters use off-road vehicles or highway vehicles to get into their hunting areas south of the Tanana, while boats, aircraft and ATVs are used to access the areas north of the Tanana. West of Johnson River is a fair producer of moose.

Subunit 20E; Fortymile, Charley and Ladue River Drainages: Moose density is low in this unit, however, the population has a good number of old-age bulls. In a recent season, fifty-five percent of the bulls harvested had antler spreads 50 inches or greater. Moose in this subunit have a larger body size than moose in subunit 20A. Harvest is heaviest in the Mosquito Fork drainage.

Subunit 20F; Central Yukon, Hess Creek and Tozitna River Drainages: Hunter success ratio averages around 20 percent in this area. The largest harvests come from the Yukon River drainage, (excluding Hess Creek) followed by the Manley-Tofty area. The population is stable.

Unit 21

Subunit 21A; Upper Nowitna, Iditarod, and Upper Innoko Drainages: Moose population is stable, with reported harvests of about 120 moose annually over past five years. Hunters fly in or float the Innoko River.

Subunit 21B; Lower Nowitna, Yukon River between Melozitna and Tozitna Rivers: Population estimates indicate about 800 moose inhabit this area. Most hunters hit the Nowitna, Sulatna and the Yukon rivers, and along Ruby Road, in that order. Populations are declining in this area.

Subunit 21C; Upper Dulbi River and Melozitna River Drainage above Grayling Creek: The moose population is low but stable. Aircraft is the predominant means of access in 21C boundary, and riverboats in the Dulbi River area.

Subunit 21D; Middle Yukon, Eagle Island to Ruby, Koyukuk River below Dulbi Slough: Harvest data on bulls sampled from this region suggest that moose from the Koyukuk drainage grow larger antlers than moose found elsewhere in the interior. Moose populations along the riparian lowlands are high and appear stable. Concentrations of bulls appear near Squirrel Creek, Kaiyuh Slough and Ruby Slough.

Subunit 21E; Yukon River drainage upstream from Paimiut-Kalskag Portage, including the lower Innoko River below the mouth of the Iditarod River, to the mouth of Blackburn Creek: Paimiut Slough is the hotspot for numbers of moose and large moose. Boat access best. Annual harvest is 100 moose for a success rate of 65 percent.

Unit 22

Seward Peninsula

The unit-wide population of moose is estimated to be 8,000 to 10,000. During the past decade, the greatest moose density and highest moose harvests have occured in subunit 22D. Moose are concentrated along two major drainages in subunit 22D: the Kuzitrin River, an area with relatively good access and high annual harvests; and the American/Agiapuk River, an area without road access and low to moderate harvests.

Unit 23

Kotzebue Sound

The unit-wide population of moose is estimated to be nearly 10,000. Good moose populations exist along the Selawik, Tagagawik, Noatak and Kobuk rivers. Access is via fly-in. Burns and willows growing along rivers in the area have provided good winter range. Excellent moose numbers in the southern portion of the unit can be found in the Kiwalik, Kugruk, Inmachuk and Goodhope River drainges. Hunting pressure near these watersheds is low.

Unit 24

Koyukuk River Drainage North of and Including Dulbi Slough

Moose population in the Koyukuk River lowlands is high, with the exception of the Kanuti Controlled Use Area located on the Kanuti Flats. The Fish Creek area, east of the Haul Road, offers good populations as do the willow stands along the Koyukuk River drainage. The area between Bettles and the Gates of the Arctic National Park and Preserve is also good. The moose population near Huggins Island, Treat Island and along the Huslia River is very low.

Unit 25

Yukon Flats, Chandalar, Porcupine and Black River Drainages; Birch and Beaver Creeks

The main harvest in this unit is from subsistence hunters. Residents of Stevens Village, Beaver or Birch Creek can get registration permits to hunt the western half of Unit 25, where numbers are still low but doing better. Moose population in eastern 25D is low and may be declining. Population in subunit 25A is low, found mostly in drainages.

Unit 26

Subunit 26A; Western Arctic Slope: Moose are well established in this area. The 1988 estimated moose population for subunit 26A is about 2,300. The population has been stable and slightly increasing, however, a poor calf survival in 1987 and 1988 may change that. Popular hunting areas include the Colville River from Killik Bend to the mouth of the Anaktuvak River, and the Anaktuvak and Chandlar rivers.

Subunits 26B and 26C; Central and Eastern Arctic Slope: These areas offer good moose hunting, however, access is difficult and expensive. Archery hunting for moose is available along the Dalton Highway.

CHAPTER 2

Barren-ground Caribou

Barren-ground caribou are probably the least understood of all big game animals found in Alaska. They are like the wind-blown sands of an arctic Sahara: their whereabouts from day to day are unpredictable. They are always moving and shifting, filling in gullies and dispersing over wide-open flats. And like grains of sand, their numbers stagger the imagination. Near the Beaufort Sea in mid-July, it's possible to see up to 50,000 caribou per square mile. Seeing these animals, or at least knowing that such numbers exist, is a truly humbling experience. Yet, this seemingly endless supply of caribou often fools the hunter into thinking that success is nearly guaranteed. Nothing could be further from the truth. The unpredictability of caribou hunting often makes for a frustrating experience.

Because of this and other reasons, outdoor writers often disparage barren-ground caribou hunting as less glamorous than hunting the woodland or mountain species of caribou found in Canada. This is nonsense. Barren-ground caribou are found in some of the most beautiful and rugged mountain ranges in Alaska. I've hunted caribou in the shadow of smoking volcanos, with the shimmering, indigo-blue expanse of Alaska's Shelikof Strait less than two miles away. I've also encountered caribou on bleak, barren tundra, where both animals and hunter have taken to the gullies for protection from a tempest of rain and hail.

Because of the variety of the arctic environment, and unpredictability of the animal, hunting the barren-ground caribou requires learning the animal's habits and developing effective hunting strategy and tactics.

In late August, barren-ground caribou—like this mature bull—are found in the high alpine country. Stalking a trophy bull requires patience and knowledge of caribou habits. (Photo by Kent Stuckey)

Life History and Habits

The barren-ground caribou, *Rangifer arcticus*, is a medium-sized member of the deer family. Males typically reach weights of 400 to 600 pounds, with females weighing from 200 to 300 pounds. The largest-bodied caribou are found on Adak Island in the Aleutian Chain. Because of the island's lack of biting insects, low caribou population, abundant forage, and absence of obstructions to movement, caribou on Adak reach tremendous size. Among the largest taken by a sportsman is a bull shot in September, 1968, that weighed 700 pounds.

The caribou is also the most abundant big game animal in Alaska. In the 1930s, Alaska had an estimated population of over one million caribou. Over the next 40 years, the various herds suffered cyclic population crashes, with the statewide total dwindling to about 240,000 in the early 1970s. However, caribou numbers throughout the state have made a strong comeback. Currently, Alaska has over 600,000 caribou dispersed in 28 major herds and two subspecies of *Rangifer arcticus*. The Grant caribou, *R. a. granti*, live on the Alaska Peninsula; the remainder are the Stone's caribou, *R. a. stonei*.

Breeding season occurs during the middle or end of October, but varies among the various herds located throughout the state. If a female fails to conceive, she can experience a second or third period of estrous at intervals of 10 to 12 days. Gestation is about 227 days, and usually the caribou calves in a herd are born within a 4-to 10-day period. Twin calves are highly uncommon. Calves weigh about 11 to 20 pounds at birth, and are able to follow the cows within an hour of being born. This is an important evolutionary factor, as in many areas predation on newborn calves is quite high. Twenty-five percent or more of caribou calves die in the first month after birth.

Caribou have a good repertoire of sensory organs that they use to their advantage. Their sense of sight is fair. Like other big game animals, caribou have difficulty in making out stationary objects, yet readily observe movement of any type. Their indifference to stationary objects or far-away moving objects—such as a hunter sneaking up a hill toward them—is not stupidity, but rather, the employment of their "danger buffer." This phenomenon is easily explained. There are no predators on the open tundra that the caribou can't outrun. Thus, a wolf at 200 yards is no threat to the animal. However, let any natural predator enter this "danger buffer" and the caribou will flee. Fast movements made toward the caribou will have the same effect. Of course, the range and accuracy of a high-powered

rifle allows the human hunter to stay out of the "danger buffer." Thus the hunter is able to take caribou without alerting their senses. In heavily hunted areas, however, caribou have responded negatively to a hunter's presence. The animals will commonly disperse over a wide range during the hunting season, or take shelter in heavy stands of timber.

Without question, caribou cows guard the herd. They are more alert and suspicious than the mature bulls, and often spend much time watching a hunter who has frozen in position. I've had caribou cows spend minutes staring at me, their noses twitching nervously. When they couldn't get my scent, they'd slowly circle around to my other side, catch my scent, and jump as if they were shocked by electricity. As long as I kept my distance, though, they'd wander off slowly. On a few occasions when I had the devil in me, I'd run after the cows, just to see them run. They'd snort, raise their tails, and lead the caribou—usually small bulls and calves—down the mountainside.

Caribou have an excellent sense of smell. How a caribou will respond to scent depends on the animal's recent experiences with hunters and humans. For example, the Porcupine herd in northeastern Alaska may not spook after scenting a hunter. Rather, they'll slowly mill around, looking at you, their curiosity getting the best of them. On the other hand, Alaska Peninsula caribou that have been hunted hard will run for miles upon scenting a human hunter at a distance of a mile or more.

However, their sense of hearing is only fair. Caribou live in a soft-sounded world where there are few "hard" sounds, like the snapping of twigs or metal clanging against metal. Herd animals, caribou are accustomed to hearing soft clicking and snapping sounds made by other members of the herd. Consequently, they pay little attention to the occasional twig crunching made by an approaching hunter. Of course, caution in stalking should still be practiced. I remember stalking one herd of caribou in the Wood River area of interior Alaska. As I cleared the ridge, I came face to face with a solitary wolf. He was off and running before I could throw up the rifle for a shot. Although I didn't get that wolf, the experience confirmed that it's best to be "soft and quiet" than "fast and noisy."

Caribou cows are often the "watchdogs" of a caribou herd. They are the first to alert the big bulls, especially when males are preoccupied with rutting activities.

Antler Growth

Both male and female caribou have antlers—the only deer species exhibiting this feature. Even the youngest caribou, a month after birth, has two spike horns. But without question, the bull's antlers are the more impressive.

Bulls begin growing their antlers in late April. During the months of May and June, the main branches appear. In July, the various tines and branches start to form and the antlers take on a mature form. In August, the antler tips fill out and the caribou begins to scrape velvet the last of August or first part of September.

A cow's antler growth is about a half-year out of phase with that of a bull. Cows lose their velvet in late October and carry their antlers until late spring. During the winter months, the hornless bulls must often give in to the cows' wishes. It's extremely common to see cows prod bulls away from choice feeding areas. This may be an evolutionary adaptation allowing the cows choice food, to nourish themselves as well as the young they are carrying.

When non-resident hunters see a mature, bull caribou rack up close for the first time, they are astounded. It sports two main beams, each sweeping back from the forehead before flaring upward and outward, stretching up to 50 inches or more. A pair a brow tines or shovels stretches out from the main beam, reaching far out onto the nose. A bez tine branches off the main beam a short distance above the brow tine. The terminal portion of the main beam is usually flattened or palmated and divided into a number of rearward-facing tines.

Antlers of a bull increase in size and dimension each year. They are at their peak when the caribou is between six and nine years of age. After that, the antlers become smaller with age. Antlers of the cow change little in size and mass after she is two years old.

The hunter looking for a good caribou trophy should keep in mind that caribou antlers come in two distinctive categories: V-shaped antlers and wide, rounded or U-shaped antlers. Getting a frontal view of the animal is usually the best way to distinguish between the two. Both types, with numerous intermediate variations, can be found in the same herd. Also, there exists a difference between herds. Caribou from the 40 Mile herd have V-shaped antlers with short, thick beams, numerous tines, and a narrow spread. Many caribou from the Alaska Peninsula tend to have U-shaped antlers with long, spindly beams and tines.

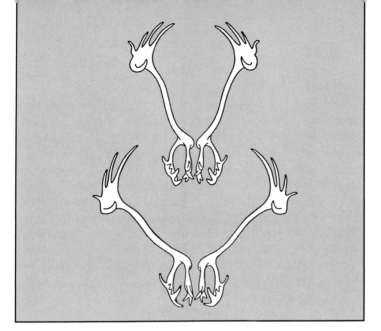

Caribou racks come in many shapes and sizes. The two most common are the "V" shape, typical of 40-Mile caribou, and "U" shape, which are common to Western Arctic and Alaska Peninsula caribou. However, both shapes can be found in any herd.

Olaus Murie (1935) conducted some pioneering work on caribou antlers. He classified them into three categories:

1. Round horns with a minimum of palmation throughout.
2. Flat horns, in which the palmation occurs as a general flattening of the beam toward the tip.
3. Palmated horns, in which the definite, somewhat circular "palm" appears at the end of the beam and principal branches.

The third category is the type usually qualifying for record-book consideration, and is of the most interest to sportsmen looking for an impressive trophy mount.

Of course, caribou antlers come in many variations, from simple to extreme. I've seen antlers that come out of the skull almost horizontally before sweeping up at the end with small but heavily tined palmation. This type of rack would never make the record book, but it's one worth taking based on its unusual configuration. Keep this thought in mind: don't expect all caribou racks to be perfectly symmetrical. The unusual-growth antlers make just as good, if not better, trophy mounts.

Some hunters are obsessed with a "double shovel" rack. In this configuration, the brow tine develops into a shovel or palmation on both sides. Normally, a mere spike and a shovel are found on most caribou. Some guides say that one out of every 5,000 caribou has a double shovel. From my experience, I'd say seven to 10 percent of the male population of a herd has a double shovel. Of course, the frequency of double-shovels varies with herd size, location, and mortality factors.

Habits

When alarmed at close range, the caribou reacts by galloping or trotting. Banfield (1951) reported caribou galloping across a frozen lake at 45 to 50 miles per hour. This speed, however, can only be maintained for a short distance, as caribou soon become winded.

When moderately alarmed, caribou break into a high-stepping trot, much like that of pure-bred, champion quarter horse. When trotting, the caribou bull holds its head horizontally, the rack stretching out over his back. He thrusts his arched forelegs out in swift, deliberate movements.

The caribou uses the trot to cover long distances quickly, and can maintain the trot speed for miles. On their annual migrations, the caribou maintain a steady pace. Trotting caribou grab mouthfuls of caribou lichen as they move along. Olaus Murie (1935) aptly compared the actions of a feeding, young bull to "...a commuter eating breakfast on the run."

To the first-time hunter, the caribou always appears to be eating. "Caribou lichen," those in the genus *Cladonia*, are one of the caribou's favorite foods. Caribou are also fond of willow leaves, dwarf birch, and grasses. Caribou also relish fungi. In both alpine and lowland areas, look for trails that lead to prime feeding areas. Windblown ridges are a good place to find caribou after a snow storm hits, especially early in the season.

The caribou is also a good swimmer. On their annual migrations, the animals frequently ford major rivers and streams. In the Western Arctic Herd region of the state, caribou herds crossing a river leave mats of their hair on the bank. Due to the excellent insulating quality of the hair, interior Eskimos often use it as stuffing for mattresses.

Hunting Techniques

If caribou hunting frustrates you, don't be discouraged. A variety of factors are responsible for the caribou's "restlessness." They are a gregarious species, always on the move for an adequate supply of food. Geographical structures (mountains, valleys, large lakes, and glaciers) also influence a herd.

Even biologists find the caribou a frustrating animal. In his 1956 thesis on the Fortymile caribou herd, Ronald Skoog wrote a paragraph about the caribou that still applies today:

> When the author first began this study, he frequently became quite discouraged, because the caribou seemed to thwart his every plan. But after three years of ex-

Caribou lichen is a favorite and abundant caribou food that is found throughout Alaska's tundra regions. Fungi and sedges are also popular food items.

perience, he has come to realize that defeat normally occurs quite often in one's dealings with caribou.''

Skoog's observations on caribou migrations are noteworthy. He said that the greatest fluctuations in movement occur day by day. A herd of caribou may be feeding peacefully in one area for several days. Overnight they'll decide to travel 40 miles to another area, and might remain there for a day, week, or month. Also, caribou holding in an area will constantly move from place to place. Individual animals exhibit even more erratic behavior.

The annual migration of caribou is generally a directional, long-distance trek. One migration usually occurs in the spring, the other in the fall. Other large-scale movements are apt to occur at any time. Insects keep caribou herds packed on top of windy ridgetops, where the animals receive some relief from the pests. Deep or hard-packed snow will prevent the animals from finding food in certain locales. Skoog said that thick fog seems to make caribou uneasy, and less likely to travel long distances; dark nights produce a similar effect. Also, salt licks and mineral springs provide a strong attraction to the herd.

Hunters should be aware of other factors that motivate herd movement. Bulls need to scrape velvet from their antlers in late August. They move down into the lower brushy areas to do this, forsaking the safety of the high alpine country. After their antlers are polished, bulls are constantly on the move in search of receptive cows.

In hunting caribou, you'll encounter various factors influencing caribou migrations. What factors are operating depends on whether you're hunting in the early season or the late season.

Hunting Early-Season Caribou

An early-season caribou hunt is exciting. The tundra is ablaze with color, berries are ripe and abundant, and caribou bulls frequent the highcountry. The bulls are in fine condition. Beneath the backskin, bulls have a layer of fat up to two to three inches thick that can weigh as much as 30 pounds. The animal puts on this fat by feeding on willow, blueberry, dwarf birch, lichens, and various types of grasses and sedges. I think that this diet is what makes the steaks, roasts, and chops from an early-season caribou much finer than the finest cuts of beef. If you're a meat hunter, an early-season hunt is the best way to go.

The early-season caribou's antlers are also in velvet, and make a very handsome mount if you're lucky enough to connect. You usually have until the third week in August before the velvet starts drying at the edges. Males over five years of age with the heaviest racks are usually the first to strip their velvet. It may take up until the end of the second week in September for the animal to have its antlers completely cleaned and polished. Younger males lose their velvet soon after the older animals shed their velvet in late-September and October.

In most areas you need to get into the mountains when hunting early-season caribou. Depending on area, you can choose from ATV, horseback, riverboat, hike-in, or the favorite: fly-in via Super Cub to get to high alpine lakes and ridges. To fly to a good caribou area without any "competition," be prepared to pay anywhere from $400 to $800 for a charter. However, the hunt is often worth the high price tag. One air taxi operator who specializes in caribou hunting had a 100 percent success ratio among all his fly-in clients during the past two years.

Getting to the caribou is often the easy part. Once you're there, the work begins. Hunting the alpine takes careful planning. Too many hunters spend the early morning and late evening hours traveling to and from their prospective hunting areas. To be successful, they should be hunting at these times rather than walking.

Be an "early bird." Pitch a spike camp near prime caribou habitat and get up very early in the morning to scout for bulls. In mid-August, this means getting up around 5 a.m. Take time only to boil water for coffee or tea. Take some snacks to munch on while you hunt. Start hunting as soon as you walk out of your tent.

Rarely do I stay in one spot during my early-morning glass-

ing. I walk around the perimeter of the mountain, glassing at select vantage points for 15 to 30 minutes before moving on. I like an area where I can glass individual alpine bowls, yet still not be far away from a point where I can glass the entire mountainside at once.

On hot autumn days, caribou and snowfields go hand in hand. The snow keeps the animals cool, and insects at bay. Have your mountain boots on, as the going is often rough!

Be prepared to act when walking through alpine meadows. You'll find yourself in head-high grass and willows interspersed amongst irregular terrain. Expect to jump up caribou as you go. While most of these will be young bulls or cows, there's always a chance that ol' mosshorn will be around the next knoll. Just take it slow and easy, and avoid silhouetting yourself against the skyline. However, if you're glassing the area properly before you walk through it, you'll usually spot caribou before they see you.

After about 11:30 a.m., either walk back to camp and cook up a meal, or unpack a stove and cook up brunch. I prefer the latter, especially when long climbing distances are involved. Besides, it's hard to beat a brunch of hot cider, cinnamon oatmeal and a chocolate/almond bar while looking for caribou on a wind-swept ridge. No restaurant can beat the view.

About 1 p.m., I'll begin scouting new areas and looking for

Early-season caribou hunts are not all work and sweat. This bull was taken in September on the Alaska Peninsula. While the temperature was in the upper 70s, the cool ocean breezes from Alaska's Shelikof Straight (upper right) made for a cool hunt. As it turned out, I had to bivouac overnight in a nearby gully with my trophy and meat. After the shot was made, a wolf pack moved in and refused to leave. I was guarding the meat until the next afternoon when the pilot landed at the pick-up site.

sign. I take out the spotting scope and glass far hillsides for caribou heading my way. I get especially excited when I find a patch of snow. Look for snowpacks in amphitheatres, gullies, hidden basins, and the northern side of mountains. Caribou will often crowd onto the smallest snowpack in an effort to cool down and keep insects at bay. On a blustery day one year while hunting the Alaska Peninsula, I saw over 50 caribou crowded onto a snowpack no larger than a tennis court.

Also keep an eye out for saddles (low areas between two mountains) and low, swampy areas on hillsides. Water often collects in these areas, and a quick check for tracks confirms whether caribou have been drinking there. If so, set up a blind near the watering hole. Better yet, camp a few hundred yards away and be ready to be on stand by first light, and if need be, throughout the late afternoon and evening hours.

On days when the temperatures are in the 70s and higher, don't bother to hunt. Take a nap or read a book. Caribou will either be on the ridgetops cooling off, or in the brush taking refuge from the sun. You may find bulls moving, but mostly things remain pretty quiet until between 4 to 7 p.m. Then, caribou start moving through the alpine country. Repeat the same hunting procedure as mentioned for early morning.

Late-afternoon glassing does have a major drawback. The animals are often hard to find in their newly grown coats of hair. Their color ranges from a light gray to a dark brown, and blends extremely well with the early morning and late evening shadows. When you are glassing a small valley with the sun at your back, any caribou walking toward you stands out clearly. The white mane of a bull reflects sunlight remarkably well, making him visible from great distances. A bull walking away from the sun, however, invariably appears dark and blends in with the shadows of the tundra. You have to position yourself so that any light works in your favor.

If you happen to see a bull, watch the animal's posture. If the bull has spotted you, he may go into an alarm pose. In this, the head sticks straight up and out, held rigidly; ears point skyward. The tail sticks out horizontally, almost vertical in position. Oftentimes one hind leg will extend out from the side. If other animals are in the group, they assume this posture also. Be prepared to shoot. If the animal that went on alert bolts, the other caribou will follow suit. Try to avoid shooting at running caribou. A study done in western Alaska showed that for every 10 caribou shot while running, two were wounded and not retrieved.

Also be wary if the bull picks up your scent before making visual contact. In heavily hunted areas, a caribou that can pick up any trace of human scent on the wind or tundra will spook up to a mile away. Before fleeing in lightly hunted areas, caribou will often walk in a wide circle, attempting to confirm what their senses have told them.

If a bull does pick up your scent and heads for other pastures, avoid the temptation to continue hunting the same location. Before a caribou bolts, you may see him rise up on his hind legs for a second or two before he bounds off. This is like the arctic hare's "spy hop," used to get a better look at the intruder. But unlike hares, when caribou are spooked, they secrete a substance from scent glands located in their hooves. Subsequently, any caribou later traveling over that same area will pick up the warning scent and spook. It must be mindboggling for the greenhorn caribou hunter, carefully hidden downwind this time to avoid spooking another bull, to observe a herd reach that spot and bolt in the opposite direction. Such a reaction could make a hunter unaware of the situation feel like an incompetent.

Here are a few other pointers to keep in mind when hunt-

When hunting early-season caribou, look for them in alpine valleys, draws and amphitheatres. Because of their migratory nature, caribou can suddenly pop into view. Therefore, always be thinking of potential stalking plans when glassing an area. Should you see caribou, you'll be prepared.

ing early-season, high-country caribou:

• If caribou are moving, always try to intercept them: never try to catch up. Plan your stalk so that you'll have plenty of time to change course should the caribou do likewise.

• Try to pick a knoll from which to shoot. On flat tundra, a caribou can be obscured by a small rise or thicket of brush.

• Take your time before shooting. Cows usually lead the herd, with the big bulls bringing up the rear. When a herd is spooked, the big bulls usually lag behind the speedy does and fawns. Take your time before shooting. Many a hunter has shot a "trophy" bull, only to find several larger caribou come walking out of the bushes minutes later.

• If you don't see any animals the first day, don't despair. Caribou are highly mobile and an entire herd can be milling around your tent by next morning.

• Be sure to make your reservations for a charter flight well in advance of the season. I frequently observe groups of hunters at the air terminal in either King Salmon and Bettles, waiting to catch a flight. On one occasion, I remember a party of hunters who waited for two days before they could get out. All they could do is watch hunters who had made early reservations fly in on a commercial jet and an hour later fly out to the hunting grounds. The sooner you can make reservations for your charter flight, the better. January of the year you plan to hunt is not too soon.

Late-Season Caribou Hunting

Your chances of taking a trophy bull dramatically increases if you hunt caribou during the late season, anytime starting from mid-September through November. In late September, inclement weather drives the caribou out of the mountains and into the lowlands near mountain bases and valleys. There they will satisfy their appetite on lush stands of vegetation nourished by underground seepage at the base of these slopes. The thick vegetation (often part of willow or alder thickets) hides caribou from the hunter. I solve the problem of finding caribou in this thick stuff by taking a few hours to climb above the jungle to where I can glass down over it. This lets me spot bulls faster than if I were on the same level. It also allows me more time to plan a stalk on a potential trophy.

As fall continues, caribou move away from the mountain basins and into the flatlands and rolling hills. There they feed on sedges and lichen adjacent to lakes and rivers. Then, these are the prime areas to look for caribou.

Late-season caribou hunting demands that you set up a base camp before you start glassing. In the first half of September, winter weather is already established in many sections of the Brooks Range. On the Alaska Peninsula, it arrives by middle October. Expect white-outs and winds of up to 70 mph, especially on the peninsula.

When flying into an area, look for concentrations of caribou.

Mountain passes or watering holes are good places to intercept migrating caribou. Remember to keep downwind!

I bagged this nice bull on a solitary hunt in late August in the mountains near Tok, Alaska. A herd of about 25 caribou were moving through a large amphitheatre at 5,300 feet at 6:30 a.m. This was the largest bull in the group.

If you spot a herd or two, have the pilot land somewhere in front of the animals. Early in the season, there are numerous lakes for a float plane to land on. Later on, after ice-up, ski-planes or tundra tires are most often used.

Since hunting the same day airborne is illegal in Alaska, you must wait until the next day before taking a caribou.

Always keep one important rule in mind. Never, never pitch your tent out on the open tundra. Find structure to break the wind: a gully, an abandoned cabin or even a patch of alders. Each year, many caribou hunts turn into disasters. A strong wind yanks up a tent and flings it like a beachball across the tundra. Without shelter, you risk hypothermia and perhaps death. Spend a few minutes each day before the hunt, ensuring that your tent is pegged down solidly.

As in early-season caribou hunting, glassing is the first order of business, especially in areas like the Cinder Flats on the Alaska Peninsula, or the hills in northwestern Alaska. Find a knoll and set up a spotting scope. I prefer a scope over binoculars because the distances on the open tundra are usually greater than in the highcountry. A 20-to 45-power variable scope mounted on a sturdy, "wind-proof" tripod is good. Unless you're hunting riparian habitat, or alder brush jungles, you should be able to locate caribou almost immediately if weather and migratory conditions are right.

Once you've located a good bull, don't put your spotting scope away. Use it to choose your route to the animal. Don't make the mistake so often made by novice caribou hunters who try to catch up with migrating caribou. It's nearly impossible to catch up with a herd of caribou on the move. Hummocky tundra is the tundra hunter's scourge. There, for every 20 feet you travel, you stumble or fall at least twice. But caribou can easily traverse this nightmarish real estate at a steady clip of six miles per hour with minimal effort!

Your goal is to plan a stalk to intercept the animals. This means utilizing any available cover, especially gullies and streambeds. If you have to walk through ice-cold creeks to reach your caribou, so be it. Often you have to crawl on your belly to get within shooting range of a prime bull. Here's a tip that might help: the ideal time to begin a stalk is when a bull beds down. With his view somewhat diminished, it's easier for you to crawl across the tundra to within easy shooting range. Just remember to take your time and remain upwind. And don't let the caribou see your form silhouetted against the skyline!

If your trophy bull is in a herd, take time out to study each animal. You might find a larger bull you hadn't seen earlier. A crucial caribou fact is that they aren't as alert when they are in large herds. They probably have a safety-in-numbers sense. If conditions are right, a hunter can use this trait to sneak to within 50 yards or less of a caribou herd. Again, take your time and be aware of wind direction.

Distances on the tundra are hard to judge, especially in hunting a lone animal. Unless you're experienced in hunting on barren tundra, a caribou at 100 yards might look 300 yards away—or vice versa. Expect few, if any trees, rocks or geographical features for reference points. While you're walking during the day, practice pacing off distances of 100 and 200 yards. Place your vest on the tundra and see how large, or small, it appears at these distances. Better yet, if you get a new scope, choose a newer model with a built-in rangefinder. This will be extremely invaluable in accurately determining distances on the tundra.

If you can find geographical or man-made structures that tend to funnel caribou together, use them to your advantage. In *Lost in the Barrens*, Farley Mowat describes the "fence posts" that Eskimos once built in areas through which caribou traditionally migrated. These posts were stacks of boulders or clumps of sod shaped to resemble kneeling hunters. Eskimos hid behind the "posts" and slaughtered the caribou as they came streaming past. The posts also served to protect the hunters from getting

trampled by the thousands of caribou stampeding after the first shots were fired.

While I don't recommend that you go out and build kneeling statues, I do recommend scouting for caribou crossings. Generation after generation of caribou generally use the same game trails. In many areas, these trails are so well worn that sometimes they are a foot or more deep. Look for a trail with fresh sign in the form of dung or defoliated shrubbery, and follow it until you find a crossing. These are geographical features like river or stream bottomlands, saddles between two hills, or gullies that tend to concentrate animals. When they come to water, caribou will usually avoid wide, shallow places, preferring narrower stretches with a strong current. Find a vantage point that allows you to glass the trail in both directions, and stay alert. Caribou always seem to pop up when you least expect them.

My friend Otto Eberle once pitched his camp near such a crossing at the end of a lake. On the morning of the second day of the hunt, he was down at the lake, brushing his teeth. Suddenly, seemingly from out of nowhere, a good-sized bull entered the lake at the crossing. Otto waited until the bull climbed out of the water on the other side before he grabbed his rifle and made his kill with one shot. Back he went to brushing his teeth, this time with a bit more zest in his movements.

One way to deal with the caribou's habitual, surprise arrival is to listen for them, especially in the willow and alder-choked mountain basins where visibility is restricted. Though caribou are not vocal, they do make a "clicking" sound when moving or trotting along. The most reasonable explanation for this odd sound is the snapping of the caribou's leg tendons. Some friends who've confessed to falling asleep on watch told me that they were once awakened by the noise. Caribou clicking can be heard up to 100 yards away, so it behooves the hunter to listen as well as look.

When deep snows arrive, caribou often stay in the lower elevations, especially muskeg areas and spruce bogs. There, they search out lakes and ponds for green vegetation. Evidence of their feeding activity is known as a crater: a large or small hole dug into the snow. Unless an area is severely cratered, you can expect caribou to return to such a feeding area for as long as food is available. These areas are easiest to reach by snowmobile.

After you've bagged your caribou, it's important to protect it from varmints and birds that can devour an entire carcass

Alaska currently has a statewide population of over 440,000 caribou. This one was bagged near the Cinder River Flats on the Alaska Peninsula.

Most caribou country is inaccessible except by small aircraft. This Super Cub is especially equipped with tundra tires, a must-have item for those hard-to-reach areas that receive little, if any, hunting pressure.

overnight. If you don't have buddies to help you pack the quarters to base camp, you might use an old Eskimo trick I learned long ago. First, remove the rack and sever the head from the neck. Next, remove the hindquarters from the hip joint with a sharp knife. Then, remove the entrails from the rear of the body. After the carcass has cooled, insert the head into the opening of the abdominal cavity. If available, pile brush over the carcass. Pack the hindquarters back to camp and return the next day for the remainder.

Caribou are a living sea of life in the arctic. To watch them move, run and frolic in herds numbering in the thousands is to go back in time to what the early mountain men must have experienced with the bison of the Great Plains. The caribou's life cycle reminds the hunter that life, wherever it's found, is never easy. This is especially true on the tundra. It is often a cruel, unforgiving place. Disease, accidents, starvation, and weather bring death. But the tundra is also the bosom of life for the caribou; the anchor that keeps this nomadic wanderer alive and well on earth.

The caribou gets its life from the tundra, in the variety of plant life that suckle nutrients from spring snowmelt and rich earth. And we, as hunters, receive our life from the caribou. We take the caribou for physical food. But the caribou offers each one of us something far more precious. By hunting it, the caribou offers us a chance to appreciate its restless soul, always on the move to find a quiet, wilderness place; a quest for the simple. Sporthunters also search out a quiet, wilderness place away from the cities, a land that is simple. A common bond in an uncommon land.

Let us respect the caribou for what it is, a symbol of our last great wilderness on earth, the Alaska tundra. Indeed, the caribou is a resource that we can't lose without losing ourselves in the process.

Where to Hunt Caribou

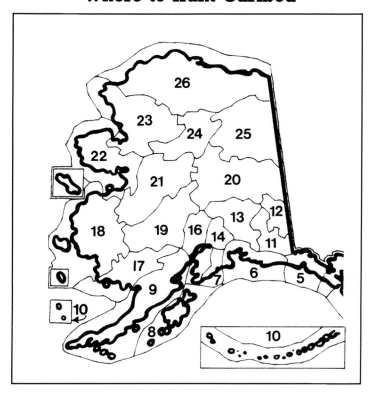

Units 22A, 22B, 23, 24, 26A

Western Arctic Herd
Population Size: 240,000, Trend: Increasing

The Western Arctic Herd (WAH), currently the largest caribou herd in the state, ranks as one of Alaska's major terrestrial resources. At a low level in the late 1800s, this herd increased steadily through the early 1900s. Before crashing to a low of about 75,000 in the mid-1970s, it contained about 242,000 caribou. The herd is still increasing, and may become as large as it was at the turn of the 20th Century.

Western Arctic Herd caribou occupy the northwest region of Alaska. In late summer, caribou are widely dispersed over the Arctic Slope. By August's end, they begin a leisurely migration south. Major migrations occur through passes in the Brooks Range and along the Chukchi Sea coast. The animals move onto the south slope of the Brooks Range in late August. Migration continues at a slow pace in October during the rut. Afterwards, the migrating pace quickens as the animals near their wintering grounds that extend through the Waring Mountains, Baird Mountains and lower Koyukuk River eastward to the Wiseman area and through the entire Kobuk and Selawik river valleys and the Nulato Hills. Sport hunting is minimal. Each year, subsistence users take approximately 90 percent of the caribou harvest in this region. The limit is five caribou per hunter, depending on residency. The season currently runs year-round, but no cows from May 16 through June 30. The best hunting is from September through November. The WAH is an excellent source of caribou trophies, but the area is expensive to reach and inclement weather is common. Local caribou movements are difficult to predict.

Units 9A, 9B, 16, 17, 19B, 19C

Mulchatna Herd
Population Size: 60,000. Trend: Increasing

The current population figures for the Mulchatna herd are the highest ever recorded. But harvest data is of questionable value since the reported harvest is a minor fraction of the actual harvest, which includes subsistence use by local villagers. Hunters can find caribou in the Lime Hills along the Stony River to the Bonanza Hills at the head of the Mulchatna River. Caribou also winter along the South and Windy forks of the Kuskokwim River, the lowlands near the mouth of the Swift River, at Nushagak Bay near Clark's Point, and along the Kvichak River. Big bulls frequent the Big Mountain area in mid-winter. In recent years, a substantial increase in caribou has occurred near New Stuyahok and Ekwok on the west side of the Nushagak River. These units are popular hunting areas for hunters chartering flights from Anchorage. Expect to pay around $800 per person, minimum, for a charter flight to this area. August and September are the best months to go on floats. Beginning December 1, three additional caribou can be taken in some areas. Then, access is chiefly by ski plane.

Units 9C, 9E, 9D

Alaska Peninsula Herd
Population Size: North—20,000. Trend: Stable
South—5,000-6,000. Trend: Decreasing

This herd has two divisions, defined by their relationship to Port Moller: those north of Port Moller, and those south of Port Moller. each herd has its own calving and wintering areas. Each year, about 2,000 animals are taken by sport and subsistence hunters. The northern herd summers in the Aleutian Range before beginning a northward movement to its wintering areas on the Egegik and the Naknek rivers. Cows and calves initiate this fall migration; adult bulls follow. By mid-September, bands of adult bulls scatter between Port Moller and Port Heiden, and a few appear around Becharof Lake. The Cinder River area offers good caribou hunting in early September and October. Scattered bands are present from Pilot Point to Port Moller throughout the winter. Caribou also winter in the region north of Becharof Lake. Caribou in the southern herd presently winter on the marshy Caribou River lowlands and westward along the foothills north of Pavlof Volcano. Total harvest varies widely with availability of animals. A popular hunting trip is to fly commercial airline into Cold Bay, rent a truck, and hunt the area by road or fly-out.

The Alaska Peninsula herd has an interesting history. The animals are highly migratory, and have often confused biologists and census takers in the past. Changes in population size were merely shifts in distribution. Russian explorers of the 1700s provided the first record of caribou on the peninsula, reporting large populations to the south of Port Moller and outlying islands. During the 1800s, the caribou population expanded northward, occupying the entire peninsula. Trading posts at Fort Alexander (at the mouth of the Nushagak River) and at Ugashik did a brisk business in caribou skins.

Between 1872 and 1874, the population peaked and then declined. Following this peak, caribou remained abundant in the northern portion, but few were found on the southern tip and outlying islands. In the 1900s, there was a reversal. The June, 1912 eruption of Mount Katmai covered the peninsula with ash up to a foot thick. The caribou survived this disastrous effect on their habitat.

Reindeer herding was popular in the Naknek-Egegik area until the early 1940s, when herding ceased and the unattended animals scattered. The Alaska Peninsula herds assimilated most of these reindeer. Even with the influx of these feral reindeer, the caribou herd reached its lowest recorded level ever. A 1949 U.S. Fish and Wildlife Survey estimated only 2,500 animals: 2,000 in the northern section, 500 in the southern section, and none on Unimak island. Today, several hundred caribou occur at some times of the year on Unimak, and the population for the peninsula is at 25,000 and increasing. The current season begins on August 10 and runs through March 31 for subunits 9A, 9B, 9C and 9E. The 9D non-subsistence season runs September 1 through October 31. The bag varies from one to four caribou, depending on time of year.

A short note about the Unimak herd. The caribou there are considered to be part of the Alaska Peninsula herd. An exchange of animals between Unimak and the mainland across Isanotski Strait, a distance of one-half mile, occurs often. Movements back and forth across the straight have been recorded since the late 1800s.

Due to its closeness to Anchorage and easy access to hunting areas, the Alaska Peninsula is one of the most popular caribou hunting hotspots in the state. However, weather is the biggest deterrent to hunting there, and hunters should be prepared for high winds, fog, and rain. Hunting for Boone and Crockett bulls, however, is good. Many trophy racks are taken from this herd each year.

Unit 10

Adak Herd
Population size: 400. Trend: Stable

Twenty-three caribou calves placed on Adak Island in 1958 and 1959 form the nucleus of the present Adak herd. By 1967, the population numbered 189. Recent harvests average 140 animals. Through sporthunting, biologists try to maintain the herd at a controllable level.

Adak caribou, now ranging over the island's entire 290 square miles, are the largest in North America. Because of abundant forage, lack of insect pests and man-made obstructions, and a low population that reduces stress, caribou there reach great sizes, reaching up to 700 pounds. The season is from September 1 through March 31, with a two caribou bag-limit.

Unit 7

Kenai Mountains Herd
Population Size: 343. Trend: Increasing

Caribou occurred on the Kenai Peninsula until the early 1900s. Around the turn of the century, loss of habitat from extensive fires and intensive hunting caused the herds to decline rapidly. About 1913, caribou became extinct on the Kenai Peninsula.

In the early 1950s, the U.S. Fish and Wildlife Service conducted feasibility studies to determine if historic caribou ranges on the Kenai Peninsula could once again support caribou. Suitable range was found in the Chickaloon River-Mystery Creek area, the Skilak-Tustumena Lake area, and the Caribou Hills north of Homer. In 1964, these areas were reappraised. In 1965 and 1966, ADF&G reestablished the herd through transplants from the Nelchina herd. The Kenai Mountains herd has increased steadily. The annual harvest is about 50 caribou. Most hunters reach the hunting area by walking; others use horses. Hunters can also find animals in the northern Kenai Mountains south of Hope and east of Tustumena Lake.

Unit 11

Mentasta Herd
Population Size: 2,400. Trend: Declining

This herd is believed to be a remnant of the Fortymile herd that ranged into the Mentasta Mountains at its population peak several years before 1932. The range of the Mentasta herd extends from the Mentasta Mountains at the east end of the Alaska Range southward onto the western slopes of the Wrangell Mountains. The annual harvest has declined from 120 to approximately 50 animals. Most successful hunters use aircraft to reach the hunting areas.

Unit 12

Chisana Herd
Population Size: 1,100. Trend: Stable to Increasing

During the late 1920s and early 1930s, great numbers of caribou from the Fortymile herd moved into the Nabesna-White River country each fall. When these movements ceased in the early 1930s, a few groups of caribou remained on the northeastern slopes of the Wrangell Mountains. The present herd may have developed from such groups (Skoog, 1968).

Because the herd does not seem to migrate out for calving or wintering, continuing rumors still hold that the Chisana herd is a species of mountain caribou like those found in parts of Canada. This is unknown. The Chisana herd now ranges through the Nutzotin Mountains and northern part of the Wrangell Mountains. The area is quite rugged, consisting of single-ridge mountains 4-8,000 feet high. Average hunter take is approximately 25 to 65 animals annually. Early-season caribou are often found on nearby glaciers, where low temperatures offer relief from biting insects.

Units 13, 14 (except 14C)

Nelchina Herd
Population Size: 30,000. Trend: Increasing

Caribou have probably ranged in the Nelchina Basin for at least 5,000 years, since the recession of the glaciers. During the early 1940s, when an estimated 5,000 to 10,000 caribou were in the Nelchina herd, the federal government was concerned about the effects of wolf predation on the herd. Following federal wolf control in the late 1940s and early 1950s, caribou numbers increased rapidly, numbering 64,000 by 1962. However, emigration, predation, weather, range conditions, and hunting continued to reduce the herd to less than 10,000. But the herd has been steadily increasing since 1972.

Caribou of the Nelchina herd wintered on the Lake Louise Flats during the early 1950s. As the herd expanded during the next decade, it used more wintering areas. These included the Talkeetna Mountains north of Eureka, the Alaska Range near Cantwell, the Monahan Flats, and the area around Tanada Lake. Today, during August, several thousand inhabit the high country surrounding Butte Lake. Later, most of the herd scatters out over the Talkeetna Mountains near the Susitna River. By October, caribou start to move eastward. One group splits off to remain in the Lake Louise-Eureka vicinity. Most of the animals head for GMU 11, between Sanford Creek and Drop Creek. Hunters who give the Nelchina herd a bit of effort have a high rate of success. Animals are spread throughout the region, and over 2,500 hunters, chosen by permit drawing or as subsistence users, hunt there. The annual harvest is over 1,500 caribou.

Units 13E, 20C

Denali Herd
Population Size: 2,400. Trend: Stable or Slowly Increasing

Most of this herd exists within or just outside the boundaries of Denali National Park and Preserve. The season is closed to both sport and subsistence hunting within the range of this herd.

Unit 15

Kenai Lowlands Herd
Population Size: 100 Trend: Stable

ADF&G recommended opening the caribou season to sport hunting by permit drawing in the fall of 1989. Three permits for bulls are available at this time. The bull:cow ratio is currently 38:100. Hunting of this herd was not permitted during the early to mid 1980s. The herd was established in 1965 and 1966 by ADF&G from transplants from the Nelchina herd. Current range is spread over subunits 15A and 15B. Population growth is currently limited by dog and wolf predation.

Unit 18

Andreafsky Mountain and Kilbuck Mountain Herds
Population Size: 400. Trend: Unknown

In the mid-1800s, caribou were numerous throughout Unit 18, but their numbers began to decline in the 1870s when heavy trade in hides and meat flourished along the Yukon. Commercial hunting on Nunivak Island eliminated all caribou from the island. In the late 1870s, the herd shifted to new ranges. Reindeer herding was extremely popular in this unit until its collapse in the late 1930s. The Andreafsky herd remains small. Hunters should concentrate on pursuing caribou elsewhere in the state.

The season in this unit runs from February through March. The limit is one caribou. Growth in the Kilbuck Mountains herd has been rapid since its closure to hunting in 1985. Additional hunting opportunities may be opened in the next several years.

Units 19, 21

Beaver Mountain Herd
Population Size: 1,400. Trend: Decreasing

Sunshine Mountain Herd
Population Size: 500-600. Trend: Decreasing

Big River Herd
Population Size: 750. Trend: Stable

Rainy Pass Herd
Population Size: 1,500. Trend: Unknown

Tonzona Herd
Population Size: 400. Trend: Unknown

Kuskokwim Mountains Herd
Population Size: 600. Trend: Decreasing

Most of the caribou in Subunits 19A (south of the Kuskokwim River) and 19B are part of the Mulchatna caribou herd. Small, distinct herds as described for Units 19 and 21 also appear in this general area. Specifically, the Beaver Mountains herd and the Sunshine Mountain herd are found in Subunits 21A and 19D; the Rainy Pass and Tonzona herds in Subunit 19C; the Big River herd (often referred to as the Farewell herd) in Subunits 19C and 19D; and several small groups (usually containing less than 150 caribou each) inhabit the Kuskokwim Mountains in Subunit 19A north of the Kuskokwim River.

The Beaver Mountains herd is probably a remnant of an old reindeer herd located in the area during the 1930s. Caribou appear along the northwest end of the Beaver Mountains in August and September. By late October, look for them in the lower Iditarod drainage.

The Sunshine herd occurs in heavy timber from the upper Nowitna and Susulatna rivers to Ivy Creek on the Nixon Fork. From late October and throughout the first part of winter, they scatter in groups from Nixon Fork Flats to near the Nowitna River.

The Big River herd stays in the foothills of the Alaska Range from the end of May until October. On occasion, they can be found in the Lyman Hills west of White Mountain Mine.

Several groups consisting of less than several hundred caribou each reside north of the Kuskokwim River and apparently represent a distinct Kuskokwim Mountain herd. Find them near Horn and Russian mountains, the Crooked Creek drainage, and in the Granite Mountain-East Fork of the George River area. But south of the Kuskokwim River, small distinct groups currently do not exist. Those that do exist south of the Kuskokwim in the Aniak and Holitna drainages and in the Taylor Mountains are part of the Mulchatna herd.

The Tonzona herd remains in the Alaska Range, mostly on drainages of the Tonzona River to near Purkeypile Mine in early fall and as far north as Slow Fork Hills in the winter.

Because the Big River and Rainy Pass herds disperse widely during the hunting season, hunting success varies in this unit. Some of the most popular hunting areas are the South Fork of the Kuskokwim River, the Alaska Range Foothills in the fall, and the flats near McGrath and Nikolai during the winter. The season runs from August to September, with extended openings in various subunits.

Unit 20A and parts of 20C

Delta Herd
Population Status: 8,400. Trend: Increasing

This herd of caribou may be descendants of the Fortymile herd that ranged into this area during the 1930s (Skoog, 1968). In 1957, Olson observed that the herd numbered approximately 1,500 caribou and was increasing. In 1963, the herd had grown to 5,000 caribou. This rapid increase in numbers could be the result of a series of severe winters causing the Nelchina herd to migrate into the wintering range of the Delta herd. Possibly some animals remained after the Nelchina herd returned to its calving grounds in the spring. Still, before slowly building up to its current level, the population had dwindled to about 2,000 animals in 1970.

Most of the area is currently open to general season hunting. Most of the 600-plus-animal harvest occurs west of the Wood River drainage. Drawing permits are required in the southwest portion of 20A. Successful hunters have taken animals near the Little Delta River, Dry Creek, Tatlanika, Ferry-Healy, Yanert and Totatlanika. The most frequently used means of access are aircraft and offroad vehicles. However, areas can be reached by walking or horseback. The general season runs from September 1 through 15.

Unit 20D

Macomb Herd
Population Status: 700. Trend: Increasing

This is a drawing-permit hunt, where about 150 permits are issued each year. Most hunters walk into the area from the road system. Motorized vehicles are prohibited within the Macomb Controlled Use Area portion of the herd's range, but fixed-wing aircraft may be used to transport hunters to Fish Lake. Popular hunting areas are the Little Gerstle and Jarvis Creek drainages. The season currently runs from August 10 through September 30, and the limit is one caribou. Annual harvest is 10 to 20 caribou.

Unit 20E

Fortymile Herd
Population Status: 16,000. Trend: Increasing

The Fortymile herd has a history of the most intensive sport hunting of any region in Alaska. The herd dwindled from a population of over 500,000 animals in the 1920s to a low between 10,000 to 20,000 in the early 1940s (Skoog, 1956). Then it decreased to a low of 5,000 animals in the early 1970s. Egress of animals to another herd accounts for the decline. An estimated

30,000 Fortymile caribou joined the Porcupine Herd in 1957; in 1964 another large exchange occurred. From 1950 to 1972, harvests consisted of fewer than 100 to 2,400 caribou per year. The size of the harvest depended greatly on when the caribou crossed the Steese or Taylor highways. Restrictive season closures were adopted in 1973, and the current harvest is approximately 200 to 250 animals per year.

At the turn of the century, Fortymile caribou moved regularly throughout the gold camp regions of the Klondike and the Fortymile regions. Miners harvested large numbers of the animals for food. Until the 1930s, the herd ranged from the Yukon Flats southeast to Whitehorse, and from the Dawson and Ogilvie mountains in the Yukon Territory to the Copper River Basin. This range included large sections of area presently occupied by the Delta, Nelchina, and Porcupine caribou herds. As the numbers of the Fortymile herd diminished, so did its range. Since 1941, the herd has moved within the area between the Yukon and Tanana rivers, and occupies a total area of about 35,000 square miles.

In early August, when the hunting season opens, caribou are in the highlands of the Tanana Hills and the upper portions of the Chena, Salcha, Charley, Goodpaster, Seventymile, and Fortymile rivers. In September, the herd moves southeast toward the Eagle Road, and, depending on weather conditions, continue to cross it until well into November. Some animals do remain in the Tanana Hills throughout the fall and winter period. Hunter success averages around 40 percent. Fly-in access is the most popular, while some hunters access the area via the Steese Highway. The season runs from August 10 to September 20.

Units 25, 26C

Porcupine Herd
Population Size: 170,000. Trend: Increasing

The Porcupine herd is Alaska's second largest herd of caribou. Accounts of the Porcupine herd before 1900 described it as composed of a large number of northeastern Alaska and Canadian animals. Considerable shifting of animals occurred, and by the 1930s, two distinct groups persisted: one ranging primarily in Canada and eastern Alaska, and the other into the central Brooks Range. In the 1950s, biologists established that only one calving area existed in northeast Alaska and therefore that caribou wintering in northeast Alaska and adjacent Canada comprised one herd, the Porcupine.

The most important migration routes include the valleys of the Kongak, Canning, Sheenjek, Jago, Aichilik, Sadlerochit and East Fork Chandalar rivers. All are important migration routes through the Brooks Range. Although expensive, hunting the Porcupine herd is generally successful. The annual harvest is about 2,000 to 6,000 animals, including U.S. and Canada. The sport hunting take in Alaska is 100 to 200 annually. Five caribou may be transported south of the Yukon River; however, most hunters can usually afford to take no more than two. Most hunters access the herd from Fort Yukon, paying from $600 to $800, including airfare from Fairbanks, depending on gear taken and amount of meat brought back out. Charters are also available from Bettles; be sure to check on prices. In most of the area, the season is open from July through April.

Units 26A, 26B, 26C

Central Arctic Herd
Population Size: 18,000. Trend: Increasing

The Central Arctic herd is a recent addition to Alaska's list of caribou herds. In the mid-1970s, it was determined to be separate and distinct from the Western Arctic, Porcupine and Teshekpuk herds. The 1986-1987 harvest from this herd was 345 animals.

Unit 26A

Teshekpuk Herd
Population Size: 16,000. Trend: Increasing

Minor Herds

Unit 21C, 20F

Ray, Galena, Wolf Mountain Herds
Population Size: 1,100. Trend: Increasing

Some hunting occurs along the Dalton Highway. Poor hunting access during the open season greatly restricts harvest. The Galena Mtn. herd is most accessible to hunters during the winter when it crosses the Galena-Huslia winter trail. The Wolf Mtn. herd is virtually never accessible, and the Ray Mtn. herd is accessible by aircraft during late summer and by snowmachine and aircraft when caribou are north of the Tanana River.

Unit 25C, 20F

White Mountains Herd
Population Size: 1,000. Trend: Increasing

Unit 20A

Yanert Herd
Population Size: 700. Trend: Stable

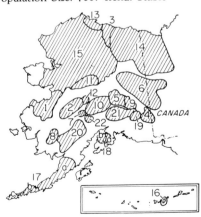

Approximate ranges of caribou herds in Alaska (1977).

Interior-Arctic Herds
1. Andreafsky
2. Beaver
3. Central Arctic
4. Chisana
5. Delta
6. Fortymile
7. Granite Mountains
8. Kilbuck Mountains
9. Macomb
10. McKinley
11. Ray Mountains
12. Sunshine-Cloudy Mountains
13. Teshekpuk Lake
14. Porcupine
15. Western Arctic

Southcentral Herds
16. Adak
17. Alaska Peninsula (a) (b) (c)
18. Kenai (a) (b)
19. Mentasta
20. Mulchatna
21. Nelchina
22. Rainy Pass/Farewell

CHAPTER 3

Blacktail Deer

For several reasons, the Sitka blacktail deer is an extremely popular species in Alaska . First, they are numerous throughout their range; hunters are awarded a five-deer bag limit in some areas of the state. Also, blacktails are wary. A big five-point that lords over an alpine meadow won't make it easy on you. He'll sneak in and out of sight so inconspicuously you'd swear it was magic. Furthermore, a deer hunt set in the alpine country is nothing short of spectacular. In early autumn, the hunter often encounters lush meadows filled with ferns and wildflowers, backdropped by an expanse of royal-blue ocean. But most of all, the blacktail is a back-up species. When a moose or sheep hunt fails to put winter meat in the freezer, a hunter can plan on a blacktail hunt to furnish him with 100 or more pounds of prime venison. For all these reasons, the Sitka blacktail holds a special place in the hearts of Alaska hunters.

The Sitka blacktail deer, *Odocoileus hemionus sitkensis*, is a recent species in geological time. This relative of the mule deer was not present in southeast Alaska until after the Pleistocene ice receded. Then their northernmost limit was the north end of the Alexander Archipelago. Geographical barriers consisting of mainland mountains on the east, icefields and glaciers to the north, and the Pacific Ocean to the west restricted the expansion of this species. Beginning in 1917, transplants extended the blacktail's range northward along the Alaska coast, throughout Prince William Sound and into the Kodiak Archipelago. Today this range extends farther north and west than any other species of blacktail deer.

The Sitka blacktail deer is smaller and stockier and has a shorter face than its cousin, the Columbian blacktail, which

Ken Schoening is pleased with his Kodiak Island blacktail. The amount of snowfall generally determines where you'll find deer. Because of a lack of snow in November, Schoening had to climb 2,000 feet to nail his trophy.

is found in British Columbia. A combination of reasons probably accounts for the differences between the species. The Sitka blacktail, isolated from its southern cousins by topography, had to adapt to a more rigorous climate.

In Alaska, the Sitka blacktail inhabits a variety of territory, from islands to coastal mainland. These areas exhibit a wide range of topographical features to which the blacktail has adapted: coastal beaches, dense coniferous rain forests and treeless alpine tundra. Often, blacktails graze in the same meadows as mountain goats.

History

The earliest record of deer harvests in southeast Alaska is a translation of a Russian report, indicating that Alaska Natives sold 2,774 deer to the Russian settlement of Sitka in 1861. In the early 1900s, market hunting for blacktail meat and hides flourished, and the deer was a mainstay in the diets of area miners and traders. During the 1940s and 1950s, the annual harvest ranged from 5,000 to 15,000 animals. The population now is about 100,000 animals, and the harvest averages 14,000 annually.

Life History

The breeding season begins in late October and peaks about mid-November. Like other members of the deer species, the male blacktail during rut is a belligerent, hyperactive animal. I remember glassing one buck in a high alpine meadow on Raspberry Island in late October. The animal bolted across clearings, occasionally rearing up on his hind legs and shaking his head. He'd frequently chase does into the nearby brush. Minutes later, he'd chase the same does away.

Several hours later, after a quiet and careful stalk, I eased over a rock ridge to within 100 yards from where I last spotted the buck. To my surprise, the buck was staring directly at me. The swollen neck and wild look in his eye indicated that maybe he was about to chase me off also. A neck shot put an end to the ol' boy's wild nature.

An interesting note is that I couldn't locate the deer after I shot it. However, I didn't have any problem smelling my way to where he was: he had rolled down the steep hillside and into an alder patch. Despite his full-rut activities, that buck was one of the best-eating deer I have ever had. Each time I look up and see his four-point rack on my wall, I get all fired up about blacktail hunting during the rut.

When Sitka blacktail fawns are born in late May or June, they weigh five to eight pounds. They gain weight rapidly during their first few weeks of life. The fawns eat some vegetation almost immediately after birth, and can survive without milk by September.

An animal's sex and condition influence its weight. blacktail does average about 100 pounds; bucks, 150 to 175 pounds. Just before rut the largest bucks can reach weights of up to 250 pounds. The average lifespan of a Sitka blacktail is relatively short. Only 10 percent of the population lives longer than five years. Some, however, do live to be at least 12 years old.

Habits

Sitka blacktail deer populations experience population fluctuations of large magnitude. In the Petersburg area, for example, biologist Harry Merriam reported that hunter harvest dropped from 3,700 in 1961 to 40 in 1974. In 1976, the season was closed. In this time frame, wolf predation was probably the primary mortality factor. But the greatest, widespread influence on deer populations was, and still is, snowfall.

Males drastically reduce their food intake during the rut, and maintain a reduced level of feeding throughout the winter. In contrast, females decrease their intake more gradually throughout the winter. The low nutritional quality of winter browse soon results in malnutrition for both sexes. Eighty percent of the deer that die during the winter months die of starvation.

A blacktail deer hunt in Alaska can be as tranquil or adventurous as you want it to be. You could opt for a quiet hunt from a tree stand in the coniferous rain forest on Montague Island, or the excitement of flying into a high-alpine lake in southeast Alaska, or the spectacle of watching deer by the hundreds on the sloping, alpine meadows while cruising the saltwater bays of Kodiak Island. The habits of blacktails vary from area to area. So do the techniques used to hunt them. Thus, a hunter of blacktail needs to consider three regions: southeast, Prince William Sound, and Kodiak.

Southeast

To maximize the chances for a successful deer hunt in southeast Alaska, the hunter needs to study three kinds of data: weather patterns, snowfall accumulation and ADF&G reports of winter mortality rates. Finding the animals is next. Deer in southeast Alaska use all parts of the coniferous forest and alpine habitat year-round. However, during the month of

While blacktails of either sex can be taken in Alaska, don't shoot the first deer you see. Chances are, one or more bucks are holding in the shadows on the inside edge of shoreline timber. Wait them out.

August, when blacktail season opens, the animals are more
likely to be in alpine tundra.

Look for densely forested areas—at timberline or just below—
interspersed with muskeg openings and alpine meadows. Also
glass high above timberline. Deer congregate in windy areas
or on snow patches that help keep insect pests at bay.

In their alpine environment, deer feed on ferns, salal, marsh
marigold, ground dogwood, trailing bramble, gold thread,
blueberry and other leafy plants. Especially favored is deer cabbage, a succulent plant that's 15 to 25 percent protein. In some
areas, it completely covers the ground. Wherever I've found
a patch of "cabbage" I've also found abundant deer sign, and
some nice bucks also. Southeast blacktails also like lichens and
mushrooms, although these items have low nutritional value.

Hunting alpine country early in the season is lots of work,
especially if you have to climb 2,000 feet or more through rainforest jungle before reaching the deer at timberline. Many
hunters prefer to charter a flight into an alpine lake and start
their hunt from there. Flying in gives you the advantage of
looking over the area you'll be hunting and spares you the
fatigue of hiking through rain forest. The thrill of hunting early-
season blacktails, perhaps in conjunction with a goat hunt,

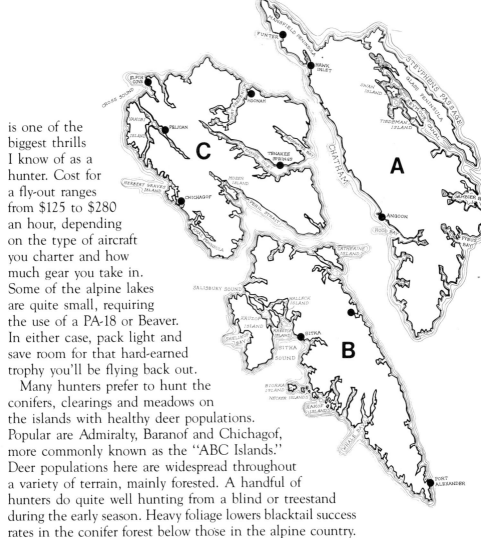

is one of the biggest thrills I know of as a hunter. Cost for a fly-out ranges from \$125 to \$280 an hour, depending on the type of aircraft you charter and how much gear you take in. Some of the alpine lakes are quite small, requiring the use of a PA-18 or Beaver. In either case, pack light and save room for that hard-earned trophy you'll be flying back out.

Many hunters prefer to hunt the conifers, clearings and meadows on the islands with healthy deer populations. Popular are Admiralty, Baranof and Chichagof, more commonly known as the "ABC Islands." Deer populations here are widespread throughout a variety of terrain, mainly forested. A handful of hunters do quite well hunting from a blind or treestand during the early season. Heavy foliage lowers blacktail success rates in the conifer forest below those in the alpine country.

The first frosts of September drastically change the deer's habits. When succulent plants freeze up and wither, deer switch to species that survive initial freezes, such as salmonberry, black currant, deer berry, fireweed, crowberry, elderberry, and cow parsnip. Deer stay in the alpine country until the first snowfall covers their food supply. How far they move down the mountainside depends on the amount of snowfall the area receives. Generally, deer stay up on the mountainside if the snowfall is less than a foot deep. Snow deeper than 18 to 24 inches throughout the alpine and upper mountain ranges causes deer to concentrate on the open beaches. Studies show that in very bad winters, over 90 percent of the deer in an area will winter within ¼ mile of the beach and lower river systems.

The ABC islands of southeast Alaska offer excellent blacktail deer hunting. However, deer populations are spotty in some areas, and racks are not as large as blacktails found on Kodiak.

In late winter, your choice of where to hunt southeast blacktails generally has a major bearing on your success. Study weather patterns and snowfall accumulations for the past few years in the area you intend to hunt. This bit of homework will maximize your chances of success. As a general rule, the southeast mainland and nearby islands usually receive heavier snowfall than those islands of the area's western archipelago. Therefore, deer densities, for the most part, except in years with mild winters, are considerably lower in areas with heavier snowfall.

A fly-out hunt in late-season can be good, but keep in mind that weather is a major factor. Always prepare to spend a few extra days. Coastal weather from late October to January can be severely inclement, and it may take several days for the clouds to lift from the water's surface before you can head afield.

The best way to hunt the southeast area late in the season is by boat. Many of the locals use open skiffs to reach their hunting areas, while cabin cruisers and sailing schooners are more often used on extended hunts to remote bays. A few guides use commercial fishing boats for deer hunting during the winter season. A large fishing boat makes a comfortable, yet mobile base camp. In fact, many a skipper-guide has served fresh-caught crab, shrimp and halibut to his clients during their hunt. Some skippers are darn good cooks, and the seafood diet is a unique feature of a late-season coastal blacktail hunt.

Prince William Sound

Deer are not native to Prince William Sound. In fact, the first big game transplant in Alaska was the introduction of deer into Prince William Sound (PWS). In 1916, the Cordova Chamber of Commerce arranged to have eight blacktail deer captured near Sitka and transplanted to Hawkins and Hichinbrook islands. From 1917 to 1923, 16 more blacktails were added. This population peaked around 1945. By 1950 the carrying capacity of the range was drastically reduced; overgrazing had done severe damage.

Extreme population fluctuations are common with PWS deer. Major die-offs were recorded in the late 1940s, mid-1950s, late 1960s, and early 1970s.

In Prince William Sound, better deer populations are found on the larger islands: Hawkins, Hichinbrook, and Montague. These three islands probably support up to 70 percent of the region's deer population. Latouche, Green, Knight (eastern side), and the Naked Island group are less popular but good

areas to hunt. The mainland of Prince William Sound is marginal deer habitat, except the area between Gravina Point and the Rude River, which consists of fair deer habitat.

As in southeast Alaska, snow conditions influence the size of the harvest of PWS deer more than the size of the deer population. Prince William Sound deer have a small home range that includes vertical migrations according to changing seasons. A 3½-year-old doe ear-tagged during March, 1967 in Port Etches was killed by a hunter on the same beach 10½ years later in November, 1977. This deer had probably moved up and down this drainage for 10 years. Such habits can be a boon to the hunter who knows the location of deer concentrations and blacktails' day-to-day habits, including prime feeding areas.

The seasonal habits of PWS deer result in three hunting periods. These periods resemble those of southeast deer hunts, yet there are some significant differences.

The first period, alpine hunting, is from August to about mid-September. Then hunting is restricted to alpine areas, where the deer are feeding on high-quality vegetation. This is the time to go if you're looking for meat. The deer are in prime shape, having fattened up from a summer of feeding on protein-rich plants. Prince William Sound deer highly favor meadows of false Lily-of-the-Valley. Also look for stands of bunchberry, trailing bramble, and blueberry. Alpine hunting accounts for five percent of the PWS deer harvest.

The second period occurs from mid-September until the first snowfall. As in southeast Alaska, deer move down into the high timber country after the first frost has killed the succulents. Deer stay in the high-timber areas until heavy snows drive them to the beach fringe. If forced to remain on the beach fringe for over two months, they usually die.

The winter period concentrates and confines deer to their winter range. A great deal of hunting effort takes place during the last few weeks of the year, when deer are widely available. Upwards of 80 percent of the annual harvest in this region is taken at this time. Most hunters charter boats or aircraft and hunt both to feed families and for sport. However, extremely snowy PWS winters often create a problem for hunters as well as wildlife managers. Biologists Johnson and Wood (1978) write in a report on coastal blacktails:

> Sometimes extreme snow makes deer very vulnerable, which poses problems of ethics and sportsmanship. This puts the manager in a "rock or hardplace" position, for

the early, heavy snow that contributes to a high hunter kill also may be the precursor of high winter mortality—the combination of which can reduce a deer population. It is ironic that severe winters, when heavy mortality occurs (both natural and hunter kill), are often followed by mild, open winters. During the latter, deer are not visible on the beaches, nor are they concentrated on winter ranges. The public has often interpreted the apparent lack of deer during the mild years as a result of mismanagement from heavy hunter kill the previous winter.

When deer are in Kodiak's high alpine country, the climb to the top is often the hardest part of the hunt. Of course, the scenery is always spectacular.

I would never think of taking a sport hunt during periods of high snowfall. It's not a pretty sight. Deep, rutty trails, oftentimes up to the deer's shoulder, stretch from beach to timber. The deer often stand in one spot, unable to move. This is a meat hunt, and nothing more. However, if you haven't bagged your moose or caribou, and the coast has been hit with heavy snowfall, do consider a Prince William Sound blacktail hunt. I'd rather see the deer go into someone's freezer than litter the beach, and be carried out to sea by the tide.

Kodiak

In 1924, fourteen deer, captured from the Sitka area, were released on Long Island, about four miles east of the town of Kodiak. Two more deer were transplanted there in 1930, and a small herd of deer became established on the island. Biologists had hoped that deer from this group would swim over to Kodiak via a series of interconnecting islands. The deer lived up to management's expectations. A 1931 Alaska Game Commission report mentioned that three does and two bucks had been seen on Kodiak. An additional transplant, this time for Kodiak itself, seemed appropriate. In 1934, four bucks and five does were released there. By then, biologists assumed that blacktails from the Long Island population had already established themselves on Kodiak.

The first hunting season on Kodiak was held in 1953 after the number of deer in the northeastern corner of the island rapidly increased. Skyrocketing deer populations continued to spread southward along the island during the 1950s. The annual harvest continued to increase as seasons and bag limits became more liberal. The average annual harvest during the 1957-59 period was about 200 bucks. Rising to over 2,100 deer in 1966, 50 percent of the harvest came from the Chiniak Peninsula. Heavy snows and severe cold in 1969-70 caused heavy deer mortality. Since, the population has increased. Reports of deer sightings in Deadman Bay, Karluk Lake, and Sturgeon River drainages are becoming more and more frequent. Afognak and Raspberry island populations are currently at an all-time high.

If I had to choose one location to hunt deer in Alaska, I'd choose Kodiak. Three conditions—less severe weather, wider dispersal of deer in winter ranges, and better quality winter range due to a shorter history of occupation by deer may explain the relatively high survival rate of Kodiak deer. Even well after the rut in late December, a hunter will see bucks with significant quantities of backfat. For these reasons, plus the fantastic scenery, Kodiak is my favorite deer hunting area.

Unlike the deer in southeast Alaska, Kodiak deer do not need spruce cover. A grass-brush-alder vegetation—interspersed with dense meadows—covers the island, supporting higher densities of deer than spruce habitat would. Cottonwood and birch occupy the lower foothills. Tundra vegetation occupies the southwestern portion of Kodiak. However, good numbers of deer can be found in the spruce forests that cover most of Afognak, Shuyak, Raspberry and much of northeastern Kodiak Island.

On all islands, in August, deer are found throughout the range of terrain, coniferous as well as alpine. However, the alpine areas receive heavy use from the deer until mid-September. Then, freezing weather desiccates herbaceous plants and snow

covers up prime forage.

On Kodiak, ferns are an extremely popular food item on steep, wind-blown and southerly-exposed hillsides. Smith (1978) reports seeing deer paw through 12 to 18 inches of snow to reach a single fern. In the alpine areas, fireweed is also a common food found before freeze-up. Deer eat some red-berried elder, Nootka rose, salmonberry and cow parsnip, willow, reedgrass and hairgrass (Merriam, 1968). Deer in the coniferous areas typically feed on cranberry, alder, spruce, and lichens.

On Kodiak, accessibility of hunting areas is what determines hunting pressure and success. Most of Afognak and western Kodiak Island have large deer populations, but are only lightly hunted because access is difficult. Fishing boats are generally used to reach these remote areas. Statistics show that boats are involved in about half of the Kodiak deer harvest. The boats range from a small skiff to access remote bays from a base camp, to a luxury motor schooner sleeping up to 12 people. On such a boat with lots of storage room, it's common for several hunters to bring back 30 or more deer after a five-day hunt.

To reach more remote areas, including inland lakes, hunters also use aircraft. Most are amphibious planes, as only a few beaches are suitable for wheel-plane operation.

Floatplanes are not a good means of access to many of the outer capes and bays. Weather and seas there are usually too rough to allow landing except on rare, calm days. And while we're on the subject of weather, do not hunt Kodiak on a tight time schedule. Weather can delay flights coming and going for days at a time. Be prepared to spend an extra two to four days

Jack Maurins is pleased with this nice Kodiak blacktail he bagged while on an outfitted hunt with Quest Charters. The bag limit for Sitka blacktails on Kodiak is currently five per season.

in town or in hunting camp waiting on weather. Boat travel is not usually restricted, except by fog and high winds.

Most deer on Kodiak are harvested during October, November and December. Then, wind-blown capes and bluffs at the mouths of bays and along ocean entrances are excellent areas to hunt. Deer readily feed there, and hunters there usually can avoid climbing as high as they'd have to further back in the bays.

Also keep in mind that the northern ends of Kodiak and Raspberry islands receive more snow than other parts of the archipelago. But at altitudes less than 500 feet, snow depths seldom exceed 24 inches. During most winters, deer in southwestern, central and western Kodiak have a far greater chance of survival during most winters. These are the places to go for trophy bucks.

Lack of good shelter on Kodiak discourages deer hunting to some extent. The Kodiak National Wildlife Refuge prohibits the use of its cabins for anything other than salmon fishing. However, there are a few private cabins hunters can use, but not all are located in good hunting areas.

Major costs for a Kodiak deer hunt would be airfare to Kodiak and the charter flight or boat ride to the hunting area. Some hunters take their cars and boats aboard the state ferry to Kodiak, and hunt the areas closest the road system. However, the limit is one deer in most areas accessible by road. A round-trip flight to Kodiak from Anchorage runs about $200. Air transportation into the area runs from $150 to $275 per hour, depending on type of aircraft chartered.

Many hunters prefer the services of an outfitted hunt. The outfitter usually provides the air transportation from Kodiak to the hunting camp, all meals, accommodations, boat transportation to the hunting areas and processing of meat. Costs vary from $800 per person to $1,250 for a five-day hunt.

I don't feel a guided hunt is necessary for Kodiak deer due to their abundance. However, a guide is worth considering if you're looking for an exceptional, trophy buck. Two years ago, the Boone and Crockett Club established a separate category for Sitka blacktail deer. While there have been numerous entries, there's still plenty of opportunity to make the record book. I'd opt for the south end of Kodiak Island, and the isolated bays such as Uyak and Uganik. Saltry Cove has also been producing some fine bucks, as are Raspberry and Afognak islands. As long as you have the time to view plenty of bucks, you're nearly assured of taking a buck with a hefty, five-point rack.

Hunting Techniques

Wherever you choose to hunt Sitka blacktails, use either alpine or forest techniques.

Alpine deer hunting techniques are basically the same as those used for hunting moose and caribou. A few minor differences are worth reviewing.

If you've been dropped off on a lake near or above timberline, great. You can glass for deer from camp. However, if you're at sea level and are looking up at deer pastures 1,000 feet or higher, then you have some planning to do.

The toughest part of an alpine deer hunt is getting to the high country. Expect a rugged climb, especially through the rainforest on the southeast mainland. If you're not carrying a spike camp, always carry an emergency overnight daysack, just in case you need to spend the night. Include Visqueen for shelter, lighter or matches, high-energy food such as candy, first-aid kit, signal flare, knife, portable saw, space blanket, and flashlight.

Before heading uphill, take a few minutes and plan your route up through the alders and/or spruce. A wrong turn can have you floundering in alders for an hour or more, with no hope of escape except heading back downhill and starting up again. It's possible your route may be dictated by concentrations of deer you'll see on the slopes in the early morning.

Two years ago I hunted Kodiak with Gary and Ken Shoening. Stan Duncan of Alderwood Retreat dropped us off on shore, and pointed out on a map a few alpine pastures where he had seen some dandy bucks several days earlier. From shoreline, we carefully laid out our course through the alders, using unusual ridges and rock outcroppings as prompts to make the required changes in direction. During the hour and a half climb to the top, we saw 12 deer, three of which were bucks. We didn't shoot for fear of spooking some larger bucks that might have been holding at the top. When we reached the alpine pasture, I opted to hunt the left side of the ridge while Gary and Ken chose the right side.

I was flabbergasted as I eased along the ridge of the mountain. It wasn't even 9 a.m., yet I spotted deer after deer, all of them looking down to the ocean for danger, and expecting none from above. Our plan of not shooting earlier had worked.

A half hour later, I eased up to a rocky outcropping. There, 140 yards away in a spruce thicket, I glimpsed a flash of gray. A quick look through my scope had me face-to-face with a massive, thick-beamed, four-point buck. The deer was sparring

with a spruce bough. As I eased into position, a rock dislodged and cascaded down the mountain. As the deer looked up, I slowly squeezed the trigger. The bullet struck home, and I was soon climbing my way down to my trophy. Later, I heard two shots, and later learned that Gary and Ken had connected also.

When alpine hunting, do not walk fast. Take a step or two, then wait and look. Don't just look 20 yards ahead of you. Look at the edges of brush, in the shadows, and 100 or more yards away. Look down at timberline, and look behind you. These areas are where you'll find big deer. I've never jumped a big buck at close range. This is either because I'm walking right by them, or I'm spotting them a long distance off. Either way, I get my share, and so do other hunters who do the same.

When in alpine country, always hunt into the wind. This is oftentimes impossible, especially in late morning when the wind is rising up the mountainside from the lower elevations. Deer can often smell you long before you reach the top. This is why I like to be in alpine country before the morning sun clears the horizon.

On your way up, occasionally slip over any side ridges and peek over. You'll often find deer packed in these gullies, especially on windy days.

When a storm is moving in, don't expect to find deer in the open. They'll move down into the timber or thick alders to wait out the storm. Be prepared to hunt the first sunny or clear morning. Then the deer come out in droves, and you'll have peerless blacktail hunting.

Even though the alpine is open country, take it slow when hunting blacktails. Take a step or two, wait, and look. You'll see far more deer. (Photo by Adela Ward Batin)

The only disadvantage of hunting alpine areas is that you usually don't spend a full day hunting, especially in the latter part of the season. On a typical day, you need from one to three hours of rugged, uphill climbing to reach the hunting area. Once on top, you have a few hours to hunt before it's time to head back down. If you get a deer, you need to take photos. You'll also need to skin and quarter it and pack it down through the alders. All these take additional time. Such daylight time may be available in August. But in late October, with little snow and deer still in the alpine country, a successful hunt probably brings you back in base camp well after dark. Walking down through alders in the dark with a deer carcass strapped to your back is not the smartest thing to do in brown bear country.

Don't pass up the possibility of making a spike camp at timberline, just for a night. If you bag a deer or two, you can hang them in the spruce near timberline and spend the next day packing them out.

Some hunters prefer to drag their deer down whole. This is too much work for me. It's much easier for me to quarter the deer and carry it in my pack than to drag it down alder chutes and steep mountainsides. If at all possible, do not leave a deer on a mountainside overnight. Chances are, a brown bear will have taken it or will be guarding it when you return the next morning.

Late-Season Hunting

Late-season deer hunting can be easy, or very difficult. If the snows have driven deer to the lower elevations, hunting them is merely choosing the animal you want and pulling the trigger. Again, this isn't sport hunting to me, and I don't recommend it as such. However, it is a necessary wildlife management practice, and an excellent way to get meat for the freezer. So if you're inclined to hunt deer in this manner, go for it. Try to take old bucks. They are usually the first to go, along with deer less than two years of age.

A deer call can be very effective in bringing deer to you, especially in their forest habitat. The basic call consists of a rubber band or thin reed placed between two pieces of wood. Hold the call between your teeth and blow sharply into it, producing a loud, bleating cry. Do this several times, wait, and repeat several minutes later. Then wait for fifteen minutes before trying again. The call is supposed to imitate the cry of a fawn, bringing in other deer to investigate. However, for big bucks,

do not imitate the cry of a fawn. Rather, imitate the cry of a distressed rabbit with the type of call predator hunters use. The bucks get curious and come sneaking right in to investigate. If you're ready, you'll get 'em.

One last tip. A day with little or no wind is best for calling. A strong wind, common to Kodiak and southeast, can muffle the call. Also, the wind can carry your scent to the deer. So if it's windy, wait.

Stand Hunting

When hunting southeast Alaska, too many hunters move around, trying to jump up deer in God-forsaken rain forest. They'd be more successful just sitting still, allowing the deer to move about and make the mistakes.

The advantages of a tree stand in the southeast rain forest are many. From a tree stand, the hunter can see down into the brush much more easily. His scent also drifts above the deer. And since blacktails seldom look up, a hunter in a tree stand needn't worry too much about moving.

Before choosing a stand, some preliminary scouting is necessary. The area should be a major concentration area for feeding, or near a trail leading to prime feeding or shelter. A hunter on stand at the end of a bay where there is nothing but spruce thickets and moss will not be as successful as a hunter who has chosen an area thick with blueberry and elderberry. Deer concentrate in the area where food is best. Look for patches of browse that have been receiving some heavy usage. But ensure that it's not entirely browsed out.

Another fact to keep in mind is that blacktails follow the path of least resistance. They'll not stray from a trail leading where they want to go. And in late winter, blacktails follow trails in search of food. These trails are most productive when snow is on the ground. The deer don't want to use any excess energy straying away from the path.

Once you've found an area, choose your type of stand: ground level or tree stand. Locate your stand so that you have a bird's eye view of the area. If your stand is in some brush, ensure the wind is not blowing your scent down the trail the deer will use.

There is a variety of ways to obtain a stand: either build one yourself or investigate the many commercial varieties available. I won't go into detail as to which works best. Your stand should be comfortable. Deer will look up if you make lots of noise and move around as a result of not being comfortable.

Your stand should be at least 10 feet off the ground. In many areas, your stand won't be in a tree. Rather, it's possible to take stand on a cliff overlooking a narrow gorge filled with alders and willows. This is an excellent way to hunt deer, as deer and brush-filled gullies go together like cattle and corn. I'm always overjoyed when I find one, as it means I'll be looking at some mighty fine bucks very soon.

The final requirement for successful stand hunting is patience. Stay on stand several hours, then, after you're sure you can't stay another second, wait another 30 minutes. Invariably a deer will show up.

Driving works well in many parts of southeast, especially when geography prevents deer from spreading throughout the rainforest. Try a drive through a patch of spruce along a steep mountainside, a narrow canyon, or alpine amphitheatre. A properly executed drive in any of these areas will kick out deer and add weight to the meatpole.

Whatever way you hunt the Sitka blacktail, from a boat, in alpine country, or from a stand in the rain forest of southeast Alaska, I'm sure that this species will provide you with the excitement, suspense, and hunting pleasure inherent to Alaska's big game species. Make plans soon to hunt Alaska's blacktail deer. It'll be a hunt you'll remember for years to come.

Where to Hunt Sitka Blacktail Deer

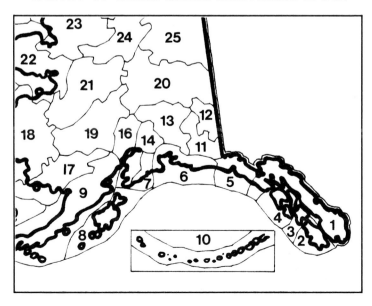

Units 1A, 2

Southeast Mainland, Prince of Wales Island

Deer populations appear to be increasing in the northern and western portions of Unit 2, yet, there are still major portions of both units where deer numbers remain low. Hecata Island has the best deer hunting in this area, folowed by Gravina Island. The harvest in the northern half of Prince of Wales Island is done mainly from the interconnected logging road system. This is very popular with hunters, as no boat travel is involved. There is record of a mule deer taken from the Stikine River Valley, but this is a rarity.

The average size of deer on the outer islands of this region is considerably smaller than in other areas of southeast Alaska. This is probably related to both poor-quality winter range and less high-quality alpine summer range within the unit. Analyses have shown a lower protein content in rumen samples from deer that inhabit the outside coastal islands than deer from islands closer to the mainland. Even within Unit 2, areas which have plentiful high-summer range produce larger deer than those with little or no alpine areas available to them. Hunter success the last six years has been nearly 70 percent.

Units 1B, 3

Southeast Mainland, Petersburg, Wrangell

Popular hunting areas include Etolin, Kadin, Sokolof, Zarembo, Wrangell, Conclusion, Coronation, Level, Vank and Woronkofski islands. The LeConte Bay and Stikine River area are also excellent. Over 80 percent of the deer harvested by hunters are taken from the islands. On the mainland, hunter success is highest south of Thomas Bay. Hunter success rates the last few years have averaged from 50 to 60 percent. The area offers excellent habitat.

Unit 1C

Southeast Mainland

A recent series of mild winters have allowed deer populations to increase. Sportsmen prefer to hunt blacktails in nearby Unit 4, especially those found on Admiralty Island. In Unit 1C, the most popular hunting area is Douglas Island, considered a 4-1 choice over any other area in this unit. The success rate at present is over 30 percent.

Unit 4

ABC Islands

The current blacktail populaton is very high, due to the series of mild winters dating back to the 1970s. Currently, over 85 percent of the region-wide harvest comes from this unit. In the past, high deer densities have occurred on Chichagof Island, with Baranof Island having lesser densities. Clear cuts and areas with disturbed habitat (loss of dense forest) are popular areas to hunt in this unit.

Unit 6

Cordova, Valdez

The deer in Prince William Sound were introduced into the area in 1916 with animals captured near Sitka. Eight deer were stocked on Hinchinbrook and Hawkins islands. Between 1917 and 1923, 16 more deer were transplanted to the same islands under supervision of the governor's office with funds provided by the Territorial Legislature.

From these transplants, deer have spread throughout most of the islands and coastal regions of PWS.

Prince William Sound deer populations are currently at high levels, although the winter of 1988-89 appeared to cause higher than normal winter mortality, especially in the younger and older deer. Hunter success from 1986-89 was near 57 percent, with 15 percent taking the limit of five deer. Hunters averaged 1.4 deer each, 3.4 hunting days per deer, and 2.5 deer per successful hunter. Successful hunters took 3.7 days per hunt. Nearly 64 percent of harvested deer were bucks.

The most popular area, Montague Island, has accounted for nearly half the harvest in the past.

Many beaches in this region were affected by the oil spill in the spring of 1989, so check with Fish and Game for current information. Deer that live at the higher elevations tend to forage in their home areas, as high as the snow will allow them in winter, and seldom go down to the beaches. Deer that live near the beach areas may be affected by ingestion of crude oil, but there is no current evidence to support this. Most of the Prince William Sound area is unaffected by the oil spill. If in doubt, hunt the higher reaches on islands with polluted beaches.

Although body size is comparable to that of deer from the better ranges of southeast Alaska, antler development is poor to moderate, and very few bucks attain the typical five-point blacktail antler. Studies show blacktails develop little more than an eyeguard and a single fork.

Unit 8

Kodiak Island Group

This unit is a favorite with southcentral and interior hunters, with annual harvests exceeding 10,000 deer. Populations are high due to light mortality and 18 years of mild winters. Over 90 percent of the hunting effort takes placce from Viekoda Bay to Uyak Bay. An average of 2.3 deer were harvested by hunters the last five years. Hunters spend approximately five to six days hunting Kodiak-area blacktails. Hunting also takes place on Afognak, Raspberry and Shuyak islands. Eastern Kodiak, due to its difficult access, accounts for lesser numbers of deer.

CHAPTER 4

Roosevelt Elk

Alaska's Roosevelt elk is not a species you're likely to see on a Brooks Range Dall sheep hunt or a Kuskokwim moose hunt. You'll have to look a bit harder and travel farther south to the "islands" to find this trophy. Yet, be wary of your expectations. Don't expect a picturesque, outdoor magazine type of setting where a royal, Rocky Mountain elk stands in an open meadow, far above timberline. More often than not, Alaska elk country is dark and dreary spruce forest, broken by clearings of muskeg or impenetrable clumps of alder. Storm clouds carry a cargo of heavy snow, dropping it on hillsides often scoured by winds blowing 60 mph and more. Yet, even in this dim, dreary environment, the Roosevelt elk is a beacon that summons hunters to partake in one of the most rugged and satisfying challenges available to Alaska sportsmen.

History

During the Pleistocene era, North America had ten subspecies of elk. Of those ten, six—including an unknown subspecies from a fossil discovered in Alaska—are now extinct (Murie, 1951). Of the four species currently found in North America, it is the Roosevelt elk, *Cervus elaphus roosevelti*, that appears throughout the coastal areas of the Pacific Northwest and two islands of Alaska's Kodiak Archipelago.

The early settlers were mistaken when they gave the name *elk* to this species of deer. The name *elk* is a colloquialism derived from the German word *elch*, which correctly belongs to the Scandanavian moose. The settlers mistook the American elk for moose, and didn't realize their mistake until much later.

Two hunters discussing the location of an Afognak elk herd. The rugged terrain and dense forests make for a challenging hunt.

In hunting circles, the elk is called *"wapiti"*, its Shawnee Indian name. The word means *"white deer"*, probably referring to the elk's whitish-brown rump patch or its bleached spring coat. Nevertheless, the elk lives up to its reputation of being one of the most impressive deer a hunter can pursue, one in keeping with its prestigious and presidential name.

Life History

In early September, Roosevelt elk bulls begin pre-rut activities of bugling and cow acquisition. To prevent competition for his harem, the dominant bull of a herd drives younger bulls out of the area. These younger bulls usually stay on the perimeter of the herd, waiting for the bull to become preoccupied with either rounding up stray cows or driving rival bulls away. Then oftentimes the younger bulls sneak in and breed with the cows.

By the second week in October, most breeding is complete. The bulls become somewhat solitary, trying to consume large quantities of food to put on the necessary fat they need to survive the winter.

Elk calves are born in early June. The usual birth is a single calf of 25 to 28 pounds. A cow tends to remain apart from other elk for two to three weeks, or until the calf is ready to travel. Then, the cows, calves, and young bulls form large herds that frequent the alpine country during much of the summer.

Roosevelt elk are the largest-bodied elk in North America. This is due to the excellent feed and mild winters on the islands. One registered guide told me that his August clients bagged two elk that provided over 1,450 pounds of quartered meat. And these were only five-point bulls!

A bull's first antlers normally begin to grow in May, and are spike horns about 12 inches long. Three-year-old bulls commonly exhibit three to four points and sometimes five points per side. The racks get heftier as the elk reaches its prime. The rack usually degenerates as the animal ages.

Hunters shouldn't expect racks of the same size as those of Rocky Mountain elk. But Alaskan elk racks are trophies in their own right. Roosevelt elk are forest-dwellers. While their antlers aren't widespread and sweeping, many do sport heavy beams as thick as a wrist. Generally, a rack on a large bull won't exceed 36 inches. Expect heavy bases to 10 inches and heavy, horn eye guards no more than a foot long. Tines are sometimes broken due to sparring and traveling through the dense spruce forests. Another characteristic of mature, Roosevelt elk antlers

is a "crown" of three or four points where the surroyals are usually located on the Rocky Mountain subspecies. Four-to six-point Roosevelt elk are available if you're willing to put forth the effort to hunt them.

Alaska's Roosevelt elk are the largest-bodied elk in North America. This is due to excellent feed and mild winters on Afognak and Raspberry islands. (Photo by Leonard Lee Rue IV)

Distribution

In Alaska, elk occur only on Raspberry Island and nearby Afognak Island. Afognak lies in the Gulf of Alaska some 50 miles below the southern tip of the Kenai Peninsula and three miles northeast of Kodiak Island. Nearly 40 miles long and averaging 25 miles wide, with an area of 780 square miles, Afognak is the second largest island in the Kodiak Archipelago. Several smaller islands, including Raspberry, belong to the Afognak group.

A transplant of eight calves from Washington State's Olympic Peninsula established the Roosevelt elk on Afognak Island in 1929. The mild maritime climate, steep terrain, abundant forage and heavy spruce timber helped the elk population grow rapidly. It reached 212 animals in 1948, and a peak of 1,200 to 1,500 elk in 1965. In the late 1960s, a decline associated with over-utilization of winter range began. Unusually heavy snow accumulations and cold temperatures during the winter of 1970

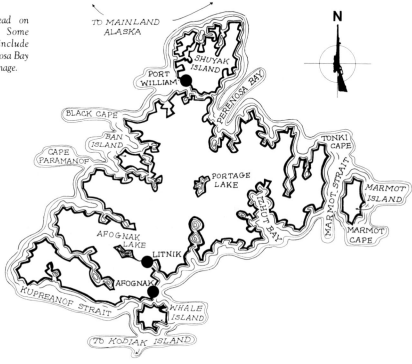

Elk are widespread on Afognak Island. Some popular areas include Kazakof Bay, Perenosa Bay and the Izhut drainage.

and 1971 brought massive die-offs. By 1972, only about 450 elk remained. Since 1975, when a census showed the herd at about 500 animals, the elk population has been gradually increasing. Today, this region is home to approximately 1,500-plus elk in six to eight different herds. Most of the population is on Afognak; the rest on Raspberry Island. The population may be declining in some areas on the eastern side of Afognak Island, where increased harvest and a relatively high take of females may be causing a reduction in herd size.

Elk hunting on Afognak and Raspberry is currently done via drawing or registration permit, the latter meaning you sign in at the Kodiak fish and game office before going afield. By law, you must also sign out after the hunt. Permittees are required to carry a transistor radio in the field and listen at specific times for closure announcements that are broadcast if the harvest quota is reached.

Biologists have predicted excellent hunting in 1989, and have recommended increasing the harvest to keep the elk population in check, and to provide additional hunting opportunities. The majority of successful hunters are unguided.

Raspberry Island and the southwestern end of Afognak Island receive more hunting pressure because of their location close

to Kodiak and other nearby seaports. The terrain is also a bit more open with rolling hills, allowing for easier hunter access.

On the northern and eastern sides of Afognak Island, however, hunting pressure is light, geography a bit more rugged, and weather more severe. The elk herds there are lightly hunted and not spooked from constant hunting pressure. Transportation fees to the area are higher, but it's worth it if you want a prime, wilderness hunt for Roosevelt elk.

The season on elk currently runs from September through October in certain parts of Afognak, and September through December on the remainder of Afognak. Many guides and hunters prefer to hunt elk during the late season. Plan a hunt around September 20, but no later than the end of October. I like that time because the onslaught of winter weather has knocked down grass and brought snow, making the animals easier to locate. Bulls are also into the rut, chasing down cows in the alpine clearings, and hence easier to catch. If you wait any later, the harvest quota of elk may have been reached, prompting an emergency closure by ADF&G. Another drawback of hunting past mid-October is that inclement weather, commonplace that time of year, can often delay a hunt for several days.

Elk hunting on Afognak often entails a rugged climb, while rolling hills and open areas are more commonplace on Raspberry Island.

Hunting Techniques

Bugling is a very effective method of locating bulls, especially if they are in the timber. While I'm no expert at elk bugling, I do know several hunters who utilize calls effectively on Afognak to pinpoint bulls. Most hunters use the commercial variety and others make their own. Excellent elk bugling tapes or records are on the market: buy one and practice, practice, practice. One friend kept his bugle in his car, and practiced in heavy traffic. The long stares of nearby drivers didn't bother him a bit. He always got his elk each year.

Calling elk is much like calling moose. If the bull is coming toward you, leave him be. If he's acting stubborn and won't budge, you'll need to make a stalk. Determine the location of the bull and slowly enter the area. Quiet is the key word here. Begin calling after a wait of 10 to 15 minutes.

Another good time to hunt elk is in early August, when bulls can almost always be found in the alpine meadows. However, not just any alpine meadow will attract elk. Look for spots with abundant grasses and browse. Especially attractive to the animals are bowl-like amphitheaters protected from severe storms and wind, with an ample supply of water and nearby patches of heavy spruce timber for cover.

The best time to hunt early-season elk on Afognak is during the first four hours after the hint of dawn and before the last rays of dusk disappear over the horizon. Elk are quite active during these times, feeding or searching out forage. Favorite elk forage includes bluejoint grass, fireweed, angelica, cow parsnip, sedges, willow, bog blueberry and salmonberry.

If elk are heavily hunted, as they are in many areas of Afognak and Raspberry, look for them in heavy brush and timber. Until evening, elk seldom move out of this type of cover. However, they take full advantage of moonlit nights, often feeding all night and resting all day. Many hunters claim their best elk hunting takes place during the new moon.

As with caribou and moose, glassing is important when hunting early-season Roosevelt elk. The use of a spotting scope or binoculars from a high vantage point will allow you to glass a variety of alpine areas, basins, ridges and clearings in forests. Concentrate your efforts in early morning and late evening.

If you locate an elk on another ridge or meadow, plan on being there later that day or at first light the next morning. Before sneaking into the area, however, consider wind and noise factors. If possible, stalk to the other side of the ridge and come over the top. If the wind is against you, stay down along tim-

Wallows are a sure indication that big bulls are using an area. Choose a stand that allows a clear view of the wallow, and wait the bull out, even if it means bivouacing overnight.

berline and cross over the top only when the wind changes direction. You can also work a stalk around the mountain when conditions warrant.

Because of the tricky wind currents encountered above timberline, I'm a firm believer in masking scents to hide human odor. If masking scents do nothing but give you that extra bit of confidence, they're worth the price. Nevertheless, don't put your entire faith in them. Always be cognizant of wind direction. Hunt as if you were not using scent. Should a crosswind unexpectedly come through the meadow, scent only deters the elk long enough for a shot. For that, it works great. Expect no more and you won't be disappointed.

Hunting Afognak late one October, my wife Adela and I were looking for a monster bull elk that was holding somewhere in the high country. We sneaked around the base of timberline, walking into the wind and glassing each nook and cranny for any indication of elk. Without warning, the wind shifted direction. Minutes later, a small elk charged up a gully, heading for alpine country. But, because we had on a masking scent, the bull stopped several times to look back and "bark" at us. It wasn't the monster we were after, but it was a good lesson in the effectiveness of a masking scent. We could have easily nailed the young bull, but decided to let him grow up a bit.

Stalking to within range—whether in dense timber or open alpine country—is a test of skill. In the high country, a stalk from above is best, but don't rule out the possibility of working up from the bottom to within shooting range. The herd's actions will tell you whether it's better to circle around and come down from above or to risk a stalk up through cover. Chances are, you'll get a better shot from above, but the elk may not stay in place for the time it may take you to work around the mountain. A lot depends on the type of cover you need to walk through. If it's alder, forget it. Alder is much too thick and noisy. If the path is interspersed with boulders and gullies, you have a good chance of using them to get within range.

Once you're within range, take a few seconds to observe the herd's behavior. Keep a low profile. If elk are looking your way, don't tarry with a shot. When frightened, Afognak elk usually head for timber or dense cover. If they are above timberline, they flee across a meadow and head down the first major gully and disappear in the forest. Oftentimes you'll see next the elk cresting the ridge on the opposite side of the valley. Elk can

move fast. Bulls have been clocked at speeds of up to 35 mph.

Some of the toughest elk hunting occurs when a major storm moves through the Gulf of Alaska. This happens all too often. The winds, with gusts of up to 100 mph, play havoc with the elk's primary means of defense, their senses of hearing and smell. Especially if snow is on the ground, one of the best ways to hunt them is to search out clearings and meadows in sections of heavy timber. Once the storm lets up, you'll see elk popping out from cover like popcorn out of an erupting popper.

Hunting elk in November and December requires a variety of hunting and orienteering skills. When the elk are in the timber in late season, a map and compass are necessary to keep from getting lost. Also, the timber in some areas is so dense that you could walk right through a herd of elk and not know it.

Heavy snowfall will usually push the elk out of the alpine areas and into the trees. With a bit of scouting, you'll find where elk have been congregating, especially if you've found a prime feeding area. Chances are you'll be able to take stand and have elk around you in a matter of hours. You can also expect to find elk near the beach and on wind-blown ridges.

Do-it-yourself hunters usually reach the bays and lakes on the islands by float plane or charter boat. Access costs run from

Late-season elk hunting is difficult. Snows have pushed the animals into timber, and finding them can be difficult. A map and compass is necessary to keep from getting lost, and perhaps spooking elk. (Photo by Adela Ward Batin)

Roosevelt Elk

This elk was taken in late October, after a heavy snow pushed the herds into the timber. The weather this time of year can be rain or snow, and always windy.

$120 to $300 per hour, depending on type of aircraft chartered, amount of gear involved, and the distance traveled. Kodiak game biologist Roger Smith said that good populations of elk reside around Malina, Paramanof and Foul bays, all located on the west side of Afognak Island. At the north end of the island, good racks have been coming from Tonki and Seal bays. Many hunters do well on Afognak's east-side logging roads.

A six-day guided hunt on Afognak or Raspberry will run from $1,800 to $2,500. Kodiak outfitters operate elk camps that include cabin, transportation to a prime elk area and basic gear (stove, utensils, etc) for about $900 per hunter. This is typical of what other outfitters are charging in the area.

While the Alaska Roosevelt elk is not the state's most lauded big game species, it does offer hunters a chance at one of the continent's most regal members of the deer family. Add the scenic beauty of hunting the coastal areas, the wilderness solitude of the alpine high-country, and the excitement of watching a herd of elk work its way, single file, into a nearby field, and you have a big game hunt that is second to none. To top it off, elk steaks and chops are a gourmet's delight. I hope the elk stays around for generations to come.

Where to Hunt Roosevelt Elk

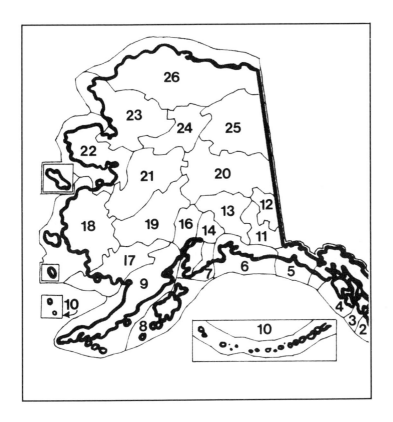

Unit 8

Kodiak and Adjacent Islands

Herds on Raspberry Island and western Afognak Island are stable and increasing in size. Approximately 200 to 300 elk per year are harvested by hunters.

Mild winters and conservative management practices have pushed the elk population to over 1,500 animals. Elk hunters should seriously consider an October hunt. The weather is mild, and sufficient daylight exists to allow for a full day of hunting.

Top areas to hunt on Afognak Island are Kazakof Bay, Perenosa Bay and Izhut Bay drainages, and Duck Mountain. At least three elk herds are accessible via the road systems.

Black Bear

The black bear, *Ursus americanus*, is a black diamond in the motherlode of Alaska big game. There's no mistaking the identity of this wilderness gem. The luster of its long, black coat is instantly apparent, whether found glistening-wet in a salmon stream, amidst the ruby-red cranberry coffers of autumn, or along the shore of an isolated, sapphire-blue sea cove. Blackie is especially coveted when found on snow-covered hillsides in early spring. The sheen of this gem, polished by months of hibernation, creates an excitement in hunters unequaled by any other trophy. As with its cousin the grizzly bear, there is a thrill, a romance in finding—and hopefully bagging—a black bear that makes it a treasure to be valued.

Alaska statewide hunter harvest figures indicate that at least 1,500 black bears are harvested each year, and that number is increasing. This is proof that the black bear is rapidly becoming an important "primary" big game species, besides being an important "secondary" species taken incidentally to the harvest of other big game animals. And there are two good reasons why the black bear should be a primary species. The season in most units is open year 'round, with a liberal bag limit of three bears per hunter. Also, the black bear is found throughout most of mainland Alaska and many of the islands of the southeastern Panhandle.

A hunter following the trail of a large black bear along the mud flats of Cook Inlet. Intertidal areas, especially those near salmon spawning streams, are good places to hunt in early morning and late evening.

Ol' blackie is a sharp-witted, keen-nosed, radar-eared game animal. Yet, with a modest show of effort, be assured that you stand a good to excellent chance of bagging a black bear, providing you are familiar with the habits, terrain, and techniques of hunting it.

Life History

Black bears are born in January or February, in the mother's winter den. The mother sleeps through the birth. The litter ranges from one to three cubs, each weighing from eight to 10 ounces. The newborn cubs will suckle and sleep for the duration of the mother's hibernation.

When the cubs emerge from the den with their mother, they weigh about five pounds. Throughout the month of May, females and cubs remain at mid-elevation areas. Males tend to stay in the lowland beach fringe, fattening up for the fast-approaching breeding season. Also, males tend to avoid territories of females. When females begin estrous and allow males to travel through mid-elevation habitat, then males are found at all ranges of terrain. Males move about quickly and extensively, foraging in new areas and inseminating as many females as possible. Cubs remain with the mother throughout their first year, and overwinter with her. The following spring, cubs are then driven off with the birth of a new litter, or when the males show up for breeding.

Spring Hunting

Depending on the severity of the winter and spring weather, blacks can be found emerging from their dens around May 1. With a late spring, this varies as much as two or more weeks. An extremely late spring in 1985 resulted in the bears emerging from their dens as late as June 25.

A good rule of thumb is to plan on the early part of April and May for islands and mainland areas in southeast Alaska, and the first of May for southcentral and southwestern Alaska. If a hunter is looking for numbers of bear, a hunt away from the crowds, and an aesthetically pleasing location, my choice for a spring black bear hunt would be Alaska's southcentral and southeastern coast. The density per square mile of bears in these coastal areas is much greater than in the interior. In many of the thousands of secluded bays and inlets of coastal Alaska, there are 10 bears per square mile. Of course, bear populations are much lower in heavily hunted areas, especially near major cities. But if I had one coastal region to hunt black bears, there are two reasons why I'd choose Prince William Sound as the best place for a hunter to pursue this species in Alaska, and perhaps, North America: bear food availability and excellent cover. Both are critical in importance. The particular qualities of each include:

1. The dense coastal coniferous forests are interspersed with many open meadows containing a lush growth of grasses, herbs and berry-producing shrubs.

2. Regular snow avalanches keep the slopes in early, sub-climax vegetative stages that offer sedges, herbs and berries, and result in areas becoming snow-free early in the spring.

3. An abundance of berry types provide excellent and necessary forage in both late summer and fall.

4. Runs of salmon provide bears with an optional food source if the annual berry crop is a disaster.

5. The absence of other ungulates and brown bears in areas of western Prince William Sound eliminates competition for food and space.

6. Large grass and sedge flats on glacial and stream tidal areas provide ideal foraging conditions in spring.

7. The habitat is complemented by numerous narrow fjords, streams and glaciers, creating a desirable place to hunt.

8. A deep snowpack common to this region helps both plant and animal species survive poor wintering conditions.

This seven-foot blackie was taken in late spring in the Chugach Mountains. Bears are often found near the receding snowline, feeding on fresh grass sprouts.

Cruising the bays and inlets in late spring is a popular way to hunt Prince William Sound black bears. The method is quiet and leaves little human scent. Here, a hunter points out a field that might hold black bear.

9. Due to the area's geography and climate, vegetation at any given growth stage is usually available to bears.

10. While bears may be smaller in size than those found in southerly climates, ecological conditions and numbers of black bears appear excellent now and in the near future.

11. The farthest a bear can be from most access points in PWS is roughly 3 miles.

An extremely popular and effective way to hunt the bays of Prince William Sound is by boat. With a boat you can access more miles of terrain than you could on foot. Many times you can effectively scout and hunt an area right from the boat. And with a boat, you leave a minimum of human scent.

A boat's effectiveness is unquestioned: about 90 percent of the black bears taken in Unit 6 are taken by boat-transported hunters during the spring season. The ports of Whittier, Valdez and Seward are major points of departure for charter boats that can reach the best hunting areas within a day or less of travel time. According to Modafferi (1982) inclement weather, not uncommon in the area in early spring, greatly affects the activities of the hunters; however, in its absence, hunter success is relatively high.

Studies of Prince William Sound spring bear hunts show that boars are the sex most commonly taken. Modafferi indicated that a greater percentage of male bears were killed by hunters in lightly hunted areas, Units 5 and 8, than in the heavily hunted areas, Units 4, 6 and 7. This was particularly evident for bears more than 9 years old. Hunters see more boars than sows, especially in bog clearings and on open hillsides, because after leaving the denning site in late spring, sows rarely take their cubs far from heavy cover (Bray, 1966). This preponderance of available boars is a bonus for hunters, as male black bears are noticeably larger than females.

Anchorage outfitter Jim O'Meara specializes in hunting for trophy black bear in Prince William Sound. O'Meara, having spent thousands of hours flying the bays and shorelines of the Sound, knows exactly where concentrations of black bear are. He operates floating cabins equipped with boats and motors, allowing easy access to the many bays in the area. He's a believer in his boat/cabin set-up for hunting Prince William Sound. For the past two years his hunters have had 100 percent success on black bears. "People will get black bear if they do what I tell them," O'Meara says. "So many will hire out with an outfitter or charter service who will just dump them off in some cove. They make too much noise walking through the brush, set-up camp and cook in the same area as they are hunting, and expect the black bear to come walking out onto the beach. It just isn't done that way."

The secret to hunting black bear successfully is in remembering that their movements are controlled primarily by available food and cover, habitat preference, and regional topography.

Look for Food Items

If you've spent a day on stand without seeing a single bear, you'll need to spend the mid-day hours searching for the forage food items that bruins like best. Frequently, finding these items is what makes the black bear available to the hunter. Otherwise, few hunters would be able to locate ol' blackie in the rain-forest-like jungle of Alaska's coast.

Hatler's (1967) study of the food habits of the interior black bear showed that relatively few items constituted the bulk of its diet. However, McIlroy demonstrated that coastal black bears forage on a variety of food items. When bears first emerge in the spring, scat samplings show they tend to feed on grass. This

Skunk cabbage grows in marshy areas where black bears are often found. The importance of skunk cabbage in the black bear's diet is questionable. However, bears feed on the new shoots of grass that are often found near these plants.

is a major food item of Alaska black bears. You can find grass sprouts in snow-free, beach-fringe habitat, on south-facing hillsides near the retreating snowline in alpine country, and along avalanche slopes.

About the third week in May, bears move down into the tidal marshes to forage. Then, beach rye grass, *Elymus arenarius*, and sedges, *Carex*, found near coastal shorelines and within the tidal marshes are the predominant forage item. Bear researchers have found that within a few days, bear carcasses left by hunters were generally cannibalized.

Bears also can be found near beds of mussels, and near the carrion of fish and marine mammals. Foraging within and near the tidal marshes starts to taper off the first week in June. However, it isn't uncommon to see bears eating *Carex* throughout the months of July and August.

During the latter part of spring, carefully glass the forest clearings that host snow-melt creeks and streams. There, succulent plants and tender shoots that bears crave appear long before nearby mountaintops are cleared of snow. Also, the subsequent snow-melt causes plants such as skunk cabbage, sedges, salmonberry, Angelica, and horsetail to sprout in low-lying marshes and swamps, both of which are also excellent areas to hunt.

Hatler's study also noted that bear activity was evident around rotted logs. He observed many rotted tree trunks torn apart and holes scooped out of open bogs. In those places, bears search for grubs and insects, and hunters should watch for these signs. Remember that coastal blacks are seldom found far from timbered areas.

The importance of skunk cabbage to black bears in the spring is questionable. Skunk cabbage contains toxic substances adversely affecting heart rate and blood pressure; it can be fatal to livestock, deer, elk and chickens (Craighead, Craighead, David 1963). McIlroy suggests that bears feed on the grasses that often grow near the "cabbage" patches. This would explain the trampling of patches of skunk cabbage I observe each year, and had mistaken for the evidence of a cabbage-stuffed bear. Skunk cabbage is a delicate plant, easily knocked over by a passing foot or bear foraging on grass or other plants.

It's important to locate a bay or cove with a marshy field or swamp at its head or base, and a mile or more away from your base camp. Be sure the wind blows away from the area you plan to hunt. Beach your craft about 300 to 400 yards away from the marsh. Situate yourself in a natural blind (logjam, uprooted tree, clump of brush) where you have a wide view of the marsh and beach. After that, it's a matter of waiting and keeping your eyes open. I prefer to hunt in this manner in early evening and at first light. Black bears are most active then.

Berry Patches

Alaska black bears are extremely fond of open areas. They travel ridges, semi-open hillsides, rockslides, gullies and game trails in those areas. They especially like second-growth areas bordering an old burn, and the burn area itself. There they spend hours digging for rodents and breaking open logs for grubs, ants and other insects. But the chief attraction is the

These blueberries are prime food for black bears. Studies show that a black bear's survival during winter depends heavily on a fall diet of berries.

berry patches. There are few forage food items that ol' blackie prefers better than lowbush cranberry, highbush cranberry, crowberry, and salmonberry, all of which are extremely abundant in Alaska's alpine regions. Hatler (1967) reported that over 12,000 berries were found in the stomach of an interior black bear. And surely, a large percentage of those were blueberries, a favorite of black bears due to their abundance and sweet taste.

In late August and September, hunters encounter ample evidence of this fact. At this time, bear dung consists of numerous mounds of partially digested berries deposited at random over a mountainside. Hatler suggests that the survival of the black bear depends heavily upon a fall diet of berries. His hypothesis has a ring of truth to it, especially when the nutritive value of spring and summer forage is compared to the fall bounty of berries. Only rarely does a fruitful berry patch escape the combine-like action of a black bear's mouth, and the subsequent deposits often make finding a safe place to put your foot scarce indeed. Yet few hunters take advantage of the situation. They'll walk around ridgetops, glass for a few minutes, then go on their merry way. Given a moderate amount of time, glassing alpine berry patches can be the most effective way to bag a nice black bear.

Modafferi (1982) commented on the relationship of berries and bears:

> It is interesting, but not surprising, that berries, a highly ranked bear food, have not evolved a mechanism to prevent bears from feeding on them. Perhaps the evolu-

tionary strategy of berry plants (blueberry and salmon-
berry) in northwestern Prince William Sound has been
to encourage, not discourage, use of their fruits by bears
as a food source to facilitate dispersal of seeds, ultimately
to increase the distribution of those particular species.
If this were the case, then the proximate strategy of berry
plants would be to produce visually and chemically at-
tractive fruits. Since the digestive strategy of bears is
to process a great deal of food inefficiently, rather than
efficiently process a much smaller quantity of food,
viability of seeds in the berries is probably not altered.

How I hunt berry patches depends on the lay of the terrain and the part of the state I'm hunting. For instance, interior blacks can often be found well out onto the alpine tundra, feeding on blueberries. Few other areas in the interior offer equal concentrations of this plant. In contrast, coastal black bears do not immediately move into the alpine areas to feed on ripened berries. Rather, they remain in forested habitat where blueberries or huckleberries are abundant. A late summer or autumn hunter flying over a coastal area at dusk is likely not to see the number of bears he observed there during the spring months. The bears will eventually move out into the open, coastal areas. You must be at the right place to intercept them.

In gently sloping, open terrain with little cover, I prefer to glass from the highest point. There, I have an eagle's view of any bear entering the area. While I'm glassing, I plan my strategy for the stalk to areas I think the bear will appear. My plans are based on topography, existing bear trails, and concentration of berries. It's important to burn individual landmarks into your mind, especially when utilizing gullies for your stalk. Once in the brushy confines of Alaska's "wilderness alleys" it's extremely easy to misjudge your location. A mountaintop, a large rock, a scraggy spruce tree, anything that you can use as a constant reference point will keep you orientated. Once the bear appears, you need but quickly review your plan and you're off. While I've seen bears feed in a berry patch the entire day, they usually feed while they move. So, if you wait too long in planning your strategy, the bear can be well out of range by the time you peek over the ridge.

Another method simply reverses the above-mentioned strategy. In areas with numerous, brush-filled gullies, you'll also find small ridges barren of alders and heavy brush. Ridges like these are common near timberline in much of the glacial-carved portions of the Talkeetnas, Alaska Range and southeast mainland. These ridges are often small: about 20 to 30 yards in length and half that distance in width. In the thick cover, bears find sanctuary, and on the open ridges, ample berries. When spooked, feeding bears merely scurry down a few yards into cover. It is in this type of environment more than any other that bears are more often apt to escape hunters' notice.

Hunting ridges is easy if you remember a few simple rules. Forget about hunting the area on foot. Trying to stalk a bear in this type of environment is an act in futility. Find a high point near timberline that allows you clear sight to several gullies and mini-ridges. Next, slowly walk the ridges until you're within range (200 yards or less) of all the gullies you'll be glassing. Also, it's important to make the first shot count, and you can do that best from a high vantage point. Take your time. I don't know about you, but I'm not too keen on tracking a wounded bear in alder thickets that offer a VHR (visual hunting requirement) of three feet or less.

If you can't take a good, solid shot at a vital area, be patient, even if the bear appears to be wandering off. Chances are, if the bear disappears, he'll reappear on a nearby ridge, unless he winded you. In that case, he's off for good, and you'll do better by hunting another area.

When hunting either alpine berry patches or ridgetops, it's important to sneak into the area well before first light. Throughout late August and September, this means being ready to hunt by 5 a.m. I've seen bears emerge from cover at first light, or around 7 a.m., give or take 45 minutes, depending on area hunted and time of year. If I've found a really hot area, I'll make a spike camp nearby, being careful to pitch it several ridges away from the hunting area. Crosswinds can betray your presence in a second, as will careless camp chatter and noise.

I can't overemphasize the importance of being on the lookout for bears when hunting berry patches. Bears can appear at any time, at any place. A funny tale exemplifying this point occurred several years ago. Two friends of mine were on an alpine hunt in the Lime Hills area of western Alaska. Jim had already harvested a nice black bear, and was hanging around camp, taking care of the hide and reading. Brad left before dawn the next morning to glass an extremely promising berry patch on the mountain ridge above camp. Bear sign there was abundant, and worth the half-hour hike through the alders.

The day dragged on for Jim, As evening approached, he began scheming to liven things up a bit. Trickster to the bone, Jim

planned to hide in the brush near camp and growl his deepest, most guttural bear growl before jumping out at Brad walking back into camp.

Alpine ridges are excellent places to hunt for black bear. Find ridges with a profuse growth of cranberry or blueberries, and plenty of bear dung. Chances are you'll have a black bear in less than three days.

About half an hour later, Jim heard the alders rustling above camp. He ran into the alders and kept his head low. When he heard Brad break into the clearing, he jumped out, shaking his hands and growled a "Rrrooooar!"

There was one minor problem. The face Jim saw wasn't Brad's, but that of a mature black bear. The bear let out a "Waaauuuggh!" that sent both of them flying in opposite directions, with the bear kicking up clumps of tundra as it barreled down the mountain while Jim dove into the tent, knocking over the cookstove and supper before grabbing and fumbling a cartridge into his rifle. About 20 minutes later, Brad arrived to find Jim sitting on a log, caressing a half-empty bottle of Yukon Jack. The last I heard, Jim had given up his prankster ways and the bear, nicknamed "ol' whiteface," was last sighted 100 miles to the east in the Chugach mountains.

Trails

A leisurely flight over any alpine region rewards the viewer with the sight of miles of criss-crossing bear trails. They stretch out like long, dead branches from hillside alders and spruce thickets, winding and weaving from berry patch to ground squirrel den. I can't figure out why hunters don't spend more time hunting such trails. For me they've been a surefire way to locate blackies.

A recent moose hunt in the Talkeetna Mountains provided a prime example of how often bears use these trails. Friend Bill Timnes and I were hunting a relatively flat plateau. Its gradually sloping sides stretched for 800 yards before dropping abruptly into an abyss of spruce and birch cover. During our ten-day stay (in which I bagged a nice moose) Bill and I counted seven individual black bears that moved via trails through our three-square-mile mountaintop. One day, using a parallel trail that ran the crest of a small ridge, Bill and I managed to stalk within 75 yards of a nice boar. But as luck would have it, the night before Bill had just finished reading a book on bear maulings. And it showed during the stalk.

I eased across the tundra on my stomach to a ledge overlooking the small ravine. The black bear, grazing in a tiny opening cluttered with small trees, was unaware that we were a mere 75 yards above him. I motioned for Bill to crawl forward.

"What do you think?" he whispered.

"He'll work his way into that clearing with all those blueberries," I said. "Get your rifle scope on him and get ready to bag him when he gets out of those trees."

Bill crawled up farther on the rock and unintentionally dropped his elbow down onto a dry piece of willow. "Krraaack!"

The bear's ears flicked to attention, miniature radar dishes straining to pick up the slightest noise that would betray our presence. I froze, not wanting the bear to locate us.

"Should I shoot? Should I shoot?" Bill questioned impatiently. I could sense the urgency in his voice. "Wait until he gets out into the opening," I countered.

"Baaaammm!" The surprise of the rifle report shocked me more than the muzzle blast. The ground exploded by the blackie's right foot. The bear swapped ends and hightailed it out of there within a heartbeat.

"Why in the heck did you shoot?" I asked incredulously. "He was going to walk out into the clearing!"

Bill looked down for a moment, then shook his head. "I feel like a horse's rear," he said. "The way that bear was looking, I thought he was going to run up that bear trail at us."

From that moment on, I've believed that bear hunters and bear mauling books don't mix! If you would be a successful bear hunter, leave such books in the bookstore until after the hunt!

As Bill discovered, hunting alpine trails requires more than just glassing. It takes the full employment of your senses on alert to any sign or indication of black bear, from the moment you get off that plane to the time you leave. For instance, when setting up a spike camp or gathering firewood, you should always hunt. Look up every so often. Take a few seconds to glass around. Blackies can appear and disappear in hillside clearings at any time. I nailed my first black bear on Mount Susitna, about 30 miles west of Anchorage. I got up early one morning for an hour hike to a clearing that had some black bear sign. I had walked no more than 20 feet from my tent when I spotted a black bear, feeding downhill about 80 yards away. One shot was all it took.

Of course, such times when the bears "come knocking on your door" are relatively rare. But the point is, always be on the lookout. And always be ready. Have your rifle in hand and shells loaded in the magazine. Have your scope on one of the lower settings, such as 2 or 4 power. The lower magnifications will help you get on your target more quickly, especially if you jump up a bear at close range. The logistics for hunting trails are the same as hunting berry patches.

Kill Sites

If you plan on hunting moose or caribou in an area with a good blackie population, don't hesitate to add a few more days to your hunt. There's nothing that attracts a hungry black bear more than a fresh or slightly ripe offal pile from a hunter-killed moose or caribou.

A few tricks can enhance the effectiveness of a gutpile. First, pack all the meat away from the kill site as soon as possible. If the weather is warm, drape the hide over the pile, and allow the heat of the sun and the insulating qualities of the hide to expedite the ripening process.

Next, find a suitable location for a blind. A high rocky out-cropping, tree-stand or brush blind in a nearby thicket are all good choices. It's best to have several blinds built, just in case the wind changes direction.

After a day or two, about the time it takes to trim the meat and prepare the cape, head back to the kill and remove the hide. Drape it over some bushes, flesh side up, to allow the breeze to carry off the odor of ripening offal to blackie's nose.

With this method, the secret of success is a comfortable seat or air pillow to prevent you from bustling around and making noise that could spook a black bear. Another aid to remaining absolutely quiet—second only to falling asleep on stand—is a good, long novel. And when packing your lunch, use crumpled paper or sandwich bags to wrap the food. Foil is too noisy. Prior to taking stand, open all paper items such as candy bars and potato chips.

I use fox or coyote urine as a masking scent with considerable success. It's a surefire way of fooling a bear. After all, these scents are what a blackie is used to. All you need to do is watch the remains of a moose or deer kill to understand what I mean.

Joe Batin bagged this fine black bear after posting watch over an intersection of several bear trails. Notice the profuse blueberry growth.

At first, the whiskeyjacks or Canada jays come flying in. They peck at the scraps, and fly off with them to nearby trees. This attracts the magpies, with their incessant squawking, which in turn attracts the ravens. Before long, and if you're quiet, you'll see foxes or coyotes stealthily move in. Despite the fact that the remains of a moose carcass is enough to feed the entire area's fox and coyote population, the animals bark, fight and howl over who gets first dibs on the remains. They'll urinate on nearby twigs and branches, marking their territory. Upon hearing this ruckus or smelling the ripening offal, ol' blackie is prompt to investigate. A dab of fox scent on your hat and clothes hides all human odor, even when upwind from the carcass and approaching black bear. My recommendation: don't take chances. Abide by the standard rules of the hunt. Position your blind downwind from the carcass. If there is a crosswind when the black bear is approaching, the masking scent may allow the black bear to get close enough for a shot.

Baiting in Spring

Baiting for black bears is like hunting over gut piles. However, baiting allows the hunter to place the bait where bear sign, migration routes or conditions best warrant it. While I personally prefer the challenge of stalking a bear, I won't underestimate the effectiveness of baiting. In areas where bear are few and far between, in dense cover where hunting bears is extremely difficult, and when limited time is a factor, baiting can't be beat. It's an art that requires the same attention to detail as stalking bruin in the high country.

The State of Alaska has the following requirements for black bear baiting:

- Intentionally baiting for grizzly or brown bear is illegal.
- Only bio-degradable materials may be used for bait; only the head, bones, viscera or skin of legally harvested fish and game may be used for bait.
- Bait may not be used within one-quarter mile of a publicly maintained road or trail.
- No person may use bait within one mile of a house or permanent dwelling, or within one mile of a developed campground or developed recreational facility.
- A hunter using bait shall clearly mark the bait station with a sign that displays the hunter's name and current address, phone number, and hunting license number.
- A hunter using bait shall remove litter and equipment from the bait site when hunting is completed.

Veteran bear baiter Richard Gardner uses salmon carcasses leftover from last season and cooking grease collected over the winter. Other hunters and guides prefer to use attractants such as a nylon bag filled with honey, or commercial scents such as anise, spearmint or even peanut butter. Count yourself lucky if you can find an old winter kill. It will attract and hold bears until it's devoured.

The container to hold your bait is as important as selecting the bait itself. Hunter John Malloy places his scraps in a piece of canvas, ties the end off with a rope and hoists the bag about 15 feet into a tall birch. On the ground beneath the hanging bag, he'll toss several scraps to keep the bears interested once they are drawn to the spot. He prefers to wire a lidless plastic trash can to a stout tree and fills it with fish scraps and "whatever smelly garbage I can find."

Be sure to anchor your bait, as the black bear is both strong and a master thief. I've heard a hunter tell of how a black bear stole his trash can filled with bait. The bear dragged it over a half mile up to an adjacent ridge. All that he could find was a set of tracks and one empty trash can with teeth marks in the handle.

It's always best to start out with too much bait than not enough. I know of several hunters who will go with nothing less than 50 pounds of salmon or meat scraps, and add to the pile as birds and animals eat away at the stash.

Once you have your bait, location is the next factor. Many

baiters prefer sets that they can easily access and replenish throughout the spring season. Since most bait is backpacked or carried in, the 1/4-mile distance from state-maintained roadways is about the limit most hunters will go. Chances of success are greatly increased when aircraft, ATVs or riverboats are used to access remote areas. A perfect example of this is the mountains and forests surrounding Skilak Lake. Access to this area is usually by boat. Here, bears are found not only on the southfacing slopes, but also on the east, west and north slopes. Most hunters prefer to set bait at the base of the mountains, and camp a half-mile down the lake. The Skilak area is one of the best hunting areas available in southcentral Alaska for blackies.

Salmon Streams

The black bear is a true omnivore. However, they often like to have a little protein with their diet of grass, berries and roots. And as most Alaskans know, the most readily accessible supply of protein in the fall months comes from spawning salmon. But hunters expecting to find hordes of black bears on salmon streams would do well to first scout an area to see if the bears are actually feeding on a select stream. Here's why:

Most black bears are found where pink and silver salmon are, usually the first 1/4 mile of stream. Often bears are found on or near salmon streams in Prince William Sound during the second and third weeks of August. Fewer bears can be found during the first and fourth weeks, although substantial numbers of fish are usually available from late July through early September. Studies show that even after bears have moved off the salmon streams, they are usually found at the mid-to-lower elevations, where they feed heavily on concentrations of salmonberry. Also in many areas, blueberries replace salmon as the bears' other major staple. This is not unusual. In other studies done by biologists, both brown and black bears have been reported to shun a readily available salmon source for berries and other vegetative foods.

Modaferri offers a reason for this behavior:

> During late summer, bears appear to be selecting a diet relatively high in readily digestible carbohydrates (plants, berries), or secondly, fats, at the expense of a diet relatively high in protein (fish).
>
> Though such a diet may not be ideal for increasing lean body mass, it would be most favorable for storing energy as deposit fat in preparation for hibernation. Even

when bears do not feed on salmon in late summer, they showed preferences for parts of fish high in fats: the head cartilage, brains, and eggs. Bears showed considerably less interest in eating the flesh of spawning fish, which is predominantly protein and extremely low in fats.

However, in contrast, during spring and early summer, bears select foods that are relatively high in protein and relatively low in nonstructural carbohydrates and fats (herbs, grasses and sedges). A diet relatively high in nitrogen must be important for increasing lean body mass and for overall growth.

Salmon are an important protein source for fall black bear. In intertidal areas, look for bear within the first ¼-mile of stream, where salmon are thickest.

Before going afield, hunters should carefully compare the amount of food available in an area to its utilization by black bears. A brief chat with biologists or fish and game staff can provide you with this type of detailed information.

Making the Shot

After a successful stalk, the next concern is breaking down the bear as quickly as possible. Following a shoulder shot with a spine or heart-lung shot is recommended. Always, always be ready to back up the first shot with a second shot. I've seen a black bear shot square in the chest get up and take off running while the hunters were congratulating themselves on a fine "kill." They finally caught up with the bruin about a mile from where they fired the first shot. Shot through the lungs, the bear just wouldn't die. If they had followed up the first shot with an immediate second shot, the bear would have succumbed to hydrostatic shock. Shock is a major factor in causing death or incapacitating an animal until another shot is made. If at all possible, and time and conditions allow, always try to take your bear from a high vantage point. Not only will you generally have a better shot, but you'll also have a bird's eye view in case the bear decides to run off after the shot.

Once the bear is down, watch it for several minutes in your rifle scope. Should it move, fire another round into it. A bullet grazing the head or paw of a bear can knock it cold for a few seconds. After you're sure the bear is down for keeps, slowly walk up to the bear from behind, ready to place the final shot into the spine or neck if necessary.

While the black bear may not be in the same prestigious company as the brown bear or Dall sheep, it certainly ranks No. 1 in my book as a superb hunting challenge. The blackie's elusive habits and keen senses tempt more hunters to pursue this fine big game species. And the hunters who have tried it are not the least bit disappointed.

Glacial Blue Bear

The glacial blue bear is a unique species of black bear, noteworthy for its elegant hide, elusive nature and the spectacular mountain and glacial country in which it thrives.

Except for the head and lower legs and feet, the pelt exhibits a gray coloration of varied intensity. The fur close to the skin tends to be a white to very light gray, while the longer tips and guard hairs are a darker gray. The mixture of the gray and black hairs is what produces the illusion that the bear has a bluish sheen. In reality, most of the "blue" is a result of light refraction. Nevertheless, a glacial blue pelt is a trophy hide possibly more coveted than any other in North America.

Other characteristics distinguishing this species include smaller teeth than those exhibited by a black, and shorter, more curved claws. Glacial blue bears are also excellent swimmers, more at home in the water than their black bear cousins.

Since there aren't many of them, glacial bears are generally not what you'd choose for a do-it-yourself hunt. You could spend months trying to find one, let alone one worth taking. To hunt glacial bear successfully requires the services of a guide.

Mike Branham has been hunting the glacial bear country out of Yakutat for over 14 years. During his career, he has had

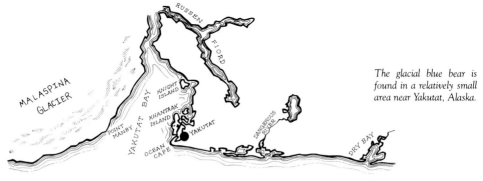

The glacial blue bear is found in a relatively small area near Yakutat, Alaska.

the opportunity to study the habits of these bears for weeks at a time.

"The habits of glacial bear are similar to the black," he says. "They will readily interbreed with the standard variety of black bear. On more than one occasion I've seen a black bear mother with twin glacial cubs. Other than the color variation, body size and mannerisms are similar. They do exhibit a marked tendency to stay closer to the edge of a snowpack than black bears."

While glacial bears can be taken during the fall months along the Yakutat area riverbeds, the best chance to harvest a good bear is in late spring when foliage is not yet a problem. Even then, locating them can oftentimes be difficult.

"More than once we've glassed bear against gray, rock cliffs or snow, only to pick out the blackish muzzle, head, and lower part of the legs. The rest of the bear blends in perfectly with its surroundings. Like any bear hunting, plenty of careful glassing is necessary," Branham advises.

The Yakutat area regularly produces glacial bears. Hunting is done by boating the coastline, hiking up valleys, setting up a stand and glassing the hillsides. Early in the season, this can mean plenty of work, especially with a late snow and early rain. You need to pack plenty of inclement weather clothing such as Gore-tex and ankle-fit hip boots. Good optics are necessary, both in rifle scope and binocs. Some hunters prefer to use a 20-power spotting scope.

Firearms are the same as for black bear. However, since brown bear are in the area, you'd be wise in carrying nothing less than a 338. Carry a choice of ammo: 200-grain or heavier boat-tail bullets for long-range shooting and heavy 250-grain slugs for brush.

Even with quality gear and plenty of luck, a glacial bear trophy can be long in coming. "Glacial bears are unpredictable," says Branham. "One client hunted with us for six straight seasons before finally bagging one. Yet, two years ago, one hunter missed shots at two different glacial bears before finally connecting on the third. It ended up being the largest unofficial record for glacial bear. It measured 6 feet, 9 inches."

Under the current record-keeping systems, all color phases of the black bear, including the glacial blue, are listed under the category of black bear. As a rule of thumb, most glacial bears run slightly smaller than a large black bear.

Most of Branham's hunters bag glacial bears in the 5 1/2-foot category. This is a respectable trophy size, considering the odds for locating, let alone reaching, another glacial blue on the same hunt are less than 10 percent. That's why most hunters who pass up a black of less-than-trophy size will harvest the first similarly sized glacial bear they see, unless it's a cub or sow with cubs.

During the past 15 years, Branham's clients have experienced a relatively high succes rate on glacial blues, averaging about 2 per year. A variety of reasons prevents a better harvest.

"Most hunters prefer to spend their time pursuing brown bear," Branham said. "Others just run out of gas halfway through the hunt. Weather plays another important part. On one hunt, a client and I located three nice glacial bears. The first one, an eagle chased away before we could get to it. The second one disappeared when a brown bear moved into the same clearing. And on the third, we just couldn't reach the bear."

Branham said that he and his guides keep tabs on the glacial bear population in their region. Their records indicate that concentrations of bears occur in select valleys. Nevertheless, biologists estimate that there are only a few hundred of these bears in existence.

A glacial blue hunt is usually undertaken in conjunction with a southeast brown bear hunt. Depending on guide and outfitter, you can expect to pay from $7,000 to $8,000 for a combination hunt. Some glacial-bear-only hunts have been going for $5,000. Of course, do-it-yourself hunts are less expensive. Depending on weather conditions, which in this area can be especially nasty and unpredictable, the best time to plan a hunt is from mid-April through May. Then, no permits are necessary to hunt glacial blues. A black bear tag and hunting license are all that's necessary.

Indeed, the glacial blue bear is a sapphire among the crown jewels of Alaska's glaciers and mountain peaks. To see one of these gems, let alone be lucky enough to collect one, should be an accomplishment of a lifetime. Let's offer the glacial blue our utmost respect and conserve its numbers so that it will be around for years to come.

Where to Hunt Black Bear

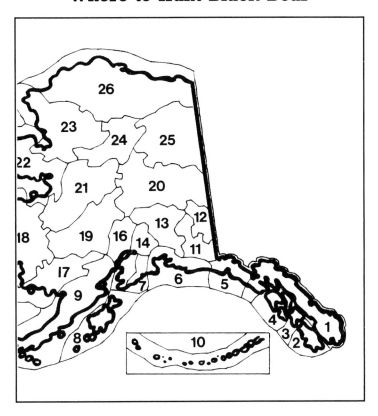

Unit 1A, 2

Black bear populations appear to be stable in these units. The mean skull size of males taken during the spring season has remained constant since 1975 (about 18 inches). The annual take is about 60 bears from 1A and 160 bears from Unit 2. Much of the hunting effort takes place on Revilla Island and the nearby mainland. In 1A, about 70 percent of the hunters use boats to reach hunting areas and 20 percent use aircraft. Thirteen percent hunt from the road system. In Unit 2, where logging roads are plentiful, nearly 60 percent use road vehicles, 17 percent airplanes and 25 percent use boats to reach hunting areas. Hunters tend to use roads more during the fall than spring seasons. Non-residents are responsible for about 25 to 35 percent of the harvest in these units, and the overall harvest for this group varies from year to year. The cinnamon color phase of black bear is found only on the mainland throughout this region. Harvests have varied from a long-term average of 82 bears to a record-high of 222 in 1986. Populations are increasing.

Units 1B, 3

Southeast Mainland from Cape Fanshaw to Lemsurier Point; Islands of Petersburg, Kake and Wrangell Area

In 1B, the average annual sport harvest is 21 bears. Approximately 50 percent are taken during the spring and the remainder taken during the fall.

It is likely that most fall bears were taken during the course of moose or goat hunting on the mainland.

The average, 10-year harvest from Unit 3 is 70 black bears. Males account for over 80 percent of the total, an indication of a healthy population. Non-resident hunters account for 30 percent of the Unit 3 black bear harvest.

The peak of the spring season in Unit 3 is in May, when about 66 percent of the spring harvest occurs. During the fall, over 70 percent are taken in September, and the remainder in October and November.

The areas with the highest kills are Kuiu, Mitkof, Kupreanof and Wrangell islands. Mitkof Island has been extensively roaded by the Forest Service for logging activities, and almost every part of the island is accessible by vehicle.

The mean skull size of all Unit 3 males is 18.2 inches; for females, 16.3 inches.

Unit 1C

Mainland Portion of Southeast Alaska Between Cape Fanshaw and Latitude of Eldred Rock

A recent black bear harvest for 1C was 95 bears, which is 48 bears above the mean annual harvest of 47.2 bears since 1974. The harvest included 10 black bears of the cinnamon color phase. Successful black bear hunters were 84 percent residents and 16 percent non-residents. Guided hunts accounted for 16 bears, all taken by non-residents.

Bears can be harvested as early as mid-April, and as late as late October. The most active harvest takes place from 15 to 25 May, when over 40 percent of the bears are usually taken.

Successful hunters spent a total of 204 days hunting black bears, averaging 2.4 days per bear. Days hunted per bear ranged from one to nine.

Distribution of the harvest in 1C show that 25 bears were taken in the Chilkat Range area (west of Lynn Canal); 28 bears in the Berners Bay to Point Bishop area; and 37 bears in the Bishop Point to Cape Fanshaw area (including 5 bears in the Gustavus area).

Modes of transportation used by successful hunters were: boat, 57 percent; aircraft, 6 percent; other, 33 percent; and unknown, 4 percent.

Unit 1D

Upper Lynn Canal

The annual harvest of black bears ranges from 23 to 60. Harvests the last few years have been as high as two to six times greater than the 1973-85 average. The fall harvest averages at least 20 bears.

Skull sizes for spring bears average 17.1 and 16.6 inches for males and females respectively; fall males average 16.5 inches while females measure 15.6 inches.

Fourteen of 45 known-color black bears harvested recently were of the cinnamon color phase. This compares to the historical, 10-year average of 30 percent cinnamon bears in the harvest.

Several hunters reported taking bears incidental to other activities, while most who hunted specifically for black bear salvaged the meat from the bears they killed.

Unit 5

Cape Fairweather to Icy Bay, Eastern Gulf Coast

This area has an annual harvest of 18 to 31 black bears. This area also has a harvest of blue or "glacier" bears. The approximate, long-term harvest has been from zero to two glacier bears per year. The black bear population is stable. Skull sizes for spring bear average 16.9 and 15.3 inches for male and female bears, respectively. The area attracts high interest from non-resident hunters, and low interest from resident hunters. About two-thirds of the harvest consists of boars. Hunters spend about 7.5 days afield in pursuit of a black bear.

Unit 6

Prince William Sound and North Gulf Coast

The 1988 black bear harvest of 292 bears set an all-time record for Unit 6. Average harvest for 1986-1988 was 266 annually, with males comprising 73 percent. Most of the harvest, 85 percent, was taken in the spring. Male skull size averaged 23.4 inches and female skull size averaged 21.2 inches.

Nonresidents took 23 percent of the annual harvest. The most productive period was May 15 to June 10 and the most productive areas were on the mainland in subunit 6D. Try out subunits 6A and 6B, which have healthy black bear populations with relatively low hunting pressure. There are no black bears on the islands of Montague and Green, and few if any on Hinchinbrook, Hawkings, Naked, Storey, Peak and Perry islands.

Units 7, 15

Kenai Peninsula

Black bears are abundant and widely distributed on the Kenai Peninsula. Research conducted in portions of subunit 15A indicate a relatively high density of 1.5 black bears per square mile of suitable habitat. (Swartz, 1981).

Hunters bag from 216 to 270 black bears each year, with much of the hunting effort taking place along the coastal area of subunit 15C, from the head of Kachemak Bay to Gore Point. The largest, accumulative harvest since 1980 has taken place on the south shore of Kachemak Bay between Halibut Cove and Jakolof Bay. There were more black bears killed in Unit 15 than in Unit 7, consistent with historical spatial distribution of harvests. The annual harvest on the peninsula has been at least 150 black bears since mandatory sealing requirements began in 1973.

The sex composition of bears killed averages 62 percent males, 33 percent females and 5 percent unclassified. Average skull size for males taken in Unit 7 is 16.7 inches; in Unit 15, 16.3 inches. For females in Unit 7, the average skull is 15.2 inches; Unit 15, 15.4 inches.

Unit 9

Alaska Peninsula

The reported harvest of black bears over the last 10 years has ranged from two to 13, all taken from the northern portion of subunit 9B.

Black bears occur in low to moderate densities in northern portions of subunits 9A and 9B. Black bears do not occur in other areas within this unit. There is a lack of data on black bears in this region.

Unit 11

Wrangell Mountains

Black bears are abundant in Unit 11, especially in riparian-forest habitats. In areas adjacent to Unit 11, minimum estimates of 5 bears per square mile were recorded by Miller (1983).

Hunters killed 10 black bears in Unit 11 during 1988. This compares with a mean annual harvest of 7.5 bears for the period 1980-87. About 40 percent of the harvest occurred during the spring while 60 percent occurred during the fall. This compares with the 12-year (1973-87) average of 23 percent for spring and 77 percent for the fall kill.

The sex composition of the harvest—90 percent males and 10 percent females—compares with the 16-year average of 69 percent males and 31 percent females. Nearly 70 percent of the successful hunters indicated they salvaged the meat, and 40 percent reported taking their bear incidental to other hunting.

Unit 12

Upper Tanana and White Rivers

Black bears exist at moderate densities throughout suitable forested habitat in Unit 12. Minimum density is one bear for every three to six square miles. Annual harvests range from 25 to 45.

Males compose about 78 percent of the known-sex harvest, with an average skull size of 16.4 inches. The average skull size of female black bears is about 15.2 inches. Interior black bears tend to be smaller than coastal bears. Popular hunting areas: along the road system near the Tanana River, along the Tok-Slana Highway, and areas south of Tok.

Unit 13

Nelchina Basin

Black bears are abundant in Unit 13, with 1 bear per 4.3 square miles along a portion of the Susitna River (Miller, 1983). Similar and even higher black bear densities might be expected in other riparian-forest habitats of Unit 13.

The 10-year take of black bears in Unit 13 ranges from 68 to 105. About 25 percent of the harvest occurs during the spring and 65 percent during the fall. This compares with the 15-year average of 32 percent for spring and 68 percent for the fall kill.

The sex composition of the harvest, 65 percent males and 35 percent females, approximates the 15-year average of 63 percent males and 37 percent females. Each year, non-resident hunters account for 19 percent of the harvest. Hunters spend about 2.4 days afield to kill a bear. To reach their hunting areas, nearly 50 percent use highway vehicles, 22 percent use aircraft, and 15 percent use boats.

Unit 14

Upper Cook Inlet

The sport harvest since 1974 has averaged 80 bears per year and has ranged from 29 to 105 bears.

About 50 percent of the total harvest is taken in the spring and 50 percent in the fall. Resident hunters are responsible for most of this harvest. The average skull size of bears taken during the spring season is 16.7 inches for males and 15.7 inches for females. During the fall season, the average skull size is 16.4 inches for males and 15.1 inches for females.

Unit 16

West Side of Cook Inlet

ADF&G observations indicate that an abundant population of black bears can be found in this unit.

Each year for the past 10 years the sport kill has averaged 140 bears, but individual annual harvests have varied from 75 to 246. Such extremes in harvest are caused by environmental conditions, good or poor berry crops, spring breakup, and other weather conditions that influence the bears' susceptibility to hunters.

The average skull size of bears killed in the spring is 17.4 inches for males and 15.9 inches for females. Of those bears taken during the fall season, the average skull size for males is 17.0 inches, and for females, 15.4 inches. These skull measurements are similar to skull size data during the past 10 years.

Unit 17

Northern Bristol Bay

Black bear harvest is extremely low in this unit. Most bears are taken on an opportunistic basis by moose, caribou and brown bear hunters. Population trend statistics are not available for this unit.

Unit 20

Central Tanana/Middle Yukon Valley

Hunters harvested 219 black bears from Unit 20 in 1987. The average annual harvest for the period 1982-86 is 130 bears. Residents take from 95 to 100 percent of the harvest. The mean skull size of 16.8 inches has changed little from the 12-year average of 17 inches. Males comprised 66 percent of the Unit 20, 1987 harvest.

The population is believed to be stable, however, overall bear numbers appear to fluctuate independent of the sport hunting take.

CHAPTER 6

Brown Bear

Ever since Neanderthals first tipped pine shafts with sharpened pieces of flint, the brown bear has represented the ultimate in hunting challenge and excitement. No more convincing proof of this exists than a successful grizzly/brown bear hunter's return from the field. It's a compelling sight. Clothes are usually soiled and torn. Hands are scratched and reddened from numerous encounters with devil's club, the scourge of the Alaska rain forest. The hunter's fiberfill vest reeks with the musky smell of bear and human perspiration. In the cook tent, the hunter's hands still tremble from the nervous tension generated by the stalk. His eyes are wide with excitement from listening to a brown bear crunch through the bones of a winter-killed moose in the pre-morning darkness. They convey the tension of easing up over the grass embankment, only to find the bear staring at him.

With quick and articulate hand gestures, and a voice an octave or two higher than normal, the hunter tells of the bear standing its ground, of the first shot, the second and third shots, and the guide's back-up shot. The story may end in the wee hours of the next morning, but the tension, the exuberance of the hunter doesn't die. It carries over into the night and the next day, and—back home—to parties, conferences and the office. The retelling of the stalk will be repeated, hands will tremble just a bit, and maybe a tiny drop of sweat form over the brow. This is what Alaska brown bear hunting is all about.

It's easy to understand why Alaska brown bears affect hunters the way they do. Maulings, sneak attacks, ambushes and almost human-like intelligence have us primed to fear, or at least greatly respect, an animal that can easily turn the tables in a hunt—

A grizzly searching for soapberries in an alpine meadow in interior Alaska. Hunters should familiarize themselves with grizzly and brown bears before planning a hunt. There are differences in size and coloration, and hunting strategies vary, depending on area.

and win! Accounts of the bear's sheer power—of absorbing six, seven, eight or more shots, when one would dispatch most any other big-game animal—kindle an obsession for hunting such a trophy, a challenge unsurpassed by any other species in the world.

And what a challenge! Fossils from Alaska show that the current species of brown bear is still very much like the giant brown bear of the Pleistocene Era. That's an animal with up to 1,300 pounds of sinew, muscle and hide covering a frame that can reach more than nine feet in height with a hind foot that can measure 18 inches long. And the challenge of the bear's physical attributes are enhanced by its unpredictable nature, making this species one of the most coveted of Alaska's big game species.

The brown/grizzly bear is distributed throughout Alaska. However, they are not found south of Frederick Sound in southeast Alaska, on the Aleutian Chain beyond Unimak Island, and on minor islands along the coast.

Hunters often become confused when deciding not only where to hunt grizzly and brown bears, but also understanding the differences between the two. This confusion is not unusual.

Since the 1896 publication of C. Hart Merriam's preliminary synopsis of American bears, the scientific classification of the brown/grizzly bear has been extremely clouded. In this and subsequent other publications, Merriam described over 30 species of brown and grizzly bears, using size, pelt color and cranial features as identifying criteria. He gave little consideration to ecological factors or to the fact that even within individual family units, bears exhibit marked physical variations.

Since Merriam's original classifications, biologists and sporting groups interested in the taxonomy of these bears have engaged in much discussion and argument. Those who think Merriam had too many classifications have deleted some or relegated them to subspecies. Rausch (1963) revised the taxonomy, treating the so-called brown and grizzly bear of the North American continent and the European brown bear as a single species, *Ursus arctos*. However, sub-specific classifications in the bears' range may be justified. For example, brown bears of the Kodiak-Afognak-Shuyak Island Group are an isolated population possessing distinctive and larger cranial features and are classified as *Ursus arctos middendorffi*. (Skull size is the criteria used for entering bears in the Boone and Crockett and Safari Club record books). Many hunters, guides and biologists include the brown bears of the Alaska Penin-

sula and southeast Alaska in the *middendorffi* group, while others claim these bears belong in a separate subspecies due to a slight variation in the bears' cranial shape and body size. Whatever. The point these groups *are* in agreement on is that the grizzly or silver-tipped bear of the interior regions, *Ursus arctos horribilus*, earns a separate subspecies category all its own.

There's a reason for the distinction between brown and grizzly. Technically, *brown bear* refers to those bears found throughout the state's coastal regions, while *grizzly* refers to inland or interior populations. Boone and Crockett and Safari Club International have different criteria for distinguishing between brown and grizzly regions. Safari Club International considers brown bears those animals taken in Units 1-9 and 14-18. Boone and Crockett defines as brown bear those that range the coastal areas from the southeast Alaska-Canada border to the Wrangells north to the Mentasta Range. Boone and Crockett's brown bear area continues west and follows the divide of the Alaska Range where it picks up the 62nd parallel west to the Bering Sea. Because the two species—brown and grizzly—both inhabit much of Alaska, the Alaska Department of Fish and Game makes no distinction between them based on geographical boundaries. Instead, it just establishes where either can be found.

When they say Kodiak brown bears are big, you'd better believe it! Veteran bear guide Joe Want guided these hunters to within easy shooting range of this 10½-foot brownie. The bear had a 29 15/16-inch skull. (photo courtesy Joe Want).

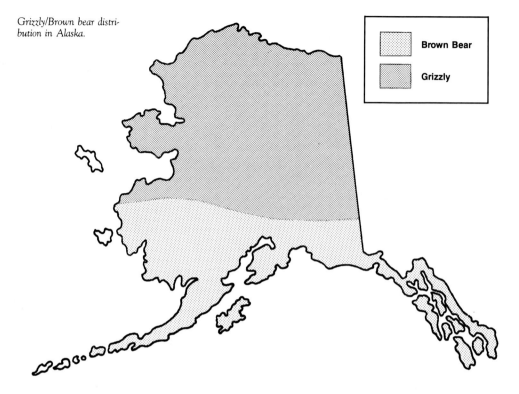

	Brown Bear
	Grizzly

Even though the two bears may be classified as the same
species, their sizes vary greatly. An interior grizzly may be as
much as 30 percent smaller than a coastal brown. Why the
difference? Nutrition and climate. Coastal browns have a richer
food supply, especially protein-rich salmon. And there's no
mistaking the coastal brown bear's love for salmon. In late July of 1961, biologist Lee Miller observed 60 browns along one
stretch of the salmon-rich McNeil River. Similar concentrations occur elsewhere throughout the state.

Coastal bears also have a foraging period several months
longer than interior bears. In contrast, interior grizzlies spend
nearly half their lives in winter dens. Coastal temperatures during the winter months can range from 0 to 20 degrees; interior
temperatures reach 50 below and colder for weeks at a time.
However, it's more than temperature that forces bears into hibernation: it's lack of food caused by the onset of cold weather.
During a mild winter, with the resulting plentiful food supply,
browns stay out as late as December or longer. But in September,
grizzlies prepare for a long winter by encasing themselves in
a layer of fat two to three inches thick.

Life History

Grizzly/brown bears breed once they reach 3½ years of age. Breeding takes place from late May through mid-July. Sows breed in alternate years unless they lose or are separated from their cubs before the next regular breeding season. After fertilization, almost no embryonic growth occurs during the first half of pregnancy and before winter denning. This is due to a delay in the implanting of the embryo in the corpus luteum, formed shortly after breeding. Implantation occurs in late October or November. Gestation lasts approximately seven months, but variations of between 194 to 278 days have been recorded.

Young are born during late January or February while the mother is in her winter den. The newborn bears are frail creatures, weighing only 8 to 10 ounces and showing only a trace of hair. Two cubs make up the normal, most common litter; however, three cubs are common and four not unusual. Females with cubs usually emerge from hibernation in late April or May, later than single boars and sows.

While the cubs accompany their mother, family ties are strong, and the sow is quite protective of her young. Occasionally a sow adopts another sow's cubs. This may explain sightings of sows with six or more cubs, or sows accompanied by both. Family breakup occurs in the fall when the cubs are 17 to 19 months old. Then, the young are as big as their mother. A still valid, turn-of-the-century study reported on the rate of bear growth over a 10-year period:

May	1901	18 pounds
January	1902	180 pounds
January	1903	450 pounds
January	1904	625 pounds
January	1905	770 pounds
February	1906	890 pounds
March	1907	970 pounds
March	1908	1,050 pounds
December	1910	1,200 pounds

Because of the similarities between the species throughout this chapter, I use *brown bear* to refer to both browns and grizzlies, unless a fact pertains just to grizzlies. Only in that case do I use *grizzly*.

Food Habits

The growth rate of a brown bear shows that they don't scrimp when it comes to feeding. Yet, when brown bears first emerge from their dens in the spring, little food is available to them. These bears are largely omnivorous, so it's not uncommon to see many freshly dug holes in the area. Known as craters, these holes are where bears have been digging for roots, particularly *Hedysarum* and peavine. As spring progresses, Kodiak browns prefer shoots of bluejoint grass, a very much sought-after food item found in and around alder thickets. Bluegrass grows on lakeshores, on well-drained slopes of 30 to 35 degrees, and to elevations of 1500 feet and over. Elderberry and salmonberry are also important bear foods; so are horsetail, cow parsnip and seacoast angelica.

Brown bears are not a significant predator of big game, except in spring when the young of moose, caribou, and other animals are most vulnerable. Bears consume little other animal matter throughout the year, except in river bottomlands and coastal areas where, in season, salmon comprise a major segment of their diet. Bears are also fond of winter-kills and feed on whatever carrion they can find. Insect larvae and rodents are their other animal foods. In rocky areas, bears will often dig out ground squirrels. Researchers have recorded some instances of cannibalism, especially boars eating young cubs.

As with other species of Alaska big game, food availability regulates bear densities. Kodiak is a good example. If food is concentrated but plentiful there, bears will often remain within a mile of the source. In the spring, hunters should search out wet, low-lying areas with plenty of forbs and sedges for the bears' spring diet. In the fall, berry patches and salmon streams attract bears.

Each of the three basic brown bear hunting areas in Alaska requires different hunting techniques. The three areas are: Alaska Peninsula/Kodiak, Southeast, and Interior. Let's briefly review each area, and what you can expect in terms of bear populations and hunting terrain.

Alaska Peninsula/Kodiak Island

The Alaska Peninsula and Kodiak Island are two of the roughest areas in the state to hunt. Both areas have maritime environments that are rainy and windy, with lots of fog and rough seas. Their alder-jungles extend from sea level to about 1,500 feet. The western and southern end of Kodiak consists of low mountains and alder jungle, while the northern and eastern end has alder jungles and dense stands of spruce forest. Much of the Alaska Peninsula has the same type of treeless terrain.

Yet, the Alaska Peninsula and Kodiak are the No. 1 producers of big brown bear in the state. Guide Larry Rivers hunts the Alaska Peninsula. It is some of the finest, yet harshest bear country in Alaska. For many years, Rivers has taken bears between eight and 11 feet, and seldom has a season gone by without a client taking at least one bear over 10 feet. However, most bears taken by his hunters are somewhere in the nine-foot category.

Scoping for Alaska Peninsula brown bear. The peninsula has some of the state's worst weather. Bluebird days such as this are rare.

According to Rivers, "We generally experience our worst weather on the Alaska Peninsula during the fall bear season, with wind being a constant factor. However, we usually see more bear than in the spring. In the fall, we hunt by glassing the mountainsides and valleys for feeding bear. The spring season traditionally produces the largest bears and offers somewhat better weather. Unusual weather can bring the bears out early, or cause them to stay in late, so again, weather is a major factor. Hunting is done by sitting in the valleys and glassing the mountainsides in search of fresh bear tracks or dens in the snow."

The peninsula bear season is currently a staggered one. The fall hunt takes place in October of the odd years, and spring hunts take place in May of even years.

For many hunters, there's no place other than Kodiak for big bears. And big they are. Last year, guide Jim Bailey guided four hunters for Kodiak browns. He had a 100 percent success ratio, with 10'3", 9'6", 9' and 8'9" bears. His clients took the bears in one, three, six and eight days, respectively. Harvests such as these are the result of a large and healthy Kodiak brown bear population. Yet, Kodiak biologist Roger Smith said that attaining population figures for Kodiak brown bear is difficult. Back in the 1960s, a couple of Fish and Wildlife Service biologists studying brown bear populations in the Karluk River

Late spring breakup can mean more work for the hunter, but a better chance for an unrubbed bear hide. This 9½-foot brown was taken in late April on Kodiak Island.

area estimated a total brown bear population at 2,000 to 3,000 animals. "It's a rough and crude figure," Smith said, "but we haven't come up with anything better to date. However, general indications from field sightings by old timers and sporthunting harvest data show that the Kodiak bear population is stable, if not increasing. Probably this is due to a decade of relatively mild weather."

Because of climate and shorter denning times, mortality rates for Kodiak browns are much lower than for the grizzlies of interior Alaska. Another factor is the number of permits issued for Kodiak bear hunting. The annual harvest fluctuates from a low of 103 bears to over 187. The harvest consists of all age types: young bears as well as old boars. This indicates healthy reproduction, vital to sustaining the Kodiak bear population.

Roughly two-thirds of the Kodiak kill occurs during the spring hunt. However, in the spring, bears are dispersed over 80 percent of the island. In fact, with a set of binoculars and recent spring snow, from the Kodiak airport you can see bear tracks on nearby hillsides.

A top bear-producing area on Kodiak has these three characteristics: good denning areas, plentiful food and cover. The Karluk and O'Malley areas are fine examples of prime bear country. They offer excellent opportunities not only to locate lots of bear, but big bear.

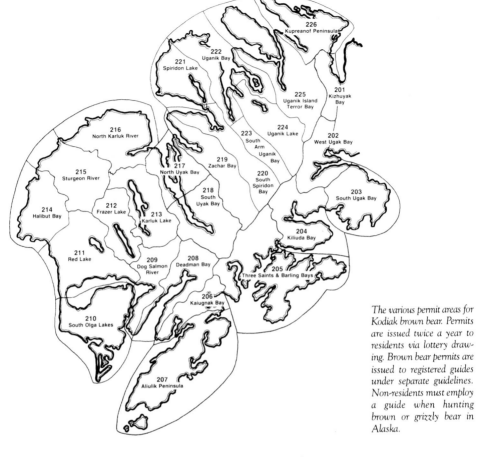

The various permit areas for Kodiak brown bear. Permits are issued twice a year to residents via lottery drawing. Brown bear permits are issued to registered guides under separate guidelines. Non-residents must employ a guide when hunting brown or grizzly bear in Alaska.

In the fall, Kodiak browns are less active. They like to stay in the brush and dig roots and eat berries. After the berries are exhausted, bears often go to rivers to feed on some of the late runs of salmon.

To draw a permit for hunting the areas with large salmon runs is often difficult. If you do get drawn, expect fine hunting. I've seen bears feed on salmon just before dark, all through the night (especially on full moon nights), and at first light. But don't concentrate all your efforts on the stream. Bears are often dispersed throughout the vicinity. Kill statistics show that in the fall, most Kodiaks are killed at the lower elevations.

Statistics also show that the earliest portion of the fall season is usually the most productive. One reason for a higher success rate is more daylight than later in the season. In early fall, it gets light around 8 a.m. and dark by 4 p.m. Also, the number of kills gradually declines as the bears enter their dens.

Kodiak Island is perhaps the top producer of big brown bear in the world. The terrain is a mixture of alders and spruce, mountains and rolling hills. In the spring, bears are spread throughout 80 percent of the island, offering a good chance for hunter success.

Before the fall freeze-up, or just after break-up in spring, hunters often charter an aircraft into select lakes in a hunting area. There they use an inflatable to cruise the lake shore and search the adjacent hillsides for large browns. Once a bear is located, they stalk on foot. Other hunters prefer hiking into smaller drainages at the higher elevations to view the slopes for a prospective trophy. They know that as a general rule, Kodiak bears prefer denning on north-facing slopes, while east-facing slopes are more often chosen by bears of the Alaska Peninsula.

A Kodiak/Alaska Peninsula bear hunt needs 15 days. Plan to spend at least five of those days held up in town or in camp due to inclement weather. Expect from one to eight days of hunting before you harvest a bear. Guided hunts in each area are running about $6,000-$8,000 for a 1x1, 10-to 15-day hunt.

Southeast Alaska

Southeast Alaska offers a world of difference in terms of terrain, bear activity and habits. Most of the islands, including the "ABC" islands (Admiralty, Baranof and Chichagof) are covered with dense stands of heavy timber. No way can a hunter hunt these hillsides by glassing, as on Kodiak and the Alaska Peninsula.

In the 1930s, Admiralty Island was recognized as a unique bear habitat. It still is. The Admiralty Island bear harvest ranks third in Alaska behind Kodiak and the Alaska Peninsula. According to brown bear researcher John Schoen, over the past 50 years, Admiralty hunters have taken about 55 bear per year. His preliminary studies indicate an island population of over 1,000 bears. However, brown bear hunting is also good outside of Yakutat and remote bays and inlets throughout southeast Alaska.

There are two ways to hunt southeast Alaska. The first technique involves trekking through impenetrable alders and rain forest to glass alpine slopes. Southeast browns den in the high mountain slopes, and hunters can often find early-season bears feeding on grasses and sedges. However, the bears don't waste much time heading for the timber. Once the bears' metabolism picks up, the only places where they find large-enough amounts of food are on the beach flats and along the shores of the myriad bays and immediate inland areas. In the fall, hunters need to hike up salmon streams in order to locate and hunt bears. Most hunters prefer spring hunting over fall.

The second technique, beachfront hunting, is useful when the bears are foraging along the coast. This foraging period usually runs from May 1 to June 1. This time and this method are the most effective if you plan on hunting southeast coastal browns. Beachfront hunting consists of slowly cruising the beaches and glassing for bear activity near the sedge flats. There, bears feed on the tender shoots a few hours in the morning, a bit throughout the day, but mostly in the evening and at night. In the spring you can expect nearly 21 hours of daylight, making for long hunting days yet allowing you to hunt the critical feeding times.

A common mistake many inexperienced hunters make when hunting coastal browns is to charter an aircraft or boat into an area and pitch a tent at the head of a likely bay. As a result, every bear in a three-square-mile radius heads for less crowded pastures. A saner plan is to be dropped off at least two to three miles away from your hunting area. An alternative is to charter a large boat and use it as a mobile base camp. Either way, you'll need an inflatable with a 10-to 25-horse motor to access the bays you intend to hunt. Many bear guides like to choose an area with two adjacent bays, so whichever way the wind blows, conditions will be right to hunt either one bay or the other.

Upon reaching the bay you are to hunt, stop the inflatable about a mile from the head of the bay. Find a place that's both

Snow can aid early-season bear hunters. Scope the mountains for tracks and visually follow them to the bear. Here, the author examines one of many Kodiak brown bear tracks he located with a spotting scope from more than a half-mile away.

comfortable and overlooks a grass flat. Stay on stand until at least 10 p.m. During the evening, bears come out to feed for a half hour to an hour before heading back into the trees. Often another bear comes out to feed after the first one has left. If you don't see any bear activity, scout potential beaches for tracks during the day when bears are in the heavy timber and you stand less chance of spooking them.

Generally speaking, guiding pressure is not as heavy in southeast Alaska as it is on Kodiak. About a half dozen guides currently work the hundreds of bays throughout the best areas. Most guides will not drop-in on hunters in or near a bay. However, expect unguided, inexperienced hunters to drop into an area you're hunting.

Whether you're hunting Kodiak/Alaska Peninsula or the southeast, it's generally your fault if you don't see bears while afield. Veteran guide Dick Gunlogson recounted a tale proving this. He saw a group of hunters get dropped off across the bay from his camp. Gunlogson saw them go out from time to time. They even went out on a spike camp hunt for several days. Towards the end of his own client's hunt, Gunlogson crossed over via inflatable to talk to the hunters. In 14 days they had only seen one bear that the nimrods jumped at close range. "The biggest mistake these hunters made was hunting brown bear like whitetailed deer," Gunlogson said. "They get in that thick brush and walk. You can accomplish much, much more by glassing and more glassing." Keep these key words in mind, especially when hunting southeast brown bear.

Interior Grizzly

Many guides feel that interior and North Slope grizzly hunting is more difficult than coastal brown bear hunting. There's fewer bear in a much larger area, and overall, the grizzly has a tougher lifestyle. This makes for an unpredictable nature. Yet hunters claim a good success ratio on Alaska grizzlies: about 35 out of every 100 hunters bag one. Some top-producing areas include the hills north and east of Kotzebue in western Alaska, the Colville and Chandalar rivers in the Brooks Range, certain portions of the the Wrangell Mountains and the upper Talkeetnas.

In most areas of Alaska, the bag limit on brown bear is one bear every four regulatory years. However, a grizzly "explosion" is happening in Unit 20E. Grizzlies in this area are preying heavily on moose calves, and the bear population needs to be controlled through hunting to allow the moose to re-establish themselves. Also, most of those areas are largely timbered, which makes for hunting the bears a bit more difficult. In fact, one guide operating out of a nearby unit lowered his prices for grizzly bear to invite hunters in and thin out the bears. Many hunters choose a grizzly hunt in conjunction with a moose or caribou hunt. A multi-species hunt generally offers a hunter a good chance of bagging a grizzly. However, I'd opt for hunting the grizzly first, as it's generally the hardest one to bag in a mixed-bag hunt.

In areas where grizzlies can be hunted during autumn salmon runs, look for them near rivers and streams. In areas where bear are hunted heavily, they feed more at night. Grizzlies especially like salmon streams close to plentiful crops of blueberries, rosehips and highbush cranberries. They'll alternately feed between the two crops—salmon and berries— which accounts for the difficulty of predicting a bear's location during the fall. An interesting note is that biologists have reported that if a berry crop is poor, some bears may even dig dens before or during the hunting season.

North Slope Grizzly

North Slope grizzlies typically move from their alpine denning areas to the flood plains in April or May. This is an excellent time to pursue grizzly in Units 22 and 23, near the village of Kotzebue. This spring hunt, usually mid-April to mid-May, requires snowshoes, snowmachines and plenty of physical effort. However, the big boars of the North Slope are almost always the first to emerge from the dens. These bears are prime

Grizzlies are about 30 percent smaller than brown bears, and lead a harder life. Many guides also consider the grizzly the more aggressive of the two species of brown bear.

trophies, with guard hair that is long and shiny, and skull measurements going 20-plus inches. On a North Slope hunt, you should be in shape and willing to cover lots of ground. Allow at least 10 days to scout for bears, since not all grizzlies you locate will be accessible, especially if you're not adept at snowshoeing and winter travel.

I'm not the first to say that grizzlies are a sneaky lot. Maybe that's why I like to hunt them so much. Too many hunters rate a successful bear hunt by the size of the hide, rather than by the personality traits and habits of the animal. When comparing the grizzly with the brown, I give the grizzly the nod in terms of sheer meanness, determination and elusive tendencies.

A prime example: Glen and Miller (1970) commented that the bears of southcentral Alaska escape or conceal themselves upon the approach of an airplane. Other biologists have noticed similar reactions in bears throughout the rest of the state, especially on the North Slope.

Because the Alaska grizzly is in such high demand, the Alaska Department of Fish and Game has implemented a permit-only system for guided and unguided hunters in most interior areas. After the drawing, the guide notifies all his successful and unsuccessful applicants. Though being drawn to hunt a particular area can take several years, getting a permit to hunt grizzlies is generally not considered a problem.

A brown bear sow is easily distinguished from a boar by her smoother, more rounded facial features. A boar has a larger, blockier head and abrupt facial lines.

In some areas, a permit is not required, only a guide if you're a non-resident. The Talkeetna Mountains in southcentral Alaska offers excellent grizzly hunting, along with portions of the Alaska Range. If you're an Alaska resident, you currently do not need a permit to hunt grizzlies in these two areas. However, you do need a grizzly/brown bear tag for hunting the bears anywhere in the state. As always, check the regulations before going afield.

Because the same techniques mentioned for Kodiak brown bear and black bear are applicable to interior grizzly bears, they're not repeated here. But you need use a bit of finesse when stalking these elusive, silver-tipped cousins of the coastal brown.

Sizing Up Your Trophy

Brown bear hunting requires plenty of intense study prior to going afield. You can do this by viewing bears in zoos, and by studying their tracks and other sign during fishing and hunting trips in Alaska's wilds. Veteran brown bear guide Joe Want strongly encourages his hunters to study bear photos prior to going afield. "They know generally what to look for once they are afield, and it's easier for them to distinguish between a trophy bear and a trophy look-alike. But once you know the criteria for judging bears, it's equally important to take time to look for the differences, and not get caught up in the ex-

The foot of this eight-foot brown bear dwarfs human hands. Tracks from big browns can measure 18 inches long.

citement of the hunt."

The first step in selecting a trophy bear is to determine its size. White claws, swayed back, pot belly and a wide rear end are some of the features that many hunters use to identify mature bears. But, while these features may indicate an old bear, they don't necessarily mean it's a large bear. Consistently identifying large bears is easy, *if* you don't confuse maturity and size.

The length of the neck and shape of the head is always a give-away. On cubs (bears less than 7 feet), the head appears merely stuck to the main body. A cub has virtually little or no neck. Cubs also have triangular-shaped heads. Look for steep, sharp angles, especially from the top of the head to the nose, and on down to the bottom rear of the skull.

Cubs will invariably carry a white "ring" or collar around their neck. This may vary in hue and intensity, and gradually disappears as the animal matures. Small bears also have ears that tend to "stick out" prominently. Cubs usually stay in groups of three or more.

As a sow matures, her head loses its triangular shape and develops a longer, smoother, more rounded face with a short muzzle. Boars develop blocky heads, with squarish facial features and larger muzzles. In both sexes the mature animal's neck is as long or longer than the head itself. Of course there are always individual variations, but these are criteria used by Alaska's top guides.

Ratio of head size to body size is what indicates bear size. Use the head (from tip of nose to just behind its ears) as a basic unit in analyzing a bear's build. The relationships between body proportions is what shows how large the bear is:

Body: 3½ to 4 head lengths . . . . a medium-sized bear.
Body: 5 head lengths . . . . a nine-foot bear.
Body: 6 head lengths . . . . a ten-foot bear.

Also look carefully at the shoulder height of the bear. If the bear's shoulder is three or more heads deep, the bear is a trophy worth taking.

Another good indicator of size for bears up to 10-feet square is track width. Joe Want, who has been hunting brown bear for nearly 30 years, considers track measurement one of the most accurate methods of determining the trophy potential of a bear. The procedure is simple:

Choose a track that is clean and undistorted, especially if the bear has been sliding in snow or mud. Take the measurement along the curve of the front pad, from hairline to hairline. Establish the width of the track and add two. The result will be the size or square of the hide (width plus length divided by two). This formula applies to bears on Kodiak Island, and is not accurate for bears over 10 feet square. For grizzlies in the Brooks Range, take the width of the track and add 1 or 1 1/2.

Don't be fooled by small bears with big feet. As a general

Chart for judging Kodiak Brown Bear

Measurements	Size of bear		
	8 feet	9 feet	10 feet
Length of nose to front of ears	15 in.	16 in.	17—18 in.
Width of front pad (Kodiak)	6 in.	7 in.	8+ inches
Height to top of front shoulder	40 in.	44 in.	48+ inches
Length from nose to tip of tail (unskinned, following general contours)	6 feet	7 feet	8+ feet

rule, young bears have tracks that are somewhat "hooked." As the bear matures, the pads square out. Mature sows have squarish front tracks while boars' tend to be oval. Also, a mature hind track is a wider "u" than the "v" shape characteristic of small bears.

I believe that hunters should harvest only mature boars except in areas over-run by females or high bear populations. Therefore, it's not only important to judge size of bear but also its sex. Here again, the track shape and dimension can help. A rectangular front pad measuring between 5.5 and 6.5 inches will probably be a mature sow. Tracks over six inches with a "hook" are probably young boars, while well-developed rectangular pads over seven inches probably belong to mature boars.

Measuring the length of the bear is another method of determining trophy size. You can do this quite easily with a spotting scope or binoculars, especially if the bear is sunning or resting. Simply estimate the distance between the tip of the nose to the tip of the tail. Add two, and you'll get the approximate square of the hide. For instance, if a bear is seven feet long, he'll square approximately nine feet. If a track of the bear is nearby, verify the bear's size by using the track measuring formula mentioned earlier. The width of a potential trophy track should be about seven inches. Using the two estimates together is an almost fool-proof way to determine the size of your bear.

Bear guides disagree about the usefulness of judging a bear's size by the way it moves. Dick Gunlogson says that large bears move more deliberately, more ponderously, while small bears tend to hop around a lot. Joe Want says he's seen large bears as frisky as cubs. Use movement only as a secondary method of judging bear size.

Other traits can indicate a bear's age. Older bears have a wider spread between their front legs: the bigger the distance, the bigger the bear. Also, darker bears tend to be older bears. Again, use these features only as secondary checks.

Many hunters use length of stride, or distance between tracks to determine a bear's size. Often, this is inaccurate. Stride varies with physical condition, personality, and actions of the bear, not to mention the terrain. The stride of a bear lumbering along a salmon stream is considerably different than a bear bee-lining it for a berry patch some five miles away. The stride only indicates a bear's attitude. No matter how long the stride or the bear's rate of moving, a hunter should never travel faster than necessary to hunt an area effectively. As Joe Want so eloquently puts it, "To do so may produce a situation where the hunter kisses the bear's butt, and the bear bites the hunter's butt!"

Hunting Techniques

One of the most reliable ways to find brown bear is to locate their dens. Most denning takes place on hillsides near alder patches or areas of thick brush. Dens look like dark holes or shadows on an otherwise lightly-colored hillside. Looking closely, you'll often see a fan of dirt below a den. If you're conscious of these indicators, you'll see dens throughout your spring and late fall hunt.

When you stalk bears near their den in the spring, realize that they may be somewhat lethargic after six months of hibernation. If so, you can easily stalk to within 50 to 75 yards of the bear. However, don't count on all bears being this way. Joe Want tells of a bear acting dopey at the entrance of its den. For almost an hour he watched the bear slowly reach out for tree limbs and paw at them in slow motion. However, when Want's client started shooting at it, the bear didn't waste any time "waking up" and getting out of there. Guide and hunter together dispatched the bear, a large nine-footer.

Another item to watch for is winter kills, especially washed-up carrion in coastal areas. Walrus, seal and whale carcasses serve as an olfactory magnet, drawing bears from miles around. The stench of some carrion might be powerful enough to cover up most human scent. Brown bears are very protective of carrion

A guide with the brown-bear-ravaged remains of a winter-killed moose. Brown bears prey heavily on moose, especially the young of the year and diseased animals.

on which they have been feeding or have fed. Find a natural blind near the carcass and plan to spend several hours watching it, especially at night and in the early-morning hours. This is especially important on the Alaska Peninsula, where bears frequently forage through the thick beds of eelgrass for dead waterfowl and washed-up marine mammals. Have a bottle of Pepto-Bismol along, just in case the stench of the carcass you find gets to be too much for your stomach.

Kodiak browns are learning that they can have a meal without the stench. Kodiak has fabulous deer hunting. With a bag limit of five deer, many hunters have been leaving part or all of their deer kill on the mountainside overnight. Returning the next day, they often find their venison gone or guarded by a large brown. It's gotten to the point that hunters report bears charging into an area after a shot has been made. Apparently, some Kodiaks have been conditioned to consider a shot as a signal that a venison supper awaits them. Keep in mind, however, that it's illegal to intentionally bait for brown bear, or to shoot deer for bait. Several fish and wildlife protection officers say that the hunter has a right to shoot a brown bear if it is stealing his deer, but I disagree. My opinion is that you should never shoot a bear because it has claimed a deer. If you pack a deer off the mountain immediately, or cache a carcass out of the bear's reach, you should have no bear problems. A bear should be shot only to defend life, and even then, only after all other means of deterring it have failed (i.e. shooting in front of it, flare guns, yelling).

Weather greatly influences brown bears, especially the larger boars. A light rain or a light wind doesn't seem to affect bears. It's a combination of the two that makes a difference. A boar may stay holed up for three or more days during a typical coastal storm. However, cubs and sows will move around, mainly due to the sows' family responsibilities and the cubs' active nature. So before heading out, consider the weather's potential to influence the day's hunt. When the wind is blowing with gale-force strength and the rain is striking the tent horizontally, hunting is usually not worth the effort. However, as soon as the weather turns nice, you'll notice plenty of activity among bears of all ages.

During the week of a full moon, bears will be more active at night and less active during the day. Then, it's very important to hunt the latter evening hours, and perhaps be prepared to stay out in spike camps to watch over prime feeding or denning areas.

According to bear guide Dennis Harms, it's not vital to get up early to hunt spring brown bear. Late afternoon, around 4 p.m., is when Kodiak browns become active. Unfortunately, if you spot a bear three miles off at 9 p.m., you're probably not going to bag him by nightfall. Note well the general location and make the stalk the next morning.

However, this doesn't mean that you should sleep in if you haven't spotted a bear the evening before. The largest number of brown bears and grizzlies I've observed were out in early morning and late evening hours: I've had fewer daytime sightings.

Don't expect to see much bear activity during mid-day. During the warmest hours, browns prefer to nap on a warm bed of dirt or roam the cool, wet gullies for food. In aerial surveys, biologists have noticed a marked difference in the activity patterns of bears from hour to hour. So constant and continual glassing is the only way to hunt both brown and grizzly bear effectively.

Rather than bust through the brush looking for bear at first light, I'll set up a spotting scope near camp at first light and glass for tracks not on the slopes the previous day. Inspect carefully every sunny area you come across. A bear often magically appears in a sun-lit area as it works its way from gully to gully. If I don't spot a bear after half an hour to 45 minutes of glassing, I walk a half mile up a valley, set up the scope, and repeat the procedure. I do this all day if necessary. To

paraphrase a popular commercial: "Let your eyes do the walking." However, if daytime temperatures get into the 70s or 80s, forget about hunting or glassing during the day. Bears seldom move about when it's this hot.

Once you locate a bear, spend some time watching it to determine what it's doing and where it's going. A fast-moving bear is a transient, one that's just passing through the area. However, watch a fast-moving bear for as long as possible. It may be heading for a nearby gully where it may slow down and begin to feed, or perhaps stop to bask in the sun. A bear moving slowly invites you to begin your stalk, as it will probably still be occupied by the time you reach it.

When stalking a bear, you must always keep wind direction in mind, especially when hunting above 1,500 feet. This is imperative. Human scent is 100 percent identification, and causes a positive reaction by spooking the bear. Winds are often unstable. The wind around your vantage point in the bottom lands may be blowing one way, while on top of the mountain it is blowing in the opposite direction. Before your stalk, glass the area around the bear thoroughly. Take notice of wind direction on bird feathers, brush, and blowing snow before initiating the stalk. If possible, take time out during the stalk to glass the bear and the immediate area to verify if the wind is still blowing in the same direction. Wind generally doesn't bother bears, unless it is very strong.

It's important to pick out landmarks while glassing from one canyon to another, or when entering a dense stand of timber on a mountainside. Establish landmarks before the stalk. Upon entering the alder or spruce jungles, it's extremely easy to get lost. If you do get lost or bewildered in the brush, do not continue to wander around. Get up on a small knoll or mountainside and regroup. Try to relocate your bear and continue the stalk.

When approaching bears above timberline, be aware of your silhouette. Bears can spot a silhouette, especially when you're highlighted against a backdrop of sky. Always keep a low profile during your stalk and utilize any rocks, trees and brush.

Stealth is another important element in a successful brown bear stalk. Bears can quickly pinpoint the exact location of a noise. Dall sheep, often touted for their excellent hearing, often disregard a noise or rifle shot, if they don't catch your scent. You might shoot three or four times before sheep start running. Brown bears are different. Fire one shot and they quickly have you pinpointed and immediately take off in the

Brown bear biologists do an admirable job of keeping close tabs on brown bear populations and harvests. Here, biologist Mark Chihuly will take blood samples from this drugged grizzly for further research and analysis. (Photo courtesy of Mark Chihuly).

opposite direction. On one stalk I took off my hipboots because the tundra was extremely dry and especially noisy. In my stocking feet, I got to within 80 yards of the bear before my watch let out a "beep." The bear was gone in a flash. And so was the watch.

Too many bear hunters place their entire confidence in the rifle they are shooting. While the caliber of a rifle is important, equally as important, if not more so, is the concept known as "field of fire." While "field of fire" applies to all big game hunting, it's a priority with bears due to their ability to absorb over a ton of energy and still keep on running.

Simply put, "field of fire" is the total area in which the bear will stay in sight and range after the first shot. "Field of fire" is also greatly affected by other variables, such as how quickly and accurately you can shoot, and how long it takes you to chamber another round. Environment is especially significant. If a bear is working a series of brush-filled gullies when you shoot, your "field of fire" is virtually nil. After being hit, the bear will disappear into the alder jungle.

However, if you're in a position to see down the gullies, or if the bear is surrounded by a couple hundred yards of tundra, your "field of fire" is greatly enhanced. Take shots only where your "field of fire" allows you enough shots to dispatch the bear.

Range and "field of fire" go hand in hand. You must select the proper range to allow for a series of shots. Most guides agree that the ideal distance to shoot a bear is from 50 to 125 yards. When you reduce the distance to less than 50 yards, as a general rule you greatly reduce your "field of fire." Beyond 125 yards, the second shot you get off at a running bear may be at 150 yards, and the third at 200 yards. These distances are much too far for successful shooting at brown bear. Any initial shot made over 125 yards greatly increases the chance of wounding or losing the bear. From personal experience, I can say that if the wind is in your favor, and you walk quietly, there is no reason why you can't sneak to within 100 yards of a bear.

However, stalking under 100 yards does have one disadvantage: detection. You are at an immediate disadvantage if the bear sees you and starts running prior to the first shot. That bear is three times as hard to put down. If you can make the first shot before the bear detects you, the bullet may be immediately effective.

Under most hunting conditions, wait for a shoulder shot, thus allowing for the greatest margin of error. Aim at the center of the shoulder. This is an area roughly 14 inches square. Even

if you're off target, the shot might still possibly do its job. If the bullet hits high on the front shoulder, it could sever the spine and arteries. A bullet striking the lower shoulder will take out the heart and major arteries. And a shot that hits the shoulder dead center usually breaks down the bone structure and enters the heart-lung area.

Generally, if a bear is hit solidly, it will go down with the first shot. Yet, hunters frequently make the mistake of not continuing to shoot while the bear is down. A brown bear is a tough animal to kill, and can quickly recover from a shot that would dipatch other big game. It's imperative that the bear not recover from the initial shock of the first bullet. Continue to shoot the bear, even though it appears to be dead or dying. Thus, you greatly minimize the possibility of the bear getting up and escaping into the brush.

Joe Want conducted an informal study of how long bears stay down between shots. He says that although everything between a 7 mm and a .500 Nitro Express (which he uses) is capable of killing bear, different calibers vary greatly in the time they take to kill a bear. Generally speaking, the smaller the caliber and foot-pounds of energy of the cartridge, the greater the number of shots required to dispatch the bear. The size of the bullet also affects the bear's "down time," the number of seconds the bear stays down after the first shot. Want reports that a bear hit with a shot from a .375 stays down longer than

Brown bear hunting does have its dangers. Here, Jim Bailey has his eyes closed, but you'd better believe they were open when this brown charged him and his client. Bailey stopped the bear with one shot from his .375. The bear fell eight feet from the hunters.

Brown Bear

one hit with a similar shot fired from a 30-06. The difference may only be a matter of seconds, but this is often the difference between another effectively placed shot or a hurried, ineffective shot.

Whatever the caliber, a follow-up shot is imperative. One well-known guide had a client stalk up to a bear and shoot it, "killing" it with one shot. After the shot, the hunter pulled out his tape and said to the guide, "Let's go measure it." By the time the guide looked up, the bear was 300 yards downhill, running at top speed. Both guide and hunter emptied their guns at it, hitting it an additional three times, but the bear never slowed down. They followed the bear for over three miles, and never did catch up to it.

Joe Want relates a story further verifying a grizzly's unbelievable stamina. He was traveling a river bottom in the Brooks Range when a sow charged him without cause. Not wanting to kill the bear, Want fired a shot directly in front of it, showering the bear with rocks and gravel. Without slowing down, the sow made a sharp right turn, and kept on running for about 100 yards. Suddenly, she lay down and started to roll her head. Want looked on in disbelief and disappointment. The bear was in its death throes. Upon closer examination, Want learned that his shot had ricocheted off the gravel and entered the sow's chest, completely destroying her heart. Joe's an understater. He said, "For a bear to run over 100 yards without a heart is somethin'."

In another instance in his guide camp, Want was carrying his .458 when he observed a small grizzly trying to kill his mules. He fired at 50 yards, hitting the bear below the throat. That's over 4,500 pounds of energy the bear absorbed. Yet, it didn't go down. The bear spun around immediately and ran for 50 yards before dropping. Upon skinning the bear out, Want found that the bullet had entered the bear's throat, destroyed the heart, continued on through the abdominal cavity, and finally buried itself in the bear's back leg. But that isn't the shocker. This bear weighed a mere 200 pounds; a mature brown can weigh up to 1,200 pounds. Ponder that, and shoot accurately and as many times as necessary to dispatch the bear. Never, ever, think you can dispatch a bear with just one shot. Trying to save shots neglects your responsibility as a hunter to dispatch an animal as quickly and humanely as possible.

When a bear doesn't drop after the first shot, but rather turns immediately and runs, you must assume your first shot hit it. You must make every effort to kill it, even if that means shooting

the animal while it is running.

Want suggests that one of the most effective ways to dispatch a bear is to shoot it in the rear. Place the crosshairs right on the tail and fire. The bullet smashes through the pelvic bone, destroys the softer viscera, and carries its shocking energy into the heart/lung area. The bear absorbs the full hydrostatic shock the bullet is capable of delivering.

Of course, this doesn't mean that your first shot should always be from the rear. Use the rear shot when the chest is obscured by brush or when the bear is escaping. Because the hunter usually doesn't salvage much, if any, brown bear meat, a shot like this is of paramount importance, especially if it prevents a wounded brown bear from escaping.

Once the bear is down, one hunter should stay back while the other carefully approaches the bear and then fires a final shot directly into the neck, just in case.

If a wounded bear runs into the brush, you have two options. You can allow the bear to stiffen up before heading in after it. If you can skirt the alder patch the bear ran into, do so. If you have to go in, do so slowly with gun ready.

The other method calls for pushing the bear immediately, forcing it to bleed. Many guides believe that bears have tremendous recuperative powers and can recover from a lung shot if allowed to rest up. Consider the merits of each method in every case, weighing density of brush, slope of terrain, shot placement, and the number of people in your hunting group.

After the Kill

Hides of brown bear taken in the fall are most likely to spoil. If you shoot a bear late in the day, and don't have time to skin it out, at least open it up to allow the carcass to cool. The heat generated from an unopened carcass is enough to cause the hair to slip overnight.

Once the hide is off, be prepared for a workout. A brown bear hide weighs up to 175 pounds. It can weigh over 200 pounds if you leave more fat on the hide than on the bear. Clean and careful skinning skills are important, and will save your back.

Speaking of saving backs, there's a practical joke that guides play on clients who shoot a large brown bear. Just before the skinning is completed, the guide will fake a back pain. He'll moan and groan to the client, saying that the only way he'll be able to pack the bear hide out is to cut it in half. The credulous and inexperienced client is usually eager to carry out the hide himself in one piece.

Once back in camp, it's important to flesh the hide carefully. Get all the fat off the hide so that the salt can penetrate thoroughly. How much salt you use isn't as important as how well you flesh the hide and rub salt into it. Twenty pounds of salt will go much farther on a properly fleshed hide than 50 pounds on an improperly fleshed hide. Once salted, the hide should be dried, but not near a fire or in the sun.

Whether you opt for the nine-foot brown bears of Kodiak Island, or the beautiful silver-tipped grizzlies of the North Slope, Alaska brown bear hunting is a sport that is unsurpassed in hunting suspense and excitement. It's an adventure of a lifetime. Experience it soon.

Where to Hunt Brown/Grizzly Bear

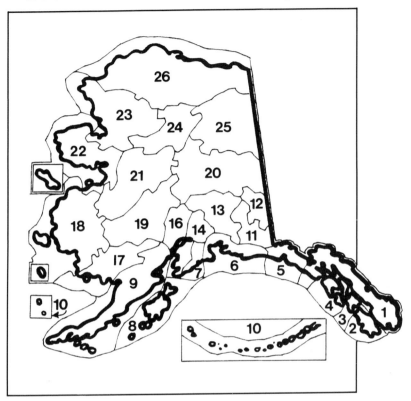

Unit 1

Southeast Mainland

Bear populations are stable. Annual harvest is 18 bears. The 23-year average for hunter harvest in this area is 15.8 bears. The average skull size is 22.6 inches. Hunting pressure is expected to increase, along with human habitation in the area. Harvest levels fluctuate periodically due to surges in resident hunter take.

Unit 4

Admiralty Island

Brown bear populations are holding their own. A recent survey indicates that Admiralty Island has a population of over 1,100. However, the last three years the harvest was 87 to 111 bears. The density of bears in the northern portion of the island is estimated to be one bear per square mile. Densities may be similar elsewhere on the island. Unit 4 is the third most important producer of brown bear in the state.

The 23-year averages for this unit are:
- Non-resident kill is 54 percent.
- Seventy percent of the harvest is taken in the spring.
- Sixty-one percent of the harvest consists of boars.
- Average skull size is 21.0 inches.

Unit 5

Cape Fairweather to Icy Bay, Eastern Gulf Coast

During the last 7 years, an average of 30 bears were taken annually by both resident and non-resident hunters. Skull sizes for bears taken average 22.3 inches and 20.3 inches, respectively, for males and females. Males comprise 62.7 percent and are 5.9 years old. Aircraft transportation accounts for over 50 percent of the access to hunting areas. Most all of the spring bears are taken in 5A. Bears with skull sizes of up to 28 inches are not uncommon in this area.

Unit 6

Prince William Sound and North Gulf Coast

The 1986-88 sport harvest of brown bears in this unit was 55 bears annually. The highest recorded harvest for Unit 6, 66 animals, was taken in 1988. During 1986-88, males made up 57 percent of the harvest. Spring hunters took 47 percent of the sport harvest; fall hunters 53 percent. Non-resident hunters took 49 percent of the harvest. Males averaged 23.4 inches in skull size; females averaged 21.2 inches. The most productive areas were Bering Glacier, Bering River, Martin River, Copper River Delta, the mainland between Valdez Arm and Cordova and Hinchinbrook Island.

Units 7, 15

Kenai Peninsula

For the past 20 years, bear harvests in this area have been steadily increasing. Since 1965, the annual sport harvest for these units has been 16 to 20 bears. The area is seeing an increase in hunting pressure, as evidenced by the 54 percent ratio of females in a recent harvest.

Unit 8

Kodiak Island

The brown bear population on Kodiak and adjacent islands appears to be relatively high; about 1 1/2 bears per square mile. All bear hunting is by permit only. Hunter success averages 35 percent for residents, and 83 percent for guided non-residents and nearly 60 percent for both groups combined. The mean age of 7.1 years for males is keeping with the 17-year average. Females average 8.4 years of age. Of all the permittees who hunt Kodiak, about 400 to 450 are Alaska residents, and 110 to 120 are non-residents.

Non-sport kill of bears by hunters is increasing and future hunting opportunities might be in danger. Biologists might be forced to take the Defense of Life and Property (DLP) kills from the total number of bears allocated to sport hunters. Many of these DLP kills take place needlessly by hunters pursuing deer during the fall months. There is a man/bear interaction over the deer carcass, and the hunter shoots the bear "in defense." Also of concern, each year hunters wound and lose several bears. The minimum caliber rifle for hunting Kodiak brownies should be a .338 or .375 Magnum.

Unit 9

Alaska Peninsula

The bear population in this unit is not only large, but stable. Hunters killed 254 brown bears in 1987; all but 12 were taken during the spring season. Boars comprised 72 percent of the harvest. The 1987 (262 animals) and 1988 harvests are at all-time peak levels. The fall 1987 take in each subunit was 9A, 25; 9B, 17; 9C, 13; 9D, 37; 9E, 171.

Questionnaires filled out by Unit 9 hunters a few years ago provided interesting information on bear hunting in this region.

Fall hunters reported seeing an average of 10 bears, and spring hunters an average of 8 bears each during their hunts. Fifty-eight percent of all respondents passed up one or more legal bears before killing a bear. Guided hunters took the first legal bear more often during the fall than during the spring, possibly because many fall hunters are also interested in pursuing other game, or fishing. For both seasons, 63 percent of the hunters overestimated the size of their bears.

Guided hunters ranked bear size first among factors affecting their decision to kill a given bear. The guide's recommendation and the bear's coat condition were secondary. Nonguided hunters clearly ranked coat condition first, and size, second, in influencing their decision to kill a bear. However, both guided and unguided hunters reported the "opportunity to take a large bear" was the primary reason for hunting on the Alaska Peninsula. Among nine factors listed as important in making a satisfying hunt, "the quality of bear taken" ranked first, while "just taking a bear" ranked seventh. Most hunters (90 percent) were satisfied with their bear. Small size was the most common reason given for a hunter's dissatisfaction; only six hunters were dissatisfied because of poor coat condition.

Both male and female mean skull sizes of bears taken by guided hunters in the spring season were significantly larger than those taken by non-guided hunters. Guided hunters in the spring were more likely to take a male than non-guided hunters.

On the spring hunt questionnaire, hunters were asked to itemize costs of their bear hunt. The average cost for non-guided hunters was $2,016; for guided hunters the figure was $10,870. Total cost for successful hunters was estimated at $1.74 million, and for all hunters, $2.0 million for the 1984 spring season.

Unit 10

Unimak Island

Brown bear hunting on Unimak Island is limited by state permits and federal wilderness regulations limiting aircraft access to beaches and existing runways. In 1988, five brown bears were killed. Permits are issued through a drawing, with seven permits allotted for spring hunts and eight for fall hunts. Normally, 30 to 40 hunters apply for each season.

Unit 11

Wrangell Mountains

In 1988, nine bears were harvested. All except one were taken by resident hunters. The 16-year, mean average of bears is 7.5. Average skull size for males is 21.6 inches and 20.2 inches for females. Grizzlies are abundant in this unit. Since 1979, however, grizzly harvests have remained low, the result of reduced hunting pressure associated with restrictive federal regulations that limit hunting activity in Wrangell-St. Elias National Park/Preserve. Recent harvest levels are about half the 16-bear average for the 18-year period prior to 1979.

Unit 13

Nelchina Basin

The 1988 harvest was 64 bears, the lowest in 10 years for Unit 13. Forty-two of the harvested bears were males, 20 were females and two were of unknown sex. The spring harvest was 18 bears and the fall harvest 46. Nonresident hunters killed 17 bears. The 16-year average age of all bears taken from this unit is 6 for males and 7 for females. The 1988 mean skull size for males was 20.7 inches, and 19.5 for females.

Unit 14

Upper Cook Inlet

The average, annual harvest of brown bears the last 15 years has been 8 bears. There is little interest in hunting subunits 14A and 14C because bear densities are relatively low. Most brown bears killed by sport hunters have been harvested incidental to moose hunts. Unit 14 has never experienced a large brown bear harvest. Subunit 14B has moderate bear densities but hunter success is limited due to poor access and dense vegetation.

Unit 16

West Side Cook Inlet

Brown bears are abundant in the Alaska Range and the southwestern portion of the unit. Historical harvests have averaged from 19 to 41 bears; in recent years harvests have averaged from 70 to 90 bears per year. Mean skull size of males is 23.6 inches, and 20 inches for females.

Unit 17

Northern Bristol Bay

During the last 12 years, the annual harvest of brown bears has ranged from 32 to 57 bears. Most bears are taken during the fall season, probably by hunters pursuing moose or caribou. Sixty-one to 72 percent of the bears taken are by non-resident hunters. Most of the hunting takes place in subunit 17B, with good numbers of bear also available in 17C. Hunting pressure throughout this unit is steadily increasing. Local residents—and incidental observations by biologists during game surveys— indicate the bear population in most areas of the unit is stable or increasing.

Unit 18

Yukon-Kuskokwim Delta

Documented (sealed) bear harvest has declined in recent years since guides have gone elsewhere in the state, and overall economic conditions have declined. Only one bear was sealed in Unit 18 in 1988. Grizzlies are most abundant in the northern and eastern portions of this unit. The record harvest of 24 bears was established in 1981. ADF&G suspects subsistence hunters are harvesting bears and not reporting kills due to bear hunting regulations and reporting requirements. The problem is confined to a few lower Kuskokwim villages.

Unit 19

Middle and Upper Kuskokwim River

Thirty-six bears were taken in Unit 19 during 1987. This harvest was near the mean annual harvest recorded for the unit for the 10-year period between 1978 and 1988. Eighty percent of the brown bears are typically taken by non-resident hunters.

Unit 20

Central Tanana-Middle Yukon Valley

About 154 to 216 grizzlies inhabit Unit 20D. The average annual harvest is 10 bears, of which 80 percent in 1987 were boars. The five-year mean is 51 percent males. Overall, biologists estimate from 740 to 1,030 bears inhabit all of Unit 20. In 20D, about 37 bears are harvested each year, and 20 in 20E. In recent years, the ratio of males in the harvest for both units has been 58 percent. Skull size for males is 21 inches, and 19.2 inches for females.

Unit 21

Middle Yukon (Tanana to Paimiut)

Hunter pressure on bears in Unit 21 continues to be low despite the recent take of bears large enough to qualify for inclusion in Boone and Crocket records. In fact, 13 of 75 bears taken the last 10 years qualified for Boone and Crockett minimum score. The 10-year annual harvest is 7 bears. An interesting note: In 1984, one bear was taken in the Kaiyuh Mountains, where it had been stealing dog food and creating a nuisance. This nuisance bear was 20.8 years old; its canines were worn down to the gumline, and it was in thin and poor condition. According to hunter reports, it had been following a larger bear, scavenging its kills.

Unit 22

Seward Peninsula

Biologists estimate anywhere from 300 to 1,100 bears inhabit the Seward Peninsula, which is near or at the record high for this area. The reported harvest has averaged 50 bears per year. Bears five years old or younger comprise up to 58 percent of the harvest; bears 6 to 10 years old, 24 percent; 11 to 15 years old, 4 percent; and bears 16 or older, 14 percent. Bears over 20 years old are taken each year. Popular hunting areas include Golsovia, Koyuk, Fish, Sinuk, Unalakleet, Ungalik and Pikmiktalik drainages.

Miners and reindeer herders were probably responsible for reducing the Seward Peninsula grizzly bear population to low numbers during the early 1900s. Following the decline of the reindeer industry in the 1920s and 1930s, grizzly bears slowly began to increase, and the population may have rebounded to pre-1900 levels by the 1960s. From 1970 to 1978, the annual harvest of grizzlies in Unit 22 was relatively low, ranging from 1 to 14 with an average of 5.6. Liberalized hunting seasons established in 1979 increased guiding activity, and the annual harvest more than tripled to at least 50 bears, of which 76 percent were taken by non-residents. Because of concern over possible overharvest in some areas, a non-resident drawing permit system was implemented.

Unit 23

Kotzebue Sound

The 1987 reported harvest was 35 bears. The August annual harvest between 1970 and 1987 is 31 bears. Boars comprised approximately 70 percent of the annual harvest since 1970 and sows accounted for 28 percent. Mean skull size of the 1987 reported harvest was 22.4 inches for males and 20.1 inches for females. Non-resident hunters took 43 percent of the reported harvest. A drawing permit is required for non-resident hunters.

The Unit 23 grizzly population appears to be stable and healthy. A 1987 survey indicates that hunters can expect at least one bear for every 55 square miles in the 2,600 square-mile Wulik and Noatak river drainages. The mean age for bears harvested in this area is about 8 years. Most of the hunting effort and harvest takes place in the Noatak River drainage. Bears in the Kobuk and other major drainages appear lightly hunted. The Wulik and Kivalina drainages also offer fair to good opportunities for hunters willing to invest the time and money to fly into this region.

Units 24, 25A,B,D, 26B, 26C

Brooks Range Drainages

Based on probable densities and food availability within various areas, the Brooks Range is presently estimated to have a minimum population of 2,200 to 2,700 grizzlies. Research shows that the Brooks Range grizzly bear density averages one bear per 100 square miles. Reduced harvest brought about by permit requirements may be allowing grizzly populations in subunit 26B to recover from previous overharvest. Population trends in Unit 24 and eastern subunit 26A are probably stabilized or increasing; numbers are also probably increasing in Unit 25, western subunit 26A and subunit 26C.

Each year since 1977, from 32 to 60 grizzlies have been taken from this region.

Unit 26A

Western Arctic Slope

The subunit grizzly population is estimated at 645 to 780 bears, which is considered to be a high for this type of environment. Since 1978, an average of 12 sport-hunted bears have been taken each year, unit-wide, although the actual figure is estimated to be at least two to three times this number due to non-compliance by area residents regarding harvest reporting procedures. Bear management efforts in this subunit are impeded by insufficient biological information.

CHAPTER 7

Mountain Goat

The mountain goat is the deity of Alaska's mountain game. From their lofty Mount Olympus wilderness, they are white-robed gods overseeing the state's coastal regions. Regal symbols, they represent the immortal qualities of nature that we as sportsmen covet: absolute wildness, being at one with the wilderness; absolute freedom of spirit not yet harnessed by the eccentricities of mankind; and of course, absolute beauty. The goat's beauty is itself the essence of dazzling glaciers, cascading waterfalls, and the perpetual fragrance of blossoming alpine flowers.

To hunt goats is to sample the wilderness fountain of youth. This fountain's gift of invigorating air and high altitude produces a euphoria unlike anything you've ever experienced. The sound of water bubbling from mountainside springs soothes ragged nerves. The taste of September-ripened blueberries sweetens the most bitter climb to the top. And of course, the spiritual renewal of setting foot on land most men have never seen, let alone hunted, is a natural rejuvenator without equal.

Yes, ol' friend, this is mountain goat country, and it's some of creation's finest sculpturing. It is not a place to desecrate with human trash and machines, nor are the goats there to pillage and waste. It is a place to appreciate with philosophical thoughts before humbly returning back to the flatlands.

Indeed, mountain goats and their kingdom are both to be enjoyed fully, yet sparingly, lest we lose them forever. And the best way to appreciate the value of the mountain goat is to understand its habits, and learn how to hunt them with the respect they deserve.

The mountain goat is a true animal of the mountains. No other big game animal is better equipped to survive Alaska's rugged alpine glacier country. (Photo by Charles Kay).

Description

Due to its shaggy appearance and stiletto-like horns, the mountain goat has often been compared to the common, barnyard variety of white goat. Nothing could be farther from the truth. Its Latin name, *Oreamnos americanus*, translates into "American mountain lamb." But the goat is neither sheep, goat, nor antelope as known in America. *Oreamnos americanus* belongs to the *Rupicaprini* tribe (Rupes=rock, capra=goat) of the family of *Bovids* (ox-like animals), whose nearest relatives are the European and Asiatic mountain-antelopes. Yet, strong disimilarities exist between the mountain goat and its foreign relatives, suggesting an American origin for this species. And according to fossil samples, the mountain goat has been here for some time.

Biologists theorize that the mountain goat was among the earliest Bovids to cross over into Alaska and Canada via the Bering Sea Land Bridge. This migration occurred sometime during the Pleistocene Epoch. Klein (1953) suggests that during the Pleistocene glaciation, the mountain goat, which had not previously spread to northern unglaciated regions, was restricted to a relatively small region, or "faunal reserve" in the Pacific Northwest. With the melting of the ice at the end of the glacial period, Klein thinks that the mountain goat was probably handicapped by being restricted in numbers, area, and adaptability. Dispersal was therefore slow, requiring build-up of population pressures in each new area before another barrier could be crossed and another new range entered. So, this slow dispersal, plus changing climactic and ecological conditions, could have delayed the establishment of goats in Alaska until modern geological times.

The first reference to the presence of the mountain goat in the Pacific Northwest was made by Cook (1784) in the account of his voyage to the Pacific Coast of North America in 1778. In May of that year, when the ship *Resolution* was anchored in Alaska's Prince William Sound, Cook wrote in his diary: *"...there is here the White Bear whose skins the natives brought several pieces and some complete skins of cubs."*

Later, the skins were assumed to be mountain goat, as polar bear are not native to the Prince William Sound area.

Until the late 1800s, the mountain goat remained an obscure animal in Alaska. As the Pacific Northwest opened up to exploration, Natives and white hunters from time to time related stories about the white beasts. The Indians of southeast Alaska's coastal regions were, of course, extremely familiar with the

mountain goat. Goat and deer were the only ruminants available to them as a source of food. The southeast Indians also favored the goat wool and hides. The meat, when not eaten immediately, was dried or broiled in large pieces and stored in the oil of the eulachon fish, commonly known as the hooligan (Oberg, 1937). Mountain goat wool was a valuable item of trade with the local mining camps. The famous Chilkat blanket, made of a combination of goat wool and fibers from the bark of western red cedar, comes from these coastal regions. Also, the Yakutat Tlingit Indians used the fatty tissue from goat as a cosmetic. The goat's waxy type of fat doesn't wash off easily with water. And a goat in good condition is layered with this fat.

Locating goats in the glacial ravaged alpine country of southeast Alaska's mainland requires physical endurance and careful planning. Here, Ned Pleus considers a possible route to another ridge that might have a few goats.

Goat hunting was considered quite dangerous among the Native peoples, and had many taboos associated with it (Birket-Smith and De Laguna, 1938). The animals were hunted before the first snows occurred in the mountains. Groups of Natives would drive the goats toward hunters lying in ambush. Dogs were also used to chase and corner a goat until it could be killed with arrows or spears.

During the Alaska Gold Rush of 1898, prospectors and miners found that the mountain goat was an invaluable source of food in many of the state's most inhospitable regions. However, the goat was not a primary goal of the major hunting expeditions that toured Alaska in the early 1900s. Then, the taking of goats

Goat country offers some of Alaska's most majestic scenery. It can also be the most dangerous, with glaciers, rock slides and inclement weather to hinder the sporthunter.

was incidental to the harvesting of other big game species such as sheep, brown bear and moose. This lack of interest is evident in the records of the annual kill of mountain goats. From 1927, when harvest records were first kept, to 1937, the total never exceeded 150 animals. As sport hunting in Alaska became increasingly more popular, emphasis shifted to the goat as a species demanding endurance, stamina and initiative to just be seen, let alone bagged as a trophy animal. Thus, the goat in Alaska acquired big game status.

The mountain goat's range in Alaska is, with few exceptions, co-existent with the coastal mountains. The animals are found from Portland Canal at the southernmost tip of southeastern Alaska, north along the entire mainland coast and St. Elias Mountains. They do not occur naturally on any of the islands of the Alexander Archipelago, but they were introduced on Baranof Island in 1923 and a sizable herd has been established there. In southcentral Alaska, the goat's range extends through Waxell Ridge (an extension of the Wrangell-St. Elias Mountains) and the Chugach and Kenai mountains. Northern extensions of the range penetrate the southern drainages of the Talkeetna Mountains nearly to Denali National Park and the Wrangell Mountains. A healthy, huntable population has also taken hold on Kodiak Island. There are currently about 11,000 goats within the state of Alaska.

Life History

Mountain goats mate in November and December, and billies may wander considerable distances in search of receptive females. They are loosely polygamous, yet some battling occurs. Bagged goats often show healed wounds and puncture scars, particularly on the rear quarters.

After a gestation period of 180 days, a single kid is born in late May or early June. Twins are not uncommon. Kids are precocious and can keep up with adults when only hours old and hardly larger than snowshoe hares. Nannies seek solitude prior to giving birth, but shortly thereafter join other nannies with newborn kids, forming nursery flocks. Kids usually remain with their mothers until the next breeding season.

There is a wide variation in goat weight, from birth on. The average weight for a billy is 175 pounds, although a mature adult may weigh up to 300 pounds in areas with good feed. Nannies are smaller, weighing about 135 pounds.

Hunters are often under the misconception that goats are as gregarious as Dall sheep. This is incorrect. While goats do gather in bands of 15 or more, they tend to remain in small groups of six or less animals until rutting season. Then, goats will group together until after the rut. Post-rut dispersal is slow. It's not unusual for several bands to remain together throughout the winter. If a careful hunter can find these herds during the rut, he stands an excellent chance of taking a prime billy.

A prime billy or nanny may live 14 to 15 years. A goat this old is a rarity. Life in the high mountains is dangerous, and many goats show healed wounds and missing teeth, indicating a high incidence of accidents, presumably from falls. An old goat exemplifies savvy and survival.

As for personality, the mountain goat is a timid animal that prefers to walk away from trouble rather than encounter it. But when forced to fight, he's an opponent with Spartan-like courage and battle savvy.

The late Russel Annabel once wrote of a freshly killed goat he found while traveling Alaska's high country back in the 1950s. Upon closer examination, he discovered that the goat had suffered from a broken back. To make matters even more puzzling, grizzly tracks were everywhere, yet, not a bite was taken out of the goat. Wondering why the grizzly didn't bury the goat for eating at a later time, Annabel followed the tracks of the bear. He found a grizzly nearby, dead, with multiple stab wounds from the goat's stiletto-like horns in its chest and stomach. It had been a battle to the death.

Guignet (1951) reported a wolverine's attack on a mountain goat in British Columbia. The wolverine, in an initial rush, seized the hind leg of a large nanny. When the goat stopped, the attacker immediately released the leg and tried for the throat. The nanny successfully evaded the rush, tossing the attacker 15 or 20 feet with her horns. The wolverine continued to haze the goat for 20 minutes before leaving the scene.

Alaska goats are primarily grazers. Their preference for plants, grasses, and sedges often varies with region and from population to population. For example, on Kodiak, rough fescue is a popular food item, along with fern rhizomes and bluejoint reedgrass. In southeast Alaska, Bering Sea sedge and arctic wormwood are popular food items, as are, to a lesser extent, common bearberry, arctic willow, alpine holy-grass, bog blue-grass, crowberry, and three-toothed saxifrage.

When snows drive goats down to low elevations, hunters need to look for different forage. In the lower areas, goats prefer grass and sedges if at all available. If not, highbush cranberry, red-berried alder, serviceberry, willow and grasses, along with conifers, will suffice. Goats will also seek out and feed on mountain ash, red currant, great western dock, black cottonwood and common bearberry.

The white pelage of the goat is one of its most interesting features. It consists of an underwool of fine fleece interwoven with white, coarse, guard hairs. After the animals reach one year of age, they shed each spring. The new coat remains relatively short until fall, when an acceleration in hair growth quickly lengthens the pelage. The thick, winter coat often makes the animal appear more blocky and massive than it actually is, a trait that causes many hunters to misplace their shots. Seton (1929) reports brown hairs along the center of the back of many mountain goat pelts. However, this is uncommon in the Alaska goats I have taken.

Judging Goat Size

Horn growth begins during the first summer following birth and continues uninterrupted until the goat is approximately 1½ years old. By then the horns are about five to six inches long. The rate of horn growth decreases after this time. However, growth rings continue to form on the horn at the rate of one per year. This occurs during the rut, when glands behind the horns give off such a large quantity of oil that the horns are softened. Permanent ridges are left after the horns again harden.

Length of horns is related directly to age. Very old goats may grow horns 11-to 12-inches long. In a study of southeast Alaska goats, one billy that had horns 9.75-inches long was 7.5 years old, while two nannies from the same group aged at 7.5 years had 8.75-inch horns.

Goat country is often desolate country. The only way to reach much of it is via Super Cub aircraft. (Photo by Adela Ward Batin)

It's often difficult for hunters to distinguish between billies and nannies. Again, horns can be an aid. Early fall is often the best time to do this. Then, the bases of horns of nannies—still accompanied by kids—are not obscured by hair or wool. A nanny's horns are slender with a gradual taper before they curve sharply back at the tip. A billy's horns have a wider base, more rapid taper, and more abrupt curve in the central area of the horn.

It's nearly impossible for the untrained hunter to judge size of horns. You need to compare horn size with a constant. Here's an aid I use. From the inside corner of its eye to the tip of its nose, an average billy will measure eight inches. It's easy to mentally transpose the horn length over the nose. Easier still, a goat's ears are about four inches long. Any horns twice the length of their ears are good. However, horns nine-to

10-inches long stand a good chance of making the record book, especially if they have heavy bases.

Also, if the hunter has patience, the manner of urination is often the only practical way to determine sex at a distance. Nannies squat to urinate while billies lower their back slightly. Also, the pelt of mature billies often has a yellowish cast, but this is not a steadfast rule. I've seen nannies that are just as yellow as billies, especially in southeast Alaska where the rainforest vegetation tends to stain the pelts.

Mature billies, both young and old, are usually solitary wanderers. They are often found in areas with no past history of goats. This is not unusual. Goats are not averse to swimming in the summer, and lakes and rivers are easily crossed when iced over in winter. Other geographical barriers, such as glaciers and narrow, fjord-like canyons, don't hinder movements in the least. Probably the only topographical barriers that obstruct goat movement in Alaska are extensive ice fields, broad timbered valleys and bodies of water several miles wide. In simple terms: expect to find big billies most anywhere.

Hunting Techniques for Early-Season Goat

The mountain goat season opens in early August and, depending on area and unit, can close as early as October (or remain open as late as December in Unit 1B). All hunts—except permit drawing hunts—are currently by registration permit, which requires the hunter to sign in at an area fish and game office prior to going afield. After the hunt, the hunter must return the permit within 10 days of leaving the field.

Base your decision to hunt goats on the area and time of year. Veteran goat hunters know there are advantages and disadvantages to early and late-season goat hunts.

The early-season hunter is more apt to enjoy himself and the hunt. Weather is milder with less precipitation, so there is a slim chance of snow. The animals are also easier to spot against the gray rock and green grass of the mountainside. Autumn goat hunts allow you to charter a plane into high alpine lakes, avoiding a grueling hike through the rain forest at lower elevations. A major disadvantage of an early-season goat hunt is that insects are still a hassle, especially in and around timberline. Also, in August and September, goats don't have their long, luxurious winter coat of hair, a must-have item for a truly impressive mount.

In areas with few or no alpine lakes, goats are usually reached by charter boat. There are charter operators out of most of

Hiking up through the timber is perhaps the most difficult way to reach goats. If a climb is necessary, carefully mark the goats' position on a topo map before starting up.

Alaska's major seaports. Boats spend a day or two getting to prime goat range. Once there, hunters glass for goats from the boat. However, when looking for goats, remember that their seasonal migrations are usually movements varying in altitude rather than range. The chief cause of seasonal migration is the availability of adequate food and shelter. During the summer and late fall, prime goat habitat is high on the mountainside.

Once you locate goats from the boat, don't get excited. Take time in formulating the logistics of your stalk. Mark your planned route on your topographic map. Once you're sure of your route, start up with enough provisions and equipment for a three-day stay. Why? Three words sum it up: Alaska rain forest.

That carpet of spruce stretching up to timberline may not look like much from the boat, but once you're in it, it's a nightmare surpassed only by the alder rain-forest on Kodiak Island. I've run into deadfalls so dense that it took about an hour to travel a mere hundred yards. Patches of Devil's Club and branches reach out and grab your pack with every step.

forward. Towards the middle and top, you'll find yourself face-to-face with sheer rock cliffs that you couldn't see from the boat. These require careful climbing or often, a major detour halfway around the mountainside.

When climbing up, keep in mind the general lay of the land. Mentally note any potential access routes, preferably one branching off to each side of your route of climb. Thus if a gorge or ravine blocks access one way—often the case—you have an alternate route. Nothing is worse than busting through alders and spruce for hours, only to break out above timberline on a rocky outcropping with no idea of how to reach the goats. Use major landmarks to help keep your bearings during the climb: a snowpatch or boulder is a good choice. And always give yourself twice as much time to reach timberline than what you figure it'll take. Alpine country looks much easier from sea level than on the edge of timberline. Distances of a few feet have a habit of increasing in football-field size increments.

In many areas, especially if you have a good billy scouted out three miles back, brush-busting is the only way to get in. I personally prefer this type of hunting. To me, the thrill and excitement of mountain goat hunting wouldn't be what it is without the physical exertion associated with the sport. However, there are populations of goats that are 10 to 15 miles back in from the coast. Here, a walk-in is foolish. Rather, if there is an alpine lake in the general vicinity of the goat, you might consider a fly-in hunt to that lake.

Most lakes in southeast Alaska's alpine country are only several hundred yards below timberline. That's what makes a fly-in hunt so attractive. Many times, you can see goats right from the lake and get within range by hiking an hour or less. You can pitch base camp on the lake, and a spike camp somewhere above timberline, all with a minimal amount of effort.

The mainland of southeast Alaska, especially around Juneau, Ketchikan, and Haines, is covered with small lakes. There, it's just a matter of finding one with a goat population nearby. Most charter pilots I've flown with know where to find the goat concentrations.

The average cost for a fly-in hunt depends on the aircraft used. With the high mountain lakes, it's usually a Super Cub or Beaver. A Beaver costs more, but can haul more gear and hunters. A Super Cub can usually haul about one hunter and gear. Prices vary with aircraft, and range from $100 an hour to $240 per hour.

Hunting Techniques for Late-Season Goats

Once the snows and wind of October and November grasp the state in their icy grip, inclement weather is commonplace for days, if not weeks at a time. Under these conditions, few bush pilots will drop-off hunters in the high alpine lakes. So, chartering a boat to hunt late-season goats is perhaps the best, and oftentimes only, way to access these animals during the winter months. Many of these boats—measuring 40 foot and larger—can travel in almost any type of weather and seas, and offer complete accommodations, including hot showers.

Once at the hunting site, you'll find that in winter, goats usually aren't as high as in the fall months. Often, winter makes their movements erratic. Storms and gale-force winds can force the goats to seek shelter in subalpine locations. If skies clear and the weather turns sunny, the goats return to the slopes that have been blown free of snow. Of course, when the forage on these wind-blown slopes has been consumed, or after more snow, a goat will return to lower elevations to eat.

Hjelgard's study of a Kodiak goat population gives a classic example of the importance of snowfall on goat movements. He writes:

> Throughout virtually the whole winter of 1968-1969, there was a permanent snow cover from sea level to the mountaintops. In March, the snow depth below the alderline averaged two to three feet. At this time, the goats were found almost entirely above timberline, at altitudes varying from 1,000 to 2,500 feet. They were

Cruising the inlets and bays of coastal Alaska's goat country is an excellent way to locate late-season goats. Plan your hunt before deep snows force goats into spruce timber. In winters with heavy snowfall, goats can often be found right on the beach.

feeding on wind-blown slopes and ridges and on south-facing rock outcrops (i.e. the alpine habitat).

During the winter of 1969-70, conditions were entirely different. At lower altitudes, most of the precipitation fell as rain or sleet. Throughout most of the winter, there was no permanent snow cover below 300 to 800 feet on Kodiak, depending on the exposure. Also, for several hundred feet above this altitude the ground was partly free of snow.

During February and March of 1970, more than 90 percent of the goat population occurred on subalpine habitat, feeding on alder-covered slopes generally adjacent to ravines coming down from the high country.

Search for goats in the "snow shadow" of coastal mountain ranges. There, plants stay green until late fall, and often the animals take on a "dirty coloration." Look for goats that are dark yellow, or even brown.

I remember hunting goats several years ago in one particular basin near Icy Bay. The peaks were covered with snow, and occasional outcroppings of boulders resembled medieval gargoyles guarding this alpine sanctuary. Once I reached timberline, I followed a set of tracks to a small glacial amphitheatre where there was no snow whatsoever. Underground springs bubbled to the surface in many places. Plant life flourished. It was a green rose on an altar of white. For an hour I glassed for the white goats, knowing they had to be using this area. Then, through my binoculars, I saw a movement. Then another: a whole herd of goats. They were smack in the middle of the amphitheatre. I hadn't spotted them before because their coats were not white, but a dirty brownish-yellow. Once I started looking for brownish-yellow goats instead of snow-white ones, I began to see them everywhere. Several hours later, I bagged a nice billy out of that group. Further research by ADF&G biologists has indicated "dirty goats" in similar areas throughout the state.

Even in late winter, sunny days will often find goats on the highest, snow-free slopes, a fact many hunters would do well to keep in mind. However, in years of extremely heavy snow, goats can be found right on the beach.

A proper knowledge of rutting seasons is also important to the late-season mountain goat hunter. Mountain goats in Alaska go into rut later than goats elsewhere in North America. The rut lasts about a month, from late November to late December. If you're hunting during this time, don't shoot the first billy you see, especially if a group of nannies is in the area. Billy goats travel considerable distances between females. Chances are you'll have the opportunity to choose between several nice billies before the hunt is over.

191

Mountain Goat

How to Hunt Goats

Goat hunting can be wonderful, or it can be some of the most miserable hunting on earth. Alaska's coastal mainland gets severe storms and high precipitation. Preparing for any situation helps to set up a trouble-free hunt, not to mention peace of mind.

Getting in sound physical condition is important before any alpine mountain game hunt, but it's especially necessary in goat hunting. The Kenai Mountains aren't too bad with their 1,500-foot elevations. But in southeast Alaska, expect peaks 3,000 feet or higher. The terrain there is also much tougher going.

Stamina is the key word here. Any hunter can climb up to goat country if he takes his time. However, it's when you have to run 100 yards uphill to head off a goat, or crawl 50 yards over an ice-glazed rockslide, that you face the ultimate tests of stamina and endurance. Without stamina, you have no business goat hunting. You could endanger your life. A ridgeback falling away to 500-foot rock cliffs is no place to have ankles shaking from overexertion. Toughen up before the hunt, 'cause your life may depend on it.

The best way to toughen up for a goat hunt is to climb mountains. There's no substitute. Not only does climbing provide stamina, but also toughens up the muscles you'll be using. I've seen hunters who had run three miles, four times a week, collapse on a goat hunt. Trying to push yourself on a goat hunt can be dangerous business.

I remember hunting with a friend for goats near Misty Fjords National Monument. About 3 p.m., my friend, who is in his early 50s, had bagged a nice nanny near the top of a rugged mountain peak. By the time we got done boning the goat out on the steep rock face where it fell, it was 5 p.m. and getting dark. The hurried descent to an alpine meadow and base camp was treacherous. With every step, nearly impenetrable alders reached out to break legs and twist ankles. Shortly after 8 p.m. and darkness nearly upon us, we walked into the meadow. Camp was still a mile of snag-filled rain forest away. My friend couldn't go on. He dropped his pack and collapsed in the field. He was totally exhausted. To make matters worse, it started to rain. We tried to go through the rain forest, but it was suicide. He was tripping and falling, and while carrying 70 pounds of goat and other gear, I fell through a deadfall that swallowed me up to my armpits. We immediately made a makeshift camp with the survival gear I had stashed away in my pack. During the

night, my friend woke up periodically, yelling in pain from severe leg cramps. It was a long night, but we made it back to camp the next morning.

As is often the case in goat hunting, you can see a mountainside of goats at first light, only to find them gone after a five-hour hike. Goats generally move to lower slopes and meadows early in the day, where they feed and bed down around noon. They return to their grazing areas and feed until evening, when they return to the rocky spires to bed down. If conditions warrant, goats remain on rock outcroppings for days, taking periodic breaks to feed and drink in a nearby crevasse or gully. However, severe storms cause goats to move to the leeward side of the mountains, or in southeast Alaska, to the fringes of heavy timber.

Gullies are often the best way into alpine country, but don't try them in mid-winter. Then, gullies are often avalanche chutes, and a simple stone can set off a slide. Rock and mud slides are also potential hazards after heavy rainfall. They can whisk you away before you have a chance to react. I prefer to climb not in the middle of a gully, but on the outer edge. There,

Gullies like this often allow you to sneak up on unsuspecting goats. Keep a low profile, and noise to a minimum. Be wary of any crosswinds that could take your scent to the goat.

In summer and early fall, goats congregate on ridgeline snow patches. Hunters wanting a long-haired goat should plan a hunt after the middle of September. (Photo by Adela Ward Batin).

I'm protected from the full brunt of an avalanche should one occur. Gullies also make for easier walking due to less vegetation to contend with.

Once you're in an area that gives you an overview of the mountain peaks, set up your scope and glass for a goat before going any farther. What you see will determine whether you stalk from below or follow the timberline around and try to get above the goat. The advice of "always trying to get above the goat" is bunk. In many cases, a sidehill stalk utilizing boulders, brush and gullies is much easier and more effective. Veteran mountain goat guide Roger Morris likes to hunt goats with a handgun or bow. On many occasions, he's used the sidehill stalk to sneak within 8 to 10 yards of a goat. I did this successfully on one occasion. It was a stalk to remember.

I was glassing the glacial-carved basins of southeast's mainland with friend Ned Pleus, then a chief pilot for a Ketchikan air taxi service. I had just spotted a goat on a rugged cliff nearly a mile away. Since we were far above the goat and looking down on it, we tried to figure some way to get to it. But the existing rocks, ice and glacial masses made a downhill hike and subsequent uphill stalk the only possible means of getting within shooting range.

As we made our way down the valley, I was positive we were hunting land where man had yet to set foot on. Slick veins of granite glistened under veils of cascading water. Pristine meadows, so beautiful you could taste their freshness, gently embraced my feet with every step I took. After a lung-searing climb up the side of a waterfall, we were finally within 200 yards of the goat. The goat was bedded down, so I wasn't in any hurry. It took me 45 minutes to sneak within 30 yards of the goat before it spotted me. One shot was all it took. I still consider it one of the most exciting stalks I've ever made. And I've never seen a more beautiful area within the state of Alaska than that high alpine valley.

The point is, take your time when hunting goats. Roger Morris, who has helped his clients harvest over 50 goats within the past 15 years, says, "Take your time and you'll get as close as you want."

Morris also recommends that hunters keep their eyes open when in goat country. Shed hair and vegetation clinging to rocks and snags may indicate that mountain goats use the area regularly. Another sign a hunter should watch for is feces, which vary in size from flat-bottomed pellets to amorphous masses. The size, color and texture depends on the diet, time of year and condition of the animal. Also, it's easy to identify the track of a mountain goat. The hoof prints are blocky and leave a squarish imprint in the snow or mud.

To warn them of danger, goats depend on their sense of smell probably more than any other sense. Remain downwind, and it's not difficult to sneak within range of a goat, even with a minimal amount of cover. However, let the hunter be upwind, and goats disappear into the rocky crags within seconds.

Be also wary of crosswinds. In the lofty heights that goats frequent, air movements are erratic and result in a rapid dispersal of odors. And after a 3,000-foot climb, most hunters aren't smelling too sweet. However, with crosswinds, a sweaty hunter might have the advantage. In erratic wind currents, goats have difficulty in pinpointing your location. If you stay hidden, and keep noise to a bare minimum, it's possible to sneak within range and squeeze off a shot.

Noise is not a major factor when hunting goats. Of course, excessive talking, unnatural noises, metal clanging against metal, and rifle shots—especially when associated with the sight or scent of the pursuer—will spook them. On the other hand,

goats often disregard natural noises such as the sound of falling or shifting rocks, as these sounds are commonplace in the rocky crags. Ironically, this indifference often contributes to the deaths of many goats in rock or snow slides. An exception to this disregard of natural noises is in areas where goats are heavily hunted, especially in the mountains close to Juneau. Goats there are habitually spooky of any noise, and require careful stalking to get within range for a shot.

Despite the arguments you've heard, goats can see moving objects both near and far. However, they have difficulty locating stationary objects, especially if the wind currents are wrong.

When observing a hunter approach them on sloping or flat ridges, goats generally move out of the area. But they'll do this slowly. If pressed hard, the goat simply quickens its pace. If necessary it will climb a ridge or rock face, and almost always look back. Here's a chance to take a shot if the animal is within range. If the goat disappears from sight, especially near a flat ridge or meadow, he may break out into a run. There is a reason for this behavior. Predators, man included, that see a goat walk slowly over the ridge and disappear from sight, will rush to the point of disappearance, hoping to find the goat standing within striking range on the other side. After being chased for tens of thousands of years by hunters, the goats know better than to wait around. And goats can run. In one area where goats and sheep were grazing together, Klein had a chance to compare their speed. When the animals were surprised, the fleeing goats ran nearly as fast as the sheep.

In areas goat use on a regular basis, watch for established escape routes. When you spot potential routes from a distant vantage point, you should have your hunting buddy stalk to within range of the route closest to the goats, especially if you intend to sidehill stalk them. A change in wind direction unbeknownst to you on your stalk could spook the animal. If your hunting buddy is watching the escape route, he may get a shot.

However, before taking that shot, ensure that you can get to your trophy. Too many goats have been lost by hunters who shot and then discovered they needed technical climbing gear to reach the goat. Again: know every inch of ground between you and that goat before you pull the trigger.

If a goat is lying down, and you are above it, a spine shot is best. If the goat is standing broadside, it's important to take out the front shoulder. You want the goat to fall where he stands. All too often, shot goats will toss themselves off the edge of a cliff, falling for perhaps a thousand or more feet before coming to a stop. And unlike sheep, goats have a tendency to keep rolling and rolling. A goat may not be in a bad area where you shot it, but it may be impossible to reach by the time it stops rolling.

Once I passed up a shot at a huge billy that I had been hunting for three consecutive years. His "throne" was on a rock pinnacle near my base camp. For two days I fished on the lake below the pinnacle, waiting for the ol' boy to make a move so I could go after him. The distance, about 400 yards, was not the question. If I shot him atop that rock formation, I didn't know if I could get there. If he jumped off, he'd turn to pulverized hamburger when he fell, and I'd lose the horns in the dense underbrush. I assumed the fellow died of old age, as he never did come off that rock, and I haven't seen him since.

For goats, carry nothing less than a 30-caliber rifle. I like a 30-06 shooting 220-grain softpoints, as it gives me the shocking power needed to dispatch goats quickly and cleanly. I rarely shoot at goats over 200 yards. For me, the thrill in goat hunting is the stalk. There's no reason why—through patience and stalking skill—you can't get within 100 yards of most any goat. Also, the closer you get to the animal, generally the more accurate your shot will be.

Whether or not the goat goes down with the first shot, be prepared to follow up immediately with a second shot. Do not give the goat time to recover from the inital shock. The same principle discussed in the brown bear chapter applies to goats.

Be careful going down the mountain with a loaded pack of goat meat and hide. It's far easier to break a leg or twist an ankle going down through the alder jungle than it is coming up. It's also easier to slip and fall going downhill. This is why I make it a point to wear ankle-fit hip boots until I reach timberline. Once I'm in the rocks, I take off the hip boots and put on a stiff pair of Vibram-soled boots. I prefer the low cuts, yet some people prefer the ankle support of the high-cut boots.

The Alaska mountain goat is more than just another big game animal. It is the main ingredient of a wilderness hunting experience that is seldom forgotten, and always appreciated. The setting is always mountainous. Sapphire-blue lakes are the remnants of a grueling Ice Age. The alpine tranquility is often shattered by a roaring waterfall, rather than the roar of generators and ATVs. Breezes carry down the refreshing briskness of an alpine glacier to cool a sweaty brow. And nesting harlequin and old squaw, rather than trash and pollution, are the only things that break the mirror-like surface of the lakes. This essence of the land, along with the mountain goat itself, offers a truly total wilderness hunting experience.

Where to Hunt Mountain Goats

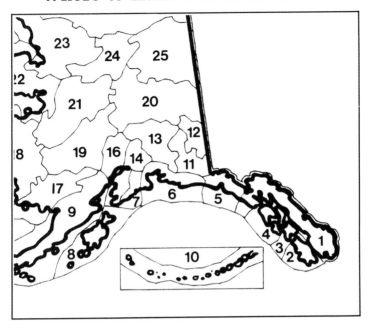

Unit 1A

Ketchikan

Goat populations are fairly stable, with a moderately high number of animals available unit-wide. Hunting is on a registration basis only. An additional goat permit is available for portions of subunit 1A and 1B to those hunters who kill a goat and return their first permit to ADF&G. Over half of the hunting effort takes place in September, with December showing the second highest effort. Weather greatly determines what month hunter effort is highest.

Airplanes are the primary means of access to the hunting area. Harvest figures indicate that 82 percent of the successful hunters and 74 percent of the unsuccessful hunters use air transportation. Boats are used by those hunters not using planes. Most of the boat use occurs in November and December. Late-season hunts from boats are not very successful.

Average harvest is as follows: Rudyerd Bay-Smeaton Bay area accounts for 35 percent of the harvest; Chickamin River-Rudyerd Bay area accounts for 24 percent. The Yes Bay-Eagle River area supplies 12 percent of the harvest, and the Boca de Quadra-Portland Canal accounts for 20 percent.

Unit 1B

Southeast Mainland from Cape Fanshaw to Lemesurier Point

Goat herds in this region are stable. Some herds are relatively untouched because of poor accessibility, while those areas easily reached are subjected to heavy hunting.

Several factors greatly influence the timing of the 1B goat harvest. After September, storm systems from the southeast and north intermittently prevent air or boat travel to goat ranges. The hunting season is purposely long to permit hunters to take advantage of brief periods of calm, clear weather dispersed throughout the five-month season. Until they freeze in late fall, alpine lakes are used as floatplane landing sites. Goats then begin to utilize the spruce-hemlock forests at lower elevations. In November and December, hunters usually travel by boat to the goat ranges.

Some of the most popular hunting areas include the Horn Cliffs area, Tyee Lake area and the Boulder Lake area.

Unit 1C

Southeast Mainland from Cape Fanshaw to the Latitude of Eldred Rock

The area has a stable population of goats, which currently remains below previous recorded levels. The Tracy Arm/Endicott area receives much of the hunting pressure. This area is under heavy pressure by Juneau residents. The area south of the Endicott River in the Chilkat Range was closed to goat hunting by the Board of Game in 1987. During the past fifteen years, November has shown the best harvest of goats.

Unit 1D

Upper Lynn Canal

Over the last decade, from 17 to 43 goats have annually been taken from this area. Over half the successful hunters use automobiles to reach the goat hunting area, while the remainder use boats. Due to logging road construction in this area, access to goats might be improved; however, too much hunting pressure will close the area for an indefinite period of time. Success rates have declined since 1982. Emergency closures have halted goat hunting in 1D on several occasions. Successful hunters take goats in September, October and November. Some of the popular hunting areas include the lower Chilkat watershed, drainages of the South Chilkat River, between Chilkoot and Taiya rivers, and the upper Chilkat.

Unit 4

Admiralty, Baranof, Chichagof and Adjacent Islands

Goat hunting on Baranof Island is hard and rugged. Most hunters pursue goats during the months of August, September and October, when the seasons allow. Nearly 60 percent use boats for access. Since 1970, harvests have ranged from 16 to a current bag of 50. Expect 30 percent success.

Unit 5

Cape Fairweather to Icy Bay, Eastern Gulf Coast

Goat populations are somewhat stable. Success per unit of effort remains high. Concentrate on only taking billies from this area. October and November are the most popular times to hunt goat. Hotspots include the Icy Bay area, Brabazon Range, Nunatak Fjord, Chaix Hills, Karr Hills, Cabin Creek, Tanis Mesa, and Emile Creek.

Unit 6

Prince William Sound, North Gulf Coast

Goat populations have experienced a net unit-wide decline in recent years while local populations have increased substantially. Areas with stable or increasing populations include Yakataga River/Glacier to Canyon Creek, between Tiger Glacier and Cape Fairfield and between Valdez Arm and Unakwik Glacier. Hunters should restrict their harvest to billies. Populations can't handle a high percentage of nannies in the harvest.

Units 7, 15

Kenai Peninsula

The current population is at a high density of 2.5 goats per square mile along the coastal areas. The early-season hunt starts in August and lasts through September. The second-season hunt starts in mid-October and lasts until late November. They are either drawing or registration permit hunts, and are extremely popular among resident hunters. Harvests average between 90 and 118 animals for both units.

Unit 8

Kodiak Island

A decrease in goat numbers has taken place in the Terror Lake area. Primary concentrations are located in the following areas: Wild Creek/Center Mountain; Crown Mountain; Hidden Basin, Terror Lake; and West Ugak Bay. The latter is extremely rugged country. In recent years, the success rate for the entire island has varied from 45 to 71 percent.

Unit 11

Wrangell Mountains

During the past three years, there has been an annual harvest of 15 to 25 goats. Hunting is by registration permit; from 30 to 50 hunters participate each year. Little change in the number of goats in this area. The population appears stable, but insufficient information exists for a complete profile. Popular hunting areas include the McCarthy area, Barnard Glacier and MacColl Ridge. Access is chiefly by aircraft and highway vehicle.

Unit 13

Talkeetna Mountains and Northwestern Chugach Mountains

The goat populations in the 14C portion of the Chugach Mountains and in the 14B portion of the Talkeetna Mountains both appear to be increasing. Hunting by drawing permit in 13D, with 26 permits issued. Annual take is about three goats per year. Little research has been done on goats in this area.

CHAPTER 8

Dall Sheep

Dall sheep, *Ovis dalli dalli*, are the aristocrats of Alaska big game hunting. With heavy, spiraling horns measuring 35 inches or more, these noble animals attract only the most avid and hardy hunters. And for good reason. Dall sheep are like noblemen ensconced in their high, mountain fortresses. Finding them is not much of a problem. However, getting to them often is. Lung-searing mountainsides, impassable glacial-carved ravines, and leg muscles that often refuse to take another step are basic obstacles the veteran sheep hunter encounters at least once, if not several times, during a hunt.

Sheep hunters overcome these obstacles because they are obsessed with not only the far-away white dots of sheep atop a greenish-gray mountain peak, but because of the challenge of the sheep's mountain aerie and the awesomeness of their many wonders. It's alpine country stretching over a barrier of jagged mountain peaks for miles. There's the alpine tundra, seemingly empty yet so full of life. Winding, glacial rivers—boiling with fury—are moats thwarting the best-laid plans. Vertigo comes easily near the top. But the sight, the view is spectacular: it's a tonic, a spur. And when the shot is over, and the sheep taken, you envy the sheep for living in a world more beautiful than any nobleman or king could ever hope to possess.

A secondary reward to Dall sheep hunting is that Dall sheep meat is some of the finest in the world. Though every scrap gets trimmed from the bone to be greatly relished, the meat is generally not the point of the pursuit. Hunters pursue Dall sheep because they are an outstanding trophy animal, often considered the ultimate North American mountain game. While sheep hunting can be as difficult as goat hunting, the

Full-curl rams are usually found in rugged alpine areas at the head of valleys, while ewes and kids are found at lower elevations in more passive terrain. (Photo by Jim McCann).

size of sheep horns are what give this animal its special quality, a prestige few big game hunters can ignore for long.

But the sheep wasn't always held in such high esteem. At the turn of the century, market hunting, and subsistence hunting by Natives, severely depleted several sheep herds in the state. By the late 1920s, populations slowly recovered as sportsmen gave their support to perpetuate Dall sheep hunting. However, a series of severe winters in the 1930s and 1940s left many of Alaska's sheep populations at low levels. They bounced back in the 1950s and 1960s, and with the exception of winter mortality in some areas, populations are currently stable throughout the state.

According to ADF&G, approximately 3,100 people hunt Dall sheep each year in Alaska, harvesting approximately 1,300 sheep in the 40-day season (10 August-20 September). About 80 percent of the hunters are residents, and 20 percent are non-residents. All hunters are required to purchase a hunting license and obtain a harvest report form. Non-residents must purchase a Dall sheep tag and also hire a guide unless hunting with a resident within a second degree of kindred.

Sheep hunters have limited hunting opportunities in Alaska. Hunting is prohibited in national parks and monuments, where about 27 percent of the approximately 70,000 sheep in the state live (Heimer, 1975). State regulations for areas outside national parks and monuments include restrictions of 1 ram per hunter, minimum horn length of rams, and area-specific restrictions regarding transportation.

Dall or dall?

There seems to be no convention regarding the misuse and abuse of the words *Dall sheep*. For instance, many outdoor writers don't bother to capitalize the letter D in Dall. This species was named after biologist W.H. Dall, whose name should always be capitalized. Biologist Lyman Nichols Jr. even goes as far to say that Dall should be in the possessive form; Dall's sheep. Technically, Lyman is correct. But like many words in the English language, the grammatically correct usage often takes second place to the usage chosen by the general public. Thus, with apologies to Mr. Nichols, I'll use the capitalized and nominative version, Dall sheep, for the purposes of this chapter.

Life History

In Alaska, Dall sheep rut starts around the last of November. By a display of horn sizes, dominant rams establish a social

hierarchy. The rams with the largest horns breed the ewes.

With the beginning of snow melt in the spring, most sheep move down from their wind-swept wintering grounds to the lower southerly slopes where green plants first emerge. At this time, they stay among alders and in or near the upper limits of timberline, much lower than at any other season.

In late May or early June, ewes seek isolation in the most rugged cliffs available to give birth to their single lambs. Escape terrain is particularly vital at this time to protect the comparatively immobile mothers and newborn young from disturbance and predator attack. After lambing, the ewes and young follow the retreating snowline upward and move onto summer ranges. Weighing about seven pounds at birth, lambs can reach 60 pounds by summer's end.

Dall sheep concentrations are largest after lambing when the sheep congregate at mineral licks. Dall sheep's dependence on mineral licks is not understood. However, biologists do know that mineral licks are an essential element in primary sheep habitat. Sheep will frequently travel several miles to use mineral licks, where they eagerly eat the mineral-rich soil. Mineral licks are of special interest to the trophy sheep hunter. Licks serve to intermingle otherwise separate populations of genetically superior sheep with average sheep, thus promoting and maintaining genetically healthy herds.

Dall sheep spend their summers grazing in alpine areas with lush grasses. Sedges and bunchgrasses (Carex and Festuca) make up the bulk of the Dall sheep's diet. Summer weather, while

Research shows that by restricting the Dall harvest to older, full-curl sheep, not only are more Dall rams available to hunters, but they are also of better quality. (Photo by Jim McCann).

not as critical to the well-being of sheep as that of winter, does need to provide an adequate growing season and enough forage to enable sheep to store sufficient body fat for winter survival. This body fat can be remarkably thick at times. Hunters are often astounded by the layers of fat on an August Dall sheep.

As a general rule, rams remain separate from ewes during much of the hunting season when rams establish their social hierarchy. The ram with the largest horns maintains order by displaying them. All other smaller rams are subordinate.

Wayne Heimer, one of Alaska's foremost authorities on Dall sheep, is pioneering research that stresses the importance of harvesting only the larger rams from a herd. When mature breeding rams (7/8 to full curl) are removed from a herd through disease, weather, or hunting, the smaller rams—which are capable of breeding at 18 months—assume the breeding responsibilities. Due to the rigors and demands required for breeding, Heimer suggests that these younger rams die off faster than normal. This increased mortality of younger rams greatly affects the overall number and quality of rams in a herd. Thus, hunters have fewer chances of taking a trophy animal, because few reach trophy size. However, by harvesting sheep eight years and older—those full-curl breeders destined to die from the effects of old age over a one-to three-year span—the smaller rams are not subjected to the rigors of rut, increasing their survival. Through a controlled harvest of these older rams, eventually, more full-curl rams will be available to hunters. Sheep taken under full-curl regs in the Alaska Range have proven this.

Geist's Dispersal Theory

The evolution of trophy Dall sheep in Alaska is the subject of many long and oftentimes heated discussions between biologists and sportsmen. According to Geist's Dispersal Theory, formerly known as his Quality Hypothesis, the ancestors of today's Dall sheep first arrived in Alaska via the Bering Land Bridge. These ancestral sheep dispersed throughout Alaska. With the arrival of the Ice Age, sheep were either stranded in refugiums in Alaska or pushed as far south as Mexico. The glaciers retreated, and the sheep stayed in isolated areas within their range. This is why sheep are found at the head of a valley surrounded by miles of glaciers or impassable terrain. According to Geist's theory, these areas have extremely fertile soil for succulent plants, and provide lots of sunlight and warmth, good for both plants and sheep.

But why do some areas of Alaska have larger-horned sheep

than others? Geist's "Dispersal Theory" again suggests an explanation. He wrote:

> "Mountain sheep evolved during post-glacial dispersal into uninhabited favorable terrain. They specialized increasingly toward delivering a more forceful clash and changed by growing relatively heavier horns, larger rump patches, acquiring more pneumation in the skull, increasing the length of the horn cores, shortening and rounding the ears, and losing the cheek and neck manes."

Elaborating upon Geist's theory, Heimer suggests that mountain sheep living in areas extensively glaciated have larger horns than those living in areas of less glaciation. Rams in glaciated areas seldom move far, a fact that assures the hunter that rams will be in the same general areas, year after year. This explains why the Wrangell and Chugach mountains, areas with high glacial activity, produce record-book sheep on a regular basis.

In Alaska, Dall sheep inhabit seven mountain ranges: Alaska Range east of Mount McKinley (ARE), Alaska Range west of Mount McKinley (ARW), Brooks Range (BRR), Chugach Mountains (CMR), Kenai Mountains (KMR), Talkeetna Mountains (TCW), Tanana Hills, White Mountains (THW), and the

John Estes Jr. with a respectable Dall ram taken from the Wrangell Mountains. Sheep hunting can be tough going, and requires the hunter to be in tip-top physical condition, with plenty of stamina.

The largest Dall sheep in the world come from the Wrangell Mountains. The area is heavily glaciated, and supports separate herds of high-quality animals. (Photo by Adela Ward Batin).

Wrangell Mountains (WMR). Each of these ranges has its own unique characteristics of terrain, weather and accessibility.

Mountains of the Brooks Range extend from the Bering Sea eastward to the Canadian Border. In Canada, the eastward extensions of these mountains are known as the British Mountains, Barn Range and Richardson Mountains. Dall sheep also inhabit the glacial refugium of the Tanana-Yukon Uplands, which may be thought of as an altitudinally lower, westward extension of Canada's Ogilvie Mountains. In central Alaska, the Alaska Range forms a band of sheep habitat running from Lake Clark northwesterly to Mount McKinley, and then generally eastward and somewhat southward toward the Canadian Border. There, it merges with the northern slopes of the St. Elias Mountains in Canada. Sheep distribution along the Alaska Range is discontinuous, interrupted near Mt. McKinley. Hence, sheep habitat is labeled as Alaska Range "east" or "west" of Mt. McKinley. Sheep distribution is also interrupted by the lowlands of the Tok River. Mountains east of the Tok River are considered the north side of the Wrangell Mountains. Just south of the central Alaska Range is an "island" of Dall sheep habitat, the Talkeetna Mountains. These mountains are not clearly identified with any major Alaska or Canadian mountain mass. The southernmost extension of Dall sheep range in Alaska is in the mountains that begin on the Kenai Peninsula and proceed northeasterly to the Turnagain Arm of Cook Inlet near Anchorage. Beyond that point, they are called the Chugach Mountains in Alaska, and they merge with the coastal portions of the St. Elias Mountains in Canada.

When deciding where to hunt, hunters wanting an average ram will do well to consider areas with large sheep populations. The higher the number of sheep, the better the success. Hunters interested in trophy animals should hunt areas with fewer, yet higher-quality rams exhibiting high growth rate of horns.

A record-book ram is an animal whose horn measurements far exceed the minimums most hunters establish for themselves. For instance, a 40-inch, full-curl-plus ram might have the length but not the bases for meeting the minimum scores of either Boone and Crockett or Safari Club. Yet, a 40-incher is a ram that most hunters would not pass up. Boone and Crocket records confirm that exceptionally large rams have been taken in the Wrangell or Chugach mountains. However, there are some flaws in using Boone and Crocket records to decide where to hunt. Record-book rams have come from most all of Alaska's sheep ranges. Even the low-quality areas turn out a record-book sheep every now and then. Also, the record books do not provide information on age of the sheep, horn increment length or other indications of growth rate. Heimer (1975) states that data reflecting average rate of horn growth provide a much better indication of an area's capability for producing "trophy" rams. This follows Geist's "Dispersal Theory."

When planning a sheep hunt, hunters also need to consider areas providing favorable winter habitat for Dall sheep. Climate appears to regulate sheep population density and thus ultimately determines sheep quality through mechanisms that are not yet understood. The importance of winter habitats in several of Alaska's sheep ranges deserves review.

The Brooks Range is not as heavily glaciated as the Wrangells, yet yields good numbers of Dall sheep. The high cost of hunting this area is a chief deterrent to the sport hunter.

(above) Most of Alaska's
Dall sheep habitat is accessible only by aircraft.

(right) Distribution of Dall
sheep in Alaska.

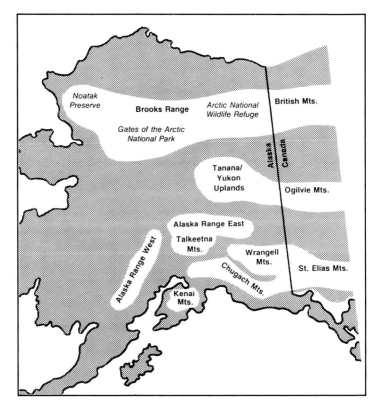

The Wrangell Mountains are the highest-quality Dall sheep habitat in Alaska. If God were to create ideal sheep country elsewhere, He'd pattern it after the Wrangells. The area is extensively glaciated, but has snow fields that are quite small in some areas. Cold temperatures, moderate snowfall and persistent winds ensure favorable winter habitat for Dall sheep. The southern exposure of slopes to the winter sun provides favorable wintering conditions.

Mountains west of the Alaska Range are susceptible to the weather patterns of Bristol Bay, and may receive more precipitation and warm winter weather than suitable for high populations of Dall sheep. Whenever environmental conditions are marginal, the animals present can be expected to be of the lowest possible quality. Year after year of heavy snows and extreme cold create stressful conditions that kill the young of the year and the older, genetically superior rams. The general trend is greater densities of sheep over a longer period of time in mountain ranges with less precipitation.

According to Heimer, the mountain range with the greatest potential for sustaining high densities of sheep is the Tanana Hills-White Mountains. This area is well-screened from all maritime influence and has the least snowfall of all Dall sheep ranges in Alaska. This area was the ancestral refugium for sheep during the Great Ice Age. While the Tanana Hills-White Mountains may have ideal climate for large numbers of sheep, habitat quality has been deteriorating with the encroachment of climax forests, making for marginal sheep habitat. Predators and mineral development are also taking their toll.

The Kenai Mountains have the second greatest predicted capability for supporting high concentrations of sheep. Although the Kenai Mountains appear to have fairly heavy snowfall, snowfall patterns reveal that sheep habitat on the Kenai Peninsula is in a snow shadow. Certain areas are especially sheltered and have the highest density of sheep of any area sampled. However, unusually severe winters have greatly curtailed the sheep population in these areas, and some biologists doubt they'll ever regain the numbers experienced earlier in the century.

The southwest portion of the Talkeetna Mountains has the greatest snowfall and the lowest sheep density, while another section located in the snow shadow of the Chugach mountains has a fairly high density of sheep. In these areas, sheep quality is least influenced by population density as are those areas sheltered from precipitation and maritime influence.

Preparing for Your Hunt

A comprehensive physical conditioning program is the first step in preparing for a Dall sheep hunt. All too often, out-of-shape hunters hack and wheeze after climbing the first 1,000 feet, or don't have the lung power to handle the 7,000-foot elevations. Not only is endurance and muscle tone needed to reach the animal, but the hunter also needs to shoot accurately without shaking from exertion.

After you've received a doctor's permission to start your exercise program, the best way to prepare for a sheep hunt is to climb mountains. However, unless you have a mountain near your home, such advice might be impractical. The next best thing is to run long flights of steps. Running steps is terribly boring, but toughens those muscles almost as well as climbing mountains. Wear a 30-to 40-pound pack when running those stairs if you really want to get in shape. Once you start toughening up, push yourself with a stopwatch. Practicing at a leisurely pace up the steps won't do you a bit of good.

It's also important to be tough mentally. There'll be times on a backpack sheep hunt, when you won't be able to take another step, except maybe to fall flat on your face. Backpack hunts are tough, and of course, my favorite. That's why I advocate pushing yourself in practice. You'll be glad you did when the sheep are moving, and you need to run 200 yards, uphill, for a shot before they disappear over the ridge. So exercise your will power as well as your body. It'll pay off in the long run.

While it's important to be in sound physical condition, it's also important to let your eyes do most of the walking, especially at the start of your hunt. Many first-time hunters don't realize that 8 to 10 hours of glassing a day is the norm when scouting sheep country. And under such rigors, bad optics—like ill-fitting boots for your eyes—can ruin an otherwise potentially perfect sheep hunt. Inferior optics can cause eye strain, fatigue, headaches, nausea, blurry vision and other complications.

Most hunters use binoculars for close-range glassing, and a spotting scope for long-distance glassing and determining the trophy potential of Dall rams. Veteran sheep hunters prefer the 8x40 or 10x40 Leitz or Zeiss binoculars costing $300 and up. However, the 10x40s get a bit wobbly when you're trying to glass after a long, arduous climb. Completely avoid the 10x28 and similar-sized, "compact" binoculars, worthless on a sheep hunt, and not meant to be used for long hours of glassing.

A 15-to 45-power or 15-to 60-power Redfield spotting scope is hard to beat. Sheep guide Ken Fanning prefers to have the

Backpack sheep hunts are physically demanding, but are very satisfying, whether or not you connect. Climbing mountains is the best way to train for such a hunt. (Photo by Adela Ward Batin)

Dave Wallace is happy with his Dall ram that he bagged after a 20-mile hike into the Talkeetna Mountains. The hike in took three days, and his party had to cross a glacial river before reaching the foothills of sheep country.

eyepiece fixed to the scope. "If it isn't sealed permanently, moisture gets into the scope when the eyepieces are screwed on and off. As a result, the scope will fog, usually when you need it most."

Some hunters think a good tripod is as important as the scope. As a general rule, any short tripod is a bad tripod. A short tripod is wobbly, often forcing you to lie on the ground or hug a boulder for a view. With a large tripod, like those used in professional photography, you can remain a good distance from the crest of the ridge, jack up the tripod to eye level, and see the sheep without giving away your position.

Also, many hunters wear glasses and take them off when glassing. Trying to find your glasses, especially wire rims, on alpine tundra is often a lesson in futility. Fanning recommends attaching a piece of fluorescent tape or cord to the glasses. You won't have a bit of problem locating them.

An ice ax is another useful item, especially when hunting the glacial sheep country of the Alaska Range, Talkeetna, Chugach or Wrangell mountains. It's extremely unlikely that you'll spook up a sheep. So, lash your rifle to your pack and carry your ice ax in your hand. The ax makes an effective anchor when climbing on ice, up shale slides or cliffs. When attached to a long pole, the ax makes a great walking stick. I won't be without one. Also, crampons are a must for glacial country. The type that straps onto a boot works well. And don't forget about 80 feet of 3/16-inch nylon rope, otherwise known as parachute cord. It has a thousand uses.

When sheep hunting, you must consider the weight of your gear. Your necessities are rifle, spotting scope, tripod, ice ax and extra clothing. There's little room for anything else, especially a full-size tent and sleeping gear. Many hunters take up a tarp and "rough it" during their alpine travels. They sleep in their clothes, and subsist on bare minimums. They generally spend three days hunting sheep in the alpine before returning to base camp for provisions. At the start of sheep season in August, this is good way to hunt, especially for those rams atop mountain peaks. The weather is often partly cloudy, with bouts of rain or sunshine. Temperatures are in the 40s to 70s. However, this practice is too risky during the latter part of sheep season, especially in the Brooks Range. September can bring snowstorms and freezing weather in the north. Then, proper shelter and sleeping gear are required.

Most hunters overdress on a Dall sheep hunt. Layer yourself in polyester and pile, and have something to break the wind during rest stops. Be sure to review the "Gearing Up" chapter in this book for layering advice and notes on other equipment.

Hunting Tactics

Finding sheep is easy: getting to them is difficult. Unlike moose or bear hunting, when the animal can stand unseen 20 yards from you in dense forest, sheep are visible high on the mountainsides from a mile or more away. Oftentimes the most difficult part is choosing the right path up the mountain.

Before the hunt, obtain a topographical map of the area. Mark down areas where several side tributaries or canyons feed into a major valley. I like to pitch my base camp in such an area for two reasons. No matter which way the wind is blowing, I can usually hunt one of the tributaries. And main valleys are close to rivers and gravel bars allowing easy pick-up and fly-out of gear and meat. Also, Dall sheep can easily be glassed from the junction of tributaries. Sometimes you see sheep right above camp, a short 5,000-foot climb straight up!

When scouting for sheep, bright sunny days are best; sunlight creates hard shadows on the snowpacks. Sunshine makes sheep tracks, possibly from the night before, easy to pick out and follow with a scope. And when you're following the tracks, remember that you're not looking for a snow-white animal. Big rams have a yellowish cast. Train your mind to pick out yellowish forms rather than white, and you'll start finding sheep where your buddies can't.

Many sheep hunters waste their time glassing for rams on the wide-open, grassy meadows or mid-elevations. Leave them be. In prime sheep country, always look for rams in the rocky saddles located higher on the mountain. There is only one exception. In areas with heavy helicopter or plane traffic, rams keep moving, oftentimes right out of their home range. Then, they can be found anywhere in the alpine.

Many hunters like to start glassing for a ram after it has bedded down for the afternoon. To me, this sounds like an excuse to sleep in. Rams are usually up and feeding by first light and continue to feed until 10 a.m. Then, they'll lie down for most of the day. I like early-morning glassing because then the big rams that usually hide during the mid-day hours are exposed. By glassing them and watching where they bed down, I can stalk them later that morning and have a sheep by late afternoon. This is why I prefer to glass from valleys. They offer a greater strategic advantage than climbing the mountains and glassing down. In some areas such as the glacial ravages of the Wrangells, it's sometimes impossible to glass from the valleys. There, you'll have to climb and glass the sidehills and peaks.

Also, when glassing from a distance, it's possible to see only the general shape of sheep. Rams and ewes are often indistinguishable. Here's a trick to distinguish ewes and small rams from large rams at a distance. Concentrate your scope on the neck. The horns on a 7/8-or-larger ram make the animal's head look separated from its body. If so, the ram deserves closer attention.

Larry Rivers is a veteran big game guide specializing in sheep. Since 1976, his clients have experienced at or near 100 percent success on Dall sheep. He has never sent a client home without at least a stalk on a full-curl ram. Most of his clients take 38-to 40-inch rams: the overall size has ranged from 35 inches to 42½ inches. There are many reasons for these impressive figures, but the most important ones are Rivers' hunting techniques and sheep-hunting savvy.

According to Rivers, many hunters underestimate the Dall sheep's sensory capabilities. He says that sheep are purported

to have eight-power eyes. "They do see you, even when you can barely see them," he said. "Their sense of smell is very good, and hearing is good. Natural sounds do not alarm them: however, unnatural sounds, such as a person coughing, gunshots and normal conversation greatly alarm them."

Rivers says most hunters make the mistake of walking up tributaries without any effort to conceal their actions. He has his hunters wear ankle-fit hip boots and he marches them through the creekbeds and gullies. From these gullies it's possible to go to all areas of the valley and glass all areas of the mountains.

Not only is Rivers keen on keeping out of sight, but he also practices keeping down on scent. He's a firm believer in the ability of sheep to smell odors from great distances. He says more hunts are foiled because hunters are careless with their "scent trails." Here's his advice:

"If you need to urinate, defecate, or dispose of biodegradable trash, you dig a hole, cover it up and put a rock on it. If not, that scent stays there for a week. Sheep can smell that hunters are in an area even before they leave their base camp. Not enough hunters consider this sense when planning their stalking activities."

Before planning your stalk, first determine the wind direction. Look up and observe the cloud flow. Is it going toward the sheep, or away from the sheep? To better understand how wind behaves in mountain country, and the problems it often

In prime sheep country, first look for rams in the rocky saddles between peaks. Here, the author is looking over some prime sheep country in the Alaska Range. (Photo by Adela Ward Batin).

Dall Sheep

The use of white overalls on
a sheep hunt is effective
when cover is limited.
However, extreme caution
and stealth is required to get
close enough for a shot.
(Photo by Evan Swensen).

creates for the sheep hunter, picture the mountain as a rock in a stream, with the wind being the water. The wind hits the rock, and breaks to either side, and continues to flow around it. If the wind is very strong, it'll go over the mountain. Also, in early morning the wind stays low, rising up the mountain as the air warms.

However, if the wind is barely moving, you may have an advantage. Here's a good way to tell. Take some cottongrass and drop it at shoulder height. See how far you can walk at a normal hunting pace before the fluff hits the ground. If the grass has kept even with you or passed you, the wind will get your scent to the sheep before you can sneak within shooting range. If you've kept ahead of the cottongrass, chances are you can keep ahead of your scent, barring crosswinds or other variables. Do this several times during the stalk to ensure the wind isn't changing.

Hunters often wear white overalls when stalking sheep. Best are the lightweight cotton type used in hospitals. Get a size or two larger than normal to fit over your hunting clothes. The old Army cotton overalls are too heavy. And nylon is equally bad, as it doesn't breathe.

The trick to using whites is to work at an angle away from the sheep, and to stay down on all fours. Sheep are not easily alarmed when they see a white object, possibly thinking that it's another sheep. Still, sheep are wary, so it's important to move slowly. Stop frequently. Pretend that you are feeding. While you don't actually have to eat the grass, some hunters go through the motion. I remember having to bite my tongue on one sheep hunt when my friend, Alan, actually went through the motions of grazing, pulling up grass in his mouth. The situation was so funny that even after Alan bagged his sheep, I laughed whenever I thought about it. I like sheep hunting, but some hunters go too far.

In considering whites, Rivers says that it is far more important not to be seen in the first place, and white is much more visible than normal hunter clothing. While Rivers carries white overalls, he doesn't recommend that his hunters use them unless in a situation where lack of cover provides no choice.

When getting anywhere near sheep, keep talking to a minimum. In wilderness areas, talking can carry for up to a mile. Rivers says that sheep can hear a normal conversation among hunters up to a half mile away. Use hand signs or whisper to communicate. If you're with friends, remind them that the time to socialize is in camp.

Judging Your Trophy

It takes years of experience to judge the size of Dall ram horns accurately. Every now and then, a ram with a weird horn configuration shows up. One guide told me of hunt where he and a client stalked to within 200 yards of a "full-curl" sheep. The guide was sure the sheep would go 40 inches, and urged his client to take it. After a successful, one-shot kill, the guide was shocked to see that the ram had a wide, sweeping curl. Total measurement? Thirty-four inches.

The first rule of sheep hunting is: If you have to ask whether a sheep is big, chances are it isn't. However, there are several things you can do to help you judge trophy Dall sheep.

Study trophy sheep by finding a mount and picking out the horn features conveying size and mass. For instance, on a good sheep, horns come out very high on the head, have heavy bases, and the length of the horn forms a complete circle. Some hunters take a photo of a Dall sheep mount and carry it with them in the field. When glassing for rams, the hunter uses the

There are several ways to judge the size of Dall sheep horns. The best is to imagine a cylinder created by the horn, and see how much of the cylinder the horn fills. To do this properly, you need to be either above or below the sheep. When viewing horns from an angle is impossible, view horns from the side. Be careful, as this angle gives the horns a deceptive appearance. Full-curl horns will create a near-perfect circle, with point touching base. Immature sheep horns appear squashed and should be passed up. A 7/8-curl ram has horns that form a near complete circle, stopping short of the eye.

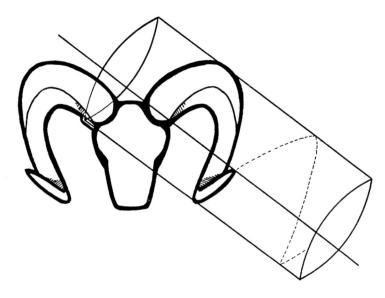

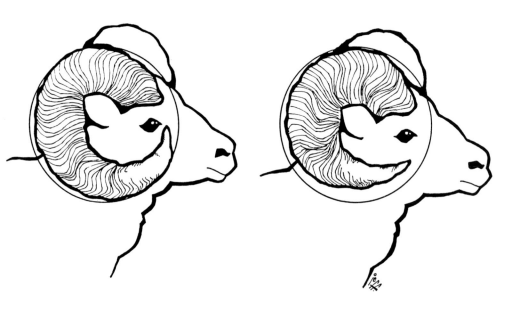

photo as a reference. This little trick helps determine whether or not a ram may be trophy-book material.

Under current regulations, the minimum-sized ram sheep hunters can take is 7/8-curl. The full-curl regulation now in effect for all areas except the Brooks Range is what usually creates a problem for hunters. The regulation says, "Full-curl horn means the horn of a mature male mountain sheep, the tip of which has grown through 360 degrees of a circle described by the outer surface of the horn as viewed from the side." Hunters should note that the definition of full curl includes no reference to the sheep's nose or eye, and that the direction the tip of the horn points is not mentioned. These items are not relevant to the legal definition.

According to Wayne Heimer, full-curl Dall ram horns typically describe a near-circle when viewed directly down the center of the horn curl. This is the best and only correct way to look at Dall ram horns to see if they have grown through the required 360 degrees. The horn curl may be said to form a cylinder. When viewed down the axis of this imaginary tube, the tip of a full-curl ram horn will meet the front edge of the horn base where it emerges from the ram's head. Since ram skulls are living tissue, the weight of the horn often pulls this imaginary tube down somewhat so that a straight side view may be a little misleading. Hunters stalking rams that may be on the border line should try to get this type of view of their prospective trophy. If in doubt, look for a larger ram.

Rams with both horns broken are also legal game according to regulations. Old Dall rams frequently break the tips of their horns by fighting. When this occurs, the horns may not be 360 degrees, but the sheep is old, legal, and certainly a fine trophy. Hunters should make sure the horns on such rams are really broken, and not simply a bit worn. As a general rule, the horn splinters when this type of breaking, or brooming as sheep hunters call it, takes place. If the horn is obviously blunt or splintered, it is truly broken. Rams with both horns in this condition are legal.

Making the Shot

If you've found your ram, and can't get to within range, don't be a fool and chance a shot. Your best bet is to go away until the next day. Chances are good the ram will still be there the next morning.

While fog, rain and snow are lousy weather for glassing, they do offer cover for a stalk. I've noticed sheep slightly distracted

Guide Joe Want washing out a Dall sheep cape in a cold, mountain stream. Blood quickly stains a sheep cape, and can ruin an otherwise potentially good mount.

from a rainshower, allowing me to sneak across a thin patch of vegetation to get within range for a shot. Mountain fog, on the other hand, makes for eerie sheep hunting conditions. Unless you know exactly where the rams are, don't bother wandering haphazardly through the fog. Not only might you spook sheep, but you could also step off a precipice. I nearly did this once on a sheep hunt in a white-out rather than fog. The intensity of light around me suddenly changed to a lighter gray. I found out why. Ten feet away, the ridge fell straight down a 2,000-foot cliff. I stayed put in a mass of boulders until the snowstorm subsided.

But I don't recommend a bivouac stay overnight in sheep country unless your camp is a good distance away from the sheep. A mile isn't too far, and should be a minimum distance, depending on wind and terrain. In some parts of glacial country, of course, this distance is impractical. Guide Jim Harrower suggests that hunters climb the mountain and spend the night in the crags. During the day, hunt the feeding areas. Another guide I know hunts by day, and comes down the mountainside by night. Allows for more hunting time, he says.

Once you're within range, take your time and get a good rest. Your rifle should be sighted in for 300 yards. As a general rule, it's harder to get closer than 100 yards. You should be able to hold your crosshairs right on the sheep and be on target within that range.

Sheep are easy to kill. Some hunters have used a .243 and done quite well. However, I recommend nothing less than a .270 for sheep, and prefer the punch of the 30 caliber rifles.

Here are two more tips on rifle care prior to the stalk. Be sure to apply a piece of tape over your rifle muzzle to keep out any slate particles, snow and dirt. Also, tape down your sling swivels so they don't squeak or come loose at the wrong time.

If you're shooting from a prone position, check the clearance between the rifle barrel and the ground. You may see the sheep in your scope, but a small rock may be in the bullet's path. Rivers says this happens to many hunters, especially those in a hurry. "We call their pulverized rock, 'stone sheep,' he says with a smile.

Once you have your trophy, take a break. Take in the sights, sounds, soak in all the feelings of accomplishment. You deserve it. However, make it short. If not washed out before it dries, blood will stain Dall sheep hair. A cold, mountain stream is all that's necessary to remove the stain. Otherwise, the taxidermist will need to bleach your cape. Bleaching makes the hair very brittle, and makes the sheep look unrealistic. Proceed to bone out the meat, and if time permits, skin out the neck and head right on the spot. If not, pack the head to base camp where you can finish the skinning.

Judging The Age Of Your Ram

Once you're in camp, you can easily judge how old your ram is by counting the rings or annuli, created on the ram's horns with each year of growth. Here's a bit of background to help you understand what to look for.

When Dall lambs are born in late May or early June, they begin growing horns immediately. A young ram's horns grow from 1.5 inches to 3 inches the first year—that is, only from late spring to early winter. Horn growth stops for a while during rutting season in late November and early December. That's when the growth is marked each year. A slight bulge on the outside of the horn and a small ring on the inside surface of the horn marks the first year's growth.

The horn then resumes growth and continues until the next rutting season. Again, growth stops temporarily and the second annulus is formed. This second "ring" is often rather wide and lumpy. Associated with puberty in rams, it is not clearly defined as other horn annuli. It usually appears as a lumpy irregularity on both sides of the horn, about four to five inches along the horn from the first annulus. The horn might

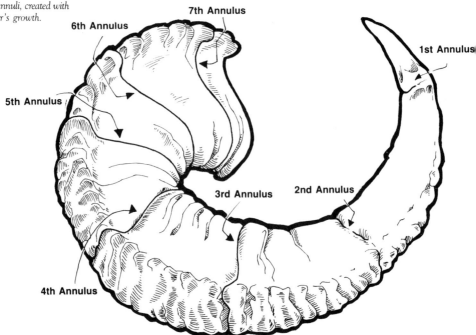

7th Annulus

6th Annulus

1st Annulus

5th Annulus

3rd Annulus

2nd Annulus

4th Annulus

have started and stopped growing a couple of times during the winter.

From then on, the annuli are usually distinctive grooves and easier to count. Still, more details can be useful. The horn is normally rough and wrinkled along its outer side; annuli are deeper than these wrinkles and they go completely around the horn. Annuli are easier to count on the inside of the horn curl. Also, as the ram gets older, the horn growth rate (distance between annuli) decreases after the third year, and the rings will be closer together.

After the sixth and seventh years, the rings become more difficult to distinguish as they get closer together. Toward the end of the ram's life at age 10 to 12 years, the rings may be separated by as little distance as the thickness of a nickel. You can usually run your thumbnail all the way around the horn in the groove of each annulus and raise some dandruff-like material from a real horn ring.

Seven-eighths curl rams will usually be from five to seven years old, and full-curl rams will usually be at least six years old with most being close to eight years of age. Rams with

broomed or broken-off horns are more difficult to age. However, it is very unusual to find a ram with a horn broken off below the third annulus. If you have trouble aging your trophy, you can get help from ADF&G Game Division sheep specialists.

Hunters often ask how long a ram lives after reaching full curl. Rams from some areas reach full-curl sooner than others, but generally speaking, a ram reaches full-curl at eight years of age. Thus, a 14-year-old ram is very old, and 10 years is old. Rams may live up to 12 years of age, and are capable of reproducing all during that time. It's interesting to note that ewes live longer than rams, sometimes reaching 19 years of age. Nichols reports on a 15-year-old ewe that died after giving birth.

How long a ram lives depends on its ability to maintain body fat throughout the rut and winter months. The older a ram gets, the less likely he's able to recuperate from the rigors of rut. With precious body fat used up during rut, the sheep must survive the winter by feeding on browse, less-than-desirable forage. In winters with high snowpack, when sheep can't reach food, they must feed on poor-quality forage, creating a negative energy balance. This means the sheep expends more energy

This nice ram with a sweeping curl was taken with one shot at 175 yards on a backpack hunt in the Chugach Mountains.

Dall Sheep

In sheep hunting, locating sheep is not difficult. Getting to them often is. John Rodrigas took this nice Dall ram on an August hunt in the glacier country north of Anchorage.

than it receives from feeding. How much fat a ram has used during rut determines its chances of survival. Worn teeth and inability to feed due to old age or disease also have a bearing on a ram's lifespan.

Many hunters are fascinated by the information that can be obtained from studying a set of Dall sheep horns. Even more incredible is how hunters perceive Alaska Dall sheep hunting, and its importance to the Alaska economy.

The preliminary results of a 1983 sheep hunter survey being compiled by ADF&G sheep biologist Sarah Watson sheds some interesting light on the subject. In February, 1984, ADF&G mailed questionnaires to all hunters who hunted sheep in Alaska in 1983. Eighty-two percent of the resident hunters, and 89 percent of the non-resident hunters returned the completed questionnaires, an outstanding rate of return.

• Residents spent an average of 5 percent of their annual household income on sheep hunting in 1983, while non-residents spent an average of 17 percent of their income on a hunt.

• Forty percent of those who answered the questionnaire said they killed a ram. Seventy percent of the non-residents bagged a ram, while only 33 percent of the residents were successful. The most likely reason for this is that most non-residents were guided.

• Forty-three percent of the residents who hunted Dall sheep in 1983 were doing so for the first time. Seventy-eight percent of the non-residents were hunting Dall sheep in Alaska for the first time.

• The rate of success for experienced, resident hunters increased as the total number of years hunted increased until experience reached 10 years. In 1983, hunters with this much experience had a success rate of 45 percent. But for hunters with more than 10 years experience, the success rate decreased to 31 percent. Watson attributes the decrease due to increase in age and/or hunter selectivity.

• Asked if whether they would hunt Dall sheep again, 95 percent of the residents and 67 percent of the non-residents said they did plan to hunt sheep again.

• Expenditures by Dall sheep hunters exceeded $5.2 million dollars, with 85 percent of the expenditures occurring in Alaska. Non-resident hunters contributed 50 percent of this total, even though they accounted for only 17 percent of the hunters. Non-resident hunters also spent over $682,000 hunting other big game species, visiting relatives, or vacationing. This brings the total to over $5.9 million. Residents spent an average of $1,519 on each sheep hunt. Ninety-six percent of this was spent in-state. Non-residents spent an average of $9,850 in total expenditures with $7,780 spent specifically on their sheep hunt. Seventy-eight percent of their expenditures went into the Alaska economy.

• Hunters surveyed in 1983 took time off work to go sheep hunting. This total amount results in $1.4 million in foregone income.

Indeed, Dall sheep hunting is what some hunters refer to as "a priceless experience." Taking in the wind-swept mountains and ravaged glacial valleys; watching a broomed-horn sheep sitting on a grassy knoll, chewing its cud; or breathing in the sweet smell of sheep tenderloin roasting over an open fire are all priceless experiences. You can't enjoy these things from the comfort of your living room. The only way to experience them is to go for them and live them, with every drop of sweat, every aching leg muscle and shoulder cramp, and every last dollar. If you're like most sheep hunters, you'll agree that Alaska sheep hunting is worth the effort!

Where to Hunt Dall Sheep

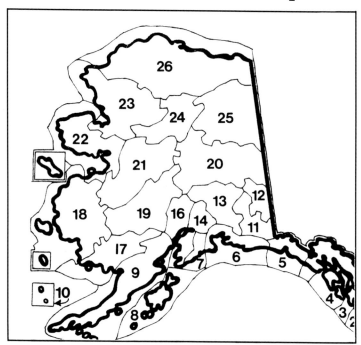

Unit 12

Wrangell Mountains

Population Status— North: 10-12,000, South: 4,000 (3,000 available to hunters). Trend: Stable

The sheep population in this region is presently in good, stable condition. Most of these sheep are on the north side of the mountain range in the Wrangell-St. Elias National Park Preserve. Rams compose about 37 percent of the population. About 400 hunters annually use the northern Wrangell Mountains, and the yearly harvest is about 200 to 225 rams. Hunter success in 1988 was 58 percent, and 48 percent in 1987. However, the number of hunters has remained low in recent years, probably due to inclement weather in the area. Average horn length from this area is 34.3 inches.

Unit 12 is managed to provide the greatest opportunity to participate in sheep hunting. Due to public demand, the legal ram definition was changed from 7/8 to full-curl in 1984. The regulation change has had little effect on sheep harvests because the harvest rate is low compared to the number of sheep present. However, populations may have declined slightly due to severe winters in 1981-83.

The remaining 4,000 sheep in the Wrangell Mountains are on the west and south sides. These sheep, (3,000) are mostly within the Wrangell-St. Elias National Park Preserve. The management plan for this area is to provide the opportunity to hunt sheep under aesthetically pleasing conditions.

About 200 hunters use this area each year, and the average harvest has been about 90 rams with 7/8-curl horns or larger. Full-curl regulations are now in effect. At the present time, no research is being done on sheep populations in the Wrangell Mountains. The largest Dall rams in the world remain under total protection from hunting because they are within the Wrangell-St. Elias National Park at the southeast corner of the mountain range.

Units 16, 17, 19

Alaska Range West of Mount McKinley
Population Status: 4,000, (3,000 available to hunters). Trend: Stable

The number of sheep in the Alaska Range west of Denali National Park is estimated to be approximately 4,000 animals. One thousand of these sheep reside in Lake Clark National Park, which is closed to hunting.

Trophy selecction in this area is rated as good. Ram harvest since 1979 has averaged 113 rams for 177 hunters for a success rate of 64 percent. The highest harvest on record, 157 sheep, was taken from this area in 1988. Almost half the hunters were nonresidents, who had a success rate of 83 percent. Success rate for residents was 62 percent. Sheep Creek and Windy Fork drainages in subunit 19C are the most heavily hunted. Other top hunting areas include the Skwentna, Tonzona and Post rivers, and the south fork of the Kuskokwim River.

Average horn size for this region is about 36 inches, with a full-curl legal minimum required. The average age is 8.9 years. In this area, the first and fifth week of the season are the best for all hunters and about 15 percent of the sheep harvested are taken on opening day of the season. Hunter effort in this region has not been widely dispersed. High hunter success, reported ram age and long horn length relative to the minimum prescribed by regulation indicate that hunting pressure is light. Most hunters use aircraft to reach their hunting areas.

Reports from guides operating in the western Alaska Range and results of hunter harvest ticket analyses indicate that sheep populations in this area are either stable or are continuing to increase. Unless hunting pressure becomes more intense or severe winter weather produces substantial winter kill, the western Alaska Range appears able to sustain very good sheep hunting opportunities.

Unit 20

Tanana Hills-Yukon Uplands
Population: 650. Trend: Slowly Increasing

The Tanana Hills-Yukon Uplands sheep are characterized by low densities that are slowly increasing in number. Surveys indicate that about 650 sheep inhabit the area. Approximately 32 hunters kill an average of 10 rams each year for a success ratio 31 percent. Six out of 10 hunters use aircraft to reach their hunting area. According to information provided by hunters, average horn length is 35 inches, and sheep average 8.8 years of age. General harvest locations are Mt. Harper, Mt. Sorenson, White Mountains, and Tatonduk-Kandik rivers. Succcessful hunts run eight days.

Heimer describes this area as, "fairly low, rolling hills; alpine habitat is disjunct with broad, timbered valleys between suitable alpine sheep habitats." This habitat is considered by many as the ancestral refugium of thinhorn sheep, and habitat character is more like the steppe habitats for sheep in northern Asia than other Alaska sheep habitats.

The most significant threat to sheep in the Tanana/Yukon uplands is displacement and habitat loss through development by the mineral industry. The most clearly identifiable threat is from asbestos and tungsten prospects being developed in areas not withdrawn from mineral entry.

Unit 20

Alaska Range east of Denali National Park, excluding Tok Management Area and Delta Controlled Use Area

Population: 9,000. Trend: Stable

The central Alaska Range contains a moderately dense sheep population that is stable. An increase from 3/4-curl to full-curl has resulted in more consecutive-year breeding and more mature rams than ever before. This area is a choice consideration for a full-curl trophy. Horn length varies from 25 to 41 inches with the average being 34 inches. The largest average horn size comes from the Totatlanika River drainage (35.5 inches) while the smallest comes from the Dry Creek drainage (32.9 inches). Hunters spend about five days afield and the overall success ratio is 38 percent. The largest harvest of sheep occurs in the Wood River drainage, while the lowest harvest takes place in the Totatlanika River drainage.

Units 12, 13, 20

Tok Management Area, Alaska Range East of the Johnson River

Approximately 2,000 sheep inhabit the Tok Management Area, where the population is holding its own. While sheep are not as numerous in this region as they are in others, it is one of the top regions in the state to bag a large-horned, trophy ram. However, hunting in this region is restricted to drawing permit hunts only to provide for trophy management. Hunter success varies from 30 to 66 percent, the latter being the figure for the 1987 hunt. Rams taken in 1988 had an average horn length of 36.7 inches, much greater than the average of 34.3 for the remainder of the unit. Ten of the 52 rams taken in 1988 had horn lengths equal or greater than 39 inches.

Units 13, 20

The sheep population in the Delta Controlled Use Area is around 1,500 animals. Hunts in this area are via drawing permits for the DCUA sheep hunts. Since 1978, hunter success has varied between 25 to 60 percent. Biological reports indicate that the Jarvis Creek wolf pack, as well as other packs, prey heavily on sheep populations in this region. Horn size ranges from 34.8 to 36 inches, and is presently full-curl only.

Units 23, 24, 25, 26

Brooks Range Herd

Population: 30,000 (15,000 available to hunters). Trend: Stable

With the passing of the Alaska National Interest Lands Claim Act, (ANILCA) more than one-third of the sheep population became unavailable to sport hunters. Approximately 18,500 of the 30,000 sheep in the Brooks Range are currently available to hunters.

At the present time, numbers are stable throughout most of the region. The western portion of Unit 24 supports moderate sheep numbers, and higher numbers exist in eastern Unit 24. In Unit 26, high densities occur just east of the Canning River, and sparse numbers exist near the Canadian Border. The 1987 season shows that 408 hunters took 274 rams. Resident hunters took 156 rams, while non-resident hunters accompanied by guides took 104 rams. Fourteen rams were taken by hunters of unreported residency. The numbers of hunters and animals harvested in 1987 were the highest since 1978, when 426 hunters took 266 rams.

In Unit 24, much of the area consists of the Gates of the Arctic National Park, and thus closed to hunting. Hunters have been concentrating on the remaining areas that are open to hunting in this unit. Forty-six percent of the hunters and 56 percent of the 1987 harvest came from drainages of the Middle Fork of the Koyukuk River and the Dietrich River along the Dalton Highway. These sheep are also managed for viewing and bowhunting within five miles on either side of the Trans-Alaska oil pipeline.

In Unit 25, hunter success was 65 percent. The Chandalar River drainage is a popular hunting area.

Unit 26 has seen an increase in hunting pressure since the passage of ANILCA. Resident and non-resident hunters had their highest success rate in Unit 26, including those areas being hunted by a large number of hunters.

In subunit 26B, hunting action is increasing in the Atigun drainage. The Dalton Highway was reported as the primary means of access to this region, even though the highway is closed to traffic north of Dietrich. In subunit 26A, nearly half the hunting and 40 percent of the harvest occurred in the mountains between the Nanushuk and the Anaktuvuk rivers. This is one of the few areas open to sheep hunting in the area and is located in the Gates of the Arctic National Preserve. In subunit 26C, hunters frequent the drainages of the Hulahula River and the Kongakut River.

The management plan for this area provides for hunting in uncrowded, aesthetically pleasing conditions. Currently, the remoteness and high cost of hunting in this area limits hunters to acceptable levels. A lottery permit system was formerly in place here, but was removed when it proved unnecessary to meet the management goal.

Units 11, 13, 14

Chugach Mountain Herd
Population: 5,000 (4,000 available to hunters). Trend: Stable or Increasing

While the Chugach Mountains contain portions of GMU 4, approximately 42 percent of the sheep population in this range is presently located in subunit 14C. Densities decrease toward the east. Dall sheep populations are quite sparse east of the Copper River, but some are found on the north side of the Chugach Mountains south of the Chitina River. In subunit 14A, populations have increased annually since 1982; within subunit 14C, the population has reached the highest level on record: 128 percent above numbers found in the late 1970s. The Unit 13 sheep population remains stable.

In Unit 14, the current population of sheep indicates a young, growing population that will experience an increase in legal rams within the next two to three years. Each year, from 500 to 600 hunters harvest an average of 130 to 158 legal rams. The mean horn size is 34.6 inches. Hunter success rate is 26 percent.

The breakdown of prime sheep habitat in this region:

Subunit 14A: The mountains between the Matanuska and Knik rivers.

Subunit 14B: The Talkeetna Mountains, above 2,000 feet.

Subunit 14C: Ship Creek, Eagle River, Peters Creek, Thunderbird Creek, Hunter Creek, and Eklutna River drainages.

Subunit 16B: Mountains above 2,000 feet in the Happy River, Styx River, Timber Creek, Crystal Creek, Muddy Creek and Emerald Creek drainages.

A large salt lick exists on Peters Creek, which attracts many sheep into the area.

Sheep habitat in the Chugach is managed to provide for sheep hunting under aesthetically pleasing conditions. In one management area near Anchorage, this goal is met through a lottery permit system. Much of this area lies within an Alaska State Park, and presents a challenging management situation because of persistent attempts by the State Parks System to manage large portions of it like a National Park, that is, exclusively for non-consumptive use. Overall, ram harvest is limited to full-curl or greater.

Units 13, 14

Talkeetna Mountains
Population: 3,000 (2,800 available to hunters). Trend: Stable

Most of the sheep are concentrated in the south and east portions of this mountain mass. Little population data is available on the sheep of the Talkeetna Mountains, however, sheep are starting to recover from the severe winter of 1984-85. In 1988, hunters bagged 105 rams. Of these, 41 animals were taken in subunit 13A, 21 were taken in subunit 13E, 23 were taken in subunit 14A, and 20 were taken in 14B. Approximately 339 hunters per year take an average of 102 rams from areas open to hunting for a success rate of 30 percent.

Two different management goals are defined for the Talkeetna Mountains. Most sheep habitat in the Talkeetnas is managed to provide for the greatest opportunity to participate in sheep hunting. However, the southwest corner has a differing management plan, to provide the opportunity to hunt sheep under aesthetically pleasing conditions.

Units 7, 15

Kenai Mountains
Population: 1,500, (1,300 available to hunters). Trend: Declining

Sheep survey data from the Kenai Mountains have many gaps and inconsistencies. Generally severe winters from 1970 through the early 1980s reduced the estimated sheep population of the Kenai Mountains from 3,000 sheep to an estimated 1,500 at this time. During the last five years, an average of 153 hunters harvested 20 rams for a success rate of 15 percent. Reports indicate that although the Kenai sheep population is at a low level, they are slowly increasing.

Rams in the Kenai Mountains usually attain 7/8-curl at 6 years of age, which is a bit earlier than rams found elsewhere. Mean horn length of harvested rams is 33.4 inches, with horn length varying from 30 to 38.3 inches. Transportation means used by all successful hunters are as follows: highway vehicle (36 percent), airplane (32 percent), boat (28 percent), unknown (4 percent).

Minor Herd Unit 23

Kotzebue Sound

Sheep populations are stable in this region, with an unofficial population of 2,000 sheep in the Baird and Delong mountains, respectively. Hunters harvested 37 rams in 1988, with 33 hunters unsuccessful. A registration permit is needed to hunt in the Baird Mountains. It can be obtained at the Alaska Department of Fish and Game Office in Kotzebue.

CHAPTER 9

Musk Ox

There's no other species of Alaska big game that offers the eccentricity of musk ox hunting. It's a sport taking you to the northernmost edge of the North American continent, a strange land where miles of eggshell-white sand dunes are frequently hammered by the frigid blasts of the Bering Sea's arctic wind. It's a hunt that replaces the tradition of a horse packtrain with the Eskimo's "iron dog": the snowmachine. Ironically, these modern-day machines are a vital link, allowing man to access this living fossil, an exotic descendant of a long-forgotten Ice Age where man was a minority in a world full of horses, camels and saber-tooth tigers. To be privileged to hunt musk ox today is to take a trip back in time.

With more nicknames than any other Alaska big game animal, the musk ox is known as polar cattle, ovibos, and arctic buffalo. The Eskimo word for it is *Oomingmuk*, meaning, "animal with skin like a beard." The Cree Indians call it *Mathehmoostoosh*, meaning "ugly bison."

Different writers have seen the musk ox as a cross between different species of animals. Whitney (1904) writes that the musk ox "appears...to be a veritable link between the ox and the sheep." Others have compared it with various breeds of cattle, calling it "a buffalo specialized for life on the polar plains" and "a South African Buffalo and a Prairie Bison combined."

Fossil remains of musk ox of the Pleistocene Era indicate little if any difference from the musk ox found in Alaska to-

Musk ox hunting in Alaska is currently on a drawing and registration permit system. Most musk ox hunters employ the services of a guide or outfitter. However, numerous hunters have been successful in handling their own hunts. (Photo by D.R. Klein)

day. The present species roamed the same lush arctic plains with the Woolly rhinoceros and mammoth bison, both now extinct. During the end of the Ice Age, the musk ox became circumpolar, following the retreating ice as far as the Alaskan and Canadian mainland would permit.

The musk ox found in Alaska today is a stocky animal with a slight shoulder hump caused by fat accumulation similar to that found in the bison. The species is covered by long, shaggy hair reaching to the ground. Coloration is generally dark brown with creamy patches of hair on the "saddle," forehead and legs. Beneath the hair is a special wool known as *qiviut*. This wool keeps the animal warm during the extreme winter months when wind chill factors can reach 80 degrees below zero. It's no surprise that qiviut is in great demand by Eskimos and commercial weavers. The wool has been compared to cashmere in texture, and is used in knitting gloves, scarves, sweaters and hats.

However, there's evidence that life-preserving musk ox hair can cause its death. On Nunivak Island, musk oxen have perished by being frozen to the ground by their hair being caught in a rapid thaw-freeze cycle.

Both male and female musk ox have horns. However, the male's much heavier skull and horns are prized most by hunters. The horns curve broadly down, out and up from the forehead. The heavy base, also known as a boss, spans the entire forehead of the bull. On cows, there's usually a patch of hair separating the horn bases.

Musk ox have cloven hooves, all four the same size. They also have dew claws, but these seldom register in tracks. As for size, cows are smaller, averaging four feet high at the shoulder and weighing about 350 to 400 pounds. Males can weigh from 500 to 650 pounds.

Life History

The breeding season begins during late August and September, when bulls start gathering harems of females two years or older. A herd's dominant bull will frequently engage in head-butting contests with other bulls, butting or goring until the rival bull withdraws, is upset, or killed. After breeding, the herds disband into individual groups that travel to wintering and calving areas. Single calves are born the following April or May and weigh about 19 pounds at birth. The newborn musk ox grow rapidly, and weigh about 150 pounds by one year of age.

Musk ox are often found in groups of 20 to 30, with older bulls frequently leading solitary lives.

History of Musk Ox in Alaska

Indigenous populations of musk ox were not found on Alaska's Seward Peninsula in recent historical times. There is evidence, however, that native stocks did occur in the area prior to visitation by early explorers. According to her 1934 report, *Status of the Muskox in Arctic North America*, Elisabeth Hone quoted letters and documents from early explorers, indicating the presence of musk ox. In an 1898 document, Frank Russell wrote:

> The oldest natives at Point Barrow say that their fathers killed musk ox, which were then abundant. (Also), evidence from the American Museum Arctic Expedition of 1908-1912 shows that in the winter of 1899-1900, there died an Alaskan Eskimo by the name of Mangi who was believed to have seen live musk ox in the vicinity. It happened in the harsh arctic winter of 1858, when Mangi and his father went inland in search of caribou. They found a herd of 13 musk ox and killed them all. Since then, none had been seen or killed near Point Barrow

Reports from the mid-1800s described large numbers of unfossilized musk ox bones along the shore of Escholtz Bay. Eskimos living in the Buckland River region were familiar with the species when contacted by Captain Beechy in 1825.

All indications are that musk ox were extirpated by human hunters from their original range on Alaska's Arctic slope in the mid-1800s. However, this "living mammalian relic of the Ice Age" was not forgotten. It was reintroduced to Alaska in 1935 and 1936 with transplants of 31 Greenland musk ox to Nunivak Island. There were several reasons for re-establishing the herds: to provide a nucleus herd from which musk ox could be taken to establish populations throughout their historic ranges in Alaska, and to serve recreational, agricultural and scientific uses for the animals.

The population grew slowly but increased rapidly after 1950. There were about 600 animals in 1965. Despite the removal of 33 calves for domestication purposes in 1964 and 1965, and the transplants of 23 animals to Nelson Island in 1967 and 1968, the Nunivak population reached abaout 750 animals in 1968. At that time, federal and state biologists recommended that the herd be reduced to equal its winter range. In 1968, The Alaska Board of Fish and Game approved a management plan involving sport hunting and transplanting. In 1969 and

Both male and female musk ox have horns. However, the male's much heavier skull and horns are prized most by hunters. (Photo by D.R. Klein)

1970, recommended transplants to several northwestern and arctic sites took place as scheduled and were successful. However, political opposition delayed the sport hunting of musk ox until 1975.

Hunting Techniques

The musk ox is a collector's trophy; the sport in this hunt comes from the area and chase. The musk ox has formidable skills in eluding its natural predators. The species has developed a nearly inpenetrable defense system in which the adults form a protective circle around the young. When attacked by wolves or bears, musk ox may stand in multiple rows while one or more adults make short charges against the predator. The species has amazing speed, agility and stamina, besides being adept at goring with its sharp, needle-like horns. Musk ox are also persistent against threats. In 1904, one explorer confronted a bull and tried throwing stones at it, only to have the bull respond by angrily shaking its head and pawing at the ground in retaliation, all the while making a low guttural grunt. Apparently not intimidated by such a confrontation, the bull remained near the man's camp all night.

One reason for the success of the herds on Nunivak and

Nelson islands is a lack of large predators (excluding man) there. The chief causes of mortality among musk ox on these islands have been malnutrition, accidents, and old age. But recently, animals have wandered off the island and were unable to return when the pack ice shifted or melted. Thus, populations must be managed intensively to keep the herds in balance with the available forage and habitat. Due to the extremely high cost of transplanting, and limited number of good musk ox habitat located elsewhere throughout the state, sport hunting is considered important in keeping the herds in check.

Musk ox hunting in Alaska is currently on both a drawing and registration permit system. Drawing permits are held by lottery, and registration permits are available on a first-come, first-serve basis. The season is closed when the allocated harvest is reached.

Due to the remoteness of the hunt, difficulty in logistics and severe weather, most musk ox hunters employ the services of a guide or outfitter. However, numerous hunters have been successful in handling their own hunts.

Before going afield, you're required to make an appointment with the ADF&G nearest the area you'll be hunting. For Nunivak and Nelson islands, this is the village of Bethel. There, you'll be given a musk ox orientation lasting no more than half an hour. This orientation consists of bull and cow identification and answers questions about the hunt area and location of animals.

Musk ox hunting is generally best in late winter. However, many hunters prefer the challenge of a fall hunt. Access to the hunting area is by a skiff or boat usually rented from a local villager for the duration of the hunt. Access to the hunting grounds is usually difficult at this time of year. The boat ride is usually exciting, with choppy seas and high winds serving to "spice up" the adventure. Should weather prevent you from leaving the island on schedule, be prepared to spend several nights in the village.

Once you're in the hunting area, expect to do a lot of walking. Unlike a winter hunt, where you can effortlessly cover miles of terrain with a snowmachine, access to the area during the fall is limited by boat. After reaching the fringe of the hunting area, both scouting and hunting is done on foot. Musk ox may be several miles inland. The terrain is typical tundra: flat expanses with a handful of low, rolling hills interspersed with a few lakes and marshy potholes. Most hunters, however, find musk ox on or near the sand dunes in the southeast portion of Nunivak Island.

It's important to glass continuously. Musk ox weave in and out of the dunes, and a small herd can be within several hundred yards without the hunter knowing. Once you're sure no animals are in the area, motor down the coast or hike inland. If you hike, you should take a small tent and pack with enough provisions to last three days. An overland hunt is tough, but many hunters claim the difficulty in finding the animals is a challenge not offered on a late-winter hunt.

Late-winter is the preferred season to hunt musk ox for several reasons. First, you're not restricted to water access. Snow-machines or aircraft are the primary modes of transportation, opening up vast sections of the islands and arctic areas. Both modes not only allow quicker access to the animals, but also the opportunity to take advantage of good hunting weather when it occurs. Late winter weather conditions consist mainly of biting-cold arctic winds, with temperatures ranging from 0 to 20 degrees. Also, expect a white-out blizzard at least once during your stay.

Another advantage of the late-winter season over the fall is that the hunter has more daylight in which to hunt. In some years, with dark, cloudy weather, an extra hour of light might mean the difference between success and failure.

Finding musk ox on the islands in late winter is easier than in the fall. Because musk ox are not adapted to digging through heavy snow for food, they are usually fond of ample supplies of grasses and sedges found in windblown tundra areas. Nelson and Nunivak islands are ideal musk ox habitat because frequent high winds there expose the vegetation on coastal sand dunes and hills, providing the animals with easy access to the forage. The highest concentration of musk ox at any time of the year occurs in late winter and early spring, when they are found in the dunes. Individual herds can number 50 or more animals.

Again, reports of recent sightings followed by hours of careful glassing will usually have you in or near musk ox on your first or second day, weather permitting.

How musk ox will react to your stalk is unpredictable. If they've been hunted hard, by either man or predators, musk ox will often flee. The only thing to do in this situation is take after them on foot or snowmachine, hoping they'll group up or resume feeding elsewhere. They can also just stand there, facing you without fear, or form a small defensive circle with other musk ox as mentioned earlier. If your trophy is packed tightly in such a circle, wait until the bull or cow has moved away from the others. Bullets easily pass through musk ox and could possibly kill other animals in the herd. If this happens, you're responsible for packing out the salvageable meat, hide and horns and turning them into the authorities upon your return to Bethel.

Older bulls, however, can be extremely challenging to track down and stalk. Use whatever cover is available, and try to get within range for a shot as soon as possible. Most of the time, a hunter can walk within easy shooting range and take the animal he wants. Because of this, many hunters have opined that musk ox hunting is not much of a sport. And granted, when compared to other species with senses acutely tuned to avoid the approach of man, musk ox hunting pales in comparison. But it is unfair to judge the musk ox as such.

The musk ox is a species that survived more than 10,000 years on its own before being wiped out in Alaska by man's greed. But man has also been its salvation. We now recognize the musk ox as a living mammalian relic, a survivor trying to exist in a modern age when man appreciates the importance of sharing this earth with such a unique species. Yet our tribute to the musk ox transcends the basic reasons for hunting this big game animal. This unique experience means breathing in the frigid, arctic air, its bite of cold racing like a venom throughout your system. It means standing face-to-face with a Bering Sea storm, defying its stinging slap of 40 mph winds that freeze your cheeks and frost your beard. It means watching musk ox form a defense circle of the type that has successfully withstood the growling charges of natural predators—from wolves to bears—for tens of thousands of years. Only by experiencing these elements of musk ox behavior and environment can you truly appreciate the Alaska musk ox, and be proud to have it as a trophy adorning your trophy room.

Where to Hunt Musk Ox

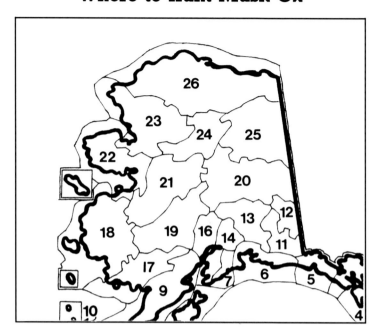

Except for the parent Nunivak herd, all musk ox herds in Alaska result from transplants from Nunivak Island conducted from 1967 through 1970. All herds are increasing, with the possible exception of Unit 23 (Cape Thompson). The Nunivak population is now at a very high level. The Nelson Island population has declined somewhat, partially due to emigration to mainland Unit 18. The Seward Peninsula and eastern Arctic herds are growing rapidly.

Unit 18

Nelson Island

The Nelson Island musk ox herd has been stable since 1981, despite the animals' movements back and forth between the island and the mainland.

In December 1988, there were 212 musk ox. The westernmost Cape Vancouver area serves as a prime wintering area for about 35 percent of the island's musk ox. Most are harvested from Erchaktruk Mountain, with smaller numbers taken from Kaluyut and Kasinuk mountains. There, they reside on rocky plateaus above sea cliffs and precipitous slopes. Hunting pressure, however, has disturbed the remaining population. Hunters and biologists have seen the animals fleeing when approached from as far away as two miles.

The Nelson Island musk ox population has produced stable annual harvests of 30 musk ox since 1984, even while contributing to the mainland herd through emigration. Hunting on the mainland was closed by the Board of Game in 1984, and that population has grown rapidly by both emigration and reproduction.

Small numbers of musk ox now roam over a wide area between the Yukon and Kuskokwim Rivers and a few have reached as far as the Andreafsky Mountains after crossing the frozen Yukon River.

Hunting will remain closed until the mainland population reaches most areas of suitable upland habitat and increases significantly in size.

Unit 18

Nunivak Island

The Nunivak Island musk ox population reached approximately 700 animals in 1988-89, slightly above the management goal of 500 to 550 for the herd.

Bulls are taken by drawing permit, and this hunt has an international reputation due to the large horns found in this herd. Cows are taken by registration permit.

The heaviest harvest of musk ox frequently takes place on the south side of Nunivak Island in the Cape Mendenhall area. Other locations include the Nash Harbor area, Chakwakamiut area, Roberts Mountain, Karon Lake area and the Bankookthleet Dunes. Other locations are scattered along the southern and central section of the island. In the past few years, many hunters have required only one to two days to take a musk ox. Of course, this depends on weather and location of animals.

Unit 22

Seward Peninsula

Musk ox were introduced to the Seward Peninsula in 1970 when 36 animals from Nunivak Island were released on the Feather River, about 30 miles northwest of Nome. In 1981, an additional 37 musk ox were transplanted from Nunivak Island to a release site near Port Clarence. Animals from both transplants have dispersed and the moving herds are expected to colonize areas not currently occupied by musk ox.

Aerial surveys by department personnel in the spring of 1988 found 527 musk ox in Unit 22. Musk ox are now widely distributed over the unit. Hunting will probably be offered in the future.

Units 26B, 26C

Central and Eastern Arctic Slope

Sixty-four musk ox were transplanted to Barter Island and the Kavik River in 1969 and 1970 to re-establish viable herds on historic ranges and to provide for high-quality recreational hunts in the future. There are about 400 musk ox in this region now; 22 percent of them are bulls. Biologists indicate that the population is increasing at an annual rate of 10 to 20 percent. Most of the population is concentrated in the Arctic National Wildlife Refuge near the Tamayariak, Sadlerochit and Okerokovik rivers. Smaller numbers have also been found near the Canning, Jago and Konakut rivers.

In 1988 the Alaska Board of Game established a fall hunting season for musk ox that runs from August 15 through September 15. Permits for bulls only were increased to 10. Five permits were issued in Kaktovik and five were issued in Fairbanks. Kaktovik hunters will hunt in all of subunit 26C, and Fairbanks hunters will hunt zones 1 and 2 of subunit 26C. Successful hunters use snowmachines and aircraft to reach herds.

CHAPTER 10

Gray Wolf

While Alaska has several species of big game that could be classified as "challenging," none match the mystique, excitement and difficulty to hunt than the wolf. Considered an endangered species in the Lower 48, the gray wolf in Alaska is well-adapted to a wide range of habitats, equally home in the rain forests of the Panhandle as he is on the arctic tundra along the Beaufort Sea.

It is both a curse and an honor for Alaska to hold the largest remaining wolf populations left in the United States. The 49th State boasts a healthy population of approximately 5,000 to 6,000 animals, and populations are stable or increasing. While this figure may not, at first, indicate a large wolf population, especially when considering the size of Alaska, many hunters and biologists believe that the number of wolves in the state justifies both aerial and traditional sport hunting methods. However, because of its endangered status in the Lower 48, wildlife protectionist groups feel the wolf should be afforded the same status as the bald eagle, and that all hunting should be banned.

But both sportsmen and biologists agree that wolves need to be harvested to allow moose and caribou populations—species that resident hunters depend on for food—to reestablish themselves in areas of high wolf concentrations. The clash between the two points of view mixes fish and game matters and politics; a practice as unconstitutional as mixing church with state. If the state allowed biologists to exercise their management options regarding wolf numbers, we'd have balanced populations of moose and wolves, rather than the current teeter-totter population dynamics between ungulates and

Wolves are widespread throughout Alaska, and are concentrated where the prey base is highest. However, they are rarely seen by hunters. (Photo by Charles Kay)

245

Gray Wolf

predators. Either way, the wolf in Alaska is here to stay.

The wolf, *Canis lupus*, occurs throughout mainland Alaska, on Unimak Island in the Aleutians, and all of the major islands of southeast Alaska except Admiralty, Baranof and Chichagof. This range includes about 85 percent of Alaska's 585,000 square-mile area.

On the average, wolf populations are generally higher in the southern part of the state. The Panhandle may have the highest densities, especially where deer are abundant. There, density can be as high or higher than one wolf per 25 square miles.

In the coastal portions of western and northern Alaska, density may be less than one wolf per 150 square miles. Although wolf distribution has remained relatively constant in recent years, densities in these regions have varied considerably, affected by availability of prey (moose, caribou), diseases, and harvests. For example, the rock-bottom wolf population in Alaska, recorded from 1900 to 1935, resulted from the lack of caribou as a food item. Populations were very high from 1952 to 1954 in the Brooks Range. In the mid-50s, Alaskans used poison to reduce wolf populations that crashed again in the 1960s. Since then, they have increased to moderate or high levels and seem stable. Currently, wolves are so abundant in areas in Unit 20 that they are frequently seen near housing developments where they occasionally take domestic animals and pets for food.

Wolves are a member of the family *Canidae*. Wolves of our *Canis lupus* species reached their greatest size during the late Pleistocene period. Early taxonomists recognized about 24 New World and eight Old World subspecies of *Canis lupus* and thought four subspecies occurred in Alaska. Recent studies of skull characteristics, body size and color suggest that differences are slight, with considerable overlap in the characteristics of various wolves from various areas. However, only two Alaska subspecies are now recognized. Wolves in southeast Alaska are darker and somewhat smaller than those in more northern parts of the state. The pelt color of Alaska wolves ranges from black to nearly white with every shade of gray and tan between these extremes. Gray and black wolves are most common, and the relative abundance of each color phase varies over time and from place to place.

Biologists offer an interesting theory for this range in wolf coloration. They account for its natural evolution by means of varying intensities of light, coupled with differences in air temperature and humidity. Wolf coloration—black in the dark forests in southeast Alaska and gray, tan and white in the snow plains of the north—provides protective coloration suited for its environment and helps to disguise wolves when stalking prey.

Life History

Wolves in Alaska normally breed in February and March and litters averaging about five pups are born in May or early June. Litters may include 2 to 10 pups. Most female wolves first breed when 22 months old, but usually have fewer pups than older females. Pups are usually born in a den excavated as much as 10 feet into well-drained soil. Most adult wolves center their activities around dens, traveling as much as 20 miles in search of food brought back regularly to the den. Wolf pups are weaned gradually during mid-summer. In mid or late summer, pups are usually moved some distance away from the den; by early winter, pups can travel and hunt with adult pack members. Biologists say wolves are great travelers, roaming as much as 50 or more miles per day in winter.

Most adult male wolves in Alaska weigh from 85 to 115 pounds, but they occasionally weigh up to 130 pounds, stretch 84 inches long and stand 35 inches high at the shoudler. Females average 5 to 10 pounds lighter than males, and rarely weigh more than 110 pounds.

Wolves are highly social animals, usually living in packs including parents, that year's pups, some yearlings from the previous year, and often other adults. The social order in the pack is a hierarchy, with separate rank orders of males and females, often referred to as alpha and beta. Within a pack, fighting is uncommon except during periods of stress, with the dominance order being maintained largely through ritualized behavior. Although pack size usually ranges from six to 12 animals, packs of as many as 20 to 30 wolves sometimes occur. Most wolf packs remain within a home territory almost exclusively theirs, only occasionally overlapping onto the ranges of neighboring packs. However, wolves primarily dependent on migratory caribou may temporarily abandon their home range and travel long distances if necessary. In Alaska, a packs' home range may cover distances from 200 to 600 square miles of wilderness.

Wolves are carnivores whose primary food in most of mainland Alaska is moose and/or caribou; they depend on Dall sheep in limited areas. In southeastern Alaska, blacktail deer and mountain goats are wolves' most important sources of food. During summer, wolves supplement their diet with small mam-

mals including voles, lemmings, ground squirrels, snowshoe hares, beavers, and occasionally birds and fish. The rate at which wolves kill large animals varies according to availability of prey and environmental conditions. In winter, a pack may kill a deer or moose every few days, while at other times they may go for days with almost no food. Since wolves are opportunistic, they prey more heavily on very young and old or diseased animals than other groups. However, under some circumstances, such as when snow is unusually deep, even animals in their prime may be vulnerable to wolves.

The author with a nice wolf pelt he took while on a caribou hunt in interior Alaska. Generally speaking, interior wolves are light colored, while southeast Alaska wolves are dark brown or black. (Photo by Adela Ward Batin)

Hunting Techniques

The current wolf hunting season in Alaska is from August 10 through April 30 in all areas except southeast Alaska, where there is no closed season. In most areas of the state, there is no limit on the number of wolves that can be taken. Wolf hunting is open to residents and non-residents alike, but hunting them the conventional way, by stalking them on the ground, can be a difficult proposition. The fact is, most hunters bag wolves incidentally to other big game species.

"It's really hard for a guide to find a pack of wolves for a hunter during the typical fall hunting season," says ADF&G Regional Game Director Dick Bishop. He said that few guides take clients hunting for wolf during the autumn months because the animals blend in too well with their surroundings.

"They are really hard to see in the autumn months," says guide Pat Witt, who hunts the eastern Brooks Range with his father, registered guide Gene Witt. Although the animals are abundant in his guide area, they are rather unpredictable. "Sometimes we run into them right on the trail or in camp. In fact, one hunter bagged an old wolf that walked into our spike camp, just like a dog looking for a handout."

Your chances of seeing a wolf on a big game hunt in Alaska depends on the area you hunt. Don't have great expectations. Witt said that although he is in a good wolf area, his hunters have bagged seven wolves and one wolverine in the last 17 years. Of course, few hunters choose not to pay for the extra days in camp pursuing wolf, but some do.

However, the best season and opportunity for a wolf trophy is during the winter months. That's when the animals sport a thick, heavy pelt. It's easy to locate a pack by using an airplane and following tracks in the snow. After the plane lands, the hunter must shoot quickly before the wolves disappear into heavy cover or run out of range. For this method of "hunting," called aerial trapping, you must have a trapping license.

Many veteran wolf hunters in the interior and western regions of Alaska prefer to hunt wolves from snowmachines. These hunts last for days and can cover up to 250 miles. Supply sleds filled with 40 or more gallons of gas, camping gear and food are pulled behind the snowmachines. It's a hard hunt, but the chance of bagging one or more wolves is good.

The main point for hunters to remember when hunting wolves is this: habitat suitable for ungulates is suitable for wolves. However, wolves do exhibit seasonal movements. For instance, wolves on the North Slope are uniformly distributed throughout the summer months. But late fall and winter finds them moving south toward the mountains of the arctic coast, following the caribou migrations. Wolves stay in the mountains for most of the winter and move back to their coastal territory in spring. In other parts of Alaska, particularly the northern game management units, wolf pack territories shift with caribou migrations.

The highly coveted, gray or white wolves are found in greater numbers as one goes north, above Yakutat. A hunter in search of a dark or black wolf should hunt the southern areas of the wolf's range, particularly southeast Alaska. Wolves there are smaller and darker than northern wolves. A black wolf mount is a stunning trophy.

The ticket to locating wolves in southeast Alaska is finding the prey base. This usually means blacktail deer, and generally speaking, where you find lots of deer, you find lots of wolves. Large numbers of wolves are on Prince of Wales Island, and in the Haines and Yakutat areas. But Kupreanof and Kuiu islands are experiencing low wolf numbers due to a severe decline in the local deer population, which, by the way, was not caused by the wolf population.

Old timers hunt wolves in southeast Alaska in several different ways that also work well in other parts of the state. The first is staking out a deer or moose kill above timberline. In the alpine country, you can construct a blind 100 to 200 yards away from the kill, and still be within effective rifle range. The best times to take stand are early morning or late evening; however, wolves do feed throughout the day, especially if enough carrion remains to entice them back. Research has shown that in a single feeding, a wolf gorges on meat. Its stomach, capable of great stretching, can weigh one-fifth of the wolf's body weight after it has finished eating.

Another popular method of hunting in fall and early winter

is to stake out a salmon spawning area. Wolves will frequent select streams to feed on spawning salmon. During the summer months, if you keep your eyes open when fishing these streams, and build a makeshift blind early enough to give the wolves plenty of time to get used to it—you set the stage for perhaps taking a wolf later in the year.

Snow machines and supply sleds are used in several western and northern Alaska wolf hunts. Expect to spend 10 to 14 days afield, with most of that being travel time. The going is tough, but the scenery and adventure is unsurpassed.

Some hunters call in wolves with an electronic predator call. This hunting method for wolves is still in its infancy, but has proven effective in areas with high wolf numbers. It's especially effective on young wolves, whose cunning has not yet been sharpened by hunting pressure. I've found that the Bill Anderson electronic call, when used with the snowshoe hare and "super bird" tapes, works extremely well in calling in all types of predators.

It's of vital importance that hunters report all wolves they've shot or harvested while afield. Biologists greatly need harvest data to regulate the wolf take and to help determine the populations of animals in other areas. By law, you are required to have your wolf hides sealed. Under a trapping license, you have 30 days after the end of the trapping season to get the hide sealed. If taken on a hunting license, you have up to 60 days from the date of kill to get the hide sealed. All hides must be sealed before being shipped from the state.

The major cause of mortality among wolves older than six months is harvest by humans. But this take is somehow compensated for by an increase in reproductive rates and greater survival of pups. Natives trap wolves as a source of income, using the pelts in the manufacture of various forms of clothing. Villagers of Anaktuvuk Pass use wolf fur around their caribou skin masks, a popular item for curio collectors the world over and an important industry in the village for over a decade.

The Alaska wolf is a trophy needing an investment of both time and money. Chances are you won't connect your first time out. But one thing is for certain. No other species exhibits the cunning shown by the wolf. And for that reason alone, most hunters think it's worth the effort.

Where to Hunt Wolf

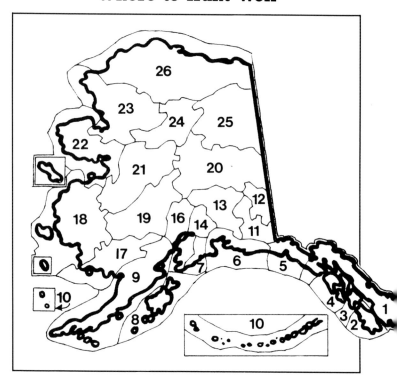

Units 1A, 2

Ketchikan and Prince of Wales

Trappers take the most wolves in Unit 1A. Recent harvest figures show from 8 to 25 wolves are harvested annually, with over half that amount taken incidentally and the others trapped. The take is scattered throughout the unit.

Units 1B, 3

Southeast Mainland from Cape Fanshaw to Lemesurier Point, Islands of the Petersburg, Kake and Wrangell areas

Hunters have reported seeing the most wolves in the Taku River, Berners Bay and Chilkat Range areas. They are also found on Zarembo and Kuiu islands. Populations in other areas appear to be stable. Recent harvest figures indicate that January and February are the most successful months to hunt wolves. However, they can be taken throughout the season.

Units 1C, 1D, 5

Juneau, Skagway, Yakutat

Look for wolves along the Chilkat River.

Unit 6

Cape Fairweather to Icy Bay

The wolf population east of Port Fidalgo to Icy Bay has increased substantially in recent years. Close to 100 wolves are estimated to be in Unit 6. Ten wolves were harvested in 1987-88. While most wolves were trapped in subunit 6C, wolves are likely to be found near mountain goat or moose populations in 6A, 6B or the eastern part of 6D.

Units 7, 15

Kenai Peninsula

Approximately 200 wolves are in this region. *They are highly mobile*, moving constantly in search of prey. Wolves essentially disappeared from the Kenai Peninsula after fires destroyed the caribou range and the caribou disappeared. They were re-established in 1960. The current sport harvest is about 50 wolves. The months of January, February and March show the greatest harvest.

Units 9, 10

Alaska Peninsula

Wolf harvest in Unit 9 has been relatively stable, averaging 23 wolves annually from 1962 to 1987. Approximately half the harvest comes from subunit 9E.

Unit 12

Tok, Wrangell, Mentasta and Nutzotin Mountains

The wolf population is high; estimated at 200 wolves. Ungulate species have suffered as a result of predation and heavy snows. The average harvest is upwards of 23 animals, but is not sufficient to control wolf numbers. The end of land and shoot taking of wolves in 1987 may reduce annual harvests.

Unit 13

Nelchina and Upper Susitna

Sport hunting accounts for roughly 65 percent of the wolf take in this unit. Most of the harvest occurs during the months of January and February, with November and December close runners-up.

Unit 17

Northern Bristol Bay

Area hunters and trappers have indicated an increase in wolf populations since 1981. Unit-wide harvests have fluctuated widely from 7 to 111 wolves per year. Poor snow conditions make wolf hunting extremely difficult throughout most of this unit.

Unit 18

Lower Kuskokwim

Possibly due to increasing ungulate populations in Unit 18, wolves are increasing in number. The current population is 25 to 50, mostly along the Yukon drainage, but also in the Kilbuck Mountains southeast of Bethel. Ten wolves were sealed in 1987-88. Wolf packs on the periphery of Unit 18 move in and out from bordering game management units.

Unit 19

Upper and Middle Kuskokwim Drainage

Based on limited surveys, there are at least 500 wolves in Unit 19. February and March are the most productive months for wolf hunters and trappers. Wolf populations are good and holding their own. It's a popular area for hunters, especially those after the Nixon Pack and the Big River pack. Some hunters prefer to hunt the Stony River area, the upper Innoko and upper Nowitna rivers.

Unit 20

Central Tanana Valley

Wolf numbers are increasing in this unit. Hunters and trappers concentrate efforts in subunit 20D south of the Tanana River. Unit-wide, the annual harvest varies from 69 to 125 wolves. This is one of the best areas to hunt wolves, with a third of the reported harvest taken by sporthunters and the other two-thirds taken by trappers. Current figures show about 1,000 wolves in this unit.

Unit 21

Middle Yukon

Successful wolf harvest in this region depends on weather conditions. Reports indicate populations are increasing. The highest number of wolves are harvested in years where flying and tracking conditions are excellent. Seventy-five percent or more of the wolf harvest is taken by the land-and-shoot method, when legal, during years of good flying weather. Biologists indicate the unit could withstand increased wolf harvest.

Unit 22

Seward Peninsula

Wolves numbers are relatively low for an area this size. However, ungulate species are high, and wolf numbers are expected to increase. They are most abundant in subunits 22A and the eastern part of 22B. The Koyuk, Shaktoolik, Ungalik and Unalakleet River systems contain nearly 75 percent of the wolves in this area. The take in this unit is usually incidental to other species.

Unit 23

Kotzebue Sound

As in Unit 22, most wolf hunting is done while hunting for other species or by Native villagers. Populations are believed to be increasing in Unit 23, but this can change depending on available food, weather conditions and hunting pressure. The banning of polar bear hunts by non-Natives also reduced the wolf take, as clients often combined that hunt with the possibility of taking a wolf. Harvest figures are elusive, as villagers often fail to comply with sealing requirements that help to manage wolf populations. In 1987-88, 93 wolves were sealed from Unit 23.

Unit 24

Koyukuk River Drainage

Wolf populations are abundant due to a high ungulate population, but only a minimal amount of sport hunting has been done to date.

Unit 25

Fort Yukon

Wolves are found in the major river valleys including the upper Wind, Chandalar, Sheenjek and Coleen. Caribou, the wolf's chief prey, are present in these valleys each fall and winter in varying numbers, depending on where they overwinter.

Unit 26

Arctic Slope

Wolves are concentrated in the mountains and foothills where moose, caribou and sheep are found. Wolves use valley bottom riparian habitat extensively to hunt and as a travel route to hunting areas.

CHAPTER 11

Bison

The bison is a living relic of the Old West. Hundreds of thousands of these great animals once thundered across the Great Plains, providing a spectacle that old timers used to talk about in glassy-eyed wonderment. To them, bison were "cattle of the early frontier." They were a favored food for mountain men and Indian alike. Mountain man literature is chock full of descriptions about bison "hump ribs" and "boudins," "fat cow" and "poor bull."

Indeed, to hunt bison today is to take a trip back in time, to mentally slip into the moccasins of Jeremiah Johnson. It's watching, as he did, the herds of bison move across fields, and employ all the skills of the mountain man to harvest such an awesome beast.

Yet, as is often the case with a plentiful resource, man's greed exploited the bison and reduced their numbers to stacks of salted hides and dried quarters of meat. Luckily, some of our forefathers realized the importance of the bison, and enacted strict conservation measures to keep them around. Today, they are holding their own in areas throughout the west, including Alaska. In a way, it's only fitting and proper that the bison should keep company with Alaska's other prestigious game animals in the "Last Frontier."

Life History and Habits

The bison, *Bison bison*, is one of the largest big game animals found in North America. It is often referred to as "buffalo" a word that, in its strictest sense, refers only to its relatives in Asia and Africa.

While the present-day bison is not a direct descendant from

Bison can be found in grainfields and muskeg areas throughout their range.

the "super bison" of the Tertiary Period, it is nevertheless an impressive animal. A full-grown bull stands five to six feet at the shoulder, is 9 to 9 1/2 feet long and can weigh more than 2,000 pounds. Full-grown cows are smaller, but have been known to weigh over 1,300 pounds. A bison's head and forequarters are so massive that they seem out of proportion to the smaller hindquarters. The characteristic "hump" is formed by a gradual lengthening of its back vertebrae beginning just ahead of the hips and reaching its maximum height above the front shoulder. From above the shoulder, the hump drops almost straight down to the neck.

The bison's headgear is simple when compared to that of caribou or moose. In both sexes, bison horns come straight out of the head and curve sharply upward. Males have larger and heavier horns than the females. If you're looking for a trophy-book mount, your bison needs to be between 9 and 12 years old.

Most hunters prefer to hunt bison late in the winter. Then, their coat is a rich, dark brown, getting progressively paler by spring. When the weather warms, the hair loosens and hangs in patches until it is completely shed and replaced by new hair.

In Alaska, female bison are sexually mature at two years of age, and normally give birth to single calves each year. The gestation period is approximately 270 days. Most bison are born in May, but the calving season usually extends from April to August. Newly born calves have a reddish coat. They are able to stand when only 30 minutes old; within three hours of birth they can run and kick their legs in the air. At about six days of age, calves start grazing. Their reddish brown coat begins to darken at about 10 weeks with the molt to dark brown complete about five weeks later.

Bison move slowly while feeding and appear to be quite clumsy. This is pure deception, for when pursued the bison is fast and has great endurance. A mature bull eventually captured at Delta Junction cleared a seven-foot log fence from a standing position (Johnson, 1978).

Bison in Alaska have been known to live to a relatively great age when compared to other hoofed mammals or ungulates. One tagged bull killed on the Copper River was found to be over 20 years old.

Alaska bison do not remain in herds, but scatter singly or in groups ranging up to 50 animals or more. They are highly migratory. Delta Junction area bison move far up the Delta River in early spring to secluded meadows where they calve. Around

August they travel back downstream, eventually moving into farming areas where they remain throughout the winter, often causing damage to unharvested crops. The Copper River herd is known to have a similar movement pattern.

Bison are grazing animals, one reason why they prefer the barley fields of the Delta area. In other areas, they find food along rivers and sedge potholes. Their diet is made up of reed grasses, various bluegrasses, ryegrass, and red-top grass. Peavine or vetch is a favored summer food found on gravel bars of the Delta and Tanana rivers. Sedges, silverberry, and ground birch are also eaten. According to biologist David Johnson, good bison range is limited in Alaska and it is unlikely that large numbers of bison could sustain themselves here.

In 1928, bison were transplanted from Montana to Alaska. About 20 animals were released in the open fields near Delta Junction, about 90 miles south of Fairbanks. The animals increased, and natural migration and transplants have created small herds at Healy Lake, Copper River, Chitina River and Farewell. Alaska currently has 600 to 800 bison.

Regretably, only a handful of Alaskans will ever be able to hunt bison within the state. With a limited number of permits for some areas, and other areas open to registration permit hunts, access to the bison is often extremely difficult. A recent application period for the Delta bison hunt, for instance, drew 3,533 applications for the 25 bull permits and 4,356 applications for the 50 cow permits. Of the 65 permits issued, 62 out of 64 actually hunted bison, and 64 bison were taken (one hunter shot three bison, and 6 hunters shot bison of the wrong sex). The Delta bison herd currently numbers from 275 to 300 animals, with a bull:cow ratio of 54:100. The total bison take provides over 40,000 pounds of meat for participating hunters.

Because hunters of Delta bison experience a high success rate, they prefer to apply for this area over the harder-to-hunt areas like Farewell and Chitina. After applying for the Delta hunt (the application fee is $10, and the drawing held in early summer) hunters who draw a permit are notified by ADF&G. Before hunting, bison permit holders must stop by the ADF&G office in Delta. The briefing includes a map showing land ownership, instructions on first obtaining permission from property owners to hunt on private lands, and sex identification of bison. The season starts the first week of October, and each permit holder is assigned a specific time period. A slot overlaps with those of other hunters. A survey indicates that hunters

Bison have a limited distribution in Alaska, yet are one of the most popular big game animals, drawing the most applications of any permit hunt. (Photo by Charles Kay)

spend about $290 each for food, lodging and transportation while hunting Delta bison.

There are advantages to hunting bison early in the season. The herd is usually less sensitive to hunters stalking through the fields. The weather is not as severe. The wind can howl up to 40 mph through the Delta area, creating wind chill factors 70 below and colder. It makes for difficult hunting, no matter how warmly you are dressed. In March, bison begin migrating out of the Delta area.

The most difficult part of a bison hunt is finding the animals. Hunters have spent hundreds of hours scouting prime bison range, and have not seen a bison all season. Others find them the first day out. Many hunters use aircraft, especially hunters pursuing bison in the Farewell area. Hunters will carefully chart the location of the herd, and land downriver from the animals. The next day, they'll stalk upriver and hunt them. When a bison is harvested, they use an inflatable to float the quarters downstream to the landing area. When bison are several miles away from the river system, hunting is more difficult.

In the Delta area, hunters cruise the backroads, glassing for bison from their vehicles. Your best bet is to contact ADF&G about the location of the herd, scout the area ahead of the season, and obtain permission to hunt likely areas. When the season opener rolls around, you can start hunting immediately.

Hunters are often suprised at how difficult it is to stalk bison. There is little cover in the fields. Gullies, hedgerows, haystacks, buildings, farm machinery and depressions are all useful for getting within shooting range. In the mid-1800s, a professional hunter would locate bison and initiate a stalk, using a gully or hill for concealment. Taking care to remain upwind, the hunter generally stalked to within 100 yards of a herd. Once the first bison was dropped, the herd rarely moved more than 150 feet before they began to feed again. If the hunter was cautious of the wind and stayed out of sight, he might expect to harvest over 100 bison a day. Do the same, and you might fill your tag.

My friend Richard Gardner and his wife Maureen learned how difficult it is to stalk bison. Last year, they drew a Delta bison permit. They were scheduled to hunt in November, well after the season opener. Richard and Maureen spent days scouting the fields for bison. For one reason or another, the bison were just not to be found or were inaccessible. Finally, after two weeks of effort, the bison were in the right location, and after a careful stalk, they managed to bag a large cow.

Once you're within range, choose your animal. Ascertain its sex to ensure compliance with your bull-only or cow-only permit. Do not shoot if your chosen bison is mingling closely with other bison. It's easy to miss and hit the wrong bison. Before taking your shot, wait until your trophy has moved off a ways, or the herd begins to disperse.

Bison are difficult to knock down. Unless you anchor them with a .338 or larger slug in the heart-lung area, they can run off, and keep going for miles. Forget the hump or neck shot. Chances are you'll only create a flesh wound. Head shots are out also. Bullets have been known to bounce off a bison's rock-hard head. If the bison doesn't go down and runs off with the herd, do not shoot into the herd! Chances are you might wound another bison. If you hit the animal solidly, he'll drop within 200 yards. Once the bison is down, immediately prepare yourself for other shots and take them if needed.

One advantage of hunting the Delta area is that local farmers are usually more than happy to offer the loan of their front loader or A-Frame to load your bison into the bed of your pickup. Hanging an animal this size sure makes quartering an easy task, especially in the dead of winter. A bison will yield about 1,200 pounds of meat, about 850 boned out. It is much like beef; marbled and delicious. It's common courtesy to share a quarter with the farmer for use of his land and gear. This action will ensure access rights for future bison hunters.

Don't forget the hide! A bison robe was a treasured possession of the mountain man of yesterday. It's worth having tanned and made into a blanket or bed spread. It will easily drape a king size bed, with plenty of hide left over for garments, if you so desire.

The bison is a big game species that few of us will ever have the opportunity to hunt. Until I get lucky enough to draw out on a Delta permit, or figure out the migration patterns of the Farewell herd, it's comforting to know that the opportunity to take a trip back in time to the mountain man era to hunt the majestic bison is still there.

Where to Hunt Bison

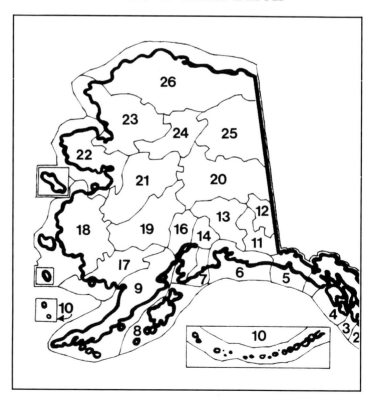

Unit 11

Copper River

Bison were transplanted here from the Delta herd in 1950. Approximately 90 bison make up the Copper River bison herd, classified as stable. Most of the herd is located near the Copper River, which makes this a popular hunting area. Riverboats are the most popular means of accessing this herd, used by 60 to 80 percent of successful and non-successful hunters. In 1986-87, successful hunters averaged 1.4 days afield. Hunters can find bison in the grasslands on the Copper River bluffs, or in the sedge-pothole country from the Nadina to Kotsina Rivers from October through May. It's important to note that all ranges are interconnected via a network of trails.

Unit 11

Chitina River

This herd currently numbers over 90 bison. In 1988, 418 hunters applied for the six permits. Most successful hunters use aircraft, while others use a riverboat as a main means of transportation. Bison potentially range from the mouth of the Tana River to the Chitina Glacier, along the Chitina River. Bison can frequently be found near Bear Island in both summer and winter.

Units 19C, D

South Fork of the Kuskokwim

The Farewell herd presently numbers about 300 animals. They are the result of two transplants: the first in 1965, when 18 bison were released at Farewell, and 20 more in 1968. The bison range in Unit 19 consists of approximately 30 miles of riverbars along the south fork of the Kuskokwim River, beginning 20 miles south of Farewell Lake, and extending a few miles into the Rohn and Hartman rivers. The bars have grasses and forbs that the bison require. In 1988, 40 drawing permit hunts were issued, 33 hunted, and 21 bison were harvested. This herd is growing and the number of permits will be increased as the herd increases. Bison continue to use the Farewell burn and the area between the South Fork and Post River. In an attempt to level off the herd's growth, 70 permits will be issued for the 1989-90 season. However, hunter access to this area is difficult.

Units 20A, 20D

Delta Area

The Delta bison herd currently numbers about 300 animals. This hunt is one of the most popular in the state. In 1988, over 9,600 applications were received for 50 available permits. Historically, hunter success exceeds 90 percent. These bison have been wintering in the Delta Aricultural Project, and are commonly found in the southeast corner adjacent to the Tanana River. They can also be found in the Clearwater farming area.

CHAPTER 12

Upland Birds—Ruffed Grouse

There are several similarities between the thunderbird of American Indian legend and Alaska's thunderbird, the ruffed grouse. The thunderbird of legend was a frightful creature that flew through the heavens, creating intense sieges of thunder and lightning at any time of day or night. As it flew, the bird supposedly created dark clouds that kept it from being viewed by earthly inhabitants.

Alaska's ruffed grouse also have a tendency to stay hidden from view. The few sightings hunters do get from these feathered bombshells are only glimpses of brown blurring as the birds skyrocket out of dense patches of willows and spruce thickets.

The subsequent thunder of beating wings can besiege the unsuspecting hunter with surprise, fright and confusion. The hunter usually reacts with a flurry of several wildly executed shots that seldom ruffle a feather on the fast-disappearing birds.

Indeed, Alaska's thunderbirds make crack shots look like amateurs, and keep the ammo manufacturing companies in business year after year. Yet despite these adversities, more and more hunters are going afield to experience the thunder of the ruffed grouse. They want excitement, and the ruffed provides just that.

Ruffed grouse occur in varying abundance in hillside woodlands and riverbottom thickets of the Yukon, Tanana, and Kuskokwim in the interior, and the upper Copper, Taku and Stikine rivers of southcentral and eastern Alaska. Ruffed grouse favor stands of birch and cottonwood with an occasional spruce thicket. There they'll look for aspens and willow buds, berries and insects. Conifers provide the shelter the birds require, especially during the winter months.

Mike Bradley is all smiles with this interior ruffed grouse (left) and bonus spruce grouse. In most areas of the state, hunters delight in a 15-grouse-per-day bag limit. But don't be fooled! Alaska ruffs are just as hard to hit as ruffs found elsewhere in the Lower 48.

During a long Alaska winter, ruffed grouse prefer dense stands of conifers for protection against wind and cold. They come out to feed during the few hours of daylight, usually between 10 a.m. and 2 p.m.

Like other grouse, ruffed grouse populations are subject to cyclic fluctuations. In Alaska, ruffs seem to peak every 7 to 9 years. Populations were high in the early 1960s, bottomed-out in the late 60s, and peaked again in the early 70s. The 1988 season saw an abundance of birds available to hunters. I spent far too many hours away from my desk grouse hunting that good year. But a hunter can burn up half a box of shells and have no birds to show for his efforts.

Description

In Alaska, the ruffed comes in two color phases: red and gray. The red phase is generally a subspecies called the Oregon ruffed grouse, whose range extends as far north as Alaska. However, the Alaska red phase coloration is less pronounced than the ruffed grouse I've hunted on the East Coast. I've yet to bag a red-phase ruff here in Alaska, although I have seen photos of reddish birds taken by fellow hunters in the southern part of the state. All the ruffs I bag in Alaska are the gray phase. This is a subspecies known simply as the gray ruffed grouse.

It's interesting to note that both color phases can be found in one family group. Biologists now believe that when snow is on the ground for long periods of time—a common occurence here in Alaska, the gray birds have an advantage over the red ones. Predators kill fewer gray birds. This may explain why the gray phase dominates in Alaska.

Ruffs are distinguishable from other grouse by the crest of feathers on their crowns. This crest is larger on the males, and slightly smaller on the hens. However, it is almost impossible to distinguish between male and female except by dissection. Ruffs also have a dark band near the tip of each tail feather. This dark band is absent in the two center tail feathers in all females and in some males. An adult measures about 18 inches long and weighs about 1½ to 2 pounds. The female is a bit smaller and seldom weighs more than 17 to 22 ounces.

Little study has been done on the ruffed grouse in Alaska. It's Latin name, *Bonasa umbellus umbellus*, describes the bird well. *Bonasa* means bison, a term early ornithologists used to liken the ruff's spring drumming to the distant thundering of a herd of bison. *Umbellus* means umbrella, describing a neck ruff that can be raised and lowered like an umbrella.

Life History

Despite the bird's popularity, only a handful of nests in Alaska have been found and reported. Most of the population data come from hunter questionnaire and fall roadside counts.

The life cycle is like that of other grouse. Males begin their "drumming," caused by air rushing through the rapidly beating wings. This noise attracts females and serves as a challenge to rival males.

Hens like to nest away from the male's drumming site, preferring the safety of a stump, a fallen tree, or a thicket of brush, especially if it's located along the edge of a forest opening. After mating occurs, the hen lays from 10 to 11 eggs. The young hatch in about three weeks and quickly leave the nest with the hen. Along the woodland fringe, broods search out and feed on a variety of plants and insects. In late September, the birds disperse in what's known as the "fall shuffle." However, groups of six to 10 ruffed grouse spend weeks together throughout the winter.

Predation on grouse is extremely high, with snowy and great horned owls, hawks, and lynx the chief predators. Probably only three out of every 100 eggs produce ruffed grouse to be bagged by sportsmen. I'm sure the same holds true for other grouse species.

I have a special liking for ruffed grouse because I can see them regularly in my front yard. Situated in a birch forest in the hills outside Fairbanks, my home is in perfect ruffed grouse country. Looking out my office window one spring, I saw a ruffed grouse strutting in my driveway. I eased outside for a closer look. At my approach, the bird flared his tail and started to bob his head and peck at gravel and nearby branches. I saw the bird had some spunk, but I didn't realize its extent until he flew directly at me, missing my head by a scant few inches. The grouse landed directly behind me, and again began strutting. I didn't want to tangle with him again. For the next week, the driveway was his.

Hunting Methods

Hunting ruffed grouse can be as simple as driving backroads, or as complex and enjoyable as spending the afternoon with a Brittany spaniel in the birch/aspen hillsides overlooking the Tanana River.

I detest road hunting: it's for hunters too lazy to get out and bust the brush. Too many hunters ride the roads, stop when they see grouse collecting grit, and powder the birds on the ground. In many areas of the state, ruffs are not leery of humans, and birds of the year are perhaps too trusting. Moreover, it's illegal to shoot birds from the road. Furthermore, shooting grouse from the road is downright disgusting. I've severed several hunting friendships because of the hunters' adherence to this unethical practice. And I'll turn in anyone I catch in the act. They are slaughterers and I want no part of them. It is the only situation that I wish the birds could shoot back. Enough. Now with that sermon out of the way, let's proceed with how to hunt ruffs in their wooded environment.

If I find grouse on a back road, I'll first flush them, then pursue them in their wooded environment. There, split-second shots are necessary and misses more frequent than kills. This is a sporting and enjoyable way to hunt ruffed grouse.

Grouse frequent alder, willow and spruce thickets of river-bottoms throughout interior Alaska. Look for stands of relatively new trees, bordered by older timber growth. Birds migrate back and forth from shelter in the big trees to their food and water supplies in the new growth along the water's edge. Look for grouse around tangles of alders bordering old clearings, around new conifer growths and at the edges of marshes. The smart grouse hunter looks for these areas with good crops of bog blueberry, lowbush and highbush cranberry, ground dogwood, and rosehip and avoids areas lacking these food items. Hunt likely areas at grouse feeding times: early in the morning and late in the afternoon.

Dogs that can stay close and obey commands work extremely well on grouse. But dogs are much like hunters: rarely is there one that lasts an entire day of grouse hunting without at least once getting scatter-brained and ranging too far.

When hunting grouse, remember that a slow, steady pace is better than a fast, erratic one. If you're lucky enough to see a grouse on the ground, walk up to it at an angle. The grouse may think you will pass it, and allow you to get closer than if you walked straight up on it.

Always be looking for the potential flight path the grouse

will take. They usually fly through the densest cover available. However, they'll often fly straight up to clear the tangles before rocketing down or across the hillside. You should fire right at the bird's apogee. If the woods are noisy with just-fallen leaves, grouse may flush far ahead. Under these conditions, wait until a rain or first dusting of snow to quiet things down a bit.

During the winter months, ruffed grouse can be more difficult to find; that's why few hunters pursue grouse in the winter months. I share with you a piece of wisdom concerning the ruffed grouse: to find birds, you must walk, and walk, and walk. There's no other way. If you're a smart bird hunter, occasionally you'll hunt in the afternoon. Then you can intercept grouse leaving their daytime roosts in the snow to feed in the tops of aspen and willow trees. Due to mid-winter darkness (interior Alaska has about four and a half hours of winter daylight) much time is spent scouting, and little time shooting. It's no wonder that interior grouse hunters are so secretive about their wintertime grouse hunting hotspots.

Expect to flush grouse by concentrating on stands of spruce and alders, or downfall offering birds protection from predators. Again, the birds can be found near the same food types available to them in the autumn. Look for these and you'll find grouse. Once November rolls around, deep snows will quickly tire the most toughened bird hunter. Grouse hunting then usually becomes a snowshoe sport. It's work, yet it's one of my favorite winter activities. Experienced skiers use cross-country skis effectively.

Ruffed grouse hunting offers the bounty of the autumn harvest, the tangy scent of newly fallen birch leaves and the sweet taste of bog blueberries. It offers a target without equal in Alaska's hardwoods, and the thunder of wings symbolizing the wilderness that Alaskans love so much. Once indoctrinated into the sport of ruffed grouse hunting, the hunter is a disciple for life.

Where to Hunt Ruffed Grouse

The ruffed grouse is concentrated in the major river systems located throughout Alaska's interior. The bird has an affinity for hardwood stands, and occupies far fewer square miles than the spruce grouse, mainly because its chosen habitat is less widespread.

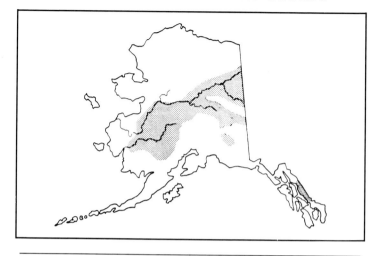

Unit 1

Panhandle

Limited numbers of ruffed grouse occur along mainland river drainages from the Unuk River north to Haines.

Unit 11

Wrangell Mountains—Chitna River, Nelchina

Grouse are found along the drainages of the Copper River near Chitina, north to Paxson, and northeast to Slana.

Units 18, 19, 21

Yukon-Kuskokwim, McGrath and Middle Yukon

Grouse are found along the river bottomlands of the Yukon and Kuskokwim drainages.

Unit 20

Fairbanks

Good to excellent populations of ruffed grouse occur throughout Unit 20. A great portion of the harvest occurs incidental to other recreational activities.

Units 24, 25

Koyukuk, Fort Yukon

Birds can be found along drainages of the upper Koyukuk and upper Yukon rivers.

Spruce Grouse

How the spruce grouse has survived in the wild for over 10,000 years is an illogical mystery. Unlike the ruffed or sharptail that will flush in a thundering roar when the hunter is 30 or more yards away, the spruce grouse sits and clucks at the approaching hunter. In fact, spruce grouse usually refuse to fly. But when they can be coaxed to take to wing—either with a swift kick or a thrown stick—spruce grouse often fly into the nearest tree and light on a branch no more than six to 10 feet off the ground. From there the grouse continues to watch the intruder, all the while pacifying itself with a series of clucks.

Early explorers used to hunt these birds with sticks, or more easily with a noose tied at the end of a long pole. People have even caught spruce grouse with their bare hands. This bird's seeming stupidity usually manifests itself in late summer and fall when the birds gather grit along gravel roads. Slob hunters drive the roads in early-morning hours, looking to blast the birds on the ground. These unethical hunters are missing out on real sport. When hunted away from the road and shot on the wing, the spruce grouse offers virtually the same excitement and wingshooting thrills as that of its cousin, ol' ruff.

Spruce grouse, *Dendragapus canadensis*, is easily distinguishable from other grouse by the rusty band on the outer fringes of its tail. However, spruce grouse found in southeastern Alaska lack the broad, brownish tip on the end of the tail, and are considered a separate subspecies called Franklin's grouse.

Spruce grouse require extensive stands of mature coniferous forests consisting of white spruce/paper birch woodlands, black spruce bogs, and in southeastern Alaska, Sitka spruce/hemlock forests. They are not found north of the Brooks Range, on the tip of the Seward Peninsula, in the Yukon-Kuskokwim Delta region, the Alaska Peninsula south of Becharof Lake, or on Kodiak and many other major islands.

Life History

The male begins his courtship strutting in mid-April, to attract hens and establish territory. By May, the males resort to aerial displays and expand their territory to roughly one acre. The hen lays five to nine eggs under a spruce tree or beneath a log. Hatching occurs in mid-June, about the same time the males stop their courting. While males don't assist in nesting or brooding, they often join the hens and chicks in late August or September. Oftentimes a single male associates with several

hens and their broods.

The groups usually dissolve in October, as the birds dissipate into dense stands of spruce. Because their winter diet is rich in fibrous spruce needles, spruce grouse will travel several miles to obtain grit. These migrations to obtain grit are the longest in the bird's life. Their grit-finding areas are riverbanks, dried-up stream beds, abandoned logging trails, and near the shores of gravel-bottomed lakes. Those are the places to find grouse. This fact holds true, especially during late autumn and early winter months when the grouse consume a large amount of grit.

Winter is a laid-back time for the spruce grouse that spends most of its time in spruce trees, feeding, resting or just loafing. The spruce trees not only offer protection from predators, but also from the cold winds and storms commonplace in Alaska. With the arrival of spring and subsequent melting of snow, spruce grouse leave their roosts and search out rose hips, cranberries and blueberries that have persisted throughout the winter.

Other areas where I find spruce grouse are sections of dense spruce bordering open swamps, old burn areas and south-facing hillside ridges with draws of alder thickets. However, if I want to assure myself of some real action, I search out the berry patches.

Spruce grouse, like all Alaska grouse, consume a wide variety of berries. In a bird's crop, I most often find lowbush and highbush cranberries, blueberries, crowberries, ground dogwood, and rosehips. Areas laden with such fruit hold birds until the deep snows hit; then the birds feed on buds and spruce needles.

Hunting Techniques

Grouse may sit tight early and late in the season, often allowing the hunter to walk by without the bird flushing. At first, a human may think no grouse are in the area, while in reality, the hunter did not hunt the area properly by producing enough alarm in the birds to cause them to flush.

At times like this, hunting pace is extremely important. Because their habitat has many predators such as lynx, marten and fox, grouse are leery of any slow-moving creatures. The hunter can use this suspicion as an aid in flushing the birds. A slow, steady pace with frequent stops usually makes the birds nervous enough to flush within close range of the hunter.

Also I've found it important to work my ears as well as my eyes when hunting grouse. I almost always hear a grouse flush before I spot it. Once my ears pick up the unmistakable whir

When hunted from gravel roads, spruce grouse offer little sport. But when pursued in thick cover, they equal the ruffed grouse in terms of challenging wing-shooting opportunities. Look for spruce grouse near gravel roads and lake beds where they can be found collecting grit.

Spruce grouse are aptly named. Hunters can usually find good populations of these birds in dense stands of spruce and birch timber. The best areas to hunt are those with a lush, berry understory.

of wings, my eyes and gun focus on the source of the sound. As I identify the bird as a grouse, I poke my shotgun through the brush and fire in one fluid movement. Spruce grouse hunting in thick timber is no place for any fancy shooting style. It's very fast shooting, rarely lasting more than a second; dense timber usually prevents any type of long shot. In fact, I'd say that the majority of the birds I harvest are within 25 yards.

Once I put a bird up and miss it or fail to spot it, I listen intently to determine the direction in which it has flown. After it's been kicked up in thick cover, a grouse usually flies short distances, oftentimes landing on a tree branch. The bird is more difficult to flush a second time, and is often content to watch a hunter pass by from a lofty spruce bough. So, check the lower and middle sections of spruce and birch trees for an added advantage.

Spruce grouse hunting is often hard work. But on a beautiful autumn day, when the winey aroma of cottonwood fills the air amidst falling yellow leaves, and ripe red berries color the forest floor, there are few sports to equal the satisfaction a grouse hunter experiences after such a day afield—especially with a plump spruce grouse in the game vest for supper.

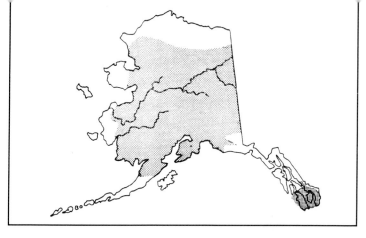

Where to Hunt Spruce Grouse

Spruce grouse are widespread throughout much of mainland Alaska. This bird is found from Nova Scotia to Alaska, and from Michigan to the Northwest Territories. Yet biologists are mystified as to why the birds have never tried to pioneer the northern forests of Siberia. In fact, none of North America's grouse, nor any of Eurasia's, have naturally established colonies on other continents.

Units 1 — 4

The spruce-hemlock forests on the mainland south of Unuk River, Revillagigedo and Prince of Wales islands have low to moderate numbers of spruce grouse.

Unit 6

Birds are common along the Gulf Coast and in Prince William Sound. The species does not range east of Icy Bay. Some harvest occurs along the gravel roads near Copper River Highway.

Units 7, 15

Spruce grouse are taken in coniferous woodlots and along the secondary roads throughout this region, especially the Kenai Peninsula and Skilak Lake Loop Road.

Units 9, 17

Spruce grouse are found throughout most of the Alaska Peninsula and north of the Naknek River drainages in Unit 17.

Units 11, 13, 14

Spruce grouse are mainly hunted from roads in these units, including the backroads leading into the Chugach Mountains.

Units 18, 19, 21

Most birds are taken along the Kuskokwim and Yukon River systems. Spruce grouse are more numerous in units 19 and 21 than 18.

Units 22, 23

The southeastern side of the Seward Peninsula offer good holding areas for spruce grouse, as do the drainages of the Noatak and Kobuk River systems.

Units 24, 25, 26

Most birds in these regions are taken along the drainages of the upper Koyukuk and Yukon rivers by Natives. Most spruce grouse harvested are used for subsistence purposes.

Sharptail Grouse

Northern sharptail grouse, *Tympanuchus phasianellus*, is perhaps the most coveted of the Alaska grouse. Found throughout the northern parts of Canada and select areas within Alaska, it is the hardiest of all the sharptail species. Yet locating sharptails is perhaps the most difficult aspect of hunting grouse. It took three years of hunting before I bagged my first Alaska sharptail. I remember it well.

My brother Joe and I drove to Tok one morning specifically in search of sharptails. We spent the good part of the morning four-wheelin' the backroads, periodically getting out and scouting suitable habitat. The action wasn't slow by any means. I had bagged a ruffed and a spruce grouse, and Joe had bagged a spruce grouse and missed a ruffed. I was two-thirds the way toward my "Grand Slam" of interior grouse. Yet I couldn't find any sharptails. I was getting antsy. It was already 1 p.m. and would be getting dark soon.

We opted to hunt another ridgetop located across a small gully. As we walked the crest of the ridge to some grousy looking cover, a brown bombshell rocketed across the ridge and flew down into a small basin. Joe and I ran over to the ridge and found a grouse sitting atop a tall spruce tree, clucking admonitions at us. It was a sharptail, and a beauty at that.

"Shoot it out of the tree with this," my brother said, offering me his .22 rifle. "You'll never get close enough to that bird to make a shot. And if you do, as worked up as you're getting, you might miss."

"Can't do it," I replied. "You know the ground rules. They have to be flying."

I inserted a special trap load into the chamber of my shotgun and inched my way down a shallow gully that led to the basin. When I was about 100 yards away, the grouse's neck stiffened, and his head began to jerk around. The bird was giving me the eye, trying to gauge if I was a threat to his welfare or just passing through.

Two feet from the bottom of the gully, the crusted snow I was walking on caved in, crumpling me to the ground. Immediately the grouse flushed from the tree. Still falling, I snapped off a shot, hoping for the best, but expecting the worst.

To this date I believe that it was mental telepathy rather than my load of 7 1/2s that brought that grouse down. My brother thinks otherwise, saying the bird died from laughing too hard at my "professional" stalk. To me, the bird was the center of attraction: It was a mature male in full plumage. The full effect of the Grand Slam hit home. I began jumping around, all excited. I've made other Grand Slam hunts since, but bagging that sharptail was one of the most exciting grouse hunts I've ever been on. And sharptails can offer you the same type of fun also.

Sharptails, also known as speckled chickens by interior hunters, were not always hard to find. Records suggest that the birds were much more abundant in the 1920s and 1930s. At that time, frequent and widespread wildfires burned over large expanses of the Tanana and Yukon River valleys. The birds thrived in the subsequent grasses and short shrubs that soon followed the fires. This "prairie" type of environment was soon closed in by successive plant growth and timber, which sharptails can't tolerate. Today, hunters can find birds on select "domes" or hilltops near Fairbanks, Eielson Air Force Base and Donnelly Dome. The Tanacross-Tok-Northway area is another good area for sharptails as are the brushy flatlands around Delta Junction.

Description and Life History

Male sharptails will weigh about 1½ pounds, with hens being slightly smaller. Coloration is about the same in both sexes, with the exception of the tail feathers. The central pair of tail feathers on the male is longitudinally barred, while the female's is cross-barred. Also, the male's breast feathers exhibit a pointed, instead of rounded, black band. They are easily identified from other grouse by the narrow, stiff, dun-colored tail and long neck.

Courtship begins in late April or early May. The males perform a dancing courtship display on communal dancing or booming grounds. The sight is impressive. Males vie for the attention of the hens by inflating the air sacs on their necks and making a "Boooooom! Booooom!" sound that often reverberates through the nearby forests. Along many gravel roads, they do this about an hour before sunrise and prior to sunset. Males may collect and mate with several females, who locate the nest far away from the "booming" grounds. The hen lays anywhere from 10 to 16 eggs in a thinly lined nest sheltered in clumps of grass or brush. Once hatched, the brood spends the summer feeding on berries, grass seeds, grains, buds and insects. In late fall, flocks are formed, and the hens and young wander considerable distances away from the breeding areas. The males, on the other hand, remain near their display areas throughout the winter.

Hunting Techniques

During the winter months, hunters can find sharptail grouse by searching out their food supply. Look for paper birch catkins, clumps of grass and grass seeds, willow and thickets, berries and fields of waste barley.

The birds are difficult to hunt due to their wariness and low population densities. They also have a tendency to flush at extreme ranges, making a 12-gauge with a full-choke barrel a matter of necessity, especially during the late autumn and winter months.

Hunting techniques and strategy are basically the same as hunting ptarmigan in alpine and sub-alpine habitat. In fact, during the winter months, smaller flocks of sharptails frequent the same wind-blown countryside as willow ptarmigan. Both species burrow into the loose snow for protection against temperatures that may drop to 50 below zero.

I cherish the sharptail grouse, and thus, won't reveal all the secret hotspots and techniques used to take it. Go out and bag your first sharptail, and you'll know what I mean. It is a special species of grouse.

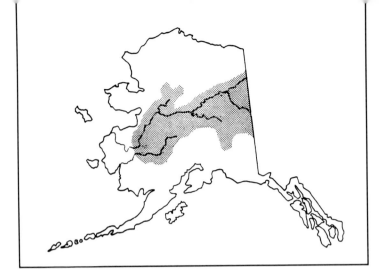

Range of the sharptail grouse in Alaska. Interior valleys and their foothills harbor practically all of the state's sharptail grouse. Occasionally, a stray shows up on the Kenai Peninsula. The species is also found in the Yukon and extreme northern Alberta.

Where to Hunt Sharptails

Units 11, 13

Small numbers of sharptails are found in the brushy grasslands along the upper Copper River from near Chitina and north to Slana.

Unit 12

Fair to good populations of grouse can be found here. The birds are found along the Alaska Highway from Tanacross to Northway.

Unit 20

Low to moderate numbers of birds occur along the Tanana River and Minto Flats.

Units 19, 21

Birds can be found on the Innoko River Flats and along the middle Yukon River.

Unit 22

Sharptail grouse have been sighted along the Ninkluk River.

Units 24, 25

Look for birds along the upper Koyukuk and Yukon rivers.

Blue Grouse

In early spring, a blue grouse hunt can be a very pleasurable experience. Enjoy it like a fine wine: slowly and with all the senses. You start on a clear-blue-sky spring morning. As you enter the forest, you'll smell the subtle bouquet of hemlock and cedar; taste the crisp, fruity flavor of winter-wizened huckleberries still hanging on the branch; and you'll study the rich, dark color of 300-year-old forests. After enjoying serving after serving of this fine vintage of Mother Nature's, intoxication doesn't come in the form of a mellowed, relaxed feeling. It comes in the form of thundering wings, a rush of adrenaline and subsequent rapid heartbeat, and then a snap shot. Whether or not you end up with a grouse in hand is immaterial. All the qualities of blue grouse hunting are what make it a pleasant addiction, one that hunters, myself included, partake in year after year.

Description

The Blue grouse, *Dendragapus obscurus*, is a species of grouse that occurs in the wet, dense coastal conifer forests stretching from Glacier Bay south to Ketchikan. It is the largest upland gamebird in the state: adult males sometimes reach up to 3½ pounds. The males, favored by bird collectors, are easily distinguished by the gray band running along the tip of a blackish tail. Females are about a third smaller than males and much browner in color. In the spring, the males develop on each side of their necks orange-yellow air sacs encircled with a rim of white feathers. The birds inflate these sacs to produce a loud "hoot" that can be heard up to a mile away, thus the name "hooter." The sound made by someone blowing across the top of a large bottle gives you some idea of what to listen for. Most hunters pursue the blue grouse during the hooter season.

Life History

We know very little about the blue grouse in Alaska. Courtship activities begin in April, starting with the male's hooting to attract a female. By late May, she lays a clutch of 7 to 10 eggs in a feather-and grass-lined nest. Throughout the summer, hens and chicks can be found near edges of swamps and muskegs, road edges and timber clearings. Near timberline, goat hunters encounter large families of blue grouse, feeding on the ripe bounty of berries and insects. However, with the approach of winter snows, blue grouse move down into the timbered areas

for cover. For the remainder of the winter, they subsist almost entirely on needles and the buds of conifers, supplemented with occasional rosehips, blueberries and huckleberries.

A hunter must be in top physical condition to hunt blue grouse in their high mountain habitat successfully. While few hunters do pursue blues during the fall and early winter months, most prefer to wait for the "hooting" season. Then, it's easier to locate birds that are calling from the top of tall evergreens near timberline. Even so, accumulated snow makes for difficult climbing, and few hunters participate in the sport.

Hunting Techniques

A father and son team in Juneau, Alaska, has developed an excellent strategy for hunting blue grouse. The son carries a .22 rifle; the father, a 20 gauge pump. After they walk through the spruce-hemlock forests to timberline, they abide by their grand plan of hooter hunting. It goes like this: with his shotgun, the father can take any and all birds that take to wing. Those that don't fly after repeated attempts to flush them with thrown sticks and moss clods are fair game for the boy's .22. At day's end, it's the boy who usually carries more birds home.

I attribute the blue's seeming lack of caution to the fact that they are seldom hunted. Just like ruffed or spruce grouse in wilderness areas, the blue will sit on a log or atop a tree, looking down at the hunter in tragic innocence. Yet, in areas that are hunted hard, the blue grouse turns into a whirling, heart-stopping projectile as it flushes in a flurry of noisy wings, rocketing its way through the conifers. Yet hit or miss, veteran blue grouse hunters, myself included, live for such moments, whether in the spring or the fall hunting season.

During the winter months, blue grouse enter a semi-dormant state. They fly to the top of evergreens, where they roost for days at a time, moving only to nip a helping of spruce or pine needles. Hunters traveling through the alpine areas rarely see blues at this time. This is just as well. In winter, the grouse's flesh is often obnoxiously strong, like pine tar.

During the spring "hooter" season, smart hunters utilize Forest Service trails to reach prime grouse hunting areas. They spend a night or two in one of the Forest Service cabins in the area. The cabins offer both a comfortable base camp in which to spend the night, and a prime location to listen for "hooters." You'll know hooting when you hear it. Most hunters prefer to rise early, and be in the woods by first light.

Once you're in the conifers, the flurry of hoots can confuse you. It takes a trained ear to pinpoint the exact tree in which blues are hooting. Just listen carefully, pinpoint the noise as best you can, and walk slowly to that general vicinity. I prefer to use binoculars and glass the conifers bordering the edges of clearings or muskeg. Trying to pinpoint the silhouette of individual birds is fine, but you'll find more birds by looking for movement. If the wind is blowing, look for a flash of white. This comes from the underlying feathers of the neck, and is easy to spot with binoculars.

Once you locate the tree the grouse is in, the next step is to find the bird in the complex maze of tree branches and con-ifer needles. I have observed that blues prefer the downhill side of the tree. There, they can better project their "hoots" out over the hillside and valleys, for all hens and rival males to hear. On a south-facing slope, look for trees that are bathed in sunlight. The birds love to sun themselves while hootin' it up. And the sunlit part of a tree is most commonly its up-per third.

When stalking blue grouse, keep talking to a minimum; your voice can quiet the birds for an indefinite period of time. Also, when approaching a blue, avoid walking directly up to the tree. Keep a short distance away. Not only will you lessen your chances of spooking the bird, but also you'll be in a better position to see and shoot if you stay to the side rather than directly downhill. Some hunters carry a beer bottle and blow across it, creating a hooting noise that often elicits hoots from blues. However, I prefer a half-gallon or gallon jug, as it gives a deeper hoot.

Blue grouse may not receive the attention accorded the ruffed and spruce grouse, but these stately birds of the southeastern rain forest offer hunting exitement and exercise sans pareil! Give a "hoot" this spring and try it yourself!

Where to Hunt Blue Grouse

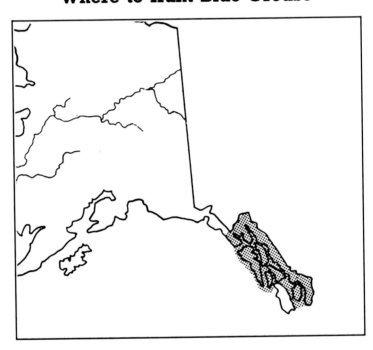

The blue grouse is a bird of the dense coastal forests of the Panhandle, or of alpine meadows and lowland muskegs within this region.

Units 1, 3, 4

Blue grouse can be found throughout Units 1, 3 and 4. They are absent from Prince of Wales Island. Individual sightings have spotted the birds as far north as the Dangerous River near Yakutat. Unlike the cyclic populations of interior grouse and ptarmigan, blue numbers are relatively stable throughout their range. Some of the best blue grouse hunting in the state takes place north of Juneau, from Montana Creek to Davies Creek.

Willow Ptarmigan

The willow ptarmigan, *Lagopus lagopus*, is to Alaska what the pheasant is to South Dakota. Both are state birds, and both are extremely popular with sportsmen. Unlike the pheasant, however, the willow ptarmigan is believed to be indigenous to North America. If fact, you could say that ptarmigan were one of the northcountry's first settlers. Fossils indicate that the ptarmigan's ancestors go back as far as 40 million years. More recent relatives adapted to the Ice Age and have evolved into the smallest grouse found in North America. Ptarmigan are the only grouse on this continent that change to a completely different plumage in winter.

Since the Ice Age, ptarmigan have spread out, and now are indigenous to virtually all of Alaska—from tundra to rugged timberline, places where few other upland gamebirds can survive. And ptarmigan are prolific: flocks of 100 or more birds are quite common at certain times of the year. So, it's no wonder that sportsmen consider the willow ptarmigan Alaska's premier upland gamebird.

Description

The plumage of the willow ptarmigan changes with the seasons. In winter garb, only another ptarmigan can distinguish between cocks and hens. Then, both sexes are an ivory white with black tails. However, it's different during the rest of the year. Beginning in early May, the cocks develop a beautiful cape of chestnut-red feathers. The cocks court the hens in this plumage, not completing the change to the brown, summer plumage until the hens have finished incubating their clutches of eggs. Immediately after the male gets this first set of feathers, then a new generation of lighter brown feathers grows on his neck and breast. This new set is never completed. In early August, the cock begins growing his winter plumage, and the cycle repeats itself.

Life History

Like other ptarmigan, the willow ptarmigan nests in sparsely timbered or treeless areas. Throughout March and April, cocks become increasingly intolerant of each other as they claim parcels of ground. Some shifting and changing of boundaries takes place, but in May, the birds have established permanent territories that they defend vigorously. Hens arrive on the breeding grounds up to two weeks later than males. They

select their nests (often the same one used the previous year) and a mate. By late May hens have laid six or more eggs and have started incubating them. Cocks go through an intense strutting, tail fanning and aerial chasing ritual that gradually diminishes as the hens take to their nests. Chicks usually hatch in late June or early July.

Male willow ptarmigan usually help care for the chicks, a habit no other North American grouse or ptarmigan practices. Cocks will often take over all family responsibility if the hen is killed (Weeden, Ellison, 1968).

The mortality rate of young ptarmigan is quite high. Inclement weather, predators and disease usually kill 65 to 80 percent of all chicks before they are 11 months old. As adults, ptarmigan fare better. Mortality is about 50 to 60 percent per year. A four-year-old ptarmigan is indeed a lucky bird.

Hunters don't understand why hundreds of ptarmigan can be found one year, and few the next. Weeden (1968) writes that the abundance of ptarmigan at any time depends on the extent of losses and the success of reproduction during the previous two years. Ptarmigan numbers can build up with astonishing speed, given favorable conditions, but they decline just as rapidly.

Families of willow ptarmigan form large flocks in early August and September. A month or so later, ptarmigan migrate: the males and females tend to separate. In much of Alaska, ptarmigan migrations range between a few miles to about 20 or 30 miles. Small groups of females generally seek food and shelter at the lower altitudes. However, hens nesting or reared on the North Slope of the Brooks Range move up to 150 miles south. They'll overwinter in the valleys of the Noatak and Kobuk rivers, or in the wooded valleys north of the Yukon River. Males also abandon their summer range, but do not travel as far as females. Southbound migrations take place in September, October and November: northward movements begin in February, peak in April, and are finished by late May. Huge northbound flocks, perhaps created by the funneling effect of river valleys and narrow mountain passes, rapidly disintegrate when the summering areas are reached. Until then, a hunter may encounter several hundred, or perhaps even thousands of birds per flock. Wingshooting is spectacular.

Where to Hunt Willow Ptarmigan

Range of Willow Ptarmigan in Alaska. Willow ptarmigan have the widest range of any upland gamebird, with rock ptarmigan a close second. The only areas in Alaska without willow ptarmigan are the broad, forested valleys of the interior, (but even there you can sometimes find willow ptarmigan in winter) and the forests of southeast Alaska. The same species also lives in Canada, Scotland, Scandinavia and Russia.

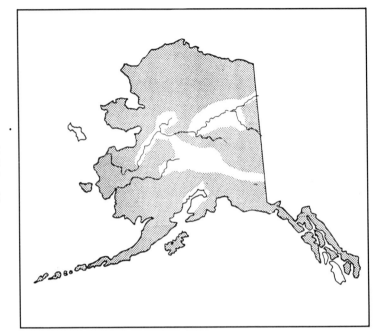

Throughout Alaska, willow ptarmigan are easily accessible by road. However, most of the huge flocks of 300 or more can be seen only in backcountry areas via fly-out or snowmachine. But you can find small flocks of 20 to 50 birds along major alpine roadways. Several trails lead to ptarmigan country from the state capitol in Juneau. Starting at about Mile 60 out of Haines, Alaska, the Alaska Highway offers excellent ptarmigan hunting across the entire nine-month season. Another good ptarmigan hotspot is the Richardson Highway from Valdez through the mountains. Many hunters prefer the grassy openings on hillsides and in open, swampy areas between Willow and Palmer and throughout the Susitna River Valley. Of course, the Richardson Highway from Black Rapids to Paxson offers world-class ptarmigan hunting, especially during the winter months. Farther north, willow ptarmigan appear along the Nome road system, and at various places above timberline between the Steese and Taylor highways.

If you're looking for a true wingshooter's vacation, try a fly-in hunt for willow ptarmigan. "Legendary" flocks of hundreds of birds gather along the northwest side of the Alaska Peninsula, the Kotzebue Sound region, and various places throughout the Brooks Range, especially Anaktuvuk Pass. Closer to Anchorage, hunters should try the east end of Skilak and Tustumena lakes on the Kenai Peninsula, and the mountains in Kachemak Bay State Park.

Rock Ptarmigan

The rock ptarmigan, *Lagopus mutus*, is a true mountain grouse. While often found near or mixed in with flocks of willow ptarmigan, *rocks*, as they are so often called by Alaskans, prefer higher, more rocky and mountainous terrain and lower growing brush than willow ptarmigan. After I find the willow ptarmigan at timberline, I need to climb another 500 to 1,000 feet before I can expect any wingshooting for rocks.

Description

Rock ptarmigan are found in nearly all treeless areas of Alaska, except the wet, coastal tundras and major treeless areas of the western and northern coasts. Some ptarmigan living on isolated islands have developed inherited, recognizable differences in color and size. The classic example is Alaska's Aleutian Chain, where seven races of rock ptarmigan have been described. These include:

Chamberlain's ptarmigan, confined to Adak Island
Everman's ptarmigan, found on Attu
Nelson's ptarmigan, found on Unalaska, Akutan and Unimak Islands
Sanford's ptarmigan, confined to Tanaga Island
Townsend's ptarmigan, confined to Kiska
Kellogg's ptarmigan, found along the western arctic coast
Turner's ptarmigan, found on Atka.

In central and northern Alaska, rock ptarmigan sport their winter plumage as early as October and remain white, except for their black tail feathers, until early May. During winter, cocks have a narrow black line or "mask" extending from bill to ear. While most hens have no mask, about one female in five has a partial black stripe fore and aft of each eye. Females turn a mottled brown by late April, and molt to completely brown before nesting season begins. After females start incubation of eggs, males begin their changeover in late May. Both sexes begin growing winter plumage in late August.

Hunters often comment about the rosy or pink coloration both willow and rock ptarmigan exhibit, especially in late winter. This glowing color, which fades slowly after death, may be caused by natural oils of the living bird's feathers. Perhaps the low angle of the sun's rays at northern latitudes emphasizes this color.

Life History

Males arrive at select breeding areas during the month of April and vigorously begin defending small parcels of ground and tundra. The females arrive soon after: then they select a nesting area and a mate. A hen commonly lays a clutch of three to eleven eggs. Males will remain on or near the breeding grounds throughout the month of June, but territorial displays subside after the hens begin incubating. By early July, most of the clutches have hatched.

The hen usually leads the chicks away from the nest as soon as they hatch. A chick lives off nutrients stored in its body for a day or two after hatching. Meanwhile the chicks learn to peck at bits of food shown to them by their mothers. The astonishing growth and development of young ptarmigan during their first 30 days of life shows how well the chicks learn the lessons of food-gathering. They double or triple their weight in 10 days, and develop a working set of flight feathers in the same length of time. They get their full set of flight feathers at 8 to 10 weeks of age.

Females and their broods continue to search out tender buds and insects near the moist ground at the headwaters of streams. In contrast, the males move to the rugged ridge-tops where they molt into their summer plumage. By late August, the hens and chicks have joined the males at the higher elevations. Females withdraw from the flocks in mid-September and migrate to the lower elevations. They remain in clearings at the fringe of forested areas until the April breeding season. Males remain at or near the breeding areas throughout the winter. Studies show that during the winter months, flocks of each sex exhibit nomadic tendencies. Weather, snow conditions and food supply keep the birds moving. The smart hunter observes these details when planning a rock ptarmigan hunt.

The food items ptarmigan prefer are easy to remember. From October to May, Alaska rock ptarmigan eat little except the buds and catkins of dwarf birch. During the early hunting season, from September to October, hunters can often find the birds feeding in alpine berry patches, especially those near birch or alders.

Chris Batin with a nice bag of willow and rock ptarmigan. Late spring is the best season for ptarmigan hunting, due to the longer daylight hours and increased bird concentrations. (Photo by Adela Ward Batin)

Where to Hunt Rock Ptarmigan

Range of the Rock Ptarmigan in Alaska. Rock ptarmigan are found in nearly all treeless areas of Alaska, except wet, coastal tundra. The species can be found throughout Canada, Greenland, Iceland, Scandinavia, Scotland, the Alps northern Japan and Russia. Some races occupy vast areas in mid-sections of continents, but inherited, recognizable differences in color and size have developed in places where ptarmigan live in isolated island situations. The classic example is in Alaska's Aleutian chain, where seven races of rock ptarmigan have been described.

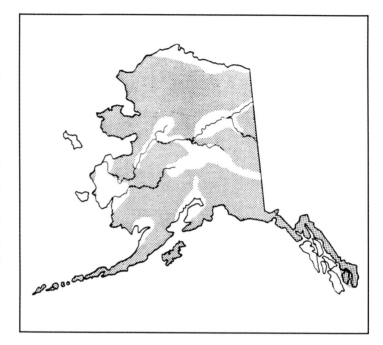

The species can be found all along the mainland coast and on Revillagigedo, Hawkins, Hinchinbrook and Montague islands. It is absent from all other major islands in this region. Snowmachiners in Turnagain Pass take a few rock ptarmigan each winter. On Kodiak, the birds are found at some of the higher elevations in the lower middle of the island. In the Susitna drainage, look for rocks in the Chugach Mountains and at the headwaters of the Little Susitna River. Birds are also found throughout Units 22 through 26, with the exception of the lowland plains and flats.

White-tailed Ptarmigan

The reclusive white-tailed ptarmigan, *Lagopus leucurus*, is an evolutionary marvel, adapting to its high-country terrain in response to territorial pressure from other ptarmigan species that claimed the lowlands. The whitetail, biologists theorize, has been adapting to its alpland existence for many millions of years. It lives in the rugged, glacially carved mountain peaks that few if any predators, including man, frequent. Nicknamed *snow grouse*, the white-tailed ptarmigan is a true bird of the mountains. It stays the entire winter in what is one of the most inhospitable areas of the northcountry: the wind-swept, barren expanse of mountain peaks. Yet this doesn't bother the whitetail. It loves boulder-strewn rockslides, dizzy heights of rocky plateaus and the massive edges of icefields.

At first glance, white-tailed ptarmigan country looks almost like rock ptarmigan country. Interestingly enough, white-tailed ptarmigan may have evolved from a group of rock ptarmigan, isolated by glaciers in alpine meadows of the western states. In the process of adapting to the new conditions, whitetails developed stronger, wider bills than their ancestors. Now, when three kinds of ptarmigan forage on common winter range, whitetails eat the widest variety of buds and twigs, including alder catkins. But, it's rare to find all three species together at the same elevation for any length of time, as the whitetail has never learned to compete successfully with other ptarmigan anywhere except in the rugged alplands.

Description

In winter, whitetails are entirely white, including the seven pairs of tail feathers. Since they shed only once a year, in mid-summer, these tail feathers are the species' year-round trademark. Even the shafts of the wing feathers are a grayish white instead of black as in other ptarmigan.

Their summer plumage is also different from the other species of ptarmigan: the general color is grayish instead of brown. The plumage is also more finely vermiculated than the other species.

Whitetails are the smallest of the ptarmigan. They weigh only 3/4 pound when mature, and are seldom more than 13 inches long, indeed, the smallest members of the entire grouse family. Anatomically speaking, the heart is also smaller than that found in the other two species of ptarmigan.

Life History

The life cycle of the whitetail resembles that of the other two ptarmigan species. Breeding begins in April, with the territoriality displays and screaming calls of the male. After mating, the hen lays five to ten eggs in a small nest in boulder fields that radiate the sun's warmth onto the eggs. White-tailed ptarmigan in the southern regions of Alaska lay their eggs about three weeks earlier than do whitetails at the southern end of Montana, Colorado and New Mexico. Biologists reason that the snow melts sooner in the Alaska Panhandle alplands than in the higher elevations of the western states.

The eggs hatch in late June, and chicks and hen remain at high elevations, feeding on tender leaves, twigs and berries at the edges of snow patches or below glaciers. Compared to the rock and willow ptarmigan, the whitetail is less migratory or nomadic, thus whitetail populations are more stable. Biologists theorize that the whitetail lives the longest of the three species.

Due to the ruggedness of the terrain in which whitetails live, hunting this species discourages all but the most ardent and avid upland game bird hunter. The only whitetail many hunters have seen are those encountered while on a goat or Dall sheep hunt. However, I've hunted the three ptarmigan species separately and on two occasions have bagged all three species in one day. Such a "Grand Slam" takes physical endurance, proper gear and proper hunting techniques.

White-tailed ptarmigan are found in a variety of terrain. In winter, look for them beneath high ridges in mountain country. Be careful of avalanches!

Where to Hunt White-tailed Ptarmigan

Range of the White-tailed Ptarmigan in Alaska. White-tailed ptarmigan are found only in western North America. Products of millions of years of evolution in rugged mountains, white-tailed ptarmigan have never learned to compete successfully with other ptarmigan anywhere else except in these rocky alplands. Whitetails range from extreme northern New Mexico to Mount Rainier and Vancouver Island, to southcentral Alaska and the Yukon.

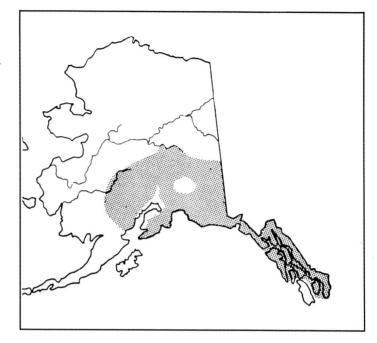

There are few places in Alaska where hunters can find white-tailed ptarmigan in less than a few hours' hiking. Some of the more accessible populations are on Mount Juneau and at the head of other glacial valleys near Juneau; in Chilkat Pass, especially at Miles 56-62 and at Mile 90 Haines Road; at Rainbow Mountain, Mile 209 Richardson Highway; in Thompson Pass near Valdez; near Healy; in the mountains surrounding Independence Mine, north of Palmer on the Palmer-Willow Road. I've personally taken whitetails in the Chugach Mountains just outside of Anchorage, and on the Kenai Peninsula.

How to Hunt Willow, Rock and White-tailed Ptarmigan

Autumn

September is an ideal time to hunt all three species of ptarmigan. Willow ptarmigan are the easiest to find. In fact, you'll often come across them when you least expect it. I remember one hunt several years ago when I was stalking a big bull moose. The animal was about 300 yards away near the edge of a canyon. The going was tough. There was plenty of grizzly sign in the area, and visibility was about 30 yards at the most. I was easing my way through the brush, confident the big bull wouldn't go anywhere if I just took my time. Suddenly, the brush to my right exploded in a flurry of rustling. I swung my rifle around, reacting to a subconscious notion that this was a bear charge. Much to my surprise—and relief—it was a flock of willow ptarmigan, dressed in their feathery suits of brown and white, perched on alder branches and croaking admonitions at me for trespassing across "their" land. I never did make it back to hunt those birds because I finally nailed that big bull and spent the remaining four days of the hunt packing meat to base camp.

While I strongly advise against hunting birds before bagging your trophy, if you manage to connect early in the hunt, you can fill out your remaining days pursuing some fabulous wing-shooting possibilities. So, I always make a point of taking a shotgun with me on all but lengthy, wilderness backpack hunts. One of the most frustrating things for a hunter in a sheep camp is to be surrounded by croaking ptarmigan. After a successful sheep hunt, a friend of mine, whom I'll call Don, shot all his available rifle ammo at the birds. With nothing else to do but twiddle his thumbs, he resorted to hunting the birds with walnut-sized rocks; dismal success. He even tried making a slingshot out of his inner-tube scope cover and a forked alder stick. By the time he got reasonably accurate with his creation, it was time to leave. The situation was enough to make a grown bird hunter cry.

The secret to finding autumn flocks of ptarmigan is to hunt the edges of willow and alder patches. Because the birds blend in so well with their surroundings, it takes a good retriever to find them in the thick foliage. My Uncle Bob's black Lab, Donovan, was equally at home flushing ptarmigan on the flat tundra near Izembek Lagoon on the Alaska Peninsula as he was in retrieving Emperor geese there. Some hunters prefer spaniels for alpine ptarmigan hunting. It doesn't matter whether the dog is a flusher or pointer. As long as the dog works an area within shooting range, you should connect.

If you have no dog, or can't seem to find birds, look for berries. They are usually the number one food source for autumn ptarmigan. You'll find a variety down at timberline, as well as several varieties atop rugged mountain peaks, where the whitetails frequently congregate. It's just a matter of working enough of the cover types previously mentioned in this section until you find the birds. However, here's one bit of information I find extremely useful. Once you've reached a section of mountainside where food and cover are plentiful, work in a zig-zag pattern around the mountainside, rather than up and down. You won't tire as quickly and you'll greatly increase your chances of locating birds.

Winter

Access to ptarmigan is much better in winter. Willow ptarmigan can be found in isolated marshes and flatlands near mountain ranges. Hunters who use snowmobiles to ride to these areas and hunt the surrounding foothills do extremely well. When you spot a flock, uncase your shotgun or .22 and the hunt begins. Look for grassy areas near heavy timber, lengthy stretches of willow and alders bordering marshes and tundra expanses, or gullies coursing through the foothills. In the mountains, search for willow ptarmigan near the edge of timberline and along gullies and the outer fringes of alder patches.

Mountain hunting during the winter months is often extremely challenging, and potentially dangerous. Deep snow usually necessitates parking the snowmachines at a lower level and tackling the slopes via snowshoes. Hunting technique starts with glassing for tracks in the snow. Ptarmigan tracks are usually in the form of erratic lines the birds make as they go from bush to bush, consuming any and all buds and twigs of willow, blueberry and birch. You'll also find small depressions in the snow, usually near heavy alders, with a collection of small droppings toward one end. This is where the birds spend the night, and are good indicators that birds are still in the immediate vicinity. A zig-zag pattern across the mountainside, hitting the gullies, ravines and alder patches will have you in birds.

Be extremely cautious of potential avalanche conditions, especially during warm weather or after heavy snowfall late in the season. Avoid shooting near steep slopes or under cornices. A shot can release tons of snow and bury you within

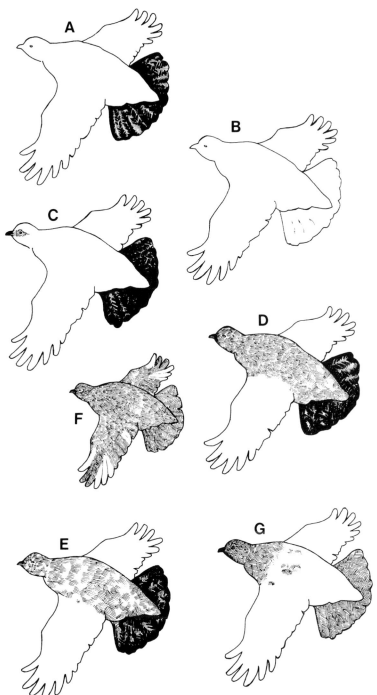

The various molting phases of the three species of ptarmigan are impressive. Identification of the different species, even when the bird is in hand, is difficult, even with experience. The whitetail easily identifies the smallest species; this is a dependable characteristic all year-long. Ptarmigan with black masks are rock ptarmigan—but not all rockers have this marking. Examples:

A. Winter plumage, willow
B. Winter whitetail
C. Winter rock
D. Summer rock
E. Fall rock
F. Rock chick
G. Spring willow

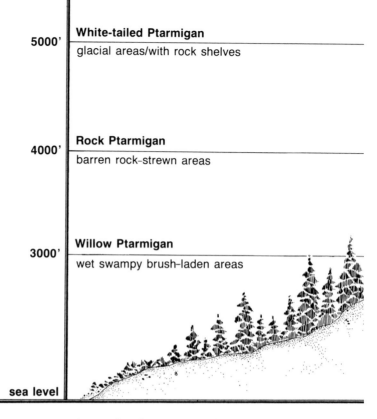

| 5000' | **White-tailed Ptarmigan** |
| | glacial areas/with rock shelves |

| 4000' | **Rock Ptarmigan** |
| | barren rock-strewn areas |

| 3000' | **Willow Ptarmigan** |
| | wet swampy brush-laden areas |

sea level

a matter of seconds. This is especially true if you're in the high, ridgetop country that white-tailed ptarmigan frequent. Another sure indication of avalanche danger can occur when you're walking across a gradual slope. Suddenly, there's a loud boom followed by a section of snowpack settling under your weight. Under these conditions, get out of the mountains and hunt willow ptarmigan in the flatlands.

Wintertime white-tailed ptarmigan hunting calls for an additional piece of equipment. Because these birds are usually found on wind-blown slopes, attach a pair of ice cleats to the bottom of your snowshoes to allow you to better traverse the wind-packed snow. On one hunt in the Chugach Mountains south of Anchorage, the mountain was so steep and the snow pack so hard that I had to chip out footholds in the snow to reach the hundred or more birds holding on a small ledge about 500 feet above me. I did that climb twice, because about halfway up, a foothold crumpled under my weight and sent me sliding down to the bottom of the mountain. Luckily, I wasn't hurt and enjoyed the unexpected ride. On another hunt with friend Mike Ticconi, a freak winter storm with wind gusts of up to 70 mph and white-out conditions caught us off-guard. It lasted

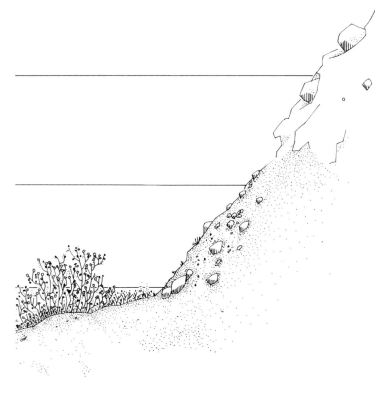

Each species of ptarmigan uses the alpine environment in a slightly different way. When the species live on the same mountain, they instinctively go to different areas where they will get along best. Typically, willow ptarmigan choose the wettest, brushiest places close to timberline. Whitetails go far uphill to boulder-strewn plateaus, rock slides and the edges of snowfields. Rock ptarmigan choose the middle ground.

Sample Environment of Ptarmigan Distribution

no more than an hour, after which Mike jumped up and bagged a whitetail, our only bird of the day.

Follow these rules if you plan to pursue winter ptarmigan:

• Don't go hunting alone, use extreme caution and check avalanche conditions for the area you'll be hunting. Let someone know where you'll be hunting and when you expect to return.

• Take a pack with emergency food, matches and space blanket in case weather strands you on a mountain peak or out on the flats.

• You'll also need polarized sunglasses, as it's easy to get snow-blinded in Alaska's winter wonderland.

• And of course, the best advice is to use common sense.

Ptarmigan are one of the most thrilling upland gamebirds Alaskans can pursue. Not only do they provide good eating and ample wingshooting possibilities, but they also keep you in shape throughout the lazy winter months. Add to that the beauty of the winter alpine tundra, with its ice waterfalls, desolate expanses and spectacular sunsets, and I guarantee you'll find winter ptarmigan hunting a sport that has no equal.

CHAPTER 13

Snowshoe Hare

The snowshoe or varying hare, *Lepus americanus*, is a mainstay in the realms of sport hunting and subsistence. Subsistence hunters in western and northern Alaska consider the snowshoe hare as a main food staple, especially when larger big game animals are not available throughout the winter months. The hare provides fresh meat that would otherwise be unavailable until spring. The hide of the animal is also a necessary element in some Native handicrafts. The fur is soft, warm, easy to tan, attractive, and best of all, plentiful.

Yet, as a sporting animal, the hare is a strange paradox of stupidity and sagacity. Often its sits under a spruce tree and innocently watches its pursuers sneak within shooting range. Other times the hare stays just out of sight of both hunter and dogs, leaving only a maze of tracks that seem to wind haphazardly through the spruce swampland. For whatever reason it is pursued, the hare is an integral part of Alaska's hunting heritage.

Two species of hare are found in Alaska: the snowshoe and the arctic or tundra variety. The latter, *Lepus othus*, is the largest of all the American hares. It can stretch 24 inches and weigh up to 12 pounds. The arctic hare is found along much of the western coast of Alaska, including the Alaska Peninsula; along the arctic coast and the North Slope of the Brooks Range, its distribution is spotty. The preferred habitat for the hare is brushy tundra and rocky slopes. The animals are also found in alder thickets. They are, however, most abundant in the coastal area tundra.

The arctic hare is probably one of the least known mammals of North America. Only a small amount of scientific literature is available on this species. Much of the life history

The snowshoe hare in Alaska is subject to cyclic fluctuations. In years of abundance, they can be found most anywhere. However, at the bottom of the cycle, look for them in only the best cover; usually alder and willow thickets along river habitat. (Photo by Adela Ward Batin)

Brush patches and gullies on the open tundra are good places to find both snowshoe and arctic hares. A snowmachine expedites travel time between hotspots.

information published on the Alaska arctic hare has been extrapolated from available information on the Canadian arctic hare. Generally speaking, arctic hares prefer open areas, while snowshoe hares remain close to willows and alders. Both species, however, prefer willows as winter forage. Biologists do know that the tundra hare, at times, is relatively abundant in the western coastal part of its range, with fluctuations in populations similar to that of the snowshoe hare.

The snowshoe hare, on the other hand, is common throughout most of the state wherever suitable habitat occurs. It is absent from the lower portion of the Alaska Peninsula, the tundra areas of the lower Kuskokwim Delta and the Seward Peninsula, the North Slope of the Brooks Range, and most of the islands except where transplanted. Hares were introduced to Kodiak and Afognak islands in 1934, and to the adjacent Woody and Long islands in 1952. Hares are sparse throughout southeast Alaska.

The snowshoe hare is well-adapted for life in Alaska's north-country. In the summer, his coat turns brown; it changes to white in the winter. The name *snowshoe* refers to its large hind feet that allow it to run easily over deep snowpacks and escape predators. The snowshoe hare can stretch 18 to 20 inches long and weigh from three to four pounds.

Mating takes place in March and April, and the gestation period is about 30 days. About four to six leverets form the average litter. In areas of excellent habitat, does can drop more than one litter a year, with the second coming later in the summer. What distinguishes newborn rabbits from hares is that the young rabbits are born furless and blind, while the young hares are born fully furred and with their eyes open.

As most Alaska hunters know, the density of snowshoe hare populations follow cyclic fluctuations averaging 10 years between peaks. The more extreme variations seem to occur in the central portions of the snowshoe's range. Interior Alaska has experienced extremes in hare density equal to any reported elsewhere. During population peaks, densities have averaged 1,500 to 2,000 animals per square mile, or even higher; some records report certain areas reaching a peak of 30,000 per square mile. The density of hares within a specific locale may differ significantly from the general population levels over a large geographical area. Even in periods of low population levels, some small area of abundance can occur in prime habitat. As the populations increase, the hares tend to disperse into less desirable habitat, and when populations decline, they disappear first from these areas. Sometimes the decline is abrupt; at other times the decline is gradual, occuring over a period of three to four years.

Snowshoe hares occupy a variety of cover, yet given a choice, especially when populations are at a low, certain types of cover are preferred. So, look for hares in subalpine areas; brushlands; white spruce-birch communities with brushy understories of willow, alder, highbush cranberry and wild rose; and especially riparian situations with an abundance of willow. Habitat disturbances such as wildfire and clearing of timber usually benefits the snowshoe, as the resulting brushy growth of fireweed provides cover and food for the animal. Perhaps this is what makes the Kenai Peninsula burn area an excellent hare hunting spot. In 1989, hunters commonly saw over 50 hares in a single outing. In contrast, a climax forest, like those found in southeast Alaska, does not provide suitable brushy understory the snowshoe requires.

Hunting Techniques

Snowshoe hares exhibit two behavioral patterns: they either sit tight, requiring hunters to kick them into jumping, or they continually dart and hop out of range of a .22 or shotgun. While weather, hunting pressure and terrain are variables influencing a hare's behavior, the constant for success is *how* you hunt an area.

When hunting hares in thick cover, most hunters walk too fast. Walk slowly in a zig-zag pattern for about 10 yards, then stop and examine the area. You should use this technique for two reasons: first, you are forced to hunt more with your eyes, rather than break brush haphazardly. I know I've lost count of the number of hares I've spotted sitting under a spruce; hares that I would have overlooked if I kept on walking.

Secondly, stopping every so often puts the jitters into hares. They think you've spotted them. The longer you stand there, the more nervous they get. They usually jump within two to five minutes. And when it does jump, a hare that's had time to get nervous won't be moving out as fast as one reacting to a charge through the brush, which helps make for an easier shot.

The second method for producing hares, especially in spruce thickets and alder gullies, is to form a drive with four or more people. One person walks or drives an area in a systematic fashion, pushing out hares to hunters waiting in select locations. These drives and their direction depend on the lay of the land and the formation of the alder or spruce thickets. If you're short on hunters, consider what I call a "staggered drive." In this method, three or more hunters form and maintain a staggered line as they drive through the cover. The hares get confused about which way the hunters are approaching, and run in a zig-zag, haphazard manner. However, hares jumped with this method usually bolt to the right or the left, so if you're on the end, be ready for 'em.

Hares are also fond of swampy terrain bordering spruce stands and alder thickets. Some of my best hare hotspots have been in thickets in swamps I needed hip boots to reach. However, during the winter months in these same swamps, look for hares in heavy tangles of grass, brush, downed timber or grown-over burns.

Hares are extremely fond of a form; a simple, slightly oval depression in the ground litter, usually located under good cover. Forms are found in places where hares can derive protection from predators and the elements, i.e. under bushes, among small clumps of trees, under logs or fallen trees, or under trees bent over by snow. These are extremely common throughout the interior during the winter. Such a snow-covered shelter is called a qali, and a hunter's swift kick into it will usually have a hare jumping out the back side.

In heavy timber such as in the Chugach Forest, hares huddle in bowl-shaped depressions in the snow at the base of spruce

trees. Pruitt (1957) used the Kobuk Valley Eskimo term *qamaniq* to describe this feature. The depth of snow at the base of the spruce is usually slight, increasing outward beyond the tree's "snow shadow" to a depth found on the less-protected forest floor. The temperature in a qamaniq is probably several degrees higher than the air temperature over the snow beyond it because the branches make a good windbreak retarding heat loss. Thus the qamaniq makes a good resting place for hares. However, hare sign at the base of spruce is not as prevalent as that found under bent-over shrubs and alders which comprise qali.

When scouting for hares, ignore the amount of droppings in an area. Droppings can stay around for several years. If at all possible, hunt snowshoes before the first snowfall of the year. Then, the animals are white and easy to see against a brown backdrop. Immediately after a heavy snowfall is another good time. Hares move extensively after such a storm and the amount

Hares often take cover in the slight depressions of snow beneath spruce trees. There, the air temperature is a few degrees warmer due to the tree bark reflecting the sun's rays into the depression. (Photo by Adela Ward Batin).

The result of a day's snow-shoe hunt on the Kenai Peninsula. The Kenai is currently experiencing a peak in its snowshoe hare cycle, offering outstanding hunting opportunities.

of sign should give an indication of the number of hares in an area.

The snowshoe is truly a "hare for all seasons." Most areas currently have no bag limit in a season open 365 days a year. While most hunting occurs in the fall, hare hunting is also popular throughout the winter and spring months. On moderate winter days, many people enjoy getting out of the house for a few hours to hunt hares as a form of winter recreation, combining it with skiing, snowmachining, or snowshoeing. And as table fare, few game animals can match the delicious taste of hare. Wild hare is 20 percent protein and 10 percent fat, with only 795 calories per pound. Beef, at 16 percent protein, 28 percent fat and 1760 calories per pound, is not nearly so healthy as wild hare, which also provides exercise. What more could you ask for in a small game animal?

Where to Hunt Snowshoe and Arctic Hares

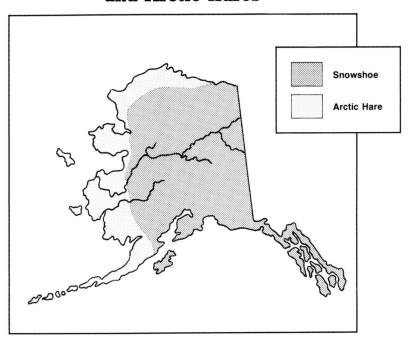

Snowshoe

Arctic Hare

Units 1 — 4

Southeast Panhandle

Snowshoe hares occur in scattered populations on the southeast mainland. Most good hare habitat is limited to major river valleys, and the coastal spruce/hemlock forests support a few hares. While fair populations occur in some areas such as Mendenhall Flats, and the Taku and Stikine valleys, hare are not common enough to be considered an important small game species in these units.

Units 5, 6

Yakutat/ Cordova-Valdez

Snowshoe hares occur in these areas, yet there is little information available on their abundance or harvest.

Units 7, 15

Seward and Kenai

Snowshoe hares are currently at the peak of their cycle in these units, especially in the Kenai burn area and near Skilak Loop Road.

Unit 8

Kodiak

In 1934, 558 snowshoe hares were released on Kodiak and Afognak islands. This transplant was very successful: in 1952, hares from Kodiak were captured and introduced to the adjacent Woody and Long islands. These introductions were also successful. On Kodiak island, the snowshow hare occurs in moderate density where habitat is best. Suitable habitat is not evenly distributed everywhere on the islands, and individual populations fluctuate sporadically. There is intense hunting effort along the Kodiak road system and in the Port Lions—Ouzinke areas.

Unit 9

Alaska Peninsula

Snowshoe hares are present in the upper portion of the unit in suitable habitat, but probably do not range far beyond the timbered areas of the Alaska Peninsula. No other information is available on snowshoe hares in this unit.

Arctic hares are found throughout the region. In 1925, Murie observed arctic hares at the west end of the Alaska Peninsula. In 1936, he reported finding abundant signs of arctic hares at Snag Point, near Nushagak, and said that they apparently inhabited alder thickets. There is no recent information on their abundance in these units.

Unit 12

Upper Tanana-White River

Snowshoe hares are cyclically abundant in Unit 12. Search streamside alder thickets and heavy black spruce forests near streams. The Tok Cutoff area usually has enough hares for a good hunt, especially in May and June.

Units 14, 16

Anchorage, Lower Susitna

Snowshoe hares are found throughout units 14 and 16. There are some localized pockets with moderate numbers of hares. They can be quite abundant in prime habitat at the height of their cycle. The Matanuska and Knik River drainages contain excellent hare habitat.

Unit 17

Bristol Bay

Snowshoe hares are abundant in suitable habitat in the unit. Areas of high concentration are Lake Clark, along the Chulitna River, Nushagak, Lake Aleknagek, Ekuuk and Kakwok rivers. There is no information about present abundance or harvest.

Units 18, 19, 21

Y-K Delta, McGrath and Middle Yukon

Snowshoe hares are six to seven years into a 10-year recovery cycle.

Unit 18. They are abundant and increasing along the Kuskokwim River in Units 18 and 19, and in the mountain valleys in Unit 19. Willow thickets and creek bottoms are preferred habitat for snowshoe hares in these areas. Arctic hares are found in Unit 18 in the coastal tundra areas. Look for them around the mouth of the Yukon River in open willow scrublands. Hares are also numerous on Nelson Island, along the Johnson River southwest of Bethel, and between the Yukon and Kuskokwim rivers north of Bethel.

Unit 20

Fairbanks/Central Tanana

Unit 20 has, at times, some of the highest hare populations in the state, and has prime hare habitat in the Yukon, Tanana and Delta River valleys. There are localized pockets of high hare populations in this region. The overall population is currently moderate to high. Hares in the Fort Greeley to Donnelly Dome area produced a bumper crop in the spring of 1989.

Units 22, 23

Nome and Kotzebue

Snowshoe hares occur in these units, particularly in the riparian willow stands along the rivers on the Seward Peninsula in the upper Kobuk Valley. The arctic hare is fairly abundant at times in some parts of the Seward Peninsula. Try hunting the Selawik Hills and Goodhope River drainages.

Unit 24

Koyukuk

Unit 24 has good snowshoe hare habitat and hares can be cyclically abundant in this unit. No additional information is available.

Unit 25

Fort Yukon

Snowshoe hares are present throughout Unit 25. Few are found in the upper quarter due to poor habitat, but they can be very abundant in drainages. Elsewhere, populations are about the same as throughout the remainder of the interior. The largest cyclic fluctuations occur in the central portion of the snowshoe's range, such as the lower part of Unit 25.

Unit 26

Arctic Slope

Snowshoe hares occur only occasionally in the southern portion of Unit 26. They were observed along the Canning River in 1973, after high population levels occurred in Game Management Unit 25 in 1971 and 1972. It is possible that the high hare populations in the adjacent units caused migration into the North Slope area. Hares are generally found in willows along major water courses when they do occur in this unit. The tundra hare has a very scattered distribution here. Most of the hares are probably in the western corner, southwest of Point Lay. Little information is available on the tundra hare in this unit, but apparently they are scarce to absent on the North Slope of the Brooks Range.

CHAPTER 14

Waterfowl

Waterfowl hunting in Alaska is a sport for the discriminating hunter. He enjoys picking his shots as thousands of geese fly through sleet-filled skies; or delights in watching his black Lab retrieve a king eider in the foam-flecked surf of the Bering Sea. He revels in hunting areas with little or no "competition." But most of all, he enjoys the quality, quantity and versatility of Alaska waterfowl hunting.

And quality hunting it is. If you crave excitement, try pass shooting for scoters out of an inflatable raft on the Gulf of Alaska; stalk wily sandhill cranes in the barley fields near Delta, or decoy emperor geese on the wind-ravaged eelgrass flats of the Alaska Peninsula.

Alaska has quantity also. Hunters enjoy a variety of species: mallards, teal, pintails, widgeons, buffleheads, shovelers, old squaw, several species of scoters, eiders, and Barrow's goldeneye to name a few. Depending on the area hunted, expect to harvest anywhere from seven to 10 game ducks per day; 15 sea ducks; up to six geese which may include Canada, white-fronted or snow geese; two black brant; eight snipe; three sandhill cranes and some of the finest hunting experiences available in North America. Even though the possibility has presented itself numerous times, I'm not one to pack eight geese per day out of the field. I mention these bag limits to give you some idea of the fantastic bird shooting Alaska has to offer. However, success requires knowledge of bird habits and hunting techniques suited for Alaska's waterfowl environment.

Robert Batin and Donovan take a break during a lull in the action on an Alaska Peninsula goose hunt. In the blind is a lesser Canada and black brant.

Lee Langbehn takes a shot at high-flying pintails passing through the Palmer Hayflats area north of Anchorage. Camo netting helps you blend into the surroundings, an important consideration when attempting to decoy birds in heavily hunted areas.

Game Ducks

Alaska currently has a 107-day waterfowl season that traditionally opens September 1. However, waterfowlers throughout most of Alaska have a limited season due to early freeze-up, which drives the birds south. In northern Alaska, waterfowl season is the shortest: about 30 days or less. Along much of the Gulf Coast and Alaska Peninsula, hunters have from 45 to 60 days of good hunting. Only in the Aleutian Islands, Kodiak, and in southeast Alaska can hunters utilize the entire 107-day season.

A recent state-wide duck harvest was estimated at about 86,790 birds, of which 79,605 were dabblers and divers and 7,185 were sea ducks. Species composition of the state-wide duck harvest has remained relatively constant during the past 10 years. About 86 percent of the harvest is composed of dabbling ducks, 10.8 percent composed of diving ducks, and 4.3 percent being sea ducks and mergansers. Statistics show active hunters take about 8 to 10 ducks per season. Daily success rate is about 1.6 ducks per hunter. Of course, these figures represent only fall sport hunting harvest, and do not consider subsistence harvest.

Hunting in September is usually good to excellent in most areas of the state for local puddle and diving ducks, that is, birds that have stayed in an area throughout the summer months. The largest concentrations of birds are near major waterways, such as the Tanana River, Susitna River, King Salmon River, lakes, larger marshes such as Minto Flats, and grainfields like those in Delta and Palmer. The Yukon Flats is pegged as Alaska's most productive duck habitat. The area has been known to support a breeding population of 99 birds per square mile in over 10,800 square miles of habitat. How good the hunting remains in the early season depends on weather, food availability and movement of birds.

There are several ways to hunt early-season waterfowl. Least expensive and fastest is to locate an area's potholes and streams. Look for areas that have plenty of natural cover and feed. Check out these areas in late afternoon and evening, when birds are moving. Mark the area, and sneak in before sunrise the next morning. Expect to jump shoot the first batch of ducks. For continued hunting action, smart hunters take along a few decoys and set them into a quiet back-eddy or cove. The decoys serve as an "all is OK" indicator for any ducks flying into the area.

Successful early-season waterfowl hunters almost always use a blind, whether they are hunting over decoys or pass shooting. If possible, construct the blind prior to the season so waterfowl can get used to it without spooking. A nearby stand of dead timber or tall grass is especially helpful in constructing a blind. Make sure the blind has easy access and blends in with the surrounding vegetation.

Blending into the surroundings is important. As grasses and sedges are the prevalent cover throughout the marshy areas in the state, I prefer green camouflage there in September, and change over to brown camo from October to season's end. On the tidal flats, gray is best, because glacial silt colors those areas.

Before establishing a blind, consider the location's accessibility to the stomping grounds of mud marchers: a term that has two meanings. The first definition of mud marchers takes into consideration those hunters who systematically jump shoot ducks in marshes rather than pass shoot or decoy. Mud marching is an effective and popular way to hunt ducks, especially when the birds aren't flying during the afternoon hours. Decoy or pass shooters often turn to mud marching in the afternoon as a means of obtaining some birds.

The other meaning of mud marching has a negative connotation: it describes people who wear bright red hats and stand in the center of the marsh without benefit of a blind, and expect birds to fly over. When none do, they walk to other areas of the marsh.

I'm not joking in saying the "bad" mud marchers, or nimrods as many people call them, are a serious problem in many of the heavily hunted areas near Anchorage, Juneau and Fairbanks. Yet, despite their crude tactics, nimrods can help keep birds moving. Locate your blind on a sheltered slough or lake edge near a popular "marching" ground. Set a dozen decoys in groups of three and four around your blind. Whenever the nimrods spook or flare birds, a quick feeding chuckle will usually draw birds into your set. I remember when a group of hunting cronies and I did just that: we placed out groups of decoys on a shallow pond near a "marchers" haven. The shooting was good all morning until one "slob" hunter had the nerve to stand on the edge of our decoys, hoping to get a shot at any of the birds that we would miss. We didn't. We dropped the next three birds that came into our set. Frustrated with our "uncanny shooting ability," the slob hunter left the area. Of course, we missed the next five shots. One thing is for certain: hunting in nimrod country can be frustrating at times, but it is never boring.

Hunting over large decoy spreads is the favorite and most effective way to hunt waterfowl in Alaska's marshes. With magnum decoys, birds drop in with feet dangling, or in the case of teal, rocket in before landing with a resounding "plop." However, not just any decoy works in Alaska marshes. Early-season waterfowl, not yet in full plumage, are in what is known as an eclipse stage. This is a rather dull coloration preceding the brighter feathers exhibited later in the year. So early in the season, make a point of using hen or drab-colored decoys until the northern birds start showing up in their full dress of colors. The drab patterns don't spook ducks as easily, and entice more wary birds to drop into range.

Size of decoy spread is another important consideration when hunting wetland marshes. The weed growth in marshes can prevent low-flying ducks from spotting your decoy spread, especially when the dekes are spread out in the standard "figure C" or fish hook configurations.

For years I used large decoy spreads on these marshes with varying degrees of success. Only when I started to set my decoys in small groups of four to six did I notice an increase in decoying both wary high fliers and low-flying birds.

Under most hunting conditions, I set out four to eight groups of five to seven decoys. Situate these groups along the shore of the stream, inlet, river, or tidal flow drawing the most waterfowl traffic. In addition to a single goose decoy, I always put

a small cluster of dekes on the opposite side of the blind. On many occasions this set has drawn in ducks and several single geese that would have passed me by.

When the northern birds start migrating south in late September or October, many hunters prefer shell decoys for both ducks and geese. These are especially effective on the glacial mud flats, where geese traditionally land for hours or days before heading south. Again, caution is required in blind construction and decoy placement. Late-season birds are not as forgiving of mistakes as birds encountered during the start of the season.

Here are a few tips on decoy rigging. Water in marshes can be clear or extremely silty, and range in depth from a few inches to six or more feet. To play it safe, I prefer a gray or black cord for anchor line. It blends in well with the underwater vegetation, and doesn't seem to spook as many birds as some of the green cord sold on the market. As for anchor weights, the wrap-around type works best. They are easily handled, stored, and rarely tangle, an important consideration when transporting a dozen or more dekes.

• During the day, try to keep glacial silt from drying on the decoys. You want to keep them clean.

• Make decoy placement and pick-up easy on yourself. Use a large pack-sack or inflatable boat or canoe for carrying and storing decoys rather than trudging through the muck and stuffing the dekes into a sack.

Decoys greatly increase hunter success in the marshy, glacial flats located throughout the state. Find open areas in the plant growth, and place decoys in small, compact groups.

Waterfowl

An inflatable or large pack-sack makes it easy for hunters to set out and maintain large decoy spreads, especially in shallow-water marshes. They're also great for transporting dekes and gear to hunting areas or from any major-access road or river.

• When traveling through the marsh, be wary of smooth areas of mud or silt. These can be quicksand traps, and can suck a hunter in to his armpits. If you you get stuck, and the tide is coming in, you may not get out in time. Use caution before stepping onto any mud, especially those areas with little or no vegetation. Always check your tidebook before going afield. Many hunters have nearly perished because the tide left them stranded on rapidly disappearing mud flats, with no escape route. There have been some fatalities.

Calling

A properly used duck call effectively complements a decoy spread in Alaska's marshes. Yet, most hunters make the mistake of using a call far too much. While it's good to know the highball, greeting, and comeback calls, the single most effective call is the feeding or lonesome hen call. When you first sight ducks, refrain from calling. Allow your decoys to do their job. If the birds seem disinterested, give a series of feeding calls to coax the birds into the area. Save the comeback call as a last resort. This holds especially true for local birds.

There is an exception to this rule: Toward late afternoon, the migrants from the north come through looking for a place to spend the night. A highball or greeting call often does the trick in turning the heads of high-flying mallards, especially if you have a decoy spread.

A few tips on calling. Never call when birds are directly

overhead: call only when they are flying away or on an outer pass circling the decoys. Keep your face down. A billed cap is essential for covering your face. Keep track of the birds by moving only your eyes. When birds are close, muffle the feeding call by placing your hand over the end of the call. To reiterate: it's always better to call too little than too much, except when ducks are circling your neighbor's dekes. Then use your best greeting or feeding call to coax the birds to your set.

You'll be able to hunt better if you wear chest waders rather than hip boots. They may be hot after a day of walking, but hunters in waders can reach far more areas than hunters wearing hip boots. In early-season hunting, the standard Marathon wader is fine. When winter blasts hit, I prefer neoprene waders because of their warmth and their ability to help you stay afloat should you fall through the ice.

To reach many of the prime waterfowl areas, you'll need a boat, preferably one with a jet unit or lift kit to get you through shallow areas. The marshes near Jim Lake outside of Palmer and the 20 Mile River near Portage are two prime areas where you need a boat to reach the best hunting. Many hunters do well with a small runabout or canoe with a 7 1/2-horse kicker, especially in the winding sloughs of areas like the Minto and Palmer Hay Flats. However, do not attempt to take such a craft on the wind-ravaged Cook Inlet, Knik Arm, or Turnagain Arm. Stay with the larger boats for these areas.

Sea Ducks

There are several reasons why I'm infatuated with sea ducks and sea-duck hunting. First, I get more time to do it. When interior waters have frozen and the puddle ducks have migrated south, I can head for the coast. There, I can enjoy up to eight more weeks of sea duck waterfowling.

Secondly, the hunting is usually fast and furious. When bad weather keeps the birds flying, you can bag a limit of 15 sea ducks in an hour or two if you are so inclined. Or, if the weather is sunny and windless, day's end may only see two or three birds in the bag. I don't mind the slow days; they're a small price to pay for the superb shooting that takes place at other times.

I also like the varied personalities, sizes and shapes of the sea ducks. There are the scoters: white-winged, common and surf. They are large ducks—about the size of a small turkey—

and are quick on the wing. Nearing fingers of land and islands, scoters are as wary as foxes and they have a unique bill structure that draws stares from greenhorn waterfowlers throughout the day.

Then there's the old squaw. It's named for the incessant squawking it makes when rafted up with others of its species on the open ocean. I think the squaw's white and gray-black plumage and long, tail feathers make it more beautiful than the pintail.

The harlequin is one of the most beautifully marked and numerous of all sea ducks. They decoy readily and prefer the quiet waters of isolated bays and points. And of course, you'll find the eiders and goldeneyes. There's one thing that is certain about a sea duck hunt: you'll not be lacking for variety.

There are two basic ways to hunt sea ducks. The first requires a large boat and outboard to reach the rocky shorelines located away from shipping lanes. Search for an area where the ducks are trading back and forth near shore cover. Pull the boat ashore to keep it from bobbing around in the surf, or anchor in a protected area. The best shooting occurs during peak tidal flows. If you've chosen an area where birds are trading back and forth, you should have steady shooting. If you're in an area with little tidal fluctuation, try placing out a few decoys in the lee of your position.

The second method requires the full complement of decoys off the tip of points or islands. Some hunters prefer to use low-lying boats anchored to one side of the decoys. Sea ducks are rather curious birds, and prefer the company of large flocks to smaller groups of birds. Make your decoy spread as large as possible, using a fish hook or raft type of arrangement. Scoters may circle the rim of a set of decoys before heading off to join a larger flock. This cursory look is the most you can expect from this species. At times, of course, they fly into the dekes, but this doesn't happen regularly. They also tend to avoid flying over points of land, so take your shots when the birds investigate the spread.

Making the Shot

All too often, sea duck hunters under-estimate the speed of their quarry. The result is shots that explode the surface of the water behind the bird. Scoters, with their large size and fast speed, can be especially deceptive. Toss that barrel out there and follow through. Don't under-estimate the length of the shot string. It's longer than you think, especially with 4s and 6s, the shot most favored for hunting sea ducks.

In stormy weather, when birds are flying close to shore, use a modified choke, as shots are seldom more than 30 yards. However, on bluebird days with no wind, or when pass shooting requires that the blind be located a good distance from the water, switch to a full choke.

Some hunters inclined to hunt sea ducks from a boat prefer a cleverly concealed inflatable or small runabout. However, shooting is greatly restricted with more than one hunter in the boat. The careful hunter passes up many shots due to the close proximity of his companion. If both parties agree, one hunter should take all shots on one side of the boat, while the other does the same for the other side. In a good area where birds are constantly working, both hunters will have ample opportunity for some fine wingshooting.

Be sure your dog is in top physical condition before taking him sea duck hunting. Alaska's strong tidal currents can easily take out to sea an over-eager dog after a cripple. Keep your dog under control at all times, and send him out to retrieve only when tidal and weather conditions allow it. Under adverse conditions, use a boat to retrieve birds.

Mike McBride, owner of Kachemak Bay Wilderness Lodge, is considered to be the foremost guide on sea duck hunting in the state. He and his wife, Diane have been guiding waterfowl hunts out of their lodge for the past 14 years. From October through December, the pair caters specifically to sea duck and puddle duck hunters and bird collectors. Many of their clients make the long trek north annually to harvest some of the area's unique species. The lodge is more than comfortable. The plushness makes a tough day of sea duck hunting an extremely enjoyable experience. The average cost for a five-day hunt is around $1,500.

In addition to spectacular sea duck hunting, Kachemak Bay is also home to the farthest north wintering grounds of mallards in the world. Yet more than locale makes these mallards different. Their wingspans can reach up to three and a half feet. Although there have been speculations as to why the birds get so large, the most plausible theory is the fact they feed on spawned-out, oil-rich salmon washed up in many of the bays.

Sea duck hunting may not have the glamour and prestige that other forms of waterfowling have to offer. And that's a shame, because in terms of numbers, excitement and shooting possibilities, you'll find sea ducks can hold their own with the best of "game" ducks. You won't be disappointed.

Cranes

One of the most challenging and seldom hunted birds in Alaska is the sandhill crane. The birds are as wary as turkeys, possess the eyesight of an eagle, and are extremely intolerant of a mistake on the hunter's part. In almost every instance, cranes choose the center of a grainfield or marsh with little cover. The choice is intentional. These areas allow cranes to spot potential predators in the distance, and to take to wing in plenty of time if they are threatened. Some crane hunters use decoys and call in the birds, while others watch what field the birds are feeding in one morning, and set up a blind for hunting the next day.

Stalking cranes requires skill. Each bird seems to be pulling sentry duty, thus making a successful stalk one to be proud of. To be successful, a hunter should be dressed in camouflage clothing, with camo face net and head netting. Expect to crawl on your stomach for several hundred yards to get within shooting range. Take advantage of weeds, gullies, forests, anything that will hide your stalk.

Cranes can attain wingspans of up to six feet, and with their long legs and necks, pose a very deceiving target for the shotgunner, especially at long range. Use nothing less than 12 gauge magnum loads of 2s or BBs.

Geese

Alaska is a goose hunter's heaven. Portage Flats, Copper River, Delta, Minto, Yukon-Kuskokwim Delta and Susitna Flats are just a few of the top goose hunting hotspots in the state. Of course, for individual species, hunters may have to hunt select areas.

For instance, of the world's 11 subspecies of Canada geese, six subspecies breed in Alaska and three of these six breed no where else in the world. Lesser Canada geese are comprised of two subspecies, while the other Canada geese are separate subspecies.

Vancouver Canada geese breed only in southeast Alaska and along the northern British Columbia seacoast. A few band recoveries have come from the Oregon and Washington coasts.

Dusky Canada geese breed exclusively on the Copper River Delta near Cordova, Alaska. Dusky populations are at a current all-time low, and efforts are being made to bolster the breed-

ing population. At one time, this subspecies was probably the heaviest harvested Canada goose population in the world. About 10 percent of the harvest took place in Alaska, while over 70 percent took place in Oregon's Willamette Valley.

Cackling Canada geese breed exclusively on the outer coast of the Yukon-Kuskokwim Delta. A major sport harvest area for cacklers in Alaska is near Pilot Point on the Alaska Peninsula.

Lesser Canada geese are comprised of two subspecies, *parvipes* and *taverneri*. *Parvipes* occur primarily in interior forested regions while *taverneri* are confined primarily to coastal tundra areas. The exact taxonomy and breeding areas of these geese is not well known or understood. Thousands of lessers stopover at Izembek Lagoon on their migration to Oregon, Washington and California. An interesting note is that before the 1964 earthquake, very few Canada geese existed in Cook Inlet. However, since the earthquake, apparently in response to habitat change, a mushrooming population of lesser Canadas is establishing itself.

The Aleutian Canada goose is classified as rare and endangered by Federal and State law. This was caused, in part, by the foxes that fur farmers released on the Aleutian Islands at the turn of the century. Having no predators on the island, the goose population quickly succumbed to the canines. Efforts to poison the foxes have been successful. The goose population is expected to take years to fully recover.

Alaska offers hunters fantastic shooting opportunities, like this rare triple on geese. Although the state's goose numbers have dropped in recent years, there is still quality goose hunting in select areas.

Even retrievers get excited when they get caught in the middle of a goose migration like this one, a common occurrence on the Alaska Peninsula.

About 60 percent of the total North American population of black brant originate from Alaska. The other 40 percent comes from northwestern Canada. Izembek Lagoon, at the tip of the Alaska Peninsula, is vital to the welfare of the entire North American black brant population. Brant arrive in Izembek by mid-September, but do not depart until late October or early November. During these weeks the brant gain several pounds by eating eel grass in Izembek Lagoon. The lagoon contains the largest eelgrass beds in the world. If this eelgrass was unavailable, the brant, and other geese, would not be able to make the long trans-oceanic flight between Cold Bay and their wintering grounds. Many birds fly nonstop between Izembek and Mexico.

Alaska is also the sole breeding grounds for emperor geese in North America. Emperors also breed in Siberia, and an interchange between Siberian and Alaskan birds is known to occur. Most of the Alaska emperors breed on the outer coast of the Y-K Delta, north of Kuskokwim Bay. In the fall, emperors leave the Y-K Delta and travel along the coast, around Bristol Bay, and then down to the Alaska Peninsula. Major concentrations of emperors can be found in the estuaries in the Egegik area, Cinder River Delta, Pilot Point, Port Heiden, Port Moller and Izembek Lagoon. Usually by late November, most emperors have left the Alaska Peninsula for their Aleutian island wintering grounds. During mild winters, emperors can be found along the Pacific side of the Alaska Peninsula and on the southern portions of Kodiak Island.

White-fronted geese in Alaska are divided into two different populations, according to their breeding, wintering and migration areas. The Pacific Flyway population breeds on the Yukon-Kuskokwim Delta. These birds leave the delta in September, pass through the Pilot Point area, and spend little time in Alaska before flying to their wintering grounds in northern California. The other group of white-fronted geese is known as the mid-continent population, and breeds throughout much of Alaska, except the Y-K Delta. Substantial numbers occur throughout the interior, in the Innoko River drainage, on the Seward Peninsula, at the head of Kotzebue Sound, and in the Selawik-Kobuk River drainages. These geese usually leave Alaska by mid-September. Their migration route is through central Canada and southward to their wintering areas along the southeast Texas coast and Mexico.

The numbers of snow geese originating from Alaska each year is minimal. A select few known breeding areas are scattered across the state. However, large numbers of snow geese pass through the Pilot Point area on their way from Wrangell Island breeding grounds in Russia, to their wintering area in central California. Other flocks migrate south along the Gulf of Alaska coast to Washington, while others migrate off the coastal areas of the Arctic National Wildlife Refuge.

Frequenting these areas throughout the season, I hunt geese much the same way I hunt ducks. However, many of the good goose hunting areas pale in comparison to Cold Bay's Izembek Lagoon, located near the tip of the Alaska Peninsula.

At first, Cold Bay appears to be a lesson in contrast. Disembarking from a turbo-prop Electra—which is the only way to reach the village—most people are immediately shocked by the barrenness of the land. Instead of grainfields and huge impoundments typical of goose hunting locations in Alaska and the Lower 48, the observer gazes upon miles of low, rolling tundra. Scrubby alders outline creeks coursing through the area. A few mountains jut their icy peaks into the typically gray skies. A short distance away, an active volcano puffs a cloud of smoke every 20 minutes. Several renovated buildings and bunkers left over from World War II, a fish and wildlife office, aircraft support facilities, and a handful of private residences make up the entire village. Leading across the tundra like a winding snake is the main "highway," a two-lane gravel road to Izembek Lagoon. Yet whatever this area may lack in modern architec-

Because of extreme tidal fluctuations in many parts of Alaska, floating dekes are often impractical. Here a hunter uses as decoys two emperors he shot earlier. When placed at the edge of an eelgrass bed, the dead birds draw in other geese that are flying the shoreline, looking for feeding areas.

ture and roads, it more than compensates for when the observer reaches the end of the road. One hears the incessant din of tens of thousands of geese and countless forms winging across a wave-capped horizon.

The waterfowler finds several species of geese at Izembek. The entire population of Pacific black brant arrives at Izembek Lagoon each autumn from its nesting areas off Alaska's Yukon-Kuskokwim Delta, arctic coast of Alaska, Canada and Siberia. Here they will stay until early November, feeding on the largest eelgrass beds in the world. Eelgrass represents what a field of shucked corn does for Canada geese.

Secondly, waterfowling's premier bird, the emperor goose, is found here in fair numbers. The species is considered by many to be the most elegant goose species in the world. The bird sports a body of light gray feathers, each outlined in black, a white crown and nape and bright orange-yellow feet. The emperor is not only coveted for its beauty, but also its rarity: the bird's range is virtually limited to a narrow strip of the peninsula that includes Cold Bay. Due to subsistence overharvest, there is currently no open season for emperors.

In addition to the brant and emperor, spectacular concentrations of lesser Canadas and a variety of sea and game ducks are also attracted to the eelgrass beds, which are protected from the heavy breakers of the Bering Sea by a natural reef, resulting in an ideal resting and feeding area for the birds. But best of all, at any given time, not more than a handful of hunters is scattered throughout the refuge. It is commonplace to hear the incessant cackling of geese throughout the day rather than the popping of shotguns, yet find out at day's end that everyone shot a quota of geese.

Few people are better qualified to discuss the waterfowling opportunities at Izembek than Ron Ozmina, owner and operator of Alaska Goose Guides, an outfit specializing in guided goose hunting trips to Izembek. Ozmina has hunted Izembek's goose populations more times than he can remember. His clients come from all over the country, and many are repeat customers. "I have one guy who has booked trips to Izembek for the past 11 years. After the first time, it becomes a traditional thing for many hunters."

Cold Bay may seem like a shortcut to the rewards of goose hunting without going through the trials and tribulations many hunters experience elsewhere in the state, such as working with large decoy spreads, waiting hours to spot a single goose, and the prerequisite of using a call to goose-foolin' perfection. However, Ozmina recommends differently.

"Because first timers are unfamiliar with flyways, hunting techniques, and dangers of hunting the area, I always recommend a guided experience first," says Ozmina. "For instance, it seldom snows at Cold Bay, but the wind and rain can freeze you to the bone. Careless hunters can become stranded on tidal mud flats, and brown bear roam the beaches. And don't expect to see the sun much, if at all, during your stay. Yet, there isn't much time for complaining when the weather is bad, because this is when goose hunting is the finest."

Ozmina explains that one week out of the month the tide becomes high enough to flow over the reef, with swells that converge upon the rafting geese. Very windy days and subsequent large waves will do the same. The extra water not only prevents the birds from reaching the eelgrass they so dearly love, but it also makes them seasick. So they mass migrate to protected bays, inland lakes and protected shorelines.

Shooting at this time is fast and furious for several hours, or until tides change and allow the geese to return to their feeding grounds. Other excellent times are at first light and toward late afternoon. To those that stick it out, full limits are possible.

In normal hunting situations, each species has its particular habits. While it is almost certain that hunters can bag all three species from one location, such as Outer Marker or the Island,

Emperor geese are the most elegant of their species in North America. They are also the most curious. These hunters are using white plastic trash bags filled with eelgrass to draw in emperors. The method works.

specialization is called for when numbers of individual species are desired.

For instance, brant almost always fly over water, staying away from shoreline. However, the trick to taking brant here is to build a blind out of eelgrass on one of the points sticking out into the lagoon, or use a boat blind. In other words, you must hunt open water if you want brant. If the wind is blowing, hunt along the protected sides of points. Just have your gun ready when they take to air, because the sky becomes black with birds.

Lesser Canadas and emperors are a different story. Shell or silhouette dekes placed on washed-up beds of eelgrass are extremely effective, especially for emperors. They are a curious and relatively unhunted species. They'll spot the decoys from several hundred yards out and fly to within range for a closer look. In fact, the emperor's curiosity is so great that white, plastic trash bags filled with eelgrass have been effective in drawing the birds into shooting range.

While many waterfowlers prefer shooting over decoys, others have success by just lying out in the tundra along major flyways between inland resting areas and the eelgrass feeding grounds. Try "Applegate" for lesser Canadas, the "Site" for lesser Canadas and emperors, and the "Outer Marker" for all species.

Because of the number of geese in the area, hunters often believe Izembek geese are easy to bring down. Not so. Since the eelgrass diet is one of the most nutritional foods available, the birds build a heavy layer of fat, up to an inch thick, under their plumage, which makes an effective "shot-proof vest." Magnum shells in ten or twelve gauge, 2¾ or three-inch in BBs and No. 2s are best. Guns must be plugged to hold no more than three shells. You should take at least four boxes of shells if you are a good shooter, and a box of low-base 7½s for cripples and ptarmigan shooting, which happens to be excellent.

There are a few precautions hunters should take when hunting Izembek geese. The area has a good population of brown bear. Each year there are reports of brown bears getting too close to hunters, who open fire with their shotguns. Bird shot does nothing but make the bears angry, and possibly instigate a confrontation. So don't shoot at the bears.

Please pick up empty shotgun hulls and trash. With the good shooting, it's easy to litter the ground with hulls. Try to keep Izembek a wilderness experience for the next hunter who uses the area.

And most of all, cooperate with any fish and wildlife biologists asking to see your birds. Field check of hunters' geese is the only way biologists have of collecting data on Cold Bay geese.

With prime waterfowling areas diminishing in the United States and Canada, it's good to know that such places as Izembek, Kachemak Bay, Kodiak Island, the Alaska Peninsula and other areas throughout Alaska offer a premier waterfowling experience. If you are thinking about a big game hunt in Alaska, plan on spending a few days afterwards pursuing Alaska's geese and ducks. And don't forget: bring plenty of shells!

Where to Hunt Waterfowl

North Slope

Seward Peninsula

Interior

Upper Yukon-Kuskokwim

Yukon Flats

Fairbanks-Minto

Minto Flats
Eielson AFB
Salchaket Slough
Healy Lake
Delta Area
Tok-Northway

Southcentral

Cook Inlet

Susitna Flats
Palmer Hay Flats
Goose Bay
Eagle River
Potter Marsh

Chickaloon Flats
Portage
Trading Bay
Redoubt Bay
Kachemak Bay
Jim-Swan Area

Gulf Coast

Copper River Delta
Yakutat Area
Prince William Sound

Southeast

Chilkat River	Duncan Canal	Farragut Bay
Blind Slough	St. James Bay	Stikine River Delta
Rocky Pass	Mendenhall Wetlands	

Southwest

Kodiak	**Alaska Peninsula**	
Kalsin Bay	Cold Bay	Port Heiden
	Pilot Point	Cinder River
	Port Moller	Aleutian Chain

Top 15 Goose Hunting Areas

Cold Bay	Copper River Delta	Trading Bay
Delta Area	Prince William Sound	Chickaloon
Minto Flats	Palmer Hay Flats	Portage
Pilot Point	Mendenhall	Goose Bay
Susitna Flats	Stikine River Delta	Blind Slough

The five-year average for sport-harvested geese in Alaska has varied from 8,000 to 15,000 birds. A recent reduction in goose numbers due to subsistence overharvest is responsible for current low hunter bag limits. Statistics show that over the past 20 years, Canada geese are the most common bird harvested by hunters, making up 70 percent of the bag, followed by brant at 7 percent, white-fronts at 7 percent, and snow geese at 4 percent. The calculated state-wide sandhill crane harvest is 1,500 to 2,000 birds annually. In 1986, the emperor season was closed due to extremely low numbers of birds. It is expected to reopen in several years.

Cook Inlet is the top goose producer in the state, due to easy access to hunting areas from the major cities of Anchorage, Kenai, Homer and Soldotna. This area has traditionally claimed over 30 percent of the state-wide goose harvest.

Top 15 Waterfowl Areas

(Determined by number of birds harvested annually).

Susitna Flats	Kachemak Bay	Healy Lake
Palmer Hay Flats	Stikine River Delta	Portage
Minto Flats	Tok-Northway	Delta Area
Copper River Delta	Prince William Sound	Chilkat River
Mendenhall	Trading Bay	Pilot Point

Species composition of the state-wide duck harvest has remained relatively consistent over the past 10 years, with 85 to 95 percent of the harvest composed of dabbling ducks, consisting of mallard, American wigeon, pintail and green-wing teal; 11 percent of diving ducks, of which the majority are lesser and greater scaup, Barrow's goldeneye and bufflehead; and 5 percent consisting of sea ducks and mergansers, of which the most commonly bagged species are the white-winged scoter, common merganser, hooded merganser and harlequin.

CHAPTER 15

Field Care of Meat and Trophies

I kept telling my brother, Bill, that after the shot is made, the real work begins. But he didn't listen, and I can't say that I blame him. He had just made a spectacular, two-shot kill on a huge bull moose in the southern part of the Alaska Range. After the bull went down for the count, he sprinted the 150 yards to the moose like a thoroughbred racehorse, leaving me in a trail of alder leaves and blueberry brush.

When I finally caught up with him, he was standing perfectly still. His arms hung limply at his side. His eyes were wide. My ears detected an almost inaudible "Oh, my Gawd" as he bent over to touch the huge beast. The animal was a freight-train of a specimen, and one of the largest-bodied moose I'd ever seen. Under a throaty grunt, Bill struggled to lift up a hind leg. It rose about two feet, only to fall back with a resounding "thud."

"Ya know," he said, "I once heard that after you pull the trigger, the work begins. How true."

"Amen to that," I said, all the while holding back a chuckle. "But if you can't turn the darn thing over, where do you start dressing it out?

It was a good question, yet it's one that needs to be answered long before the start of a hunt. Because I was with Bill on his first moose hunt, we finished field dressing his moose in a matter of hours, including caping out his trophy. But for the hunter unprepared for game meat handling and preparation, the results could mean the loss of what many people consider better eating than the best, corn-fed beef. I'm not talking about a few choice cuts, but rather 500 to 650 pounds of boneless meat from a moose, 200 pounds from a caribou, and 800 or more pounds

To field dress a moose, first turn the animal on its back, with head uphill. A good knife and steel are essential.

from a bison. I know one moose will keep my family dining on choice steaks, chops and roasts for two years. During that time, we don't spend a penny on beef. Thus, it's not only economical to spend as much time as necessary to ensure safekeeping of meat, but also unethical for us as hunters to do otherwise. How you care for meat in the field will greatly determine how well it will taste several months later.

Equipment

Proper meat preparation starts with using the right tools. And the most versatile is a skinning and/or butchering knife. Forget about that Bowie knife you have tucked away in your trophy room. Such a knife with a 12-inch blade is nothing more than a weapon. On an Alaska big game hunt, you need a functional tool: one that's lightweight, holds a good edge, and feels comfortable in your hand. You have two choices: a one-piece sheath knife or a folding knife. The decision depends on your preference. I find the modern folding knife to be especially advantageous on a wilderness hunt. Unlike a one-piece sheath knife, whose handle and guards usually stick out of the sheath and catch on limbs and snags, a folding knife is usually completely encased within a compact belt sheath. Not only is snagging minimized, but there's less length to jab the hunter in the leg, especially when climbing uphill.

A folding knife is also efficient. With one you can bone out an entire moose carcass, and leave so little scrap on the bone that the ravens will croak admonitions at you as you leave the kill site.

I prefer a folding knife with two, five-inch blades. One has a wide blade for meat cutting and scraping, while the other narrow blade is used for skinning chores and the detail work required in caping. I carry a back-up folding knife in my pack, along with a pocket knife in my pocket or camera bag. Should I happen to lose one, I won't be out of luck.

Skinning out a thick-skinned animal like a bison or bear will eventually dull the sharpest knife. When both blades get dull, stop and sharpen each on a steel. The best tool I've ever found that can sharpen a blade to a razor's edge is a Neivert Whittler. A variation of a sharpening steel, the Whittler is a tool used for sharpening dental instruments and scalpels. It is equally adept at putting a keen edge on knives, axes and other tools. And after four years of heavy use, my Whittler has yet to show the slightest sign of wear.

You'll need a few other items before starting to field dress your trophy. Pack at least 100 feet of nylon parachute cord or 1/4-inch nylon rope. You'll need it for lashing meat to a pack frame and for hanging meat back at camp. And don't forget a small backpack saw or ax. Each has advantages and disadvantages. The saw makes for neater cuts—especially when cutting the rib cage—but definitely requires more elbow grease to use. The ax is quicker, yet a tad crude. On hunts for species larger than moose, I take both, and use both. Use the ax to split the pelvis and backbone, and the saw for cutting up rib cage and separating legbones. Using an ax to split the rib cage can create sharp, jagged edges. These can not only cause serious injury to you, but also puncture your inflatable if you're on a float trip.

Surgical gloves work very well in preventing the blood from caking on your hands. They are especially invaluable on August sheep hunts and during the early September moose season. Then, white-sox and no-see-ums are out in plague force. They love to bite into hands caked with blood. After several hours of skinning and quartering without gloves, insect bites can turn into half-dollar-size welts that ache and remain swollen for days. Surgical gloves keep your hands bite-free in addition to protecting them from minor nicks and cuts incurred while skinning.

Field Care of Meat

Once the animal is down, and the congratulations have been passed out, spend anywhere from 10 to 20 minutes on photos. I know of an instance when a float hunter was sucked into a sweeper on a remote Alaska river. He managed to swim away from the incident, but not without losing his 60-inch moose rack, meat, and all hunting gear. As fate would have it, he always carried his camera in his shirt pocket, and despite the dunking, the film was undamaged. The photos of his hunt and trophy moose were the only defense he had when he got home, when he had to explain to his suspicious wife that he was actually moose hunting and not gambling in Las Vegas!

The skinning and quartering procedure is basically the same for sheep, goats and members of the deer family, which includes moose and caribou. The procedure is different with bears, especially 10-foot Kodiak brownies.

If at all possible, turn the animal on its back, with its head uphill. Proper positioning usually requires the help of some 1/4-inch rope and plenty of heave-ho. Once you get the animal on its back, anchor the moose by jamming the rack into the ground. Anchor the legs with lengths of rope, and you're set.

(left) Insert the knife beneath the breastbone; slit open the abdominal wall, and cut free the testicles and penis.

(right) Split open the pelvic bone, cut loose the intestines and organs.

Preparing smaller game such as deer, goats and caribou requires that you simply prop the shoulders with logs or stones to secure it for skinning and quartering.

The first step is to locate the sternum or breastbone. Insert your knife horizontally directly beneath the sternum. Keep the blade edge pointing toward the sky when making this initial cut. I do it this way because when the animal is propped on its back, there's a small air pocket beneath the brisket. It's easier to insert a knife into this pocket, and starting there minimizes the chance of puncturing the digestive tract. I also prefer to skin the belly section before opening up the carcass. I find the entire skinning job is easier when started this way.

After making the cut through the abdominal wall, insert the index and middle fingers of your non-cutting hand into the cavity. Use them to guide your cutting. With your fingertips, push the viscera aside before cutting. And, by cutting from the inside out, you cut less hair that can taint meat if not removed soon after butchering.

Skin down to the testicles and penis and cut them free. This makes cutting a straight line to the anus much more convenient. Next, cut down to, but not through, the anus. Cut it free from the pelvis and tie the end off with a piece of string. Find the bladder, and tie it at the urethra. Cut down to the the pelvic bone with a knife. Once you can see bone, take the ax and gently split the pelvis in order to free the bladder, urethra and anus. Once you have the anus and large intestine cut free, cut the bladder loose.

Reach inside the chest cavity and cut the diaphram, keeping your knife as close to the rib cage as possible. Pull out the heart and liver, and wrap them in a plastic bag for dinner later that night. Cut the windpipe and blood vessels as far forward as possible.

Split the breastbone, cut open the diaphram and remove lungs, windpipe and heart.

Now, the entire digestive tract and chest cavity organs can be removed in one pull and deposited to the side. Many hunters prefer to remove the abdominal organs before tackling the chest cavity. This is perfectly acceptable. The important thing to remember is to keep from puncturing the digestive tract or bladder.

After pushing the gut pile aside, begin to trim the inner carcass of fat, kidneys, and connective tissue. Make sure the animal is propped up so that it can properly drain. Do not use water to wash out the cavity. Water can spoil meat, especially if you're going to be in camp for another five or more days. The first priority is to cool the meat, clean it, and allow it to crust. Water delays crusting. I remember one goat hunt when I shot my goat two days before a friend shot his. We both hung our meat in elk bags to keep off the dust and flies. However, after five days, his meat was beginning to acquire a strong odor, while mine had developed a nice, cherry-red crust. The reason? He had shot his goat in the rain, and hung the meat in damp game bags. The meat never had a chance to crust. The meat cutter had to discard about 20 pounds of it as trim.

339

Field Care

While small animals such as blacktail deer and goat can be left unquartered overnight if the temperature is cool, I don't advise this practice for moose, elk or bison. Even if the temperature is 15 degrees, the meat and thick hide serve as an effective insulator in locking a carcass' heat. The adage, "Heat will sour meat" holds true, especially for moose. An incident that took place last year near Fairbanks proves this.

State Troopers received a report that a moose had been shot on a side road near 17 Mile Chena Hot Springs Road. After a brief search of the area, Fish and Wildlife officer Jane Schied found the dead bull at about 9 p.m. "The moose was concealed with saplings, and hadn't been gutted," she said. "I decided to wait and see if anyone would return to recover the moose." She hiked to the top of a nearby hill and waited.

At about 1 a.m., a truck pulled up to the covered carcass. Schied said she saw a man get out and light a lantern. He fired a shot into the air.

Schied suspects the poacher thought that the rifle shot would explain the carcass to anyone who came to investigate, since it was now September 1, the opening day of moose season.

She continued to watch the poacher for several minutes. When a car drove by, he extinguished the lantern until the car passed. He then got down to business and entered the woods to butcher the moose. That's when the poacher received his first lesson in what not to do in field preparation.

Separate ribs, backbone and neck and pack out.

Undisturbed and ungutted for many hours, the carcass had filled with gases. When the poacher cut into the belly, the abdomen exploded.

"The explosion so surprised him," Schied said, "that he ran back behind his truck. It took him several minutes to get over the shock, but he eventually returned to butcher the animal."

That's when he received his second lesson. Schied made her way downhill, walked up behind him and said, "Good morning. I'm Trooper Schied."

First, the poacher told Schied that he had just found the moose, but later admitted to shooting it. He was later charged with taking a bull moose in a closed season and failing to salvage game meat.

The moral of the story is twofold: First, poaching doesn't pay. And second, always gut the animal and prop it open to cool if you need to leave it in the field overnight.

Once the viscera has been removed, concentrate on the front and rear quarters. They are held in place by muscle and cartilage, and can easily be removed with a knife. I prefer to start with the hind quarters, and then take off the front quarters. I saw the ribs off, then neck and rack, and finish up with the fine tenderloins and backstrap along the backbone.

When you have to skin out a moose by yourself, try the filleting method. As the name suggests, you "fillet" the moose, starting by removing the hide. Start at the head and cut down the backbone, down the inside back leg, and up the belly to the jaw. Skin off the hide before removing the front and rear quarter. Next, bone out the neck, backstrap, flank and ribs. Place the sections in game bags or on the skinned-out hide. Remove the antlers, and flip the moose over onto its "filleted" side. Repeat the procedure. The digestive tract and organs remain inside the carcass for a relatively unmessy and easy field dress.

If you plan to leave camp in a day or two, or when hunting by yourself, boning is a fine way of leaving lots of weight at the kill site, especially for sheep or goat. However, if your plane won't arrive for three or more days, leave the bones in the meat if at all possible. Here's why. Every time you make a cut in the meat, whether by cutting deeply or by boning out a hindquarter, you trap bacteria and moisture in that cut. Air needed for proper crusting can't get in and spoilage occurs. And in warm weather, spoiling can take place in less than two days. Besides, keeping bones in the meat makes for easier handling and hanging in camp. That's a prime consideration when you're looking at a hindquarter of 135 pounds or more.

Just before your pick-up date, bone out the meat by taking your knife blade and simply carving the meat from the bones. Keep the knife blade pressed against the surface of the bone as you cut. Any missed pieces can later be trimmed away for stew or hamburger scrap. On a successful moose hunt in western Alaska, friend and former professional meat cutter Max Grill showed me how to salvage an additional 20 pounds of hamburger meat by digging out the meat from a boned-out neck and the muscles of the head. "Man-o-man I tell you," he said in his German accent, "I made sure not one scrap of meat left my meat-cutting shop by hanging to a bone. Small pieces add up to hundreds of dollars in a few days."

Since then, I've used Max's boning techniques to salvage an extra five to ten pounds of meat from a kill. The "scraps" make an excellent camp stew.

When finished boning or sectioning, you should have two hindquarters, two front quarters, neck, two rib cage halves, flank and tenderloins and miscellaneous meat from the backbone.

Before hanging, it's important to clean the meat of any fat, dirt, grass, hair, maggots or other organic substances that can cause the meat to spoil. Also, cut out any and all bloodshot

areas in and around the bullet entrance. Sometimes this damage can be quite extensive, as the hydrostatic shock that kills the animal can rupture blood vessels a foot away from the bullet wound. Also remove any excessive coagulation that may collect on the outside of the meat.

Once in camp, clean meat and hang in the shade.

Next, individually bag each section and quarter. Game bags keep the meat clean, not only while hanging, but also during transport back home. Do not use the "two for a dollar" wide-meshed game bags. These are practically worthless, as they fail to keep both insects and dirt off the meat. Quality game bags are close-knit mesh, and four bags cost anywhere from $10 to $14. You'll need eight bags to properly bag an entire moose; six for a caribou, sheep or goat. If treated with care, the bags can be washed and reused the following year.

In camp, nothing can beat a make-shift meat pole for hanging and aging wild game. Select an open, relatively breezy area where the wind can cool and crust the meat, and keep the insects at bay.

However, in many places like the Alaska Peninsula or Brooks Range sheep country, trees are non-existent. There, you'll have to prop the sections onto a brushpile. The main point to keep in mind is aeration. Place the meat on a pile of alder, willow, or birch sufficient to allow aeration from the ground up and to keep the meat out of the dirt. If there is no brush, prop the meat on a windy knoll against some rocks.

Whether you're using a meat pole or brush pile, it's wise to have a tarp ready to cover the meat, just in case it rains. Should I go out for a day of hunting, I always make a point of

covering the meat with a tarp. The tarp should be suspended from a rope hanging over the meat, and not placed directly on the meat itself. When in camp during good weather, remove the tarp and allow the meat to aerate. A tarp also serves to keep whiskeyjacks and Canada jays from tearing open the meat sacks and having a feast.

Your meat is most susceptible to the ravages of Alaska's insects from the time you section it until it forms a hard crust. Insects, especially blowflies, require a moist surface for laying their eggs. They can find the tinest hole in your game bags. And when they do, it's only a matter of several hours before the laid eggs turn into wiggling, squirming maggots that feed on your hard-earned meat.

If the meat is crusting properly, flies don't have a place to lay their eggs. That's why it's extremely important to check the meat about twice a day. Ensure that the surface of the meat stays dry. If the bags are wet from blood or water, dry them out on a bush or over a fire before slipping them back over the meat. Properly crusted meat exhibits a dull-red color and a hard, glazed surface. It's possible to leave a properly crusted, unbagged hindquarter on a meatpole during fly season and not have it infested with maggots 24 hours later. But don't try this unless the meat is crusted hard.

If insects are particularly bothersome, liberally dust any section of meat with black pepper. This is especially important at the tie-end of game bags, and where the bag comes in contact with the meat. Also, if the meat isn't crusting fast enough, smear blood over the sections. Hang them immediately and allow them to air-dry. This makes for an armor-like crust. If you don't have a supply of moose blood, try vegetable oil. Liberally smear it over all exposed surfaces. Flies hate it.

Most hunters prefer to hang their meat from three to five days at a temperature ranging from 38 to 50 degrees. Hanging allows the enzymatic action that occurs naturally in the flesh to tenderize the meat. Some sourdoughs claim a moose should be hung 10 days prior to butchering.

At the risk of incurring the ire of aged-meat connoisseurs, I say that hanging meat for more than 72 hours is not necessary. I once had a moose processed the day after I shot it, and it was some of the best eating meat I ever ate. Aging of meat often results from waiting for your bush pilot to pick you up. Then, you have no choice but to age your meat. Under ideal conditions, (cold, windy weather) aging will certainly enhance the tenderness and flavor of the meat. But rarely do you ever have ideal aging conditions in hunting camp.

In warm weather, meat need not be hung long since the aging action is accelerated at temperatures over 55 degrees. So, whether it's aged two days or five days, as soon as I get into town, I have my meat processed. However, aging is not productive if you've cut open the intestines, allowed blood clots to remain in the meat, and maggots to set in. Proper field care is the key to enjoying your steaks, chops, and roasts in the months to come.

Shipping Your Meat

A big heartache for many non-resident hunters who have successfully hunted big game in Alaska is the need to leave all or part of their meat with their guide or outfitter. Costs of air freight between Alaska and the Lower 48 can run up to $500 to shipping four quarters. However, by doing a little preparation yourself, you can eliminate 50 percent or more of this cost.

Depending on the amount of meat you want to take back, you'll need three to eight freeze-lock boxes. Available from meat and processing outlets in Alaska's major cities, freeze-lock boxes are specially corrugated and waxed containers usually used to ship fish and seafood. Although they come in various sizes, choose the type rated for 70 pounds. They run about $12 each, assembled. Divide your meat into piles of 60 pounds each and wrap in heavy-duty garbage bags. Pack the meat evenly throughout the box. If you have a couple of gel-packs, place them on top of the meat. They'll help keep it cool during the flight.

For added insulation, put newspaper or cardboard on under the lid. Meat processing outlets in Alaska have strapping machines where you can seal your carton. If not, regular strapping tape is a good substitute.

Airlines allow you to check up to three bags not exceeding 70 pounds each. Check three boxes of moose meat. It's important that you advise the counter clerk of the boxes' contents at the time of check-in. If the meat is delayed for whatever reason, many airlines will store the meat in a freezer until the next available flight. Check your hunting gear and rifle as excess baggage (the fee is usually $25 per piece; still cheaper than air freight). If you have any meat left over, ship it air freight. Shipping is on a per-pound basis, and the cost varies according to destination. Figure on $1.50 per pound as an average cost.

If you don't want the hassle of doing it yourself, or if you are pressed to catch your flight, there are several meat and fish processing outlets that can take your meat, package it, and air freight it wherever you want. Count on prep charges of $20 per box before delivery and air freight charges.

Good field care of meat is not difficult. All it takes is attention to detail and neatness. And when you sit down to that prime top sirloin moose or sheep steak several months later, you'll be glad you made that extra effort.

Trophy Care

Several years ago, I was talking to a local taxidermist about a few choice locations to try for spring black bear. Halfway through our conversation, we were interrupted by a hunter walking in with a beauty of a Dall sheep rack. The horns stretched 39 inches on one side and 40 inches on the other. They were heavily beamed and extremely close curled, a record-book ram if I ever saw one.

"I'd like to get this stuffed," the hunter said. Brad, my taxidermist friend, lit up with a smile.

"Why, it would be a honor to mount a trophy like this," he said, taking the horns from the hunter. "Where's the cape?"

The hunter looked around uneasily for a few seconds, then pulled out a bug-eaten, half-bald sheep cape that didn't even include all of the neck.

"Well, it was sorta hot in the mountains, and I forgot to take along some salt for the cape. The hair started to fall out after the fifth day. But I got it figured out." He reached into a bag he brought in and pulled out bits and pieces of tanned

sheep skin, the type used in fly tying.

"I was thinking that maybe you can cut the rotten sheep skin out and sew this good stuff in," the hunter said. He was as convinced that it would work as the owners of the Titanic thought it unsinkable.

My mouth was doing all sorts of contortions to keep from laughing out loud. Yet my jaw soon dropped in disbelief when Brad accepted the "cape" and horns, and said he'd call the hunter in a couple of weeks. The hunter left, happy as could be.

"You can't be serious," I said incredulously. "It can't be done."

"I know it and you know it," he said. "But I get so many ruined capes in here each year that I'm prepared for it. Before sheep season starts, I spread the word that I'm offering $300 for each properly fleshed and salted sheep cape that comes in. I then use them on mounts like this," he said, pointing to the bug-eaten cape. "It saves me a lot of business, and makes a lot of guys happy. I'll call this guy in a week or two, and let him know I have a cape available. I'm sure he'll jump at the chance, despite the extra cost."

If you're spending hundreds, and perhaps thousands of dollars on an Alaska big game hunt, it only stands to reason that you'd want the very best care given your trophy. If you're on a guided hunt, no problem. Most guides are extremely well-versed in proper trophy care. However, if you're by yourself, it's up to you to provide that care until a qualified taxidermist can take over.

Now taxidermists can only do a job as good as the material they have to work with. And judging by the poor condition of hides and capes they receive from many hunters, I'm surprised they're able to salvage anything at all. To give you an idea of the responsibilities you have in field care, I've compiled a list of the most common problems associated with hides and capes one taxidermist received last year:

- Capes with partial field care
- Ears turned halfway
- Faces of moose and caribou not fleshed
- Meat not removed from inside of nose and muzzle
- Nostrils and nose areas not skinned out or fleshed on moose or caribou
- Moose and caribou feet with joints left in the hooves
- Moose bells not split (especially rope bells)
- Bears not fleshed properly
- Bear noses not skinned
- Toes left in bear feet

This is only a partial list, but enough is enough. Familiarize yourself with the guidelines set forth in this chapter, and you'll be one of the few who will receive the taxidermist's thanks and praise rather than his guttural mumblings. But best of all, you'll have a first-class trophy hanging for all to see in a place of honor in your trophy room. It's hard to beat that type of satisfaction.

Take Photos

Before making any step toward caping your trophy, take plenty of photos, especially close-ups of the head and neck. The photos will aid the taxidermist in duplicating the form of your mount as closely as possible. Head-on shots, side shots and shots depicting any special markings are all helpful. Have these developed before taking your trophy to a taxidermist, and use them to explain exactly how you'd like your trophy to be mounted.

The Shoulder Mount

The shoulder mount is the most popular of all mounts, and one of the easiest to skin out. First, make an initial cut about three inches behind the foreleg, followed by a circular cut up and over the back and down the other side. Make a bit of a dogleg right at the junction of a circular cut that will help the taxidermist center the tanned skin on the form. Also cutting three inches behind the front legs will give the taxidermist a bit of extra hide to work with for repairs or patch-jobs. Indeed, extra hide on a cape is a prized rarity in many taxidermy shops. Taxidermists frequently complain that the most common problem they have with capes is that hunters cut them too short. Heed this warning and keep well back of the front legs.

From the circular cut from behind the front legs, cut up the back of the neck, ensuring that you stay along the ridgeline, and branch off in a "T" configuration for deer, elk and bison, and "Y" configuration for sheep and goats.

Next, start skinning and peeling the hide from the top of the neck down and forward to the head. Disjoint the head at the first vertebra. The remainder of the skinning job can either be done on-site or in camp, as conditions warrant. However, don't wait too long; hair slippage occurs as quickly as overnight.

The next step is to skin the hide away from the base of the antlers or horns. This can be easy or extremely difficult. I carry a screwdriver and a separate knife for this chore. Using the screwdriver for prying, and the knife for cutting, I can get the hide off the horn bases in no time. These tools are especially useful on difficult-to-skin animals such as sheep and Roosevelt elk.

Skin down to the ears, and sever them where they meet the skull. Continue skinning down the side of the head to the eyes. Be particularly careful there. When coming to the corner of the eye and the tearduct, use your fingernails to pull up on the hide. Then, while holding the knife at about a 90 degree angle to the skull, cut down into the eye membrane in short, even strokes. This technique minimizes any accidental cuts to the eye lid in this critical area. A cut eye or tear duct is extremely difficult for a taxidermist to repair.

Continue skinning down the nose. Keep the knife blade close to the skull as you skin out the lips, making the incision as close to the teeth as possible. Leave the lips attached to the skin and split them, after which they require an immediate dousing of salt. On large animals such as moose and bear,

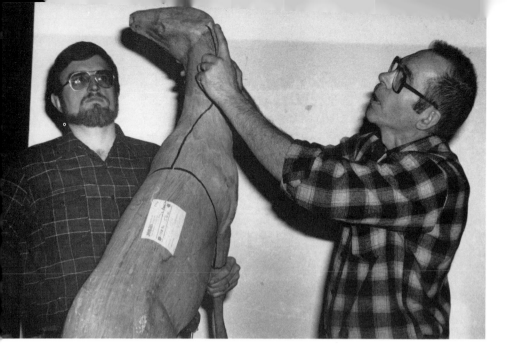

Taxidermists Darrell Farmen (right) and Brent Jones explain the proper cuts to make when skinning for a shoulder mount. Many hunters make the mistake of not starting their cut behind the front legs.

remove excess fat and tissue commonly found in and around the mouth and ears. If necessary, make additional cross slits to allow the salt to work into the tissue. When in doubt, it's always better to use too much salt than not enough.

Continue skinning out the nose. Take your time on a moose, as the nasal passageways are very hard to skin out and flesh. Here's a tip: keep right in the center of the white membrane as you're skinning it out. Also, a thin-bladed knife, such as a muskrat skinner, will help get the job done faster.

Once the cape is off, it's extremely important that you scrape all flesh and fat off the hide. An ulu is the best tool for this (see bear fleshing section). No matter what species the animal is, salt will only penetrate about 1/8-inch of fat and at the most, 1/4-inch of meat. By the time it reaches the hair follicles on an improperly fleshed hide, the salt has lost its effectiveness.

After the hide or cape has been completely fleshed, completely skin out or "turn" the ears. This is often tedious work, but of paramount importance for a quality mount. Spread out the cape and with the hair side down, liberally apply a layer of salt about 1/4-inch deep to all fleshed areas. Take care to rub sufficient quantities into the edges of the cape and any other nooks and crannies that might otherwise get neglected. Stretch the cape out to dry in a cool, airy place for about 24 hours. This allows the salt to draw out any excess moisture from the hide. Tilt the hide on an angle to allow this moisture to drain. This moisture can measure a gallon or more, which is

Remove the antlers from the head while in the field. A trophy moose rack can weigh up to 70 pounds, and the head another 50 pounds. For a European mount, however, you'll need to pack the entire head back to camp.

why it's imperative to shake off the wet salt the next day and reapply a fresh layer. Next, roll up the hide, hair side out, and position it so that it can drain properly again. If in camp for any length of time, reapply salt to the hide every third day.

The final job is to saw the horns or antlers from the skull. Make a cut that runs in a straight line through the eye socket. Clean out the brain cavity and set out the skull plate for the magpies and whiskeyjacks to clean up. Do not split the skull if it's a potential Boone and Crockett trophy. Doing so will automatically disqualify the rack.

Dall Sheep

The Dall sheep is a white, hollow-haired animal, and its cape is very susceptible to blood staining. Above all, do not let the blood dry on a Dall sheep cape. After you've caped it out, stick it in a plastic bag and find a snow-melt creek. There, soak the bloody area for 10 to 15 minutes. Only after the blood is completely washed out should you begin fleshing and salting. A standard sheep cape will use about one to two pounds of salt.

Field Care

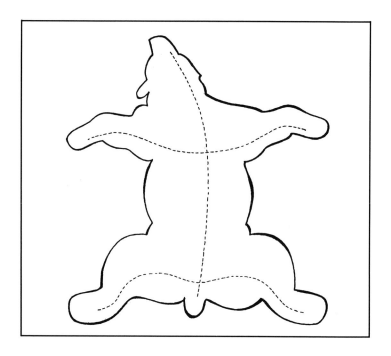

Bears

Skinning out bear rugs is relatively simple, if you follow a few basic guidelines. First, make a cut from about six inches up from the vent straight up to the underside of the bottom jaw. From this central incision cut down the inside back of each leg to the back edge of the footpad. On the hindquarters, be sure to stay within a couple inches of the rear seam, where the thick hair of the hide meets the sparse hair of the underleg.

For bear rugs, you can cut through the center of the pads. On lifesize mounts, cut around the pads. Cut the paw off at the wrist joint, but don't forget you'll need to skin every knuckle out once you're back in camp. Next, cut from the vent to the tip of the tail. Finish skinning out the bear, giving the same special consideration to the eyes, ears and lips described earlier.

If you only do one thing to your bear hide, please take off all the fat. Nothing else ruins a trophy hide more quickly than fat. And nothing else can take off bear fat more quickly than an Eskimo knife or ulu. The ulu has two big advantages over regular hunting knives: a wider, rounded blade, and the ability to apply pressure directly over the blade, rather than from the side. Both allow for a more effective and easier fleshing job.

To flesh a bear hide in camp, find an old log about 10 inches in diameter and peel off the bark so that it's perfectly smooth. Shave down any bumps with a knife or ax. Next, place a section of hide over the log and push the ulu blade into the fat and down the hide, being careful not to cut into the hair roots. With a few hours practice, you'll be able to flesh a brown bear hide expertly. And don't forget to completely turn the ears, and to salt them thoroughly.

After fleshing, liberally salt the hide with fine, granular, non-iodized salt. For an Alaska brown bear, plan on using at least 50-pounds of the stuff. If you have a tarp to store the hide under, salt the hide and stretch it out under the tarp for about two days. Otherwise, roll it up, hair-side out. Forty-eight hours later, scrape the old salt off and reapply new salt, making sure the hide is propped up to allow excess fluids to drain.

Many hunters forget to rub flat the edges of the bear hide. You must work salt into these tiny folds, or hair slippage will occur.

Skulls

Bear skulls are unique trophies, and you should not pass up the opportunity to add one to your collection. After skinning, remove the skull at the first vertebra and boil in a pot of soapy water. Simmer until the meat falls off the skull. Darrell Farmen of D and C Expediters in Anchorage says that bleaching the skull in household chlorine bleach will yellow it. He recommends a solution of 55 percent chlorine bleach and 45 percent hydrogen peroxide and magnesium carbonate. Let the skull soak in this solution until it's bone white. Remove, dry, and brush on a mixture of 50 percent water and 50 percent Elmer's glue. This seals and protects the skull. When dry, lightly spray with an acrylic plastic.

If the skull is record-book material, be sure to have it scored prior to preservation.

Antler and Horn Preservation

First, remove all meat and brain tissue from the skull cavity. Next, cut off any and all pieces of hide from the skull, especially around the burr at the base of the antler. Dust with salt or borax and allow to air dry.

Good field care of your trophy capes, hides and horns is not difficult. All it takes is a constant awareness of what needs to be done, and the time to do it. And each day as thousands of hunters the world over look at their favorite Alaska big game trophies, most will agree it was worth every bit of effort!

CHAPTER 16

Planning Your Guided/Outfitted Hunt

One day while writing a moose hunting feature for Sports Afield magazine, I received a call from a New Jersey hunter named Mark. His tale, which took over 70 minutes to tell, was a sad one. For the past five years he had been scrimping and saving a few bucks here and there for an elaborate, multi-species, Alaska big game hunt. Mark said that he could afford only one such hunt in his lifetime, and he wanted it to be a good one. He insisted on a competent guide who had his camp in an area with lots of trophy big game. A blue-collar factory worker, Mark had to take a second job moonlighting at a sporting goods store to save enough money for the hunt. He didn't want to touch his family's savings or children's college education fund.

Mark was not lackadaisical in doing his homework. He talked with guides at the local sport shows, wrote to hunting guides advertising in the outdoor magazines, and even visited a hunting consultant. He finally settled on a guide who had a proven track record for over eight years, and a good success ratio for caribou and moose. It wasn't coincidence that this particular outfitter also charged more than the other guides. "You expect to pay more for quality," the guide told Mark.

The hunt started out a bit confusingly. First, the guide wasn't at the airport, as promised, to pick up Mark. Eventually, a teenager employed by the guide showed up and drove Mark around town, helped him purchase a hunting license, tags and gear, and got him on the flight to the hunting camp. Upon arrival in camp, Mark was a bit dismayed. Weather-worn tents, rusted camp gear, and firewood strewn around the cook tent didn't fit the picture of the "quality" hunt the guide said Mark

To many hunters, a guide is worth the few extra dollars over the cost of a do-it-yourself hunt. Hunters don't have to worry about cooking meals or taking care of basic camp chores. The guide's knowledge of an area is equally as important, and can often make or break a hunt.

would be paying for. Nor did it resemble anything in the guide's brochure. Even when the cook tossed a load of dishwater out of the tent and into the main path, Mark reserved judgment.

But as the hunt wore on, Mark's worst impressions were confirmed. The head guide stayed in camp and assigned a young assistant to guide Mark for a trophy moose, his first and foremost preference. The assistant guide spent the next three days walking the alder patches, glassing, and walking some more. Overall, very little glassing was done. To make matters worse, the spike camp was extremely cramped and the food was second rate: mostly freeze-dried rations. Five days later, the assistant guide urged Mark to shoot a "nice" 40-incher they had spotted in a valley about half-a-mile from the main camp. Of course, Mark refused and demanded to be taken back to base camp. There, he planned to express his extreme displeasure with the hunt to the head guide. However, the scene back in camp was unacceptable. Mark was stunned to find that the camp's other two assistant guides had gone out and bagged two huge caribou bulls for themselves. Mark demanded to be taken back to Anchorage and issued a refund for the unused part of his hunt.

Mark was audibly upset as he continued his story. To make matters worse, the guide had sold his business after the close of the hunting season and had yet to provide Mark with a refund. He asked me if there was anything he could do. I gave him the names of people at the Guide Licensing and Control Board, plus a few other contacts, and wished him luck. I never heard back from Mark again. Chances are the only thing he could do was to chalk up the entire nightmare to experience.

Checking into the problem, I found a few mistakes made by the hunter. First, he fell victim to what I call the "Alaska: Game-and-Fish-Behind-Every-Bush" syndrome. Because the state is touted as the "Last Frontier," and "wilderness extravaganza," many out-of-state hunters believe that their dream of a successful, three-species hunt is impervious to failure. But in cases like the one Mark experienced, failure finds its mark all too often.

I have two commandments that hunters would be wise to follow when considering a guided or outfitted big game hunt in Alaska.

I. Thou Shalt Not Have Unrealistic Expectations:

In Alaska, trophy game animals are not behind every bush. Much of the state consists of mucky swampland, impassable glaciers, barren tundra, and uninhabitable mountains. Game

populations are concentrated in select areas, which may be hundreds of miles from the nearest road. Hunting near populated cities such as Anchorage, Fairbanks, and Juneau continually requires new techniques as game animals respond to increased hunting pressure.

Wilderness hunting can be potentially dangerous to the inexperienced hunter. Inclement weather, glacial rivers, rock slides, avalanches and tides can all cause severe injury or even death.

II. Thou Shalt Not Believe Only Thy Outfitter:

When you purchase a used car, you don't take the salesman's word that the engine has been rebuilt. You ask for evidence or receipts that indicate the work has been done. You should do the same with a guide or outfitter. The fact that an outfitter is in business is no indication that he has the qualifications, ethics, or hunting knowledge to handle your needs. Shop around. At last count, over 49 master guides, 388 registered guides, 162 class A assistant guides and 1,062 assistant guides are licensed within Alaska. Most of these are competent and well-respected. Yet, according to the State of Alaska, guide violations vary from one or two violations to as many as eight per year. Violations range from not operating with an air transport license to herding brown bear with dynamite to violations of the Lacey Act.

When an Alaska guide is charged with a minor violation, the court can revoke his license for a specific period of time. More serious violations can result in the license being revoked permanently. In that case, all guide-area privileges belonging to the guide are redistributed by the state to other guides.

Usually five years after their conviction, guides can reapply for renewal of their licenses. The guide must take a written exam to ensure his proficiency and current knowledge in first aid, ballistics, animal habits, and other topics, and must also take an oral exam before the licensing board. It is up to the board to determine the guide's sincerity in pledging to keep within the ethics of his profession. The state can either withhold the guide's license for an indefinite period of time, or reinstate his license. However, the re-licensed guide must apply for new guide areas just as a newly licensed guide does.

So, how do you go about choosing a competent guide and avoiding a renegade outfitter with a bad track record? First, hunters can try phoning the Alaska Fish and Wildlife Protection Office, (907) 269-5675. Give the name of the guide, and ask for a list of any game violations on his record. You can also call the Alaska Big Game Commercial Services Board for pertinent information regarding the board's agenda on guides and guided hunting.

Another way to check out a guide or outfitter is through friends and acquaintances. If they've had a hunt with a guide within the past year, they're more apt to tell you the nitty-gritty of the operation. Also, hunting or outdoor columnists in Alaska-based publications are good reference sources.

On a national level, *The Alaska Hunter*, (P.O. Box 8-3550A, Fairbanks, Alaska 99708) is without question the best publication for keeping track of both good and bad hunts, guides and hunting conditions, hunting techniques, where trophy big game animals are being taken, and complete information on guided as well as fly-out hunts. Regular features of this high-quality newsletter include Hunt Area Specifics, Secrets of Alaska's Hunting Guides, Alaska Hunter News Updates, Guide/Outfitter Issues, Hunt Reviews, and the popular Do-It-Yourself Alaska Hunter, which offers complete information on how you can duplicate the author's success on a particular hunt. All of Alaska's big game species, as well as waterfowling opportunities, are covered. The publication is available by mail-order subscription only, and is produced in Alaska by Alaska's top hunting writers. It's well worth the $49 a year pricetag.

Paid advertising is another effective way to learn about which guides are offering what. Many advertise in the national magazines and special interest publications such as *Western Outdoors*. Read the ads for specific information. With that in mind, here's a bit of advice that I'm passing on to you, free of charge: Semantics are the lifebuoy in the roily sea of hunting advertising and hype. If there is any mention of a "guaranteed" hunt in either the ad or the brochure, immediately look elsewhere. Not only is a guaranteed hunt unethical, but it's illegal within Alaska. A guaranteed hunt often prompts a guide to resort to less-than-ethical practices toward the final days of the hunt, especially if the client has been unsuccessful. The guide stands to lose some bucks if the client collects on his "guarantee." No one likes to spend $7,500 on a hunt and come back without a trophy. But then again, if you need to kill something each time out, you're missing the whole purpose of hunting. The Alaska hunting experience is here to enoble us, to allow us to better appreciate the world around us. If you need to kill something, go shoot rats at the dump.

However, just because a guide or outfitter doesn't advertise doesn't mean you shouldn't contact him. Many of Alaska's guides and outfitters are booked through word-of-mouth references based on past performance. Typically, they can be booked for two or more years in advance. This is especially true with popular species such as Kodiak brown bear and Dall sheep. If you really want to hunt with a particular guide, phone him and explain the situation. If he can't do it, he may be able to recommend another guide who can offer the same services.

Don't overlook the local fish and game office and taxidermists as alternate sources of information. They know the top guides in the area, and the trophies they've been producing in recent months. Beware of booking agents. Many are fly-by-night operators. Booking agents that have been in the business for five to 10 years, however, are relatively safe. Be especially wary of part-time consultants, especially those with their main offices in the Lower 48. When in doubt, ask for references.

The Alaska Hunter Information Service is an excellent and fail-safe source of information. The information service is not a booking agency, nor do they receive any remuneration or benefit from recommending one hunting area, guide or do-it-yourself hunt over another. They provide any and all information that hunters need, from the best gear to buy, to quality guides and air taxi operators, to game statistics and success ratios in a particular area. You pay at the time of your call with either a Visa or Mastercard number. The minimum charge for 15 minutes of consultation is $30, and their toll-free number, 1-800-446-2286 or 907-456-8212, makes this a service that is well worth the investment. It's easy to spend three times this amount in doing your own research. Call between 10 a.m. and 6 p.m., Alaska Standard Time. Have your questions ready.

Remember that planning is crucial to success. A hastily planned hunting trip, or one based on advertising hype rather than fact, can have hunters spending their time staring at barren tundra rather than herds of caribou.

I have two reasons for hunting with a guide with an unblemished record. First, guiding is a very demanding business. If a guide forgets about applying for a transport license, chances are he might forget other items such as enough salt for your cape or worse yet, the boundaries of open and closed hunting areas. Such an error could result in the loss of your trophy, hunting privileges and/or a fine.

Second, established guides tend to take care of their areas, and promote the health of their game populations. They know what animals are where, and it's this knowledge and experience that you're paying for. Fly-by-night operators do little, if any, scouting. They try to take the easy way out in terms of equipment, sportsmanship, and ethics. In fact, one guide, before being caught and convicted, used to fly around, shoot moose from his airplane and leave them for bears to feed upon. He would then fly around and "round up" the brown bears with sticks of dynamite and herd them to nearby hunters.

Why these tales of horror? So that you can understand what an ethical, professional guide is. They are masters of their trade, and worth every penny of their asking price. Don't settle for anything less. Now that you know what you need, let's go about doing it.

How to Deal with an Outfitter or Guide

First, figure out how much money you can afford to spend on the entire hunt. I sit down with some representative prices and make a list detailing each aspect of an Alaska big game hunt, and any side trips, such as a fishing or bird hunting trip I might want to take while I'm in the area. Here's a rough outline for a typical bear hunt:

Side Trips...$300

Souvenirs..$100

Taxidermy fees..$900

Air freight trophy home.................................$275

Back-up/emergency fund................................$250

Airfare (rt from Chicago to Kodiak, Alaska)..........$700

Accommodations (four nights)...........................$240

Meals (four days)...$100

Taxi, ground transportation.............................$40
Hunting equipment and clothing
that needs to be purchased (ankle-fit hip boots,
new rain gear, new socks and shirt).........................$300

License fees and tags....................................$410

Guide fees and tip.....................................$8,000

Total...$11,615

Write down your total available for the hunt and start sub-
tracting from the top down. The guide fees and tip should be
the last item on the list, as these are most important. The total
should give you some indication as to whether you can afford
a 14-day, multi-species hunt or just a single species, 7-day hunt.
I use this method of computation to avoid missing any major
area. Always stash extra bucks away for accommodations and
meals. In Alaska, weather is the Number 1 culprit for strand-
ing hunters before and after their hunts. I always get stranded
at least once a hunting season, requiring an overnighter or two
at a local hotel.

Making Contact

When you have a working budget and a list of potential
guides, write an identical letter to each one. Introduce yourself
and state the type of hunt you are interested in. Ask for a copy
of the guide's current brochure, price list, and other literature
explaining his services. Also, ask for at least three and preferably
half a dozen references. The guide will probably already have
a list of references printed up in his brochure or information
packet. Ask for others. The prepared list may contain hand-
picked friends or relatives, or the hunters on a select hunt the
guide had planned for promotional purposes. Make sure the
references are recent, preferably within the last two years, and
from different hunts offered by the outfitter. They should contain both addresses and phone numbers.

Next, divulge in as few words as possible a bit of personal
background. Tell him your age, physical condition, (smoker,
overweight) and previous hunting experience. Briefly list any
expectations in terms of services you expect him to provide
and the minimum trophy and the preferred trophy you will
accept. I prefer to include a SASE with my query. This shows
the guide you're serious, and usually initiates a prompt response.

When you receive your replies, compare and analyze them.

Before the hunt, be sure to advise your guide or outfitter of any special eating habits such as a low-sodium diet or allergies to certain foods.

Using identical query letters helps in comparing the different guides' personality, attitude and timliness in responding. Don't expect great volumes of prose and elaborate dialogue on the hunt offerings. Guides are not journalists. Forgive their misspellings and read for information, quality of experience, and cordiality. One of the best guides I know is a horrible speller. But he can look at a bear track and tell if it's male or female, its approximate weight, and whether or not it's pregnant. And for skills like that, I'm not going to be critical about spelling.

Check Out References

There are several reasons why I always ask for telephone numbers when I request references. A phone call may cost more than a letter, but hunters are more apt to divulge information over the phone because it's more convenient than responding by mail. You also get a quick response and "feel" for the hunt from the hunter's choice of words in describing the hunt. But whether you decide to call or write, you can make reference checking easier on both of you by having your questions thought up and written down beforehand. Some basic ones include:

• Was this your first hunt with this guide/outfitter in this area?

• What did the price of the hunt include? Were there any hidden charges, such as extra fleshing or trophy fees not specifically stipulated up front?

• How knowledgeable was the guide on game habits and hunting technique?

• How many hunters were in camp, and what was the total number of trophies taken? Was the hunt physically demanding?

• How many hunters and support people were in camp? Number

of assistant guides? How many hunters per guide? Were camp personnel friendly? Were they clean and tidy?

• In what condition was the camp equipment and tentage? Quality of food?

• What is the referee's opinion of the guide/outfitter? What things would he change about the hunt? Would he take the hunt again? Why?

When listening to or reading the responses to your questions, be wary of biased opinions. Hunters find it easy and soothing to the ego to blame their personal shortcomings on the guide. An out-of-shape hunter will say the guide walked too fast; "the game was spooky" means the hunter was a lousy shot; and "didn't hunt an area thoroughly enough" means the client should have booked a 10-day hunt instead of a four-day package.

I've had many people call me over the years and ask me questions about everything from guides to the best rifle to take for brown bear. Most callers are usually apologetic for disturbing me. Don't apologize. I believe that hunters share a common bond in helping each other out. Just don't overabuse the privilege. Keep it short, to the point, and courteous. Besides, if you're one of the few lucky ones that manage to catch me at home, you deserve to have a question or two answered.

A common mistake a few hunters make is to contact a guide, find out where he hunts, and set up their own hunt in the same area. I think this practice is unethical. Yet as fate would have it, the effort usually backfires.

While on an outfitted moose float in western Alaska last year, four raftloads of hunters stopped at my hunting party's camp toward the end of our hunt. We offered them each a cup of coffee and light snack. It was apparent that they were envious of our camp, chef, and accommodations. Conversation revealed that they had contacted a guide about moose hunting on a nearby river, only to cancel out when he wanted $4,000 a head. Not wanting to pay the full price for a fully-guided hunt, they managed to find a seasonal air-taxi operator who was willing to outfit them with inflatables and camp gear and fly them into the same area where the guide had his moose camp. One of the hunters said that before they sent the charter operator a deposit, the operator assured them that they would all get their moose, or at least a shot at one.

As it turned out, the group of eight had seen only one moose during the nine days of their hunt. With two more days left, they weren't too enthusiastic, especially when they saw our racks and learned that our camp was five for five, with the smallest rack measuring at 50 inches.

The hunters were misled, but in a way, it was their own fault. None of the hunters had previously hunted moose, and obviously never learned, at least on that hunt. They were unaware of the techniques used to hunt moose in that area, which are quite different than those used elsewhere in North America. And of course, they got what they paid for. From what I figured, they saved a mere $1,300 by taking on the extra hassles and troubles themselves. As my Dad used to say: "If it's worth doing, it's worth doing right." In the case of those hunters, a guided hunt was the only way of doing it right.

Closing the Deal

Once you've made a decision, contact the guide for more information. Advise him which references you have contacted, and any questions that may have arisen from those contacts. Now is the time to fire off the detailed questions you have about the hunt. It's not unethical to ask what your chances are (percentage) of bagging the trophy you're after. Indicate that you're in the final decision-making process on your hunt, and need the nuts-and-bolts information to make the final move. If you haven't already done so, inform the guide of any special diet you may require, or physical handicap you may have. Many guides protect themselves as well as clients by using a contract that details the terms of agreement. Read the fine print. Avoid any commitment that specifies a certain firm to do all the taxidermy work from your hunt. Hunting and taxidermy are two separate services, and should be treated as such. Guides often get a "kickback" from the amount of business they provide to certain taxidermists, and vice versa. You should be free to take the recommendations of the guide, and make your own choice.

It's imperative that you tell the guide exactly what you want out of the hunt. If you won't settle for anything less than a 40-inch Dall, tell him so. But be honest! If you smoke two packs a day, and the most exercise you get is taking your shoes off to go to bed, tell him that also. It's much easier to be disappointed with a "Can't help you," than the excruciating embarrassment you'd feel as you sit wheezing at the 500-foot level of a 5,000-foot mountain.

The trouble is that most hunters hear what they want to. Tundra is interpreted to mean flat, easy walking, when in reality, it's some of the most difficult walking found anywhere in the world. Be sure to ask your guide exactly what type of terrain you'll be hunting in, and relate any exercise program you've been pursuing (or intend to pursue). He'll give you the facts as he sees them. And don't forget about any medical conditions. I have a relative who was in a horrible car accident. He can't walk very far without the help of a cane. He came to me two years ago, wanting to go on a moose and grizzly hunt. We found him a guide who uses a trac vehicle, and he bagged a nice, 60-inch bull and almost bagged a nice, toklat grizzly. But he was open with the guide, and the guide catered to his requests. Enough said.

Once you've decided on a hunt, make your deposit as early as possible. A guide I know says that over half the requests he receives are for "information only." A deposit indicates to the guide that you're serious about the hunt, and is a prompt for him to start planning your hunt or scouting for that special trophy during his pre-season trips.

It's not improper for you to initiate a contract if the guide doesn't provide one. Keep it simple: a letter that briefly details the expectations of the hunt and the services to be provided. Send this registered mail in ample time for the guide to receive, sign, and return to you.

Plan on paying anywhere from 25 to 50 percent of the hunt price when making your reservation. You can use a personal check, cashier's check, or money order. The balance is usually due before the start of the hunt. Expect to pay the balance in cash, cashier's check or money order. Most guides won't accept a personal check for the hunt itself. Why? Because for too many years, many unethical hunters—upset with a hunt for reasons which may or may not have to do with the guide—have stopped payment on the check after the hunt, and refuse to pay the guide. Other hunters have stopped payment on a check prior to the hunt, not telling the guide until they have harvested their trophies. If they don't connect, the guide doesn't get paid. Abide by the payment system your guide suggests, and keep a folder of all correspondence in your duffel, just in case a question comes up before or after the hunt.

By following these guidelines and booking your hunt as early as possible (two years in advance is ideal, one year is the absolute minimum), you'll discover that half of the excitement of the hunt is in the planning. It's awaiting the daily mail, reading up on Alaska in the local library, and talking to the guide, especially about the ol' mosshorn he has scoped out for you in a secret meadow. Indeed, if they had homework like this in school, I'd still be in college!

CHAPTER 17

Gearing Up

Veteran Alaska outdoorsmen know that a successful hunt takes more than a thorough knowledge of big game habits and hunting techniques. The proper selection and use of clothing is an integral part of a successful hunt. A hunter who is shivering and stupefied from the cold of a wet down jacket, cheap raingear, and poor-quality footwear has not only wasted his time in the field, but also has made himself a prime candidate for hypothermia. Hunting takes 100 percent effort and concentration, whether it be in gale-force winds on the Alaska Peninsula or in the sunshine of an August afternoon in the Brooks. Indeed, how well you enjoy your Alaska hunting trip greatly depends on how well you are dressed.

Clothing

Alaska's weather is unpredictable. Seventy-mile-per-hour winds, blinding snowstorms, 40-below-zero temperatures, or days of cloudless, sunny weather can all be experienced in a week's time, in the same location. The hunter whose careful planning lets him dress properly for a variety of inclement weather conditions such as these stands a greater chance of bagging that trophy.

Recent advantages in fabric design and manufacturing leading to lightweight man-made materials have given new meaning to the term *layering*, a manner of dress that provides the best protection in all weather conditions. The strong argument for layered dress is that no single garment is best in all conditions. With layering, you can loosen or take off a layer when climbing the hills for sheep, and once on top, you can add a layer or fasten up the cuffs and neck for increased warmth. Also,

A pile jacket has many advantages on a hunting trip. It's warm, dries fast and is durable. It's also "quiet" when stalking in dense brush.

a proper selection of layered garments for a week's hunt can be packed in a small duffel. But before you pack, you need to understand how each of the layering elements works separately, and together, to keep you warm and comfortable.

Foundation Layer

The choice of a foundation layer (or underwear by its traditional name) is extremely important to the hunter. The purpose of the foundation layer is to wick moisture from your skin and transport it to an outer layer of clothing.

Until recently, the cotton "long john" was the most popular undergarment. While it provided warmth in fair weather conditions, it was unsuitable as an insulating layer. When soaked or wet, cotton underwear loses its insulating properties, and can actually cause hypothermia.

Polypropylene has revolutionized underwear in recent years. Because polypropylene is a "plastic" type of material, it doesn't absorb water. In fact, it wicks moisture vapor away from the skin and into outer layers of clothing where it can evaporate without chilling you.

The main disadvantage of polypropylene underwear is that it loses its "wicking" ability after several washings. It also is extremely sensitive to heat. Once when I sat by a campfire in my polypropylene underwear, a spark popped out of the fire and landed on my arm. The polypropylene exploded and fizzled, much the same as fishing line does when thrown into a fire. I could have easily been burned, but wasn't.

The new fabric on the block—polyester—surpasses polypropylene in several ways. A polyester foundation layer's wicking ability is superior to polypropylene's. Polyester is also warmer, softer against the skin, and unaffected by high temperatures. Unlike polypropylene, polyester undergarments can be tossed into the dryer without disastrous effects. Polyester garments come in various weights: five-to eight-ounce garments will handle most Alaska hunting situations.

Insulating Layer

Once the moisture and perspiration is wicked away from your skin, it needs a place to go for evaporation. Enter the insulating layer. Garments in this category must be breathable and allow for adequate ventilation of body heat. The hunter has a variety of insulating layers from which to choose. Because most Alaska hunts take place in cold, wet weather, pile is the favored, and often best choice. It is quick-drying, warm, breathable,

Clothing List

☐ Army Duffel Bag (to carry gear)
☐ Qualofill or down sleeping bag
☐ Air mattress or pad
☐ Ankle-fit hip boots
☐ Leather or camp boots
☐ Breathable raingear
☐ PVC raingear
☐ Thinsulate vest
☐ Insulated outerwear
☐ Wool or chamois shirts and sweaters
☐ Corduroy or wool blend pants
☐ Insulated hat and billed cap
☐ Polyester underwear
☐ Polypropylene/wool socks
☐ Polypropylene/wool gloves
☐ Extra shoelaces

and non-binding on the arms and shoulders. Pile retains its loft and stays warm when wet. It has the edge over both wool and down in that it can easily be dried by vigorous shaking in the open air. When you add a waterproof shell, you increase its wind resistance and warmth.

Protective Layer

Your outerwear deserves careful consideration. The supporting layers are useless without a quality, protective layer both to resist the wind, rain and cold, and also to maintain a comfortable environment for your body to function in.

In early August caribou or sheep hunting, you usually need nothing more than a shell to protect you from the wind. Shells made from Gore-tex or similar fabrics offer protection from light rain, and breathability—a necessary element on both hot and cold days.

For wet/cold conditions, keep in mind that Gore-tex is not waterproof. It is highly water resistant. It also leaks from time to time. For complete waterproofing, you need a polyurethane or PVC two-piece suit. In fact, I carry both two-piece Goretex and PVC suits. After a week of steady wear in wet weather, the Goretex suit tends to get a bit clammy, despite continual "dryings" in the cook tent. In most hunting situations except those requiring lots of exertion, I wear my camo PVC suit with good results. After the Gore-tex is dry, I hang up the PVC suit to dry.

Some hunters prefer a poncho, which if necessary, can be made into a make-shift shelter. A poncho is big, roomy and allows you to cover your day pack and keep your rifle dry in a rainstorm. But ponchos often leak, and contribute little to the total layering system. They do work well when worn over Gore-tex garments, especially in torrential downpours.

In snow/cold conditions, an insulated Gore-tex jacket, coat or shell works extremely well. However, if you're going to be hunting the brushy forests of southeast Alaska, wear an outer layer of wool or "soft" fabric: one that isn't "noisy" in the brush. I prefer a heavy wool jacket and carry my raingear, along with my lunch, in a small daypack.

Shirt: Many hunters prefer chamois, flannel or wool-blend. If the shirt gets wet from body perspiration, just remove it and hang it to air dry. I've been warm in the worst weather conditions with just the polyester underwear, pile jacket and outerwear.

Pants: Keep in mind that you'll be hiking in some of the world's toughest terrain. Snags, devil's club and alder all slash away at your legs. When hunting in the mountains, your legs do most of the work, and perspire heavily. In cold, wet weather, it's hard to beat worsteds or wool pants. In less severe conditions, I like Corduroy because it is durable and dries quickly when wet. For outer wear, Gore-tex leggings work very well in most situations. Be sure to buy them large enough to allow freedom of movement. For added warmth, try the Thinsulate type of bib overall.

Headgear: Remember that 60 percent of all body heat is lost through an unprotected head. For wet-weather hunting, the water-resistant caps with a synthetic insulation are a good choice. Eyeglass wearers, be sure the hat has a bill to protect your glasses during rainy spells. During September and November goat, deer and moose hunts, I like to take along a wool hat for early morning and late evening glassing. If you find wool uncomfortable around your head and ears, find a hat

with a polypropylene liner.

Gloves: For most hunting conditions, polypropylene/wool gloves are the only way to go. They resist abrasion and dry very quickly. When waterfowl hunting, or when weather is extremely wet, insulated Gore-tex-lined gloves keep fingers nimble. Choose the 200-to 300-gram insulation models; they're much warmer than 150-gram gloves.

Footwear: No matter what the conditions, the best footwear for Alaska hunting conditions is the ankle-fit hip boot. Advancements in technology have allowed manufacturers to construct a boot that withstands the ruggedness of Alaska terrain. I've tried them all, and found the Marathon ankle-fit is by far the best. One season I wore the hip boots on a grueling goat hunt in Ketchikan, a caribou hunt in the interior, a moose hunt in the Talkeetnas, and an elk hunt on Afognak, and they performed flawlessly. Not a single blister or chafed area on either foot. Ankle-fits are snug around the ankles, which prevents your feet from sliding around in the boots when climbing or on a long-distance walk. Marathon hippers have an aggressive tread that offers sure traction in all conditions, including snow and ice. They're the next best thing to Vibram-soled boots that I've seen.

Speaking of Vibram soles, there is only one occasion when I do change over to stiff-soled climbing boots: that's when I'm goat hunting. I'm a climber, and I like to scale the precipices for those solitary billies. Stiff, vibram-soled climbing boots are the ticket here. On a late-season goat hunt, rocks are often glazed with ice, and can be treacherous for the hunter. If I'm carrying a pack up, or goat meat and horns down, the stiff-soled boots offer additional support to handle those icy, narrow ledges. Once I get back down to timberline, I take off the climbing boots and put on the ankle-fits.

The Gore-tex type boot liner is a must-have item to wear inside your ankle-fits or leather hunting boots. In past hunts, my feet used to be soaking wet after a long day afield. However, with the new Gore-tex liners and polypropylene socks, my feet stay fairly dry; not completely, but better than they were before. And dry feet are the first step to preventing blisters.

The disadvantage of ankle-fit hip boots is that they offer virtually no ankle support. They are not for hunters with weak ankles. However, if you're in shape, and you should be, there's no reason why ankle-fits won't do the job. I've packed thousands of pounds of moose out on my back in ankle-fits, and have yet to twist or turn an ankle. Just use common sense and take it slowly.

Many guides have tried, and rave about the plastic, Koflach climbing boot for both sheep and goat hunting. The Koflach offers the features of a quality climbing boot, and the water-proofing of hip boots. They're a bit stiff and take some getting used to, but worth the expense, according to some owners.

For types of leather boots, I prefer the low cuts because they allow me increased ankle movement when climbing for goats and other mountain game. But most hunters should consider higher-cut boots for these reasons: they provide better ankle support, keep feet warmer and drier and keep debris out. I personally don't care for the leather and fabric-composite hiking boots. They're useful for blacktail or grouse hunting. But when you're up in the rocks, they don't offer the protection your feet need. Better to have that leg-weary feeling of carrying heavily constructed, four-pound boots at the end of the day, than to have feet battered and bruised from the insufficient protection offered by these lightweight boots. There is one good use for lightweights. Wear them in camp when your hippers or climbing boots are hanging to dry. Camp shoes help your feet relax at the end of a long day. Take whatever is comfortable, from jogging shoes to rubber-bottomed "pacs."

A few important reminders on boot wear. Always break in your boots before hunting. Before going afield, waterproof them thoroughly according to the manufacturer's instructions and keep them treated with a water-seal or a silicone dressing throughout the hunt. With ankle-fit hip boots, always carry a patch kit for emergency repairs. And with all your boots, dry them out after a day afield. Stuff them with old newspapers or scrap paper. This will help absorb the moisture, helping them dry for the next day's hunt.

Socks: Wool, nylon and polypropylene socks are extremely warm and serve to whisk perspiration away from feet. They are an absolute must when wearing ankle-fit hip boots. I prefer the knee-high sock. They help reduce chafing from hip boot wear, and keep the blood circulating through the lower leg and feet in cold weather.

Better yet is the two-layer sock system. When conditions are dry, first put on a pair of silk socks. They keep your feet dry and comfortable, and they're the only way to go when your boots lack room for two heavy socks. Over the silk sock put on a medium-weight, wool-blend sock. And take enough socks for each day of hunting. Wearing dirty socks is a sure invite for blisters, athlete's foot and other problems.

Sleeping Bag: The sleeping bag is one of the most important items to take on a hunt. After a grueling day afield and a hearty meal, you're ready for a good night's sleep. If a drafty or wrongly chosen bag interferes with your sleep, you're not going to be at your peak the next day. Within three days, you'll be reduced to a jittery mass of nerves and irritability.

Most hunters prefer a mummy bag made either of goose down, the best of natural fibers, or Qualofill, the best man-made fiber available today. I prefer the Qualofill bags because they remain warm, even if wet. Once down becomes wet, it loses its insulating properties. On my moose hunt last year, it rained for nine out of 10 days. The temperature hovered above freezing during the day, and below freezing at night. There was never the chance to dry out the sleeping bags. Hunters with down bags began to complain about being cold at night, while those of us with synthetic-fiber bags didn't have a bit of trouble sleeping like babes.

For everything except long backpacking trips, I use a five-pound Qualofill bag rated for 20 below. On the longer trips early in the season, I use a three-pound fiberfill bag or goose down bag, depending on weather conditions. With the heavier Qualofill, I've been warm in temperatures to -40. However, this was only possible with a liner. Sleeping bag liners can add as much as 7 to 20 degrees to the bottom end of your "comfort zone." I prefer a flannel liner during the autumn months, and pile for the winter months.

Of course, one of the keys to staying warm is to air your bag each day, weather permitting. It's important to fluff up the fibers that provide the insulating effect.

Air Mattress: The best bag won't do you a bit of good without a proper mattress. The foam pads are best, but are large and bulky. Therma-rest makes an inflatable foam mattress that's both compact and warm. The choice depends on the type and duration of the hunt. On long backpack hunts, I prefer a quality air mattress, mainly for its compactness. The long backpack hunts are usually in August and early September, when temperatures are not too extreme and the extra insulation offered by the foam pads isn't necessary. Later in the year, especially if I'm hunting from a base camp, I'll take my one-inch Therma-rest. Here again, the amount of loft is a matter of choice. Some hunters can sleep on a one-inch mattress, while others need a minimum of three inches. Use what's most comfortable for you.

Equipment

Optics: A good pair of binoculars and/or spotting scope is as important as the hunter's rifle and ammunition. To hunt without quality optics is an exercise in futility.

Spotting scopes are for long-distance glassing. Choose a scope with a 15-to 45-power variable eyepiece. Variables are quick and easy to use, with no fixed eyepieces to misplace. Also, the act of changing fixed eyepieces while in the field allows moisture to get into the scope, which can blur a sight picture. It may not be noticeable at first, but after eight hours of glassing, expect eye strain and blurry vision.

Expect to pay several hundred dollars for a good scope. Eyestrain from glassing through inferior optics can cause headaches, double vision, loss of hunting drive and overall fatigue. Bausch and Lomb makes a good scope that stands up well under field use.

Binoculars are equally as important. But to purchase a pair of binoculars for power alone is asking for trouble. Most binoculars range from 7 to 10 power and are sold as 7x35, 7x50, 10x28, 10x50 and so on. The smaller number (7, 10) refers to the power, while the higher number is the diameter of the objective lens in millimeters. As a general rule, the larger the objective lens, the better the light-gathering properties. But the lower-power binocs are a tad better in low-light situations than high-powered binoculars. For hunting in Alaska, choose a pair of binoculars with good, light-gathering properties. Avoid the high-powered, small objective lens binoculars such as the 10x28s. These are worthless as big game binoculars because they make locating game difficult, especially when you need to glass for hours at a time. Go with the 7x35s or 10x50s made by either Zeiss or Leica. These and other quality optics allow you to glass all day with little or no eyestrain.

Scopes are a matter of choice. Most guides recommend a variable scope. Usually the 1x4 power is best for brown bear hunting, while the 3x9s or 4x12s offer more versatility for other types of Alaska big game hunting. For tundra hunting, where

(left) A variable scope, like this Bushnell 4x12 Rangefinder, is good for most Alaska hunting situations. However, if most of your hunting is for sheep and goat, you might opt for a lighter scope in 3x9. Brown bear hunters often prefer a 1x4.

(right) Good optics are important to prevent eye fatigue and headaches. These Bushnell 7x50s with rangefinder are fogproof and waterproof, necessary features when hunting in Alaska's oftentimes inclement weather.

distances are deceiving, the rangefinder scopes are hard to beat. To test them out, I've used the rangefinder feature on my Bushnell to determine distances of game after I've guessed the range. Usually I'm on, but on two occasions I missed by a bit less than 75 yards. The rangefinder does have several disadvantages. It takes time to use, and is worthless when an animal is fleeing. Also, its ability to determine range depends on the animal's being a certain size between brisket and back. Animals with larger than normal proportions tend to toss the rangefinder off a bit. But for most hunting conditions, especially if you're not used to judging distances on the tundra, a rangefinder scope might be a good investment.

Some bear guides swear by a detachable scope mount. They need to. If a bear gets wounded, the fast sight picture that iron sights provide is essential, especially if the guide needs to go into the brush after the bear. This is the only situation requiring iron sights in Alaska big game hunting, unless of course, you prefer to use iron sights.

Camera: To capture the adventure of the hunt for later re-savoring, a good camera is important. If you're going to invest several hundred to thousands of dollars on a hunt, invest in a 35mm system. A 35mm takes much better prints and slides than the 110 models. Many of the quality cameras available today are no larger than a pack of cigarettes. Their only disadvantage is they don't have interchangeable lenses, which can be disappointing if you want to spend time photographing moose or caribou after you've bagged your trophy. So I recommend a compact 35mm system with interchangeable lenses. Whatever camera you choose, keep it in a zip-loc bag to protect it from dirt and moisture.

First-Aid Kit: For backpack use, a first-aid kit containing a few items is all that's necessary. My kit includes:

- [ ] Suture kit (for sewing up deep cuts)
- [ ] Antibiotics (for my own use only)
- [ ] Antibacterial soap
- [ ] Actifed
- [ ] Aspirin
- [ ] Band-aids
- [ ] Moleskin
- [ ] Antiseptic cloth in foil pouch
- [ ] Kaopectate (for GI distress)
- [ ] Flagyl (treating ingestion of water organisms)
- [ ] Robitussin DM (respiratory infections)

If you do get into an emergency situation, don't forget the directions for making emergency signals located on the back of your Alaska hunting license. They are invaluable when signaling to aircraft that you need help.

Extra Eyeglasses: It's extremely easy to lose, break or crack a pair of eyeglasses on a hunt. Always carry an extra pair of glasses or contact lenses in your daypack or stashed away in your duffle back in camp. An old pair is better than no spare.

Food: For long float hunts or hunts from a base camp, food is not a problem. You can have steak and lobster every night if you so desire. Planning for food and its weight comes into play when hunting in the mountains. Pack food items that are nutritious, provide high energy, yet are lightweight. Generally, the options are instant foods, freeze-dried foods or the "ready to eat" meals in a foil pouch.

Freeze-dried foods are lightweight, great for long-distance hunts, especially when supplemented with canned or ready-to-eat foods and meats. Yet after several days on a diet of nothing but freeze-dried, many hunters feel sluggish, and lack the necessary energy for wilderness hunting.

Max Grill, Sr. cooking up a tasty dinner of moose stroganoff. Foods with heavy gravies stay with you longer, and provide ample energy for those long climbs or cold weather. How you eat on a hunt usually determines how well you hunt. Feast out at base camp, but choose items carefully for spike camps and overland treks.

Ready-to-eat meals, available in a variety of entrees vacuum-packed in foil pouches, need no refrigeration, and have a shelf life of up to five years. To prepare, just drop them in a pot of boiling water, heat for five minutes, and serve. I like the meals with heavy sauces and gravies. They stay with you longer.

For lunch, pack the creamy type of instant soup. They don't run through you as quickly as the broth type of soup. Also, summer sausage, meat sticks, jerky and cheese are good sources of protein. Trail mix is excellent. Many guides make their own by combining nuts, M&Ms, granola, coconut, raisins, corn-nuts and dried fruit. Some hunters have been known to subsist off this mixture for days at a time.

For breakfast, make something quick and simple. Instant oatmeal is a favorite item; so are the granola bars or granola and milk. If you like a heavy breakfast, go for it. Many hunters prefer to eat a larger lunch than breakfast. Their reasoning is simple: they want to get out in the field and start hunting. Although unorthodox, the Ramen Cup-O-Noodles is a nourishing getter-upper with its dried egg and noodles. However, you need to unpack it from its fragile styrofoam cup, which usually cracks in transit and takes up space. Of course, coffee or tea is important, and hot chocolate is ideal for those chilly mornings. Always take extra food on your hunt. Your floatplane or boat is likely to be delayed by weather or mechanical failure. Food not eaten during the course of the hunt can be put into reserve, just in case.

Shelter

A free-standing dome tent with metal or fiberglass poles is the best, all-around choice for Alaska hunting. It should be quick to assemble and easy to take down, especially if you're hunting on the Alaska Peninsula or in high mountain passes. There, winds can gust up to 60 mph and destroy a standard dome tent in seconds. The tent should also be water-resistant and breathable, and include a rain fly.

However, a tent is often unnecessary weight when hunting sheep in the alpine areas in early August. If you don't mind roughing it, a piece of Visqueen is sufficient protection when strategically placed between two boulders.

Of course, the best shelter is a cabin. There are numerous trappers' cabins spread throughout Alaska's wilderness areas. These cozy little shacks offer a bit more comfort and room than a dome tent. Many cabins are privately owned. It's best to request permission to use these cabins prior to going afield.

Camp Gear

A single-burner stove is best for backpack hunts. I personally like the Coleman Peak 1 stove. It's compact, lightweight, and puts out a hot flame. Under normal use, a tank of fuel will last about three days. As for cook gear, it's a toss-up between aluminum and stainless steel. Over the past few years, aluminum pots and pans have received some bad press regarding their potential toxicity. I don't like to boil water for coffee in aluminum cookware because of the aluminum aftertaste. Stainless steel is my choice. It's more durable, and although weighs more, imparts no aftertaste.

Another good item is a backpack lantern. A small lantern is worth the extra weight, especially in late autumn when you have from 12 to 14 hours of darkness. Flashlights just don't provide the light output needed for several hours of reading or other activities. Also, a lantern serves as a portable heater on those cold nights. It'll keep a two-man tent warm and cozy.

As for packs, I'm sold on the Peak 1 frame also manufactured by Coleman. Unlike aluminum pack frames, the Peak 1 frame won't break or snap under a heavy load of moose meat. Manufactured from a space-age plastic called Ram-flex II, the pack frame can bend completely in half and snap back to its original position. Best of all, the packframe conforms to the shape of your back, and is extremely comfortable, even with a heavy load.

For personal reasons, some hunters prefer a solid frame to pack in gas cans, food boxes and the like. Then, the moose freighter-type of pack is best.

There are other items to take on a trip. Map and compass are important items wherever you go, especially in the rain-forests of southeast Alaska or Afognak Island. Always have an extra supply of parachute cord. It's great for a variety of uses. And don't forget a fishing rod. Some of the best fishing in Alaska is in those remote areas that anglers seldom frequent, yet hunters do.

Many of the smaller airlines serving Alaska's villages have a weight limit of 60 pounds per person, including gun. If your gear weighs more, it goes standby, and may not get to your destination when you do. If you have a bush plane or outfitter waiting for you at the other end, such a delay can easily ruin a hunt. Also, if you access an area via Super Cub, it'll take additional trips (read more money) to pack out your trophy and gear if you pack over 60 pounds. Keep it light, and you should have no problem.

A smart hunter will pack light, yet still have everything he needs for a successful hunt. A Super Cub aircraft has room for only one passenger and gear and perhaps a sheep, goat or similar-sized animal. Pack more than 60 pounds of gear and your pilot may have to make two trips. (Photo by Adela Ward Batin).

Rifle

The rifle is a personal choice for hunting in Alaska. One thing is certain. Much of the talk about the .270 and 7mm cartridges being adequate for such species as moose, bear, and goat are just that...talk. Rifles suited for mule deer and whitetails in the Lower 48 are not especially suited for Alaska's big game. Besides, most of us don't get enough field practice to place the shot precisely where it needs to be to dispatch an animal quickly. Plus, there are always variables to consider such as unexpected wind gusts, bullet deflection and the toughness of the animal. For aesthetic reasons, and to reduce the chance of crippling and perhaps loss, I stick to the larger calibers, preferring a 30-06, .300 or .308 as minimum, all-around cartridges. I don't believe any of these cartridges are "overkill." For Alaska brown bear and grizzly, a .338 or .375 is needed. It should be a pre-64 bolt action, with a clip capable of holding at least three shells. Of course, these recommendations are my personal opinions. However, Joe Want's information (see Brown Bear chapter) on knockdown power is something to consider when choosing a rifle for Alaska big game hunting.

As for ammo, I favor the round-nosed bullets. They seem to dispatch game faster than pointed soft-points. I don't like silver-tip bullets because for me, they don't perform as effectively as soft-nosed slugs. Here's another bit of advice. Use the same caliber of rifle as your guide or hunting buddy. That way, if you lose or run out of ammo, you'll still be able to hunt with your own rifle.

As for a shotgun, the versatile 12 gauge will allow you to hunt everything from snipe to big emperor geese and not be undergunned. Vary the loads to match the game.

Gearing up for an Alaska hunting trip takes homework and common sense. Use the above advice as a basic outline for the type of equipment you'll need. Of course, it's always best to get advice from your outfitter or guide before your trip. He'll help you choose the items you'll need on your particular hunt. As a final, all-around rule, take the items or equipment that increase your confidence in the field. As I'm sure you know, confidence makes for a better hunter.

* * * * * * * * * *
Epilogue

Since the start of this book, we've become better acquainted with Alaska's big game species, and the techniques for successfully hunting them. I know I've learned a bit more about myself as a hunter and how I fit into Alaska's hunting realm. I hope that you, too, took time for some introspection in understanding your place as an Alaska hunter. Whatever conclusions you've come up with, I hope that respect for the resource is at the top of your list. Only by showing our respect and admiration for Alaska's game animals do we better ourselves as human beings, and perhaps realize our place in this wonderful world the Creator has made for all of us to enjoy. On a hunt, game doesn't need to be harvested to be appreciated, nor is its abundance a key element for success. It's man's philosophy of vanity and greed that says we must kill to be successful. Nothing could be further from the truth. It's tuning in to the other, oftentimes overlooked aspects of a hunt that enoble us as hunters. It's washing your hair in an ice-melt mountain stream or gazing at white-capped mountain peaks and glaciers. It's sampling tart cranberries after missing a shot at the sheep of your dreams, or telling stories by lantern light while the northern lights blaze away overhead. These, my friends, are just a few of the many elements that make up an Alaska hunting trip. With that in mind, I'll divulge my last, but perhaps greatest hunting secret. It is patience, with both yourself and the game you pursue. Take time to study Alaska's wildlife, and allow their habits and fascinating lifestyles to be the basis for your hunting philosophy. Once you've made that effort, the rest will fall into place, naturally. All I ask is that you allow it to happen. See you in the field.

CHAPTER 18

The Hunting Experience: Ethics

Editor's Note: This story was originally titled "An Eye to the Heavens" and ran in the December 23, 1984 edition of the Fairbanks Daily News-Miner. It later went on to win First Place in the Bausch and Lomb National Hunting Writing Awards Competition, and another First Place in the Northwest Outdoor Writers Association Annual Writing Competition. Many consider it one of the best stories Batin has ever written.

The snow swirled in miniature whirlwinds around the decoys, enveloping them in a shroud of icy crystals that sparkled in the orange-pink, pre-dawn aura. A large boar muskrat, his brownish head cutting a wake through the black river water, twitched his whiskers once, then dove into the inky-black liquid with a resounding "plop." Less than a minute later, he popped to the surface with jaws stuffed with succulent aquatic vegetation. The muskrat quickly scampered up a nearby log and shook vigorously. His fur rolled on the layers of fat beneath his prime pelt. Partially obscured behind a wall of grass laced with hoarfrost, the old duck hunter observed all this, smiled and shook his head.

"It's seems you've been eating good this winter, ol' friend," the old man said to the muskrat. He poured himself a cup of coffee, turned to the furbearer and said, "It's good to have breakfast company for a change."

Just as he lifted the steamy brew up to his lips, the sharp adrenalin-pumping honks of Canada geese broke the early-morning tranquility. Silhouetted against snowy mountains, the black forms winged their way closer to the blind. The old man answered back with an old wooden call, faded from years of exposure to the elements, but perfected in tonal quality through years of practice. The geese, looking for company in the storm, immediately responded and set their wings on a beeline course into the old man's dekes. He inched further down into the blind and slowly flicked off the safety on his Model 12 shotgun.

The man stood up and quickly admired the beauty of the big Canadas as they hung with tilted wings over the decoys. As always, he did not feel the shot as he swung on the lead bird. The large Canada folded its wings and landed with a soft thump in the deep snow on shore. The remainder of the flock beat their wings frantically to regain altitude, but unbeknownst to them, there was no more danger. The old man didn't need to shoot a limit of geese to make a successful hunt. He smiled as he watched the birds fly off in the distance, then laughed when he heard the geese calling in unison. He thought they were either cussing him out or thanking him. Either way, he gently picked up what was to be his Christmas goose, a nice 10-pounder, and softly stroked its breast feathers. He then held up the bird, with arm outstretched to the rapidly disappearing flock. He was paying tribute to these birds and the excite-

Author Chris Batin taking a break during a September hunt to read his favorite philosopher, Plato. A big game hunt is a good time to contemplate the spiritual and emotional rewards of interacting with big game animals and their wilderness environment.

ment of hunting waterfowl in Alaska.

But the old man's smile didn't last long. A volley of shots rang out from where the geese last disappeared from sight, followed by a pause, and more shots. The old man had a hunch that made his stomach turn. He had heard that sound many times in his life: someone was hunting geese with an unplugged shotgun. After all, he had only seen one set of tracks going out to the point early that morning. He quickly picked up his dekes, stashed them in the weeds, and walked down the trail that led to the point. The old man took a stand near an old spruce tree and waited. He was going to confront this lawbreaker.

Twenty minutes later, he narrowed his eyes at the approaching figure. It was worse than he thought. A mere boy, not more than 14 years old, slowly worked his way down the edge of the trail, keeping to the inside shadows. He was hunched over with a packbasket loaded with geese. A shotgun stuck out from the basket, and he had another one slung over his shoulder. The old man fought off the impulse to take the lad and dangle him over his knee. Instead, he would confront this young lawbreaker in his own manner.

The old man eased down the riverbank and scurried ahead of the lad. About 50 yards away, he turned back and started whistling Christmas carols while slowly walking up the center of the trail.

He soon met the boy, also standing in the middle of the trail, but without the pack and extra shotgun. The old man reasoned that the boy must have hid them when he heard him approach.

"How's it goin'?" the man asked with a nod to greet the boy.

The lad was fidgety and frightened at having been interrupted in his escape. "Not many snowshoe hares around today," he replied.

"Oh. You hunting hares?"

"Yep."

"How about you?"

"Geese. I'm a *waterfowl* hunter. The old man emphasized waterfowl intentionally.

The boy became visibly upset, yet wouldn't make the first move to walk on. It was obvious he wanted to stay near his cache of birds. The boy's actions indicated that he was not a dyed-in-the-wool poacher. Too fidgety. The old man decided to get to the bottom of things. He cleared off the snow on a fallen birch and unpacked his thermos of coffee.

"Care for a cup? It has cream in it."

"Might as well," the boy replied. "I'm waiting for some friends to meet me here so we can drive through this side of the woods to roust out some hares."

"You hunt with your friends much," the old man asked, trying to piece the puzzle together.

"Every chance I get," he replied. "I have to. We have contests to see who can bag the most hares. It sharpens our hunting skills for other game like deer and grouse."

The reply hit the old man like a load of bricks. He would bet his prize antique decoy that the boy was having a contest with his friends to see who could kill the most birds in one morning. The old man felt that the boy was a victim of peer pressure, and maybe, just maybe, there was a way to turn him. If not, he'd turn him in.

"I used to shoot limits all the time," the old man said. "Used to catch limits of fish also. But that was before I became a member of the prestigious Category Five Group."

"Category Five Group?" the boy asked with interest.

"Sure. It's the most honored sporting group I know of. You see, there are five basic groups of sportsmen in this world. The first consists of the greenhorns and novices. They are happy with anything they harvest while afield because they have yet to acquire the outdoor skills that you and I have.

"People in the second category are the mass harvesters. They show their friends what great hunters and fishermen they are by taking limits of game or fish. To them, numbers mean everything, and they have no satisfaction unless they've bagged a limit.

"People in the third category are trophy sportsmen. After numbers, they want records; the bigger the fish or horns, the better. And usually they do pretty good...for a time being. However, soon trophy harvesting loses its pizzazz, which leads to the fourth category: the purists.

"These individuals delight in catching 70-pound kings on two-pound-test line and hunting grizzlies with archery gear. However, the lucky ones snap to their senses early on in the sport, as they quickly realize this is the shortest lived of all groups."

The boy laughed. "I know several people like that."

"In the fifth and final category are the respectors. The individual that's a member of this group is a pleasure to watch in the field. The angler in this category releases most of the fish caught. The ones that are kept are dispatched immediately. There is no underlying need to harvest the fish to satisfy a macho outdoorsman ego. He realizes that he has the power of life or death over this creature, but has evolved beyond the need to kill every chance he gets. He feels a kindred, a bond with the fish and game he pursues. He knows them and their habits better than he knows most people. He can't help but to ponder over a fish such as the salmon that has, through its eyes, seen the secrets of the ocean depths, roamed as a free spirit on the high seas for several years, and survived freshwater and saltwater hazards, diseases, predation by birds, bears, mammals, killer whales, fishing nets and pollution to return and spawn! To the respector, it's the greatest survival story ever told! And every year, one of those survivors can be held right in the palm of your hand.

"A respector receives life from the fish...not his biological life from eating it...but a spiritual life from knowing that each fish is a wonder of creation, each with its own personality, habits, and beauty. He appreciates the softblue gill plate on a dime-bright sockeye just in from the ocean; marvels at any of the 700 teeth in the mouth of a northern pike, which serve the fish as one of the most efficient paralyzers in the fishing realm; or delights in the delicate smell of thyme exhibited by a freshly-caught grayling, which is the reason for its Latin name, *Thymallus*. You can almost say this behavior this attitude is a love for the fish, as the definition of love is a one-way street; you give without expecting to receive anything back. I do believe it is love a respector has for the resource, as the fish will not intentionally give anything back."

The boy was visibly impressed, but soon looked down at his boots, kicked the snow in what seemed to be defiance and said, "But I'm a hunter. It's different with us."

The old man poured the boy another cup of coffee after which he pulled out his pipe and drew on it long and hard several times before speaking.

"Ah, but that's where you're wrong, lad. Hunters in this respector category have the same basic attitudes, only they're usually much more involved. I often wish that, after bagging a goose or ptarmigan, that I could wind it up and let it fly again. It may come as a shock to you to hear me say that I greatly dislike to kill. Sometimes it bothers me for days after."

"Then why do you hunt, Mister, and what has this all got to do with being in this respector category?"

"It's a hard question to answer with words. I hunt because it is the best way I can show respect for the resource God has given to me. For example, I'm sure an avid hunter such as yourself would be enthused if you won a special, one-of-a-kind permit to hunt polar bear or walrus? I'm betting you wouldn't be able to talk straight for a week. I know I couldn't! It's that feeling of excitement, of anticipation, of thinking through the hunt a thousand times, of the thought and emotional processes of being on the hunt that serves as a basic element in the overall chemistry of respect for the resource. Having this euphoria, this appreciation is what both fishing and hunting is all about. But this same intensity of feeling should not just be restricted to polar bear, walrus or prestigious game and fish species, but also with everything you pursue, from a 10-inch grayling to a merganser. If you have no other feelings when hunting these animals, you not only disgrace the resource, but are guilty of ignoring this special gift available to each and every one of us. These feelings, in part, are what make our reasons for hunting different than those of a fox or wolf.

"Naturalist Sigurd F. Olsen once wrote, 'When one finally arrives at the point where schedules are forgotten, and becomes immersed in ancient rythms, one begins to live.' And *living* as one with the outdoors is one of the benefits belonging to the respector group. Do you follow me?"

"I think so," the boy replied. "But where do you get this feeling and how do you make it stay?"

"It comes from within, son. To put it in terms you can understand, it's much like the *force of life* in the movie 'Star Wars.' This deep-down appreciation for the resource is the *force of life* in the outdoors. It fills your very being, makes your heart skip a beat and butterflies converge upon your stomach en masse. It is the very *essence* of the sport. These feelings transcend the idea of 'killing something' and make it an ultimate tribute to that particular species. And I'm sure if the fish or animal had its choice, this would be the way it would choose to go rather than end up in the stomach of another animal."

"I've sorta felt that way, but my friends said it was sissified to be like that," the boy said as he looked the man straight in the face.

"Well, they don't yet have the qualities to belong to the respector group. They have some learning to do. But you can help them most by not going along with their games of 'bagging the limit.' You become a full-fledged respector when you can do more than just explain the techniques of a particular sport, the safety aspects, or even explaining some of the aesthetic reasons why people hunt or fish. You must pass on the feelings and emotions of the sport as it comes from the *soul*. And you can't be hypocritical about it. You either have it or you don't. And what is the best way to find out if you have it? That's simple. Your actions when you're alone in the field. In *Sand County Almanac*, Aldo Leopold wrote, 'A peculiar virtue in wildlife ethics is that the hunter ordinarily has no gallery to applaud or disapprove of his conduct. Whatever his acts, they are dictated by his own consciousness, rather than that of onlookers. It is difficult to exaggerate the importance of this fact.' "

The boy looked down at the goose that the old man had pulled out of his pack to cool. He touched its breast feathers gently, and tenderly stroked its white cheek patch. "And they told me I was a sissy if I felt that way," the old man barely heard the boy mutter.

The boy looked up with tearful eyes and started to speak, but didn't. He kicked the snow around with his boot for several more minutes. He pretended to blow his nose while wiping his eyes, so the old man wouldn't see his tears. The old man, touched by this reaction to his words, put his arm around the boy's shoulder.

"Son, you and I are lucky to be Alaskans and enjoy the bounty of fish and wildlife in one of the most scenic geographical areas in the world. We have plenty to be thankful for. I would like to share a moment with you doing something I usually do by myself. With those feelings of respect and appreciation I talked about earlier, let's spend a few quiet moments on reflection and give thanks to God for allowing us the privilege...yes it is a privilege...to appreciate the fish and wildlife resources He has given us."

The two spent a few moments in silent reflection before the old man continued his words.

"Yep. Through hunting and fishing, it's possible to get closer to God than you never before realized. It hits you like a brick, like a painting that finally makes its message clear. The master plan becomes evident. Soon, you are catching fish, not for the fight, but to see and marvel in the palate of colors that radiate along their flanks, or to feel their pot bellies after they have been feeding on helping after helping of salmon egg omelet. You admire a ptarmigan for clucking admonitions at you for invading its territory, and you keep your shotgun on safety, hoping that such spunk will best be served in perpetuating the species rather than on the dinner table that night. Or even the simplest things, such as the funny, yet functional shape of a surf scoter's beak...something that you would have passed up before...intrigues and stands out as something special the Creator has made for us to enjoy. These and all the outdoor treasures available to us deserve our time, appeciation, and most of all, respect."

"Mister,...by the way, what's your name anyway?"

"Just call me John."

"John, I need to tell you something. This morning, my friends and I had a contest about who could shoot the most geese and I ..."

"Ah, save it for now," the old man replied. He stood up, brushed the snow off his pants, and pointed up the trail. "Go over there and get your geese. We need to get back to the road before dark."

"You mean you knew all along?" the boy asked incredulously. Slowly, a look of admiration replaced the astonishment on his face. The old man pretended not to notice. He clinched down hard on his pipe stem. He felt his heart soar as emotion filled him. This boy craved the "respector" philosophy, something his now full-grown sons couldn't understand, or didn't want to understand.

The boy slowly walked over to his pack, picked it up, and joined the old man already walking down the trail.

"Ya know," the boy said, "I think the best way to show my respect for these geese in view of the wrongdoing I did them is to offer the birds as Christmas dinners to needy families. Do you think it would, someday, help me become a 'respector' like you?"

The old man took the geese and loaded them in the truck, along with the decoys. "I think you already qualify," the old man said. "By the way, we respectors have to stick together, ya know. How about a goose hunt next week, if your parents say it's OK?"

As the pair drove down the road, the old man again saw the boy admiring the goose he had shot.

"Ya know, John Muir was one of the best respectors of our time. He wrote a few words I'd like to share with you. He said, 'I used to envy the Father of Our Race, dwelling as he did in contact with the new-made fields and plants of Eden; but I do so no more, because I have discovered that I also live in 'creation's dawn.' The morning stars still sing together, and the world, not yet half made, becomes more beautiful every day.' "

The boy looked down a moment, reached over and stroked the breast feathers on the goose. He shook his head as if to understand, swallowed hard, then looked up and smiled.

"You know, John, I think this is a beautiful day. And even though I barely know you, I wish I could give you a Christmas present, just to say thanks."

The old man didn't speak until he pulled into the boy's driveway. "You've already given me the best Christmas present I've ever had, son. Merry Christmas."

The Hunting Experience: Excitement

Editor's Note: Brown Bear hunting produces thrills and excitement unlike any other type of hunting in the world. Batin conveys these feelings in his feature entitled "Brown Bear Guides I Have Known," which originally appeared in the April, 1983 issue of Sports Afield. Later that year, the article won First Place in the Hunting Article category in the Northwest Outdoor Writers Association's Writing and Photo Competition.

Johnny Luster pulled back on the reins of his mud-splattered horse and gazed intently over the tundra. Behind him, a green curtain of spruce ran a tattered border along the edge of timberline. The brilliant morning sun brightened the towering spires of the Talkeetna Mountains. A light veil of snow crowned the precipitous ridgebacks while the lower slopes were vested in a shiny cape of blueberry foliage and intricate crystals of autumn frost. But Luster's guard was not relinquished by this beauty. Sixty years of mountain life had taught him otherwise. For half those years, he had allowed the packhorses he uses on his fall bear hunts to feed in these wilderness meadows. There were never any problems...until this year.

His grey-flecked eyebrows narrowed sharply as he squinted and dissected every potential hiding spot along the horse trail as it coursed up the rocky, alder-infested mountainside. The trail, worn deep into the tundra mud, resembled a winding rattlesnake, and possessed the same deathly potential. This was the back door of the brown bear that had attacked and killed two of his horses. Luster's lips pursed tightly as he recalled the most recent kill. The mare was dragged 50 feet from the main trail and partially covered with a layer of alder saplings and caribou lichen. The heart and other organs had been devoured. Luster vividly remembered the 16-inch-long by eight-inch-wide tracks that cratered the nearby kill site.

The puzzle was grim, but easily deciphered. There is not a more dangerous animal than a brownie whose speed and senses are worn down by time. The bear had been ambushing his horses along the trail because they were easy game. It was just a matter of time before a client would be riding one of those horses.

Traveling slowly through the scattered patches of alder and stretches of open tundra, Luster sensed something wasn't right. Off to his left, two backpackers popped into view on a higher horse trail on the mountainside.

"Why all the fool...," Luster thought as he watched the couple trek past a willow and alder thicket. But there wasn't time to finish the thought as he focused on the thicket. A large brown bear was crouched on the edge of the alders, his face hidden behind a small clump of grass.

Before Luster could yell a warning, the bear lurched forward and crept stealthily toward the backpackers. In one motion, Luster grabbed his 44 caliber rifle from its saddle case and jumped off his horse. He yelled several warnings to the couple, but to no avail. They kept on walking, oblivious to danger.

Luster quickly leveled on the bear and fired. Upon impact, the bear spun violently on his hindquarters and charged along the bullet's path, straight for Luster. Quickly ejecting the spent cartridge, he desperately tugged on the rifle lever. The feeding mechanism had jammed. Nothing existed now except snapping jaws and muscles rippling under a gray-tipped hide. Luster grabbed the rifle barrel and swung hard as the bear rushed past him and disappeared into the brush. He coughed to expel the bear's foul breath as it lingered in the air.

Two weeks later, Luster outfitted two hunters that found and shot the bear as it was hiding in an alder patch near the same horse trail. Luster's foresight had been correct. The bear's teeth were rotted and worn to the gumline; its face swollen from the decay. Upon skinning the bear, Luster found his and two other slugs buried in the front shoulder. This bear was a monarch: the hide squared out at 10 feet.

And what about the backpackers? Luster smiles and shakes his head. "After the bear disappeared into the alders, they came running over to me yelling, 'Don't kill that beautiful animal. It belongs in the wilderness. Why don't you leave it alone?' "

Man's fascination with the brown/grizzly bear has spanned the ages. This man-bear relationship was the start of the best known and durable form of worship known by anthropologists as the Cult of the Brown Bear, which had its start back in Neanderthal times and persisted until the late Paleolithic Era, covering a span of approximately 40,000 years.

Today, a similar cult exists between brown bear and the guides who hunt brown bear. Instead of paintings on cave walls, the brown bear guide creates a one-of-a-kind experience with a hunter that is more vivid and durable than any art form. A bear hunt can be recreated a hundred times over in the retelling, and still hold people spellbound because there are no forgeries in this realm. It would be difficult for an artist to recreate the hair-raising excitement a hunter feels while listening to a brown bear crunch the bones of a moose kill before first light, or the dark, piercing eyes of an alerted, nine-foot brown bear on a wilderness mountainside as rifle slowly meets shoulder.

For guides like Johnny Luster, brown bear hunting is the essence of life. He started hunting bears and other big game when he was 14 years old. Sixty years later, he's still guiding bear hunters with all the eccentricities of a veteran brown bear guide. Luster can't recall the number of bears he's harvested. But he does fear one thing, and surprisingly it isn't brown bears. "I live a safe life because I stay away from automobiles. Darn things are death traps," he stresses with sincerity.

Whether Luster's life as a bear guide has been safe is a matter of perspective. For instance, on a late-season hunting trip in the Talkeetna Mountains, Luster was taking a snooze in camp after putting the horses out to feed for the evening. His hunters were busy fishing for grayling in a nearby creek. Sleeping on his side, Luster felt a hard nudge. Without opening his eyes, he semiconsciously groped for a nearby stick to smack the "horse" on the snout. Upon hearing a snort and fading footsteps, he dozed off again. But it was short lived. Moments later, his clients came running up and began shaking him. Even Luster's bushy gray eyebrows raised when he saw the back-end of a large brown bear exiting camp.

However, an Alaska registered guide, who prefers to be known only as J.M., encountered a brown bear that needed a bit more coaxing than Luster to awaken. J.M. and his client had been glassing the Alaska Peninsula for three days when they finally spotted a large brown bear sleeping smack in the middle of a mile-wide stretch of tundra expanse. J.M. was sure the bear would make the record books. It would be a tough stalk, calling for a half-mile crawl through cottongrass and scrub willow. What would be tougher yet would be crawling within shooting range. His client carried a bow.

Two hours later, the pair had crawled, stalked and fought to within 50 yards of the bear. Perfect range for a lethal shot. Then minutes later, J.M. shook his head. It was obvious his client had just taken up bowhunting; five arrows stuck in the ground surrounding the bear. With one arrow left, the archer took careful aim and lobbed an arrow that was a direct hit...right into the bear's foot. Of course, an arrow in a bear this size would be like a rose thorn in an elephant's foot. The bear shook his foot and kept on dozing.

The situation posed an unusual problem. The client wasn't about to walk up to the bear and retrieve his arrows, and he was adamant about not taking the bear with J.M.'s rifle. The hunter shook his head and walked back to camp with J.M. He was satisfied with the hunt, although grudgingly admitting he needed a bit more practice. Two hundred yards from the sleeping bear, J.M. looked back, smiled and shot a hole into the air with his .375 H&H Magnum.

"That bear didn't waste any time heading for the river a mile away," J.M. recalls. "I was surprised he didn't trip over any of the arrows on his charge out!"

J.M. has experienced plenty of brown bear action in his quarter century of guiding in Alaska's wilderness. Yet he stresses by no means are brown bears as lethargic as the one encountered with his bowhunting client. J.M. was hunting the Alaska Peninsula country for caribou. A large migration was going full tilt, and the riverbank was ankle-deep in caribou hair the animals shed while fording the river. J.M. sat down near the fording spot and waited. Surely this would be the place for a trophy bull.

It wasn't long before he heard the crashing of brush and hooves clicking. A nice bull with an impressive rack popped into view on a small knoll above the river. Yet something strange about the animal's behavior kept J.M. from shooting. It's eyes bulged wildly as it gazed nervously in the direction from which it fled. Like coiled springs, the caribou's back legs catapulted it into the river seconds before a silver-tipped grizzly came charging over the knoll, kicking up dirt and furiously biting nearby willows.

The bear neither saw nor scented J.M. He wanted that bull and immediately jumped into the river after it. However, the caribou's buoyant hair permitted it to swim the river faster than the grizzly. Climbing out of the river, the caribou ran down the bank a distance and stopped to watch the grizzly. Upon reaching the other side, the bear scented the air and growled furiously. The caribou had jumped back into the river and headed for the opposite shore.

With a bit more reluctance this time, the grizzly followed. In midstream, the caribou switched directions, as if to further tantalize the bear. At this point the grizzly ignored the caribou and continued swimming toward shore. Moments later, both dragged themselves from the swift river with tongues hanging out and necks hung low in an exhausted posture.

J.M. chuckled as he concluded, "Both eyed each other for a short time and ambled away; the caribou to rejoin the migration, and the grizzly, a try for a dinner that was a bit slower, like ground squirrel."

While brown bear hunting is dangerous in its own right, the danger, along with the excitement factor, increases dramatically if a bear becomes wounded and needs to be tracked down.

Master Guide Clark Engle has survived several charges and forays after wounded bears in the brush. He was taught the ropes of brown bear hunting by one of Alaska's greatest guides, the late Hal Waugh. And it's apparent Engle inherited his mentor's obsession with brown bears by simply listening to him describe the highlights of his 23 years as a bear guide.

One of Engle's favorite encounters with brown bears was also his first as a registered guide. He was guiding a New Jersey doctor for Kodiak Island brownies, a subspecies of bear that has earned its own classification—*Ursus arctos middendorfi*—due to its size, habits and geographical isolation from other bear species.

One glance at Kodiak Island left no doubt in Doc's mind that this was a brown bear heaven: miles of virtually impenetrable alder thickets, spongy ground, isolated stretches of rocky, uninhabited coastline surrounding rolling hills and bog valleys. But despite the barrier this subarctic wilderness and miles of tough walking presented, Engle encountered no problem locating a large boar in the thicketed bottomland. After several hours of careful planning and maneuvering, they stalked to within 100 yards of the bear, who was busy foraging for roots and carrion.

"Aim for the front shoulder," Engle advised his client in a whisper. "Ain't never seen a bear run off with a busted shoulder."

Engle waited in anticipation as Doc lined up the crosshairs. The boar raised his head to sample the wind. "Now."

Doc's .338 slug found its mark too far back. The bear bit madly at its side and charged quickly into an alder thicket and disappeared. "Damn, a lung-shot bear. Nothing to do now but sit down, have a smoke, and let the bear stiffen up a bit."

As the hour slowly ticked away, neither could hear any movement in the dense alders. Engle reviewed the situation, like a chessman foreseeing every possible move his opponent could make. Only losing here could mean death.

A narrow creek ran down the center of the alder patch, and the guide hoped the bear was lying there...dead.

But as the pair entered the alder thicket, they saw no bear. Engle remembered Uncle Hal's teachings about the unpredictability of brown bears. He was sure this bear would be no exception. Time is not measured in seconds or minutes when stalking a brown bear. It's measured in heartbeats and drops of sweat. Inches seem like miles. Senses are acutely tuned to reflexes.

The warm blood flecked with foam on the tea-brown carpet of leaves told the story. Engle stood up, but didn't have time to motion Doc forward. The alder stand above the creekbed was transformed into a hideous symphony of crashing brush and growls as the enraged brown charged.

Thinking requires too much time. Instincts and reflexes dominate. Engle quickly hammered the charging brownie in place with a shot from his .375 Magnum, after which he sat down and smiled. "I don't know who was more proud, me or the hunter," Engle recalls.

Upon piecing the puzzle together, Engle discovered the bear had entered the alders and made a wide circle. Then it lay down to watch its backtrail.

Such staunch determination and courage is only one side of a guide who hunts brown bears. Humor is another, and this elite group loves to immortalize tales about greenhorns and brown bears.

The favorite is about the greenhorn who traveled all the way to Alaska from the East Coast in search of a brown bear. The local outfitters grubstaked him with all the necessary gear: ropes, food, ammo and the like. The greenhorn started out, and later that day, came to a narrow bridge. He was half across when a huge brown bear also started across from the opposite end. They met each other midway, and the bear, snarling, let out a large *Wooof!*

Since the greenhorn's rifle was packed away, he had no alternative but to growl and *Wooof!* Both bantered this exchange several times before the bear turned and walked into some bushes, left a huge pile of dung, and walked off. When the town residents asked the greenhorn what he did, he replied, "The same thing the bear did, only after the first *Wooof!*

Both brown bear and brown bear guides are prime examples of survival of the fittest. For the guide, survival means not only learning a skill that demands educated guesses that are right the first time, but also learning to enjoy and cherish the sight of a brownie chasing a salmon; to take pleasure in a nap on a wilderness knoll; or to confidently take a client down a bear trail worn three feet deep by its ancestors. In the life of a brown bear guide, there is rarely a second chance. And if there were, it wouldn't be brown bear hunting.

The Hunting Experience: Adventure

Editor's Note: This account of a hunt the author took in interior Alaska in 1984 won First Place in the Hunting Article category in a writing contest sponsored by the Northwest Outdoor Writers Association. When the story appeared in the March, 1985 issue of Alaska Outdoors magazine, it generated a response more favorable than any other hunting article that had previously been published in that magazine.

The rocky spires of the Alaska Range reached up like a massive hand as the Super Cub climbed for altitude. Holding onto my seat, I peered out the window while casting an occasional nervous glance up toward pilot Art Warbelow. Looking down into the precipitous canyon, I spotted an eagle soaring above a more passive piece of terrain.

"You sure caribou are up this high?" I asked Art as the two spires passed to what seemed to be feet of the wingtips. "Even the eagles are reluctant to fly this high."

"The warm weather has pushed the caribou to the top of the ridges," he said over the whine of the engine. "You'll like the area. Why, there are some caribou right over on that ridgetop, and there's a sheep right next to them."

Art banked the Cub for a closer look. Sure enough, two small caribou bulls were near a sloping ridge, while an immature Dall sheep stood on the rocky face of the peak. The caribou shook their heads at us as we passed over them. We continued on to the area I was to hunt.

"This Steese-Fortymile caribou herd is something else," Art said as we flew down a winding river valley. "There's over 12,000 animals in the herd. Right now, the animals are beginning to group up and migrate south to their wintering grounds, which will give you an excellent opportunity to look over several bulls and choose the best one. Best of all, I'm sure you won't have nearly the hunters or the hunting pressure that you experienced last year on the Alaska Peninsula."

"Don't remind me," I said rather disgustedly.

The Cub soon approached the landing strip, which was nothing more than a flat section of alpine ridgetop. The plane bounced down, and vibrated to a stop on the shale-covered ridge. I quickly unloaded my gear. "See you in three days," Art called before shutting the window and lifting off the ridge into the mountain-studded skyline to the south.

The first hunt of the year is a special occasion. I always experience euphoria when the plane disappears from sight, leaving me with a one-on-one challenge with the terrain and my quarry. Plans laid months ago finally begin to gel. Hours spent studying maps and planning strategies pay off with quick decisions and confidence. Now it was time to put it all together.

I reviewed a few facts in my mind as I scanned the rugged alpine landscape. Since caribou are highly migratory, success greatly depends on choosing the right area to intercept the herds as they move through an area. I had a good feeling about a saddle between two peaks about three miles distant. Within minutes I was on the trail, breaking through tangles of blueberry bushes, their winey aroma slowly cleansing the pollution and smells of civilization out of my lungs and nostrils.

I quickly found a caribou trail and followed it, only later to discover that it was in actuality a bear trail. Minutes later, I blamed my shortness of breath on my loud whistling and off-key singing that I always recommend when "trespassing" on bruin property, especially through bruin berry patches.

With the berry understory quickly disappearing in the distance, I began trudging through head-high willow and alder thickets, my legs more accustomed to the inactivity of months of fishing rather than the weight of a 75-pound pack. I cursed the branches and the sweltering heat. Sweat ran freely. My pack bit into shoulder muscles not yet toughened by miles of overland packing. An hour later, I sat down to rest on a piece of quartz. Slowly but surely I felt my body toughen up for the upcoming hunt. Mixed feelings of challenge, excitement and accomplishment ran rampant in anticipating the upcoming events. I breathed deeply as if to savor each one. If only someone could invent a pill that would produce this feeling during the rest of the year. But then again, one reason these feelings are so special is that they come only from hunting. I pushed on.

The saddle lies between a peak at 5,300 feet and one at 4,400 feet. It's a barren piece of ground, with a few patches of sedge and some scattered scrub bushes. With all the rain that fell the week prior to my hunt, Art said there would definitely be water nearby. I set up camp, unpacked my container and started looking. No water to be found. I thirstily eyed a small stream about 3,000 feet below me, but the setting sun kept me from trying any such foolhardy marathon. I would need to make the hike first thing in the morning, before hunting. That would be a hike that I would not look forward to.

While scavanging handfuls of berries to satiate my need for liquids, I found a boggy section of tundra. Remembering some long lost bit of advice from an old, boy scout manual, I dug a hole in the bog. Slowly, it filled up with blackish water. An hour later, the sediment settled and I had a delightful cup of cold, spring water, located not more than 30 feet from my camp. I wasn't about to dine on freeze dried food sans water, so I cooked up a feast to celebrate my discovery and prompt cancellation of my 6,000 foot, round-trip hike for two gallons of water.

With the blue flames of the small cookstove hissing away, I busied myself checking minor details to prepare for the hunt: sharpen knife, select the cartridge that has my trophy caribou's name on it, ensure the camera is working properly, and prepare one of three shots of

Yukon Jack for a toast to the area and the hunt.

Chores finished, I sat down to eat my celebration feast when I heard a rock tumble down the rocky mountainside behind me. Thoughts of the grizzly whose real estate I earlier trespassed upon instantly came to mind. I slowly turned, rifle in hand, only to lay eyes on a small herd of caribou: ten cows, seven calves and two small bulls. They grazed slowly down the slope toward my tent. Smiling, I ate my supper while watching them. TV could never match this live showing of "Caribou Capers." Occasionally, one of the bulls would raise its snout and sniff in my direction. Eyes would bug glaringly at me whenever I moved about, usually followed by a few curious steps forward. As the herd moved down into the saddle and up the mountainside that loomed directly opposite my tent, I made a toast to the caribou, the wilderness area in which they lived, and the opportunity for being there. Ol' Jack never tasted sweeter.

The pre-aura of daylight painted a pinkish streak across the horizon at 4 a.m. Frost covered my water bucket, and the cold nipped at my face. These conditions, which would normally send me crawling back under the covers, encouraged me to get up and experience every tingling goosebump, the cold, clammy boots, and the anticipation of some fresh-brewed coffee on a ridgetop where not another human being, machine or civilized mechanism could neither be seen nor heard. The hunter was becoming part of the hunt.

As my swamp water boiled, I looked around. Not a caribou to be seen. A quick cup of coffee, some food bars thrown in the pack, and I was soon hiking a quick pace to a gradual sloping ridge about 500 yards west of the saddle. From the tracks in the tundra, this is where the caribou that I observed the previous night had come down.

Shadows hung heavily on the west side of the mountain. I searched every depression, every ridgetop for a white mane that signaled a big caribou. Seeing nothing, I started to glass the timberline. I never finished. Two clicks on the hillside to my left riveted my hand to my Austrian-made, 30-06 Voere. The sound was a dead giveaway: the clicking of caribou tendons. Turning slowly, I could only pick out gray images against the sunlit ridge. A splash of white against a black background grabbed my attention. Throwing up my rifle, I searched the scope for an image. Anxiety rushed through my limbs as I focused on a heavily tined caribou looking directly at me. I quickly scanned the herd, and found another good bull, but not as impressive as the one in my scope. I centered the crosshairs. The distance was far: about 300 yards. Seemingly impatient with my indecision, the bull started to walk away with the cows. I acted on instinct. I crouched down and scooted through the brush for about 50 yards. Yet the bull was walking too fast, and would soon disappear over the ridge. I sat down, adjusted my rangefinder scope, held slightly in front of the shoulder of the walking bull, and squeezed off. The recoil of the 165-grain boat tail kicked my head back and eyes off the animal and into the sun. But I heard the bullet hit home as I pulled the rifle down to ready myself for another shot if need be. The bull took two steps, stumbled and fell.

I was soon running over the tundra and up the hill toward my trophy. The other caribou snorted and leaped into the air before taking off down the ridge. I stopped and jumped in the air, a bit of hunting success insanity taking hold. A gust of wind blew through my hair, and at that very moment, I was not a hunter, but the hunt itself, of everything that comprises it: the behavioral tendencies of the caribou, the freedom of soul, the skill of a predator once again fulfilling an age-old desire to harvest a resource. But above all, appreciation and respect for the caribou for bringing this all about swelled within me. In silent reflection, I gave thanks.

I slowly walked up to the bull, a handsome animal with 37 tines and heavy beams. It was extremely fat and would provide many a caribou dinner during the upcoming winter. Adhering to European tradition, I cut two scrub spruce shoots: one I placed in the animal's mouth to signify its last meal, and the other dipped in the blood and placed in the band of my hat. This covenant between man and animal completed the hunt. Now there was work to do.

The next two days were spent quartering, prepping and packing the caribou back to the ridgetop for pickup. Steep hillsides were handled without the shortness of breath or lower leg pain. Feet toughened up, and eyes were quick to spot the slightest movement. Thoughts of the hunt were mentally replayed over and over again during the pack. Ptarmigan were observed and studied. I even treated an ermine I met on a ridgetop to a few handfuls of caribou scrap. I would see caribou from time to time, but the cold weather had sent most of them down toward timberline.

The last day was spent contemplating on a ridetop. I watched the endless horizon of mountains change colors like a giant kaleidoscope as the sunlight spotlighted carpets of red cranberry and yellow alder through slow-moving clouds.

When the drone of Art's Super Cub in the distance forced me to head for the strip, I felt a part of me remain on the ridge. Yet I quickly captured the feeling...a feeling only a hunter who opens himself to the philosophy of the hunt can appreciate...and locked it in my mind. They'll be times when I'll gently unlock it, when work schedules keep me from going afield, or when old age wears down my physical stamina to the point of retirement. And I'll reminisce and relish the memories. But at the time I was living it to its fullest, and as I eased on my pack, I made one last toast: To caribou hunting in the Fortymile area. May it provide similar rewards to all those who favor a true Alaska hunting experience.

The Hunting Experience: Camaraderie

Editor's Note: This story originally appeared in the 1982 Sports Afield Hunting Annual. It has won first and second places in local and regional outdoor writing contests. Batin shows that no matter what the language or nationality, hunting is the basis for developing one of the highest forms of camaraderie known to man.

For brief moments, the setting sun produces kaleidoscopic colors under Alaska's autumn sky. The cold blue of a distant glacier is transformed into a glowing orange. Birch and blueberry foliage are illuminated in vibrant, pastel droplets. And a subtle breeze sends fire-orange waves across the lofty fields of cottongrass.

A battle-scarred moose beligerently strikes an alder to signal his readiness to dominate this valley. On a nearby esker, patches of tundra grass slowly metamorphose into a nomadic herd of caribou. These knights of the tundra are also responding to the enchanted season. Slowly, like mice to a piper, they travel down a ridgetop toward their wintering grounds to the west.

Also responding to the spell of the season, three intruders share a temporary home of canvas. German and English voices incongruously mingle in the shadows, and the aroma of fried caribou heart hangs heavy in the stale air of the tent.

"*Gute Essen*," Gothard Schnitzler exclaimed as he raised his fork. Nearby, Otto Eberle busied himself making adjustments on his rifle scope.

"This is good hunting you have here in Alaska," Gothard bellowed in faultless English. "In Germany, you always know where the game is. But here, you must always look and wait."

I nodded in agreement. Several years ago, Gothard and Otto had been lured to Alaska from Germany. Earlier that year, I had heard of their plans from their guide, Jim, and made arrangements to hunt moose and caribou with them in one of Alaska's finest hunting areas: the Alaska Range. It would be a unique experience to share the excitement of such a hunt with them and learn something of the German hunting methods and tradition.

Otto spoke between mouthfuls of chocolate pudding—his fifth can that evening. Gothard listened and translated.

"Otto thinks we should hunt the far ridge tomorrow for moose. He saw a huge bull there yesterday while skinning my caribou. You agree?"

"Sounds good," I replied as I unrolled my sleeping bag. But before I could crawl in, Gothard gave me some advice.

"Make sure you have many large sticks tonight to throw at Otto. He is a bad sleeper."

As I drifted off to sleep, I remembered what Jim told me as he flew me into camp.

"The Mulchatna herd, which you'll be hunting with Otto and Gothard, is moderately hunted. It's not uncommon for a hunter who puts out some effort to see 50 to 1,000 caribou on a ten-day hunt. It's an area favored by hunters searching for large meat animals or trophies.

"One reason more trophy caribou aren't taken is that nonresident deer hunters usually shoot the first animal they see. To them a small caribou rack is large when compared to an eastern whitetail.

"Trophy moose are also here in good numbers, but they require a bit more work. The calf and yearling mortality rate has decreased in recent years and that has provided a good, but well-scattered moose population.

"Otto has never hunted in Alaska, but Gothard has hunted here twice. They may need some advice on occasion."

"A hunting symposium in the grandest arena of all—the Alaska wilderness," I mused.

Lesson No. 1

The first thing Gothard taught me the next morning was my need for more physical conditioning. He had the gait of an ostrich with a wolf on its tail and the stamina of a chicken-stealing weasel. Gothard would head toward a ridgetop and start glassing before I'd even reach the base. By the time I crawled up, he'd be on his way to the next ridge. It was time for Lesson One.

"Wait, Gothard. Let me fill you in on these moose we're chasing," I gasped between breaths. "Moose hunting in Alaska calls for covering a lot of ground with your eyes, not with your feet."

Gothard glassed the area quickly with his binoculars. "No moose here," he replied.

"Moose have learned to remain motionless in any kind of cover, much like the redd deer you have in Germany," I said. "When I was grouse hunting last year, I saw a flicker of movement and moved toward it, hoping to flush a grouse. As I busted through the brush, my 'grouse' turned out to be an oversized ear with a moose attached. So it's not only glassing, but interpreting what you see.

"Before the rut, bull moose are often hard to find," I continued. "They'll stay in high-mountain meadows and spruce thickets, coming out only under the cover of darkness. However, the approach of rut makes them more vulnerable. Over a period of several days, I've seen as many as eight bulls roam through an area searching for receptive cows.

"The trick to bagging one of these bulls is to find a crossroad where their paths come together, perhaps in that valley between those two long ridges over there," I said as I pointed. Gothard began glassing the area intensely as I continued my wilderness oration.

"Large bulls will usually dominate such an area, keeping lesser bulls on the run. In this country, bulls of 24 to 40 inches don't argue much with those 50-to 65-inch monsters.

"And bulls can wander everywhere. During the rut, you might find them in swamps, above timberline or right in camp."

"Bull," Gothard replied.

"It's the truth," I snapped back.

I suddenly realized the significance of Gothard's remark and threw up my binoculars in time to see a cow moose walking into a distant clearing. A mud-stained bull with a 50-inch rack followed, his brown back hairs standing straight as sentinels. He playfully bit the cow several times on the rear.

"Lovesick for sure," I said to myself. It was a perfect set-up, and we made plans quickly. Gothard would walk straight toward a small knoll that overlooked the clearing. I would walk around to the opposite end of the field in case the bull spooked.

I tried to calm myself as I snaked through the knee-high alders. The moose trail I was following was worn deep, with abundant sign. As I reached the marsh, I couldn't tell whether my legs were wobbly because of the spongy tundra or from excitement.

It seemed to take hours to reach the clearing. At any second, Gothard's 30-06 might reverberate off the neighboring snow-capped peaks. The situation made me question the logic of a mere 180-grain slug bringing down a 1,200-pound moose.

Suddenly I heard a rustling of alders off to my left. The moose was coming my way. As my ears strained to pick up another sound, my "moose" began spewing out German words in a tone that signaled something was wrong.

Gothard filled me in when he reached me. He had been within 200 yards of the bull, which was partially obscured by thick cover. While he was waiting for a clear shot, the moose had simply vanished!

We glassed the ridge again for a full hour. Except for a small herd of caribou in the distance, not a movement anywhere. I shook my head.

"It's as if the earth swallowed him whole, right Gothard?"

"Must be a pretty big hole for a moose that size to fall in," he replied with a grin.

Meanwhile, we heard a rifle shot echo down by camp. Otto must have bagged a moose! We skimmed across the marshy areas back to the tent like diving ducks taking to wing.

We arrived to find Otto bent over by the lake dressing out a nice caribou bull. Otto's smile wasn't the least bit hampered by his thick moustache. The usual flurry of German ensued and I waited for a translation from Gothard.

"Otto had finished moose hunting for the day and decided to grab his 12 gauge and stalk some ducks he had seen earlier. But he saw a caribou swimming across the lake. Instead of his shotgun, Otto grabbed his rifle, waited for the bull to climb out and bagged him. Ha, less than 150 yards from the tent too!

It was a good animal with 39-inch, polished beams and a double shovel. A real trophy. As we finished dressing the animal, I couldn't believe the skillful manner in which Gothard had done the skinning. Not an ounce of meat or fat was left on the hide.

"Do you skin many deer in Germany, Gothard?"

"Last year I shoot 73 redd deer," he replied. "This is the quota for the land that I hunt. Each year, German hunters must shoot their quota, whether it be ducks, rabbits or deer. We must employ a professional hunter who is also the caretaker of the tract we hunt. But this is not real hunting. This is." I agreed as I hung a caribou quarter on the meat pole.

Fresh caribou steaks sizzled in the pan that night as Otto performed miracles from our food stock. I was served ample portions of *heiss kartoffelsalat* (hot German potato salad) and *kaltes bohnen salat* (cold bean salad). Our overwhelming appetite was matched by our hunger to learn more about each other's hunting customs and traditions. We managed to get our points across, despite our destruction of the German and English languages.

The most curious interlude was a lesson in how to make popcorn, which they put away as fast as I could make it. As the fourth batch of exploding kernels complemented our excitement, we planned our last day's hunt. We would split up for moose, whether it would be one for the wall or for the freezer.

Glassing For Moose

The soft bite of approaching winter arrived with the dawn. Skim ice had formed over the lake's edge during the night, and intricate frost crystals enveloped the low-lying vegetation. My destination was a far ridge about two miles from camp. Otto had hunted it several days earlier, and had spotted two cow moose and much bear sign. As I trudged through some scattered alders, snowshoe hares scurried everywhere, their summer-brown coats showing first signs of whitening.

Before long I was glassing three areas from a rocky ridgetop: both sides of the ridge which ran for several miles, and a marsh off a nearby point. As the sun dispelled the early-morning aura of pinks and orange, the grandeur of the area once again nearly overpowered me. Spiring mountains, scarred by the glaciers of another age, loomed several thousand feet into the cloudless sky. A skein of snow geese was answering a distant call. This is a cold and heartless country, but ruggedly beautiful. My glassing lasted until the blushing morning sky transformed into a brilliant azure blue. The area was pocked with bear and moose sign, but the sun's rays kept the animals hidden in spruce patches and alder thickets.

"Maybe there's some activity at the marsh," I said to myself as I walked the mile-long ridgetop for a better view. I studied the marsh intensely, but saw only a narrow creek coursing through a maze of grass and willows. Before I continued cross-country to the next ridge, I glassed the area I had just covered. My heart jumped as I focused on a cow moose trudging toward the swamp.

"There has to be a bull nearby, there just has to be!"

I all but forced the wish through my glasses, straining to see any part of the quarry I knew was there. As if my magic, another form emerged behind the cow. A bull!

I forced myself to calm down and review the situation. Very likely my walk along the ridgetop had spooked the animals to the marsh below. But the pair was ambling toward a thick patch of spruce on the far side of the marsh. If they entered, I'd lose them for sure.

I calculated about 500 yards to the bull, and 600 feet down to the marsh. I could feel every nerve throbbing with excitement as I busted through the brush on the far side of the ridge. Minutes later, I cleared the ridge and spotted the bull, about 275 yards distant and gaining ground.

I sat down, placed the crosshairs over the bull's neck and fired. My scope returned to the scene just in time to see the bull drop like a stone. Not a movement as I walked down to the marsh. It was a young bull, sporting a 27-inch rack and weighing about 950 pounds. My jumping and shouting could have produced seismic tremors in China!

It seemed to take only several minutes to cover the two miles back to camp where Otto and Gothard were having lunch, finishing the popcorn from the previous night. A magpie on a nearby limb seemed to join the celebration on hearing the cheering and commotion as I broke the news.

When we arrived at the moose, and before I started quartering, Otto and Gothard indoctrinated me into a German tradition. Otto cut two small twigs from a nearby spruce. He placed one in the bull's mouth, and the other in my grubby hunting cap.

"In Germany, the twig in the mouth represents the animal's last meal," Gothard explained. "The twig in the hat honors the hunter."

Otto took my hunting knife and held it in his outstretched hand. I placed my hand over the knife and repeated a few German phrases commemorating the successful hunt. I was honored by the ceremony, but then it was the ol' pat-on-the-back and congratulations.

It would have been much simpler to pack the entire camp, including the wood-burning stove to the moose rather than vice versa, I thought as I labored under 100 pounds of boned hindquarter. We had boned out the moose so carefully that the magpies and ravens were yelling insults rather than praise. As I trudged into camp with the first load, I realized the truth in the saying, "Moose hunting becomes work *after* you make the shot."

Ten and a half hours later, I arrived in camp with the last of the moose: the hide and rack. My body ached, my shoulders were sore, and I reeked of moose and tundra, but I blessed every minute of it!

I was surprised to find Jim at camp, loading the Beaver with gear and meat. "Bad storm headed this way. You timed it just right."

I climbed into the backseat of the aircraft and felt that a part of me remained onshore as the floatplane taxied on the lake. Everyone was quiet as we gazed over the land. We could still feel its spell tugging at us as the Beaver lifted over the mountain peaks.

Wolves howling, the crashing of fighting bulls, and long evenings by the cookstove fire still replay over and over in my mind. The spell of Alaska's autumn magic is strong, and I'm sure to answer it again—soon.

Appendix

Resident—

Hunting License ....$12.
Hunting and Fishing License ....$22.
Tags—Musk Ox Bull: Nunivak Island ....$500.
        Nelson Island and Unit 26C ....$25.
Tags—Musk Ox Cow: Nelson and Nunivak Islands, Unit 26C ....$25.
Tags—Bear, brown or grizzly (not required for
  Unit 20E,) ....$25.

Non-resident—

Hunting License ....$60.
Hunting and Fishing License ....$96.

Tag—Black Bear	$200.	Tag—Roosevelt Elk	$250.
Tag—Brown/Grizzly Bear	$350.	Tag—Moose	$300.
Tag—Bison	$350.	Tag—Mountain Goat	$250.
Tag—Caribou	$300.	Tag—Musk Ox	$1,100.
Tag—Dall Sheep	$400.	Tag—Wolf	$150.
Tag—Blacktail Deer	$135.	Tag—Wolverine	$150.

Resident and Non-Resident—

Drawing Permit Application Fee ....$5. each Drawing
Permit Application Fee (bison and musk ox) ....$10. each
Alaska State Waterfowl Stamp ....$5.

Hunting Information

  Hunting licenses may be obtained from any designated issuing agent or by mail from the Department of Revenue, Fish and Game Licensing Division, 1111 W. 8th St, Juneau, Alaska 99801. Hunting licenses and tags are valid for the period January 1 through December 31, inclusive, of the year for which they are issued. No license is required of an Alaska resident under 16 years of age, for hunting or trapping. Licenses and big game tags are required of all non-residents, regardless of age, for any big game animal. Residents intending to hunt brown/grizzly bear are required to possess a brown/grizzly tag.

  Non-residents are required to have a guide or be accompanied by an Alaskan resident over 19 years of age within the second degree of kindred by blood or marriage when hunting brown/grizzly bear and Dall sheep.

  Marine Mammal hunting is presently controlled by the federal government. Contact the U.S. Fish and Wildlife Service for information on hunting walrus, polar bear and sea otter. Contact the U.S. Department of Commerce for information on hunting seals, sea lions and beluga whales.

  Portions of the Alaska State Park System are open to lawful hunting. However, the law pertaining to the discharge of firearms vary from park to park. Many state parks closed to the discharge of firearms are open to hunting by other means, such as bow and arrow. For specific information, contact the Alaska Division of Parks, Department of Natural Resources.

  Portions of the National Park System titled **Preserve** are open to sport hunting. Those areas titled **Park** or **Monument** are closed to all hunting except by those who qualify under federal regulations as subsistence users for areas allowing such uses. Hunting seasons and bag limits are in accordance with state regulations.

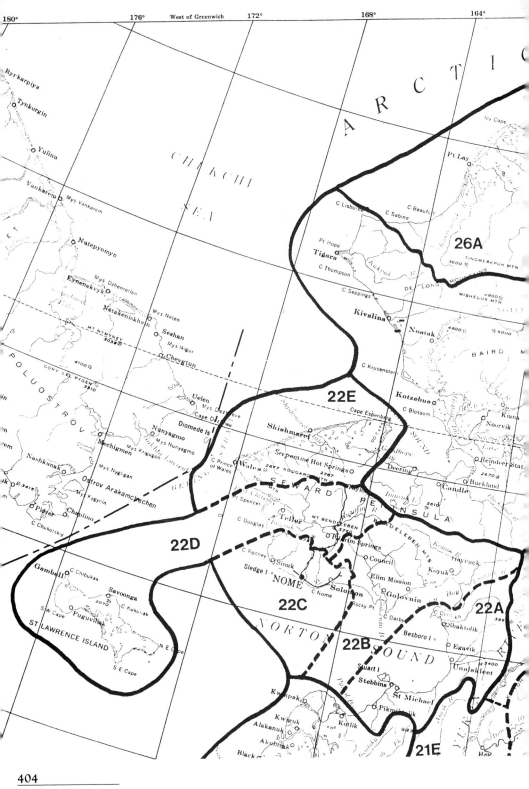

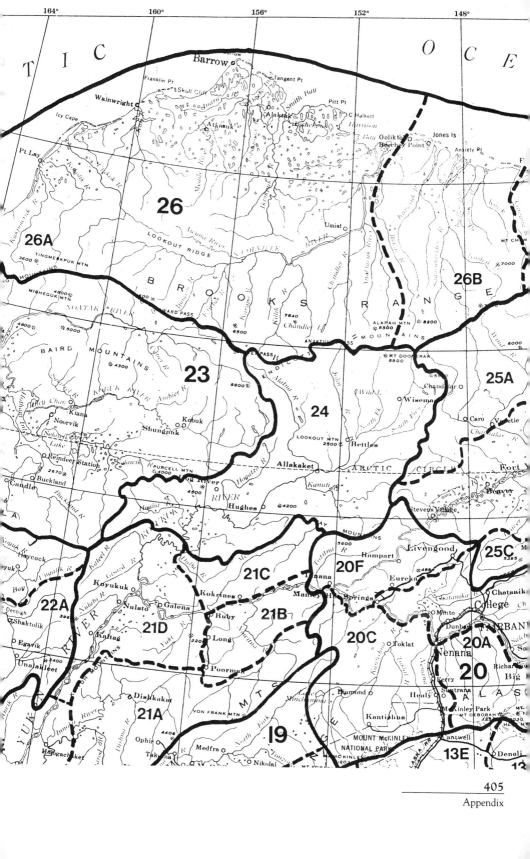

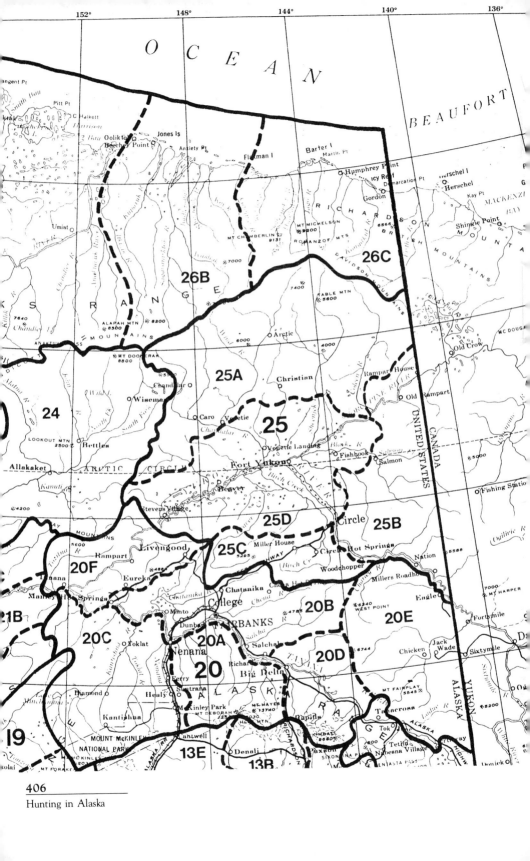

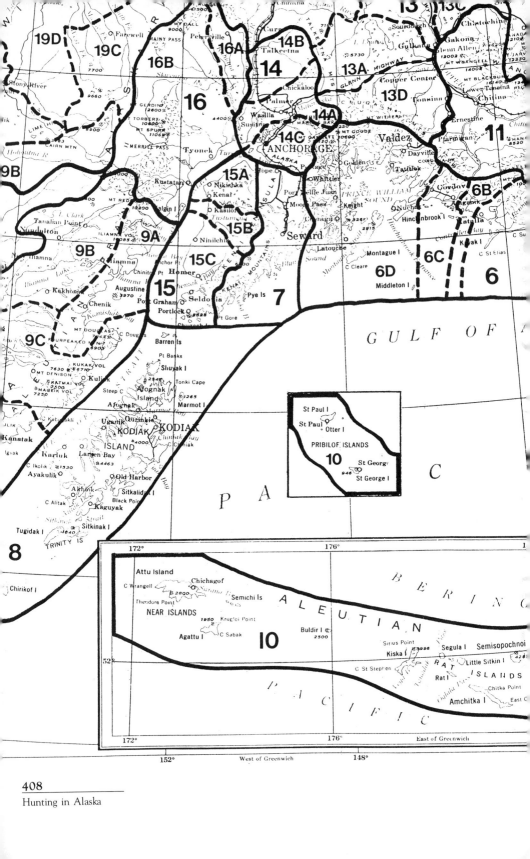

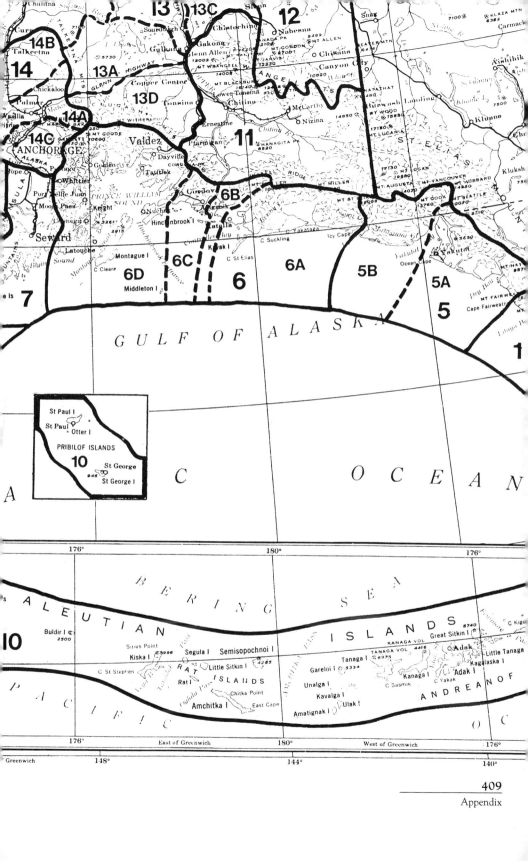

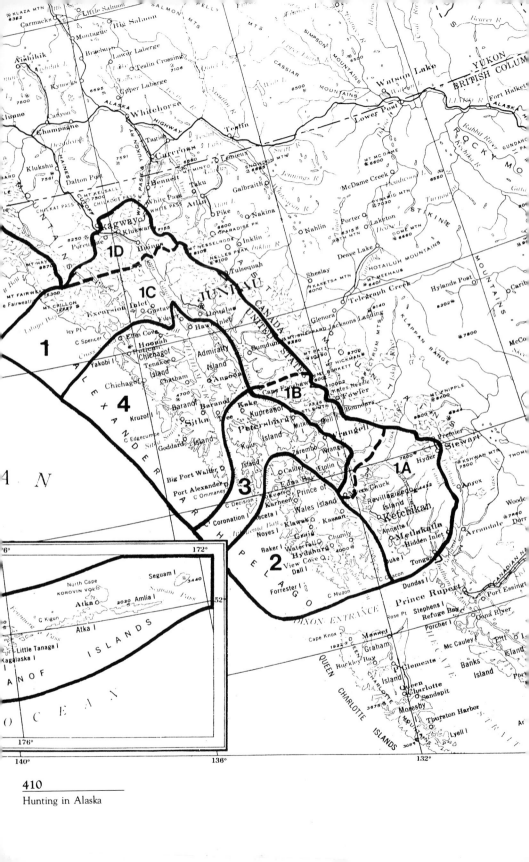

Index

Ordering Information

Hunting in Alaska: A Comprehensive Guide, by Christopher Batin. ISBN 0-916771-07-5, 6"x9", 416 pages, softcover, **$24.95**

The Alaska Hunter. Newsletter for those who want the very best in Alaska hunting. Features include do-it-yourself hunts, guide reviews, hunting techniques, trophy hunts and more. The most timely, complete information available on Alaska hunting. 8½"x11", 8 issues a year (year-round), **$49.00 postpaid.** (Canada $59.00, Europe $69.00 postpaid) Custom-binder with Alaska Hunter logo, **$14.00 postpaid.**

The Alaska Angler. Newsletter for those who want the very best in Alaska sportfishing. Features include lodge reviews, fishing hotspots, angling reports and new techniques for fishing Alaska waters. The most timely, complete information available on Alaska sportfishing. 8½"x11", 8 issues a year (year-round), **$49.00 postpaid.** (Canada $59.00, Europe $69.00 postpaid). Custom-binder with Alaska Angler logo, **$14.00 postpaid.**

Bear Heads & Fish Tales, by Alan Liere. Alaska outdoor humor at its best. A collection of zany outdoor stories to tickle your funny bone. Illustrations by Jeff Schuler. ISBN 0-916771-05-9, 5½"x8½", 144 pages, softcover, **$9.95.** (Canada $10.95)

How to catch Alaska's Trophy Sportfish, by Christopher Batin. The most comprehensive book written on sportfishing in Alaska. Both novice and veteran anglers will benefit from this book. Over 120 action-filled photos. Detailed information on 18 sportfish species found throughout the state of Alaska. 16 full-color pages identifying Alaska's trophy sportfish plus the best lures and fly patterns used to catch them. Detailed charts and illustrations. Illustrations by Adela Batin. ISBN 0-916771-03-2, 6"x9", 368 pages, softcover, **$24.95.** (Canada $27.95). Collector's Edition, (limited edition), hardcover, ISBN 0-916771-01-6, **$60.00**

Fishing Alaska on $15 a Day, by Christopher and Adela Batin is the first comprehensive guide to inexpensively fishing the best steelhead, trout, char and salmon waters in Alaska's 23-million acre Chugach and Tongass National Forests. Profusely illustrated with over 50 maps and 105 photographs and charts, this book provides you with hundreds of practical and indispensable tips on accommodations, fish migrations, stream and lake locations, as well as valuable fish-catching and hunting advice. Anglers experienced in the world's best sportfishing, as well as novices, will benefit from this book. ISBN 0-916771-25-3, 6"x9", 320 pages, softcover, **$19.95**

Add $4.00 shipping & handling for one book, each additional book add $2.00. Allow 6-8 weeks for delivery. Airmail delivery add $2.00. Foreign orders add $15. U.S. Funds only.

TO ORDER, send your name, address, phone number, and check, money order, Visa or Mastercard number and expiration date to:

ALASKA ANGLER PUBLICATIONS
P.O. Box 83550, Fairbanks, Alaska 99708
or call (907) 456-8212

Credit card orders call TOLL-FREE 1-800-446-2286